The Soviet Economic System

About the Book and Authors

A comprehensive analysis of the Soviet economy from a legal perspective, this book discusses the Soviet theory of legal regulation of economic activity and the formal structure of economic legislation. The authors argue that two contradictory tendencies characterize the Soviet economic regulatory system: reform and retreat from reform. Legal reform efforts usually result from the attempt to increase economic efficiency, which typically involves according greater independence to lower-level economic organizations. The danger that political power might be undermined, however, eventually leads to the reestablishment of the dominance of the central authorities over lower-level decisionmaking. Drs. Ioffe and Maggs also examine the tensions in labor law, which must reconcile the needs of the economy for job mobility and high worker morale with administrative ideals of strict discipline, and the legal aspects of technology transfer. In addition, emphasis is placed on the ways that economic legislation is developed and applied in practice; the authors note in particular the progress that has been made in systemization and codification of economic legislation.

Olimpiad S. Ioffe, professor of law at the University of Connecticut, taught for thirty-two years on the Faculty of Law at Leningrad State University. **Peter B. Maggs** is professor of law at the University of Illinois. He studied at the Leningrad State University as a graduate student and later taught at Moscow State University.

The Soviet Economic System

A Legal Analysis

Olimpiad S. Ioffe
and Peter B. Maggs

Routledge
Taylor & Francis Group
LONDON AND NEW YORK

First published 1987 by Westview Press, Inc.

Published 2019 by Routledge
52 Vanderbilt Avenue, New York, NY 10017
2 Park Square, Milton Park, Abingdon, Oxon OX14 4RN

Routledge is an imprint of the Taylor & Francis Group, an informa business

Library of Congress Cataloging-in-Publication Data
Ioffe, O. S. (Olimpiad Solomonovich), 1920–
The Soviet economic system.
(Westview special studies on the Soviet Union and Eastern Europe)
Includes index.
1. Industrial laws and legislation—Soviet Union.
2. Soviet Union—Economic policy—1981– .
I. Maggs, Peter B. II. Title. III. Series.
LAW 1987 343.47′08 86-33971

ISBN 13: 978-0-367-29597-4 (hbk)

ISBN 13: 978-0-367-31143-8 (pbk)

Contents

Introduction 1

The Soviet Economy in the Soviet System 1
The Soviet Economic System in Soviet Law and Soviet Legal Theory 8
Notes 15

1 **The Fundamental Structural Elements of the Soviet Economic System** 19

Ownership 19
Production 25
Distribution 31
Exchange 37
Notes 43

2 **The Soviet Legal System in Connection with the Soviet Economic System** 46

General Structure of the Soviet Legal System 46
Subjects and Methods of Legal Regulation 48
The Branches of Law 49
Notes 58

3 **Ownership and the Law of Ownership** 59

General Principles 59
The State's Right of Ownership 66
The Right of Personal Ownership 83
Notes 96

4 **Production: Its Legal Organization** 101

General Principles 101
Agencies of Planning 105
Agencies of Production 115
Notes 131

5 **Production: Research and Development** 134

General Principles 134
Planning, Financing, and Organization of Research and Development 136
Enforcement and Encouragement 144
Other Legal Forms of Modernization of Technology 148
Notes 153

6 **Production: Labor Force and Labor Law** 157

General Principles 157
The Labor Force Planning Process 159
Law, Plan, and the Formation of the Employment Contract 161
The Labor Contract and Its Terms 166
Termination of the Labor Contract 169
Procedures for Deciding Employer/Employee Disputes 174
Notes 175

7 **Distribution and Its Legal Forms** 179

General Principles 179
Planned Distribution 183
Unplanned Distribution 197
Notes 208

8 **Exchange: Its Legal Regulation** 210

General Principles 210
Economic Contracts 217
Non-Economic Contracts 246
Notes 264

9 **Legal Protection of the Soviet Economic System** 269

General Principles 269
Institutional Basis of Protection of the Economy 270
Types of Protection 278
Protection of State Property 284
Responsibility for Mismanagement of State Property 288
Prevention of Violations of Plans and Rules 290

Prevention of Other Threats to the Economic System 294
Notes 299

Conclusion 303

Afterword 311
Index 319

Introduction

The Soviet Economy in the Soviet System

The intrinsic nature of the Soviet economy depends not only on this economy itself but also on the Soviet system as a whole. Western Sovietologists, oblivious of what is happening around the Soviet economy and concentrating on purely economic matters, often make mistakes inexcusable in light of elementary facts that are readily available.

Sometimes these mistakes are not very important and result more from the juggling of words than from errors in substantive analysis. Thus, John H. Wilhelm contends, with reference to his own arguments and relying upon Eugène Zaleski,[1] that "the Soviet Union has an administered, not a planned, economy": while a planned economy means that "the plan and the planning process constitute the dominant mechanism by which economic coordination and decision making are achieved," in the USSR one finds, "instead of a plan and planning process governing economic operations, . . . an ever-changing process of administrative corrections of 'the plan' actually characterizing economic activity."[2] Yet, it is apparent that economic planning can be implemented only administratively and in no other way. Had Wilhelm combined his study of the Soviet economic system with appropriate information gleaned from the Soviet legal system, he undoubtedly would have avoided this obvious error. As the most significant Soviet legislation on civil law provides: "civil rights and duties arise from . . . administrative acts, including . . . planning acts."[3] Consequently, planning acts are only a species of administrative acts, and therefore there is no point in contrasting a planned economy with an administered one. Actually, Wilhelm unconsciously substituted the contrast between stable and non-stable plans with a contrast between planning and administration. However, changeable planning is still planning, and moreover, under certain circumstances, it is preferable to rigid unchangeable planning. But regardless of the stability of Soviet plans, an administered economy arises owing to its planning as such, not to the character of this planning. Unfortunately, there are more significant errors arising as a result of the academic insulation of the Soviet economy, not from the Soviet legal system, but from the Soviet political system. Hardly any other Western work describes the Soviet economic mechanism more faithfully than does the universally known book written by Alec Nove.[4] Even a hypercritical reader can find, at most, only a few inaccuracies and no evident mistakes. However, once Professor Nove attempts to suggest the measures that should be employed in order to improve the economic situation in the USSR,[5] any interest previously engendered by his book disappears without a trace. His innovations possess no originality: liberalize economic management and economic miracles will be achieved. But how would this economic liberalization affect the Soviet political system? Professor Nove must sincerely think that the two, his economic reform and the Soviet political system, are basically compatible. Otherwise, the question "Is a within-system reform possible?," the title of his paper at the 1985 Geneva conference on the USSR, could not have been positively answered as it was in this paper.[6] It is true that the call to economic liberalization has not brought Professor Nove to the extreme expressed by his supporters at the same conference who insisted without a trace of humor upon the compatibility of the Soviet political regime with the economic model of Taiwan and Singapore. Nevertheless, like his supporters, Professor Nove makes no attempt to argue the correctness of his assertions with reference to the substance of the Soviet political system. He entirely disregards this system, preferring a bare postulate of the invulnerability of the political regime even in the face of essential economic modifications. But just as a postulate does not bind its author, it also need not impress its addressees.

Who are these addressees? At any rate, they are neither the Soviet rulers, nor anti-Soviet activists. The former have never followed the suggestions of their Western advisers, and there is no reason to assume that anything has recently changed in this regard. Anti-Soviet activists, in turn, demand economic modifications incompatible with the Soviet system, i.e. modifications that either are not suggested by Western Sovietologists or cannot be introduced without the politically suicidal support of the Soviet rulers. The only "consumers" of Sovietological "production" are Western democracies interested in discovering the truth in order to prevail in their competition with the USSR. To be equal to the singular task of making their work valuable to their readers, Sovietologists must strictly observe certain fundamental principles which require them: (1) to study the Soviet system as it really is and not as one desires it to be; (2) to ascertain the actual forms of social improvement determined by the Soviet system itself and not those invented by its explorers; (3) to discover whether these forms are potential sources for the strengthening of the Soviet regime and to refrain from instructing this regime how to overcome its weakness; (4) to elucidate specifically Soviet processes with reference to all aspects of the Soviet system and not as isolated phenomena. With this last guideline in mind, it is convenient to begin by considering the Soviet economy as an important ingredient of the Soviet system.

The predominant component of the Soviet system is the unlimited political power of the ruling summit. Domination of this summit does not mean, of course, that its representatives directly manipulate all of the governing apparatus. Mikhail Voslensky is unquestionably right, in emphasizing the distribution of such functions among all of the ruling agencies, from the Politburo to the local executive committees.[7] As he says, the Politburo would never appoint the chairman of the collective farm: this must be left to the appropriate district committee of the CPSU (the Communist Party of the Soviet Union).[8] However, despite the actual distribution of governing functions, not the entire "nomenclature," as Professor Voslensky calls the Soviet bureaucracy, but only its highest pinnacle wields unlimited political power, whether this pinnacle is represented at a given historical period by collective or by personal dictatorship. As Professor Voslensky himself recognizes, "the Politburo, certainly, may appoint . . . a chairman of a collective farm," but this "would be an outrageous violation of established rules and would be met with silent perplexity by the nomenclature (if, it were not, of course, a question of demotion . . . of some one of the high-ranking persons included in the nomenclature of the Politburo)."[9] This means, in other words, that the power of all other agencies is restricted by their functions, while the Soviet summit, though fulfilling only certain functions, possesses supreme and not subordinate, all-embracing and not partial, or, to be brief, unlimited and not restricted political power.

The subject of this power is the Soviet people, as the next component of the Soviet system. This component, being the largest in quantitative terms, does not occupy a qualitatively appropriate position. While political dominance is effected from the top of the system, the Soviet people, as subordinate subjects, are at the bottom of it. However, this bottom level is not homogeneous. There are different social strata. Official Soviet ideology distinguishes workers, peasants, and intelligentsia.[10] In fact, the social stratification of the USSR is even more complex than the Soviet Constitution acknowledges.[11] Unskilled labor and the "working aristocracy" are united under the general notion of "workers," well-to-do and extremely poor members of collective farms are called by one name "peasants," to say nothing about the intelligentsia, which, in Soviet parlance, includes everyone except workers and peasants—from the new millionaires among a section of the highly paid intellectual elite down to ordinary clerks with miserable salaries and without any hope for the future. The actual stratification of the Soviet people demands an application of different approaches toward various groups, and, accordingly, one stratum will be somewhat more politically dominant than another. But this, in principle, does not change the basic situation. The entire population lives under the fully unrestricted weight of the elite's political might, and the Soviet regime would cease to exist if the relationship between the ruling pinnacle and the subordinate masses were to be destroyed or even shaken. From this point of view, distinctions between the nomenclature and the remainder of the Soviet people are of little significance, whether one considers the nomenclature as a new dominating class or as a privileged part of the dominated people.

The means that support political domination are the functions of the next components of the Soviet system: propagandistic persuasion, on the one hand, and organized suppression, on the other hand. Although Soviet propaganda is generally notorious as the most boring in the world, one must recognize its capacity to elaborate a certain stereotyped mode of thinking adapted to the totalitarian system and capable of explaining social events or phenomena in light of the official attitude. As a result, even the invasion of Afghanistan, despite its duration and the suffering involved, is not properly understood or interpreted by the majority of the Soviet people. As to organized suppression, its implementation is ensured by the special work of punitive agencies (the judicial system, the procuracy, the police, the KGB, etc.) as well as by the routine methods of governmental activity (legal regulations and administrative orders, formal and discretionary solutions to the daily problems of the executive process, etc.). As a result of the activity of these agencies, even the dissident movement, despite the personal boldness of the majority of its participants, has lost any substantial significance, though it continues to show itself now and again. However, strong as they are, propagandistic persuasion and organized suppression can be utilized only in the performance of relatively specific tasks and for the achievement of comparatively limited purposes. The general task of holding each individual and the entire population in check is beyond their capacity.

The efficient execution of this task, essential to the dominant summit, is ensured by another component of the Soviet systems—by the Soviet economy. The most important peculiarity of the Soviet system consists of the fact that the holder of unlimited political power is at the same time the economic monopolist in the USSR. It keeps in its grasp all more or less significant economic ingredients, beginning with land, factories, and means of transportation; ending with housing funds, retail-trade enterprises, domestic service, etc. Here, in the economic monopoly of the ruling stratum, one can find the explanation for Soviet-style economic miracles: technological backwardness in one area and high technical achievements in another, shortages of material resources for some industries and unrestricted abundance for others. Owing to its economic backwardness the USSR does not have the capacity to maintain an optimal correspondence between supply and demand in general. But, possessing at its unfettered disposal the entire economy of one-sixth of the world, the Soviet leadership does concentrate as many resources as are needed to solve those problems which the Soviet regime regards as being of paramount importance. Mikhail Checinski does not take into consideration this peculiarity of the Soviet system, when he contends that in the USSR "a dramatic shift in the allocation of resources is extremely difficult."[12] In fact, just the opposite is true. In the United States Congress may waste years or even decades in argument and debate; the Politburo, as the actual holder of unlimited power and economic monopoly in the USSR, can obtain an unanimous decision in five minutes, as soon as a new leadership, overcoming a short period of political struggle, manages to consolidate its power after the replacement of previous rulers. Economic monopoly has, however, not only this but also another, incomparably more substantial, importance for the Soviet system: it is the main source of the unlimited political power of the dominating summit in the

USSR. Other methods for the maintenance of dictatorship have been encountered in human history, if not in identical shape, than at least with an extremely similar nature. However, in the entire history of humanity no other regime has possessed political omnipotence of such magnitude as does the Soviet regime. Such an extraordinary phenomenon becomes understandable only when one recognizes that, owing to this economic monopoly, each individual in the USSR is permanently and inseparably dependent on the political power. Withdraw the economic monopoly from the grasp of the Soviet rulers, and they will lose their unlimited political power; withdraw from the grasp of the same rulers unlimited political power, and they will lose their economic monopoly. Only the combination of unlimited political power with economic monopoly gives rise to and assures the continuance of the Soviet system, and, conversely, were the Soviet system to be deprived of either of these two components, it would as such cease to exist.

The Soviet leadership knows no less than do Western Sovietologists that the liberalization of economic management would have positive economic effects. At the same time, the Soviet rulers understand their own interests better than even their good-natured critics and advisers from the West. They are not so naive as to rely upon those who strive to assure them that the acceptance of a "combination of certain capitalist elements with state property and the state interference in the economy—convergence‘is not dangerous' for the regime as such, for the highest and middle links of party and state machinery."[13] Soviet rulers know that at the very moment when a liberalized economy is permanently introduced, their political power will be doomed.[14] This must be seriously taken into account by those Sovietologists who, in professing to lending a helping hand to the Soviet regime, are actually suggesting the means of its destruction. They must also not forget that, because of the correlation outlined between economy and politics, the Soviet system presents substantial contradictions.

First, the Soviet state as a political organization cannot directly implement economic activity. Such activity must be imposed upon economic entities recognized as state organizations (economic associations, state enterprises, etc.) or disguised as non-state economic units (collective farms, consumer cooperatives, etc.). Thus, the economic monopoly of the political rulers exists in the USSR under an inevitable separation of economic activity from economic domination. This is the determinative contradiction of the Soviet system which, in the final analysis, leads to all other insoluble conflicts.

Second, in order to directly implement economic activity, Soviet economic entities need a certain economic independence from the Soviet state. Where the necessary independence is not assured, the state substitutes itself for its entities in the realm of economic activity, activity which requires initiative, not merely the carrying out of orders issued "from above." Such substitution has always resulted in economic failures, since political organizations are incompatible with the direct implementation of economic activity. Conversely, if economic entities attain the necessary independence, then the state itself actually loses its economic monopoly, which assumes an absolute, not simply a relative, governmental control. Such a loss of control has always resulted in political failures, since unlimited political power is incompatible with the economic independence of those who are politically dominated.

Third, the permanent attempts to find a way out of this vicious circle by the Soviet leadership have always necessitated maneuvering between economic centralization and economic decentralization. Economic centralization (Lenin's War Communism, Stalin's rigid planning, Brezhnev's economic and industrial associations[15]) corresponds to the nature of the Soviet system, in supporting an economic monopoly as the primary source of unlimited political power. But this entails an economic collapse and thus threatens the entire system. Economic decentralization (Lenin's NEP, Khrushchev's *sovnarkhozy*,[16] Kosygin's 1965 reform[17]) contradicts the nature of the Soviet system, in undermining the state's economic monopoly and in weakening, as a result, its unlimited political power. But, it is necessary to prevent an economic collapse, even though economic decentralization threatens the entire system with political collapse. In this regard, it is very remarkable that new Soviet leaders—Andropov and his successors, including Gorbachev—have appeared at the stage where the economic cycle attains the point of the turn to decentralization. Andropov actually purported to move toward decentralization, but employed the cautious method of an economic experiment.[18] Instead of introducing an economic reform, Gorbachev's line continues to be ambiguous, expressing tendencies toward both centralization and decentralization.[19] But under all circumstances, the Soviet economy develops in a cyclical continuum,[20] each cycle beginning with centralization and ending with decentralization.[21]

The Soviet economy, as described above,[22] has both strong and weak points.[23] The former are expressed in the efficiency of this economy and the latter in its inefficiency.

The Soviet economy is efficient, however flabbergasting this assertion may appear from the viewpoint of *communis opinio doctorum*. Any system can be evaluated by a number of criteria, but if one is not to misconceive the nature of a given system, one must measure its efficiency by the criterion that best mirrors its primary aim. In a society that subordinates politics to economic success, productivity constitutes the chief criterion of efficiency, on the condition that the level and structure of productivity corresponds to the level and structure of demand. So it is with efficiency under a market economy. But one must avoid the mistake made by Ljubo Sirc who identifies efficiency of a market economy with any economic efficiency.[24] In a society that subordinates the economy to politics, the criterion of efficiency must be found in the degree to which the structure of the economic system guarantees the unlimited dominance of the political rulers. So it is with efficiency under the Soviet economy. Efficiency of this kind is the source of the phenomenon noticed but not explained by Vladimir Kontorovich's words: "The Soviet political structure differs from most others in that it is very well insulated from the consequences of economic failures."[25] It is really insulated from these consequences because no economic failure can undermine unlimited political power so long as the state's economic monopoly remains inviolate. Once this point is grasped, one will never ask certain questions so fashionable in the West: why cannot the Soviet leadership make the economy work, why does one economic failure follow another, why is every new economic measure more stupid than the last? In fact, the Soviet leadership has made the economy work splendidly as the source of its dictatorship. In this regard, Soviet economic policy has never suffered a single real failure, and each new economic measure has appeared at least as effective as any previous one.

However, being efficient, the Soviet economy is simultaneously inefficient, however inconsistent such an assertion appears from the viewpoint of the unacceptability of any form of *contradictio in adiecto*. Although efficiency in the meaning of a market economy has never been and could never become the goal of the Soviet system, this kind of efficiency may not be entirely disregarded, first of all, because of domestic problems. There are natural limits below which the standard of living of a human being cannot be lowered, and the Soviet regime would be doomed, were it to ignore this natural factor. This explains, for example, why the Soviet government, greedy as it is with respect to gold and hard currency, does not hesitate to buy grain abroad in order to maintain the standard of living of the Soviet population at least at the level of natural limits. On the other hand, external problems also push the Soviet regime toward economic efficiency in the market meaning of these words, and among these problems military superiority plays the most important role. Therefore, all Soviet leaders, even Stalin, have been concerned with economic efficiency in its common sense, without which it is impossible to resolve other significant tasks, except the task of maintaining of political dominance based upon economic monopoly. Thus, the insulation of the Soviet political structure from the consequences of economic failures does exist, but this insulation is not absolute because of the impossibility, even for the Soviet regime, of entirely ignoring certain aspects of economic efficiency intrinsic to the market economy. At the same time, such efficiency can be achieved, within the limits of the Soviet system, only if the system itself is inviolable, i.e., on the condition that political power is unlimited, and the economic monopoly is in the grasp of political rulers.[26] This, the most fundamental contradiction of the Soviet system, entails both its ability to survive and its impending doom.

The general conclusion which follows from what has been argued above must be sufficiently clear. Cyclical development on the basis of an alternation of opposite reforms—from centralization to decentralization and then back to centralization—as an objective law of economic development in the USSR ensures the existence and retention of the Soviet system. However, the real potential of such maneuvering is not inexhaustible. On the contrary, its actual force undergoes continual weakening with the transition from one stage of economic development to another because of the incessant intensification of the contradiction between efficiency and inefficiency of the functioning economy. As a result, the Soviet system must collapse under the effects of its own nature. However, until its collapse occurs, this system needs to be explored rather than interred, and genuine exploration assumes the ascertainment of objective reality by all available means, among which Soviet legal theory and Soviet law play especially significant role.

The Soviet Economic System in Soviet Law and Soviet Legal Theory

Soviet sources concerning the economic problems of the USSR suffer from a substantial lack of terminological coordination in the area under discussion. Thus, one can come across such terminological designations as "the economic system" and "the economic mechanism," employed with the same or, at least, with a similar meaning, and yet these terms are not identically interpreted by different sources. Various conceptions are united only by the recognition that: (1) the economic system (the economic mechanism) in the USSR is a broader phenomenon than the economic basis (the total set of dominant production relations) as the most fundamental category of Marxist doctrine; (2) this system (mechanism) includes all links of economic activity and all methods of economic management (centralized planning, self-regulation, etc.); (3) the essential feature of this system (mechanism) is represented by the established forms of ownership of the means of production.[27] It follows from these generally accepted theoretical prerequisites that during "the transitional period from capitalism to socialism"[28] there was no unitary economic system in the USSR because of the poly-economic structure of the Soviet society where socialist ownership existed along with private ownership. "Only after the end of the transitional period and under the victory of socialism was this system created in its principal features."[29] As to the mature system of new economic relations, it appears only at the stage when so-called developed socialism has been achieved.[30]

These theoretical declarations correspond completely to the appropriate legal provisions, and it could not be otherwise: the content of those declarations became part of the 1936 (Stalin) Constitution, and since that document was promulgated, these Constitutional principles have enjoyed both legally and ideologically binding force. Strict adherence to the standard interpretation has been required in all cases, except where a principle may be ambiguous. Any other deviation by a legal theorist from constitutional formulae has been persecuted to the same degree as would be an outright violation of the corresponding legal provisions.[31] It is, however, another question as to whether legal theory and law, while certainly corresponding one to another, are in conformity with Soviet reality.

The Soviet legislation of the 1920's did not use such terminological designations as the economic system or the economic mechanism. This legislation distinguished between state, cooperative and private ownership, without employing the terminology "socialist ownership" either as a general notion for state and cooperative ownership or as a specific term denoting state ownership. Nevertheless, state ownership received the most privileged support in this legislation, while private ownership was substantially restricted.[32] As the law stated, "legally existing cooperative organizations may possess various kinds of property to the same degree as may private persons."[33] Thus, in principle, cooperative ownership qualified as private ownership, though the cited rule provided for cooperative organizations certain advantages in comparison with those provisions addressed to private persons. It is obvious therefore that the Soviet legislator of that period of time could not employ even formal pretexts (to say nothing about the actual situation) as bases for proclaiming that a unitary economic system had been established in the USSR.

The legal and the appropriate doctrinal positions, supported by Lenin and other Soviet leaders as well as by representatives of Soviet jurisprudence during the NEP period, were, in essence, adequate for the circumstances.[34] Some phenomena called by Lenin "excesses of NEP" appeared, of course, now and again. Namely, certain persons strove to engage in prohibited trades (for instance, private credit operations) or to exceed the limits established for private activity (for instance, hiring more than five workers). Judicial practice unfailingly applied measures of confiscation to such enterprises, if the violations committed were the issue of a penal accusation or of a civil law suit. However, these violations cannot be considered as symptoms of the creation of an "underground" (or of a "second") economy in its contemporary interpretation. A "second" economy arises as an illegal antipode of the "first" or the only allowed legal economy. Since there was no economic monopoly of the Soviet state at that time, the objective circumstances that could give rise to an underground economy did not exist. Strange as this may seem, the underground economy is a specific anti-socialist product of the so-called socialist economy. When "under the victory of socialism" the Soviet economic system was created "in its principal features,"[35] the underground economy appeared in nascent form. After the new economic relations were proclaimed to have attained the level of maturity,[36] the underground economy entered the stage of genuine prosperity.

The "victory of socialism" was effected by measures initiated in the late-1920s—early-1930s. First, the Soviet authorities implemented the compulsory collectivization of agriculture and the mass expropriation of retail trade and other private enterprises by means of exorbitant income taxes and extra-judicial repression. A 1930 decree prohibited hired labor in districts of complete collectivization,[37] and a 1932 decree precluded the creation of private enterprises in general.[38] This legal development, prepared by illegal activity when the Soviet authorities "moved the law aside," as

Stalin cynically recognized, was finally crowned with Stalin's 1936 Constitution. The new Soviet Constitution proclaimed "the liquidation of the capitalist system of economy" and "the abolition of private ownership of the . . . means of production."[39] In fact, the terminology "private ownership" entirely disappeared from the Constitution, regardless of whether it dealt with means of production or with consumer goods. With regard to individual peasants and artisans, whose activity was still allowed, though within very restricted limits, the Constitution introduced the designation "small-scale private economy," instead of private ownership.[40] In all other cases, individual property was subsumed under a new legal category—the right of personal (not private) ownership.[41] At the same time, the Constitution put into legal circulation a notion previously employed only in political declarations and theoretical works: socialist ownership.[42] Simultaneously, the terminology "the socialist system of economy," the predecessor of the category of "the socialist economic system," appeared for the first time in Soviet legislation.[43] "The socialist system of economy and socialist ownership of the . . . means of production" qualified as "the economic foundation of the USSR."[44] However, "the socialist system of economy" was "the predominant" but not the only existing form of economy in the Soviet Union: along with it, "small-scale private economy of individual peasants and artisans" was also "permitted by law."[45] This could leave one with the impression that two different, though not equivalent, economic systems functioned in the USSR. But the predominance of the "socialist economy" attained such a level, and "small-scale private economy" was so weak and uncoordinated, that contrasting the two economic systems would not be realistic or truthful. Since the time of Stalin's Constitution, the economic monopoly of the Soviet rulers has been firmly established, and, as a result, their unlimited political power has been ensured. Stalin's purges were important only from the viewpoint of determining the personal holders of the established dictatorship. As to the dictatorship itself, it is based upon economic monopoly, the creation of which results from a series of measures beginning with the "nationalization" carried out directly after the seizure of political power in October 1917 and completed by the "collectivization" and other forms of expropriation undertaken in the late–1920s—early–1930s.

The rules cited and the terminology mentioned were transformed into the dogmatic arsenal of Soviet doctrine. Only certain problems of secondary importance were disputed owing not so much to the complexity of these problems as to the vagueness of the relevant parts of the Constitutional text. What is the substance of the right of personal ownership? Does it allow the possession of small means of production? If not, then how is one to interpret the collective farm household, bearing in mind Article 7 of the 1936 Constitution, which entitles the owners of such households to possess minor agricultural implements? If so, then does the small-scale private economy of individual peasants and artisans qualify as personal ownership or as a specific kind of private ownership? Should it be neither one nor the other, what kind of ownership is represented by legally allowed private economy? Such were the economic problems that figured prominently in Soviet doctrinal discussions from the moment of the promulgation of the 1936 Constitution until its replacement by the 1977 Constitution.[46] Other economic issues of theoretical analysis, far more significant than those enumerated above, were not directly connected with Constitutional provisions and, therefore, despite the established dogmatism, a relative freedom of doctrinal exploration was not entirely precluded. In contrast, analyses of the Constitution could not exceed the limits of pure explanatory commentary.

It is, however, well worth noting that the 1936 Constitution and, after it, Soviet legal theory in fact supplied the designations for all of the most substantial modifications which had occurred in the Soviet society by this period of time. Unfortunately, the designations employed, instead of being adequate, are extremely distorting. But, replace the misleading Constitutional jargon incessantly repeated in doctrine with clear terminology supplemented by proper interpretation, and a true picture of the Soviet society will supplant the legally confirmed propagandistic farce. So-called socialist ownership actually was and is ownership by the ruling elite, and since this elite keeps in its grasp the Soviet state, one can treat "socialist ownership" as state ownership, and there will be neither a distortion of the truth nor a complete break with the official language of Soviet legislation. Further, the predominance of "the socialist system of economy" terminologically camouflages the predominance of the economic power of the Soviet rulers over all other components of the Soviet economy. Finally, the dependence of the latter on the former finds direct expression in the 1936 Constitution where this states that the right of personal ownership primarily comprises citizens' labor income,[47] and that each collective farm household has its own farming operation "in addition to the basic income from the social collective farm economy."[48] Only the small-scale private economic activity of individual peasants and artisans was restricted not by subordination to the dominant economy, but by established legal limitations.[49] Since, however, these limitations stemmed from the same source from which economic domination emanated, this legal subordination did not essentially differ from economic dependence.

The only economic phenomenon omitted by the 1936 Constitution was the underground or second economy. But this omission should not be assessed as a gap in the Constitution, which, according to its nature, was to deal with permitted, not with prohibited, types of economic activity. At the same time, the new situation summarized by the Constitutional provisions provided stronger encouragement for illegal economic activity than had the circumstances prevailing during the USSR's early years. The collectivization of agriculture led to rampant starvation. Rationing of the food supply was continued until 1935. The expropriation of private property in urban areas marked the beginning of the Soviet system's inability to meet consumer demands, which has since become the chronic disease of the Soviet economy. Owing to these events, the black market, which had vanished after the replacement of war communism by NEP, reappeared after NEP was destroyed by the "victory of socialism." Furthermore, the 1936 Constitution, legally allowing for the small-scale private economy of individual artisans, restricted this economy to the extent that it had to be based upon the personal labor of artisans and not upon the use of other persons' labor. Therefore, openly acting as a laboring artisan and secretly functioning as an employer of hired workers, one could illegally perform that which previously had been assessed as quite legal activity. Secrecy also was useful in evading legislation that made certain types of trade legally unavailable to individual artisans. Thus, as always, actual demands were stronger than legal prohibitions, and although the underground private economy of the period of the "victory of socialism" did not attain tne scale of the legalized individual enterprise of the period of NEP, this economy was, nevertheless, a concealed supplement to the official system. And any small openings resulting from the weakness of the official system were immediately filled by such concealed supplemental economic activity despite the danger of persecution and suppression.

The present stage of doctrinal development and legislative innovations is connected with the promulgation of the current 1977 Constitution. From this document the entire world learned that the USSR seemingly not only had achieved the "victory of socialism" but also boasted the creation of "a developed socialist society."[50] The official announcement of such an historical event entailed a number of consequences. However, despite the purely propagandistic character of the announcement itself, its results are, at least to some extent, quite significant. First of all, in contrast to its predecessor, the new Constitution employed the terminology "the economic system" (not "the system of economy") and dedicates to this topic a separate chapter[51] (instead of several words). In this latest version, socialist ownership of the means of production plays the role not of "the economic foundation of the USSR" but of "the basis of the economic system of the USSR."[52] Neither private ownership nor small-scale private economy are mentioned. Individual ownership qualifies exclusively as personal ownership.[53] However, a new provision addressed to all Soviet citizens, whereas the older version was directed only to individual artisans, states: "In the USSR individual labor activity is permitted in accordance with the law in the sphere of handicraft, agriculture, domestic service to the populace, and also other forms of activity based exclusively upon the personal labor of citizens and members of their families," but at the same time "the state shall regulate individual labor activity, ensuring its use in the interests of society."[54]

The two formulas cited have different purposes. The first formula, generally allowing individual labor activity, on the one hand, sanctions the actually established situation previously legal only for individual artisans and illegal for workers and officials, and, on the other hand, it formally confirms the common knowledge that the "socialist economic system" cannot satisfy the needs of the populace without individual labor activity. The second formula, in subordinating such activity to state control, entitles the appropriate governmental agencies to introduce limitations on individual labor (prohibitions on certain trades, or on the expansion of individual economic activity, etc.) that serve to maintain the absolute predominance of the "socialist" economic system "in the interests of society," as the law euphemistically expresses itself. Actually, however, this represents only a measure by which the holders of unlimited political power can retain their economic monopoly, while allowing a certain amount of private activity.

Further, the Constitutional proclamation of the "socialist" economic system is combined with a characterization of the USSR's economy as "a single national economic system."[55] This system embraces "all links of social production, distribution, and exchange within the territory of the country."[56] Because individual labor activity also is connected with production, distribution and exchange, one may quite logically conclude that it too pertains to the "links" of the national economic system. Such an assumption, however, finds no confirmation in a subsequent part of the same provision, which reads: "The direction of the economy is carried out on the basis of state plans for economic and social development, taking into account branch and territorial principles and combining centralized management with the economic independence and initiative of enterprises, associations and other organizations. Economic accountability, profit, cost of production, and other economic levers and stimuli shall be actively used in this connection."[57] Neither "direction," "planning," nor "organizations," to say nothing of economic accountability or similar "other economic levers," are compatible with individual labor activity.

Thus, the Constitutional interpretation of "a single national economic system" is more narrow than the Constitutional definition (all links of production, distribution, and exchange). But just these logical defects render the appropriate Constitutional provision, in fact, irreproachable, because "a single national economic complex" is only the official jargon substitute for the dictatorship's economic monopoly which relies upon the "socialist" economic system as opposed to individual labor activity. One may also notice that "the socialist economic mechanism," a category introduced by the Soviet legislature in the early 1980's,[58] originates with the "single national economic complex" and the methods of its direction outlined in the 1977 Constitution. As a result, the economic monopoly of the politically ruling bureaucracy has, at last, found consistent legal confirmation in the multifarious, though conventional, terminology of the Soviet Constitution as well as in the Soviet theoretical writings based upon this terminology.

Finally, as to the underground economy, it is not, of course, mentioned in the Constitution, but it exists and prospers, despite the post-Brezhnev battle against corruption and money-making. Yet only in the period immediately preceding the proclamation of the epoch of "developed socialism" and since that proclamation has the underground economy of the USSR finally attracted the serious attention of Western Sovietologists.[59] This could occur only because at that time development of this economy attained its zenith. While, seemingly, the all-embracing predominance of the official economic monopoly should leave no room for its antipode, in reality, this antipode has managed to infiltrate the "socialist" economic system itself. While continuing to manifest itself in the traditional areas, the underground economy has also been appearing in numerous new forms, namely: (1) private production as a part of "socialist" production (where private equipment functions as a part of equipment of a state enterprise); (2) private production under the mask of "socialist" production (where an enterprise, though registered as "socialist," is in fact private); (3) "socialist" production for the purposes of private gain (where a state enterprise, fulfilling its planning task, also produces "*nalevo*," i.e., illegally and not for the benefit of the state); (4) "socialist" production and private wholesale (where the distribution of "socialist" output is partly implemented by private persons evading the channels of planned supply); (5)"socialist" production and private retail trade (where articles produced by a state enterprise are sold directly to customers by workers and officials of the enterprise).[60] Such expansion of the underground economy under "developed socialism," strange as it seems at first glance, appears as quite natural when viewed as a spontaneous reaction against the barefaced polarization of Soviet society. In the broad sense, there is a process of just, though illegal, correction of the legal, though unjust, distribution of goods established in the USSR. In aspect of interests of different groups of the Soviet population, the underground economy functions as a source of a monetary supplement not only to the beggarly salaries provided by the state, but even to the living standard that legally is available only to the Soviet official elite.

This contemporary peculiarity of the underground economy has proven to be so impressive to certain Sovietologists that with reference to it they sometimes deny the economic monopoly of the Soviet political rulers. Such a view results, however, from an obvious misunderstanding. First, the number of people enriched by illegal economic activity represents only a small part of the Soviet population. Thus, it is normally not the underground economy but the official economy that determines the living standard and source of income in the USSR. Second, the underground economy is illegal, and it can be engaged in only under the constant risk of probable prosecution. One must not forget that, because of the significance of the official economy as the primary source of unlimited political power, economic crimes are ranked among the most dangerous crimes in the USSR, and the death penalty, inapplicable to such infractions in free countries, is the common reaction of the Soviet regime against its sworn enemy. Third, to engage in illegal economic activity a Soviet citizen must occupy an appropriate legal position as a worker, an official, or a member of a collective farm. Otherwise he will be punished if not for an economic crime, then for malicious evasion of socially useful work. Therefore, even those who could ensure a high living standard for themselves by participation in unofficial economic activity remain dependent on the official economy. Fourth, the underground economy is prohibited by Soviet law. As a result, similar to the political monopoly of the Soviet rulers which exists despite illegal dissidents' movement, the economic monopoly of the same leadership cannot be abolished by illegal economic activity. Because of these arguments there is no need to directly deal with the underground economy in the subsequent analysis.

Henceforth, the only object of our study will be the phenomenon officially called in the USSR the socialist economic system. Since, however, this system is developed on the basis of individuals' labor, representing the principal or often even the exclusive source of individuals' income, economic relations in which Soviet citizens take part cannot be entirely disregarded. At the same time, the purpose of this book is to analyze the Soviet economy not from an economic but from a legal standpoint. Therefore, a general characterization of the Soviet legal system in its connection with the Soviet economic system is inserted (Chapter 2); ownership, production, distribution and exchange are considered in their legally established forms (Chapters 3–8); and, finally, the legal protection of the Soviet economy is be considered (Chapter 9). However, as a logical premise of legal analysis one must explain the Soviet economic system as a whole and as a combination of its fundamental elements (Chapter 1).

Notes

1. Eugène Zaleski, *Stalinist Planning for Economic Growth* (Chapel Hill: University of North Carolina Press, 1984), p. 484.
2. John Howard Wilhelm, "The Soviet Union Has an Administered, Not a Planned, Economy," *Soviet Studies*, 37, (January 1985), 118–119.
3. Fundamental Principles of Civil Legislation, art. 4.
4. Alec Nove, *The Soviet Economic System*, Second Edition (London: George Allen and Unwin, 1980).
5. Ibid., p. 293–328.
6. The Second International Congress of Professors World Peace Academy, 1985, Panel No. 1, Paper No. 4.
7. Mikhail Voslensky, *Nomenklatura—Gospodstvuiushchii klass Sovetskogo Soiuza* (London: Overseas Publication Interchange Ltd., 1985) pp. 148–149.
8. Ibid., p. 149.
9. Ibid.
10. 1977 Constitution, art. 1. This grouping, mirroring the evolution of the official ideology, actually results from stratification of the Soviet society, the genuine character of which is, however, deliberately distorted. Marx emphasized only establishment of the dictatorship of the proletariat (Marx i Engels, *Sochineniia*, Second edition, vol. 28, p. 427). The 1936 Constitution, proclaiming the victory of the dictatorship of the proletariat, characterized the USSR "as a socialist state of workers and peasants" (Articles 1–2). At the same time, the Soviet intelligentsia qualified not as a class but as a "stratum between classes" (Stalin, *Sochineniia* vol 14, p. 145). The 1977 Constitution (Art. 1), contending that the USSR is "a socialist all-the-people's state," enumerates workers, peasants and intelligentsia as the three groups of this "all people," without reference either to "classes" or to "strata."
11. For Western Sovietologists this has long been an open secret. E.g.: Interests Groups in Soviet Politics, ed. by N.G. Skilling and P. Griffith, Princeton, 1971.

12. The Second International Congress of Professors World Peace Academy, 1985, Panel No. 1, Paper No. 2.

13. Igor Birman, *Ekonomika nedostach* (New York: Chalidze Publication, 1983), p. 168. This consolation sounds especially persuasive after the author's warning that "affairs will get worse before they become better" (ibid., p. 169). In a very peculiar interview given to the a magazine *Vremia i My* 86 (1985), p. 125) a famous American economist, Nobel Laureate, Milton Friedman, the author of the book *Capitalism and Freedom*, answering the question if the introduction of a free market economy in the USSR would cause any major disturbances, formulates ideas even more encouraging for the Soviet rulers: "No disturbances will occur. Only advantages will be realized, because the Soviet economy is so inefficient that as soon as a market system will be introduced, literally in a month everybody will actually live better, except for the *nomenklatura*." Thus, the *nomenklatura* will be defeated, but no perturbation will occur! An excellent prediction!

14. References to the experiments of China and Hungary, usually employed by the proponents of the opposite view, do not seem persuasive. As to China, only the future can prove whether this is simply one temporary reform in an overall cyclical pattern that will eventually lead back to centralization (then, nothing has occurred) or "a new deal" has been permanently established (then, the system itself will be modified). In assessing the situation in Hungary, one must not forget that under the umbrella of the USSR this country has the opportunity to operate a relatively decentralized economy and at the same time to retain centralized political power. As a matter of course, the Soviet Union cannot employ an identical approach under the umbrella of Hungary. Therefore, both examples have no demonstrative value.

15. See the section of Chapter 4 ("Production: its legal organization") on "General Principles."

16. *Sovnarkhozy* replaced industrial ministries and administered economy of regions subordinate to each *sovnarkhoz*.

17. See note 15.

18. *SP SSSR*, 1983, part 1, no. 20, item 109.

19. See note 15.

20. In contrast to Vladimir Kontorovich's assertion that "there are no cyclical fluctuations in the Soviet economy" (Second International Congress of the Professors' World Peace Academy, 1985, Panel No. 1, Paper No. 1).

21. Therefore, not "some" Soviet reforms have been implemented in contradictory directions, as Professor Nove claims (Note No. 6), but each reform is opposite to the one that preceded it.

22. See also Olimpiad S. Ioffe, "Law and Economy in the USSR," *Harvard Law Review* 95 (1982): 1591–1625); Olimpiad S. Ioffe and Peter B. Maggs, *Soviet Law in Theory and Practice* (New York: Oceana Publications, 1983), pp. 10–13, 75–88, 119–132.

23. In order to ascertain these points not all of the schemes of Soviet society disseminated in Western literature seem helpful. Let the reader judge for himself on the basis of the most recent publication which summarizes its discussion of the Soviet society as follows: it is "not characterized by class conflicts" because "the relations to the means of production are socialist in the sense of there being collective ownership of the means of production"; "Soviet society is not a classless society" but is "a unitary class society involving the domination of the state acting on behalf of the working class"; "planning has replaced the market," and "full employment has eliminated the'reserve army' of labourers"; "the pattern of dis-

tribution . . . is unequal," and "this gives rise to various forms of hierarchy"; and, finally, "inequalities and incompatibilities . . . are of a qualitatively different kind from notions of class conflicts developed by traditional Marxists." David Lane, *Soviet Economy and Society*, (New York: New York University Press, 1985), p. 97.

24. Second International Congress of the Professor's World Peace Academy, 1985, Panel No. 1, Paper No. 5.

25. Second International Congress of the Professor's World Peace Academy, 1985, Panel No. 1, Paper No. 1.

26. These limitations stemming from the Soviet system itself are entirely disregarded in the reassuring perspectives outlined in the book *The Soviet Economy Toward the Year 2000*, ed. Abram Bergson and Herbert S. Levine (London: George Allen and Unwin, L1983), to say nothing about the official optimism expressed by the Twenty-Seventh Congress of the Communist Party of the Soviet Union (*Izvestia*, Feb. 26-March 9, 1986).

27. E.g., P. G. Bunich, *Khoziaistvennyi mekhanizm i ekonomicheskaia politika partii* (Moscow: Nauka, 1980), p. 49; *Sovershenstvovanie sotsialisticheskikh proizvodstvennykh otnoshenii i effektivnost' proizvodstva* (Moscow: Mysl, 1980), pp. 5–11; D.P. Evstigneeva and R. N. Evstigneev, *Sotsialisticheskii khoziaistvennyi mekhanizm* (Moscow: Ekonomika, 1981), pp. 3, 6, 45, 62–68.

28. Marxist doctrine proceeds on the premise that after establishment of the dictatorship of the proletariat this dictatorship itself will ensure the liquidation of classes and the creation of a classless society—socialism. The time period required for such an achievement is called in the same doctrine "the transitional period from capitalism to socialism" (Marx and Engels, *Sochineniia*, vol. 28, p. 427).

29. *Sovershenstvovanie sotsialisticheskikh proizvodstvennykh otnoshenii*, p. 9.

30. Ibid.

31. As an illustration one can point to the fate of Academician I. P. Trainin, who lost all of his official positions in 1949 as one result of his attempt to draft a system of teaching Soviet Constitutional law organized on a basis different from that outlined by Stalin's Constitution.

32. 1922 RSFSR Civil Code, art. 52–55.

33. Ibid., art. 57.

34. E.g., I. B. Novitskii, *Pravo sobstvennosti, kommentarii k st. 59–65 Grazhdanskogo kodeksa (Moscow: Izd-vo iuridicheskoi literatury, 1925).*

35. Above, note 29.

36. Ibid.

37. SZ SSSR, 1930, no. 9, item 105.

38. *SZ SSSR*, 1932, no. 38, item 233.

39. Art. 4.

40. Art. 9.

41. Art. 7 and 10.

42. Art. 5.

43. Art. 5.

44. Art. 5.

45. Art. 40.

46. E.g., compare R. F. Mazhitova, *Osnovnye problemy prava lichnoi sobstvennosti* (Moscow: Izd-vo iuridicheskoi literatury, 1949) with A. Eroshenko, *Lichnaia sobstvennost' v grazhdanskom prave* (Moscow: Iuridicheskaia literatura, 1973).

47. Art. 10.

48. Art. 7.

49. Art. 10.

50. 1977 Constitution, Preamble.
51. Chapter 2.
52. 1977 Constitution, art. 10.
53. Ibid., art. 13.
54. Ibid., art. 17.
55. Ibid., art. 16.
56. Ibid.
57. Ibid.
58. See above, in the present section.
59. There is no need to enumerate the boundless Western explorations of this topic. It seems, however, important to make special mention of F. J. M. Feldbrugge's article "Government and Shadow Economy in the Soviet Union," *Soviet Studies* 37 (1984): 526–543, where one can find a general theory of the phenomenon discussed here: the definition and morphology of the Soviet second economy, the interdependence of the first and the second economy, the second economy within the Soviet political system, and the governmental treatment of the second economy. The same article lists the most important publications on the Soviet underground economy (pp. 442–443).
60. O. S. Ioffe, *Soviet Law and Soviet Reality*, pp. 103–108.

1

The Fundamental Structural Elements of the Soviet Economic System

Ownership

In his work, "A Contribution to the Critique of Political Economy," (published in English in New York in 1904), Marx characterized the economic system as a phenomenon based on a specific type of ownership. He described the system as consisting of production, distribution, and exchange; and also of consumption insofar as it consisted of what he called "production consumption" and thus embodied a component of production. This scheme is the only one legally recognized in the USSR. At the same time, the doctrinal terminology stemming from Marx is supplemented by official terminology created by the Soviet authorities and expressed in their theoretical dogmata or even in legal provisions. Such terminology, taken as a whole, is binding, regardless of its objective correctness, for Soviet scholars, and regardless of their subjective attitudes. Bearing in mind the issue of our research—legal analysis of the *Soviet* economic system, we also will employ this official terminology, emphasizing wherever necessary, however, its adequacy or inadequacy with respect to Soviet reality. This approach determines the sequence of the forthcoming discussion: first ownership and then production, distribution, and exchange.

According to Marx, ownership is the first fundamental element of every economic system. The Soviet economic system presents no exception to this general rule. What constitutes a purely Soviet feature is the divergence between ownership as such and its legal and doctrinal interpretations. In addition, while these legal and doctrinal points of view have evolved, ownership in the USSR has not changed in substance.

The 1936 Constitution distinguished between two types of ownership: socialist and personal.[1] Production purposes were connected with socialist ownership, while personal ownership was designed to satisfy the citizens' needs as consumers. As collective ownership, socialist ownership could be exercised by two types of collective bodies: (1) the Soviet state and (2) collective farms or other cooperative organizations. Correspondingly, two forms of socialist ownership were distinguished: state ownership and cooperative/collective farm ownership.[2] Personal ownership may be ownership by one individual, by several individuals, or by a specific group of individuals, such as the collective farm household.[3] Ownership by the collective farm household, i.e. the household of a member of a collective farm and his family, is subject to special legal rules, particularly rules based upon deeply rooted Russian customs preventing the fragmentation of a rural family's estate. Another peculiarity of the collective farm household is that, while personal ownership usually assumes consumer purposes, this particular form of personal ownership is inseparable from production activity. Because the 1936 Constitution did not characterize ownership of a small-scale private economic operation as a particular type of ownership,[4] Soviet legal theory, while relentlessly following the Constitutional text in all other cases, showed in this specific instance a degree of independence: one group of scholars considered it as a separate type of ownership, another found nothing but a variety of personal ownership.[5]

The first question that arises in connection with these legal and doctrinal postulates is a question that relates to state ownership. Why does state ownership qualify as socialist ownership? Because, as Article 4 of the 1936 Constitution says, it constitutes the wealth of all the people? But this Constitution, in contrast to the 1977 Constitution that has replaced it, did not rely upon the idea of the "state of all the people." Then, how could state ownership be ownership by all of the people? The 1936 Constitution relied upon the idea of the dictatorship of proletariat,[6] and this meant, according to Marx, the creation of a state in which the "proletariat [is] organized as the dominant class."[7] Consequently, at best, only the proletariat, not all of the people, could qualify as the holder of state ownership under the 1936 Constitution. But what kinds of actions could this collective owner implement under circumstances where the jurisdiction of various state agencies taken as a whole exhausted all of the opportunities to which the owner was entitled? Or, could it be that socialist ownership of the Soviet state was only a euphemistic designation for the economic domination of the Soviet bureaucracy? On the other hand, why is the second form of socialist ownership personified by collective farms and other cooperative organizations? It is true that, in contrast to the proletariat, which even formally has no rights with regard to state ownership, members of collective farms or consumer cooperatives are entitled to take part in the management of these entities' activities, at least according to the wording of cooperative/collective farm statutes. However, Article 11 of the 1936 Constitution established that "economic life in the USSR is determined by the state national economic plan." This formula, dealing with the "economic life of the USSR" makes no mention of any exceptions for collective farms or other cooperative organizations. They too are subordinated to the state plan, which is by nature strictly binding and precludes any deviation, except those directly provided for by law. As a matter of course, neither collective farms nor other cooperative organizations may manage their operations otherwise than in the manner indicated by the state plan. Thus in the final analysis, the highest disposition of cooperative/collective farm property is in the grasp of the same dominant bureaucracy, regardless of whether the members' rights to participate in the administration of common affairs are fictitious or genuine. As a result, the distinctions between the two forms of socialist ownership are not so palpable as the 1936 Constitution might suggest.

Finally, if any kind of collective ownership in the USSR is a form of socialist ownership, why are there only two such forms? Consider the most important examples that do not fit in the narrow limits of these two forms: ownership by trade unions and ownership by the Communist Party. Neither one nor the other can qualify as cooperative/collective farm ownership. At the same time, their correlation with state ownership is very peculiar. Trade unions, whose membership includes almost the entire adult urban population, possess a tremendous amount of property. But this property is subordinated to the state no less than are the trade unions themselves. Therefore, implementation of certain state functions by trade unions does not change anything either in the nature of these functions or in their economic substance. Ownership by the Communist Party of the Soviet Union is very different. State agencies exercise no control over the Communist Party's internal economic activity, and, consequently, one cannot argue that ownership by the Party and ownership by the state are identical on the basis of state control. But it can be shown that the two types of ownership are identical, starting from an examination of Party control. The Party, represented by its appropriate agencies, directs the administration of state ownership and, if necessary, employs state resources for the fulfillment of purely Party tasks. Owing to these circumstances, it does not matter whether the Soviet Constitution touches upon trade union and Party ownership or passes over these issues in silence. In all cases, there is one, and solely one owner—the ruling bureaucracy. Only the methods of ruling differ. As soon as this becomes clear, the Constitutional parlance ceases to be an obstacle to the ascertainment of the truth, and one begins to understand the actual situation concealed by the words "socialist ownership" and its "various forms."

The Constitution, as a law and not a text-book, does not, of course, explain its provisions. Therefore the questions formulated above remained unanswered even after the promulgation of the 1977 Constitution. Subsequent legislation could not leave unfilled the gaps in the 1936 Constitution connected with the omission of the ownership of so-called social organizations. The 1961 Fundamental Principles of Civil Legislation, paying no attention to the constitutional dual classification, enumerates three forms of socialist ownership: "state ownership (or ownership by the whole people); ownership by collective farms, other cooperative organizations, their associations; ownership by societal organizations."[8] This new classification was transferred in the draft of the 1977 Constitution. However, a number of scholars, mainly economists, disagreed with this solution when the draft was discussed publicly. They contended, citing Marx, that only ownership of the means of production could be characterized as the basis of the economy, while ownership by societal organizations served primarily non-production purposes. Because of these arguments, the drafters of the 1977 Constitution adopted, in Article 10, another wording: "Socialist ownership of the means of production in the form of state (all-the-people's) and collective farm/cooperative ownership constitutes the basis of the economic system of the USSR. The property of trade unions and other social organizations needed by them to carry out charter tasks also is socialist ownership." The new definition, clumsy as it is, actually implies three forms of socialist ownership, two of them as parts of the basis of the Soviet economic system and one outside of this basis. One can hardly explain what such a differentiation means in terms of Marxist doctrine where all social phenomena are distributed between "the basis" and "the superstructure," while the ownership by social organizations belongs neither to "the superstructure" (as ownership!) nor to "the basis" (as the Constitution provides!). Let, however, the Soviets themselves rationalize their laws from the Marxist point of view. For those who study Soviet laws in the West the fact of the constitutional recognition of another form of socialist ownership, along with the two forms previously proclaimed, is the only matter of significance. Moreover, the 1961 Fundamental Principles of Civil Legislation, which, in contrast to the Constitution, deal with ownership in general, not with its specific substance as "the basis" of the economic system, have retained intact the legal provision confirming *expressis verbis* three forms of socialist ownership, instead of the "two and a half" mentioned in the 1977 Constitution.

Thus, the law in force multiplies the forms of socialist ownership in comparison with former legislation. This law also rejects certain contradictions inherent in the earlier legislation, if not actually, then at least in words. It combines the interpretation of state ownership as "all-the-people's" wealth with the characterization of the Soviet state as an "all-the-people's state." In substance, nothing has been modified, and "all-the-people" as a whole dispose of state property to no greater extent than did the proletariat in its nominal role as the dictatorial class. As in the past, the ruling bureaucracy, not the people, keeps this property in its grasp. But the obvious contradiction contained in the abolished legislation has been doubtlessly eliminated by the new legal provisions. Unfortunately for their compilers, however, these new provisions engender their own contradictions. With respect to the discovery of the true nature of the Soviet regime, these contradictions are incomparably more significant than those that have been eliminated.

The 1936 Constitution did not characterize the Soviet economy as a unitary economic system. Therefore, it could distinguish different types of ownership and different forms within the limits of socialist ownership. The 1977 Constitution uses the notion of the "economic system of the USSR"[9] as an integrated phenomenon which, by definition, cannot be based upon different types of ownership or even upon different forms of one type. While this conclusion is purely theoretical, the Constitution in force renders it practically indisputable, in proclaiming that "the economy of the USSR constitutes a single national economic complex" and that all components of this complex are directed by "state plans of economic and social development."[10] Could a unitary economic complex and its centralized management exist along with socialist ownership of three various forms encumbered by a vast multitude of rightholders? And because the former really exists, the latter is no more than a propagandistic declaration. Only as the actual holder of so-called socialist ownership can the ruling bureaucracy treat the Soviet economy as a single complex under the rulers' domination. However, because it is expedient to apply different approaches to exercising its ruling powers does the bureaucracy consider it reasonable to proclaim the existence of "socialist" ownership in three different forms.

Gorbachev has already eloquently demonstrated that for Soviet leaders economic dogmata are one thing and economic practice is entirely another. Under Gorbachev's leadership, the Twenty-Seventh Congress of the Communist Party adopted a new edition of the Program of the Soviet Communist Party.[11] Communist programs are purely propagandistic documents, and as such they assume strict observance of Marxist dogmata. Therefore, like Brezhnev's Constitution, Gorbachev's Program speaks about socialist ownership, its forms, and the distinctions between these forms.[12] The Program also outlines the direction of future development, which must lead to the merging of these different forms of socialist ownership and result in the establishment of an integrated "all-the-people's" ownership in a stateless communist society.[13] Thus, comprehensive "all-the-people's" ownership is a matter of the communist future, according to Gorbachev's Program. But it is considered as a *fait accompli* when Gorbachev addresses problems of contemporary practice. In order to centralize the administration of agriculture, a new agency, the *Gosagroprom* of the USSR (the State Agricultural Industrial Committee) was created in 1985.[14] *Gosagroprom* has republican and local agencies. As an extremely centralized system, it absorbed not only five Soviet ministries, but also the whole system of consumer cooperatives and all of the collective farms of the country. Is this compatible with the recognition of collective farm/cooperative ownership as a specific form of socialist ownership? From the propagandistic viewpoint, it is not. But propaganda can easily be adjusted to new circumstances by means of appropriate verbal manipulations. From the viewpoint of practice, however, nothing extraordinary has occurred. Since the ruling bureaucracy deals with property under its exclusive ownership, this bureaucracy itself is entitled to decide which method of property administration must be chosen in each specific case.

Soviet theory pays no attention to such practices, assessing the character and differentiation of Soviet ownership in conformity with the Constitution, as if the latter existed in a vacuum, and as if it was in no way connected with Soviet reality. In those rare cases where theoretical constructions deviate from constitutional provisions, the authors of these constructions strive to be more Catholic than the Pope. For instance, the compilers of the 1977 Constitution mention ownership by trade unions and other social organizations only incidentally in order to divert attention from the economic area, where Party ownership is concentrated. Certain Soviet commentators go farther, contending that collective farm/cooperative ownership and trade union or other social organization ownership are the same phenomenon: collective ownership in contrast to state (all-the-people's) ownership.[15] The same compilers distinguish between socialist and personal ownership. This fiction seems insufficient to certain Soviet scholars. One of them proclaims that personal ownership also is socialist ownership.[16] Another thinks that the socialist type of ownership is of two kinds—collective and individual, provided that the former is represented as state, collective farm/cooperative, trade union, and other organization ownership, while the latter is expressed in the form of personal ownership.[17] Thus, instead of the usual fiction of socialist ownership of the means of production, this peculiar interpretation proclaims the fiction of an all-embracing socialist ownership comprising not only collective but even individual property.

The actual situation, however, bears no relation either to constitutional orthodoxy or to doctrinal super-orthodoxy. The economic substance[18] and legal regulation[19] of property relations under the Soviet regime lead to the following conclusions.

First, socialist ownership does not exist in the USSR at all. Utopian socialism in all its variants, including Marxist doctrine, maintains that socialist ownership is only that which belongs to a collective body based upon the equality and labor of its participants. In the USSR, personal ownership is based upon the labor of proprietors, but each proprietor is an individual, not a collective body. In contrast, the Soviet bureaucracy as a proprietor is a collective body, however, this collective body relies upon hierarchical rather than equal relationships, and employs not its own labor but rather that of other persons.

Second, the dominant bureaucracy, functioning under the title of the Soviet state, is the sole proprietor of the Soviet economy, there being only certain insignificant exceptions. Therefore, this economy can be called a state economy, and correspondingly, socialist ownership actually is state ownership. Following this interpretation, the terminology "the state economy" or "state ownership" is used in the remainder of this book.

Third, for political and economic reasons,[20] the actual proprietor of the state economy is interested, on the one hand, in disguising the real situation, and, on the other hand, in managing economic activity by using both direct and indirect methods of administration. The goal of disguising the actual situation is achieved by proclaiming that all kinds of property, except for personal property, are held under socialist ownership. Differentiation between direct and indirect economic management results from designating the most important part of the Soviet economy as objects of state ownership and from categorizing other, less significant, components of the economy as the property of collective farms, cooperative and social organizations. In fact, however, a disguise can not transform state ownership into socialist ownership, and different methods of management do not diminish the comprehensive nature of state ownership. The latter exists either under its own name or under the name of the property of collective farms, cooperative or other organizations.

Fourth, as a general rule, the ownership of collective farms, cooperatives and other organizations is state ownership in a modified form. As an exception to this general rule, there exist organizations such as housing cooperatives or garage cooperatives that free the Soviet state from substantial expenses, which are paid instead by the citizen-members and are repaid to these same citizens upon termination of their membership. Cooperative organizations of this kind represent modified ownership, ownership not by the Soviet state, but by Soviet citizens.

Fifth, once individual labor activity has become available to any Soviet citizen, regardless of whether he is an individual artisan or a hired worker or official, distinctions made between personal and non-personal individual ownership no longer make any sense. All Soviet citizens possess or may possess their own property, and the source of its acquisition—income from individual labor or salaries received for hired labor—no longer affects the resulting economic or legal characterization. However, because Soviet legislation does not employ the terminology "individual ownership," it seems preferable to use the terminology "personal ownership" in order to avoid purely verbal difficulties in legal analysis of the Soviet economic system.

Production

Ownership of the means of production is a "dead" prerequisite of production activity. In order to transform this prerequisite into a component of the production process it must be connected with human labor, a "living" prerequisite of the same activity. Different social epochs develop different forms of connecting human labor with the means of production. These forms are reduced by Marxism with respect to the presocialist period to economic and extra-economic coercion. The latter was employed in the slaveowning and feudal societies where slaves and serfs worked for the benefit of their owners, because they were compelled to do so, not because of the absence of other sources of income. The former, economic coercion, according to orthodox Marxism, is typical in a capitalist society where workers, deprived of other sources of income, have no choice but to work for the benefit of their employers. Addressing the future, Marx predicted (and addressing the present, the Soviet rulers contend) that socialism assumes the free labor of individuals for their own benefit and simultaneously for the benefit of society. Regardless of whether one consults Stalin's or Brezhnev's Constitution,[21] Khrushchev's Party Program or Gorbachev's Party Program,[22] one will find the characterization of the specific socialist method of connecting labor force with the means of production expressed identically not only in content but even in wording. However, serious doubts arise as to whether any of these documents guarantees a Marxist Utopia when one examines them more closely.

The Soviet Constitution, announcing that Marx's prophecies have become realities in the USSR, provides for both a right to labor and a duty to work.[23] Why must the right to labor be combined with a duty to work? If labor is free, the appropriate right should be sufficient; but if there exists a universal duty to work, labor lacks the element of freedom. One's suspicions are strengthened by a textual comparison of the legal provisions concerning this right and this duty. The right to work is guaranteed only economically ("by the socialist system of economy"),[24] while the duty to work is enforced by the threat of punishment for its violation ("avoidance of socially useful labor is incompatible with the principles of a socialist society."[25]) Does this not mean that economic and extra-economic coercion, separated from one another under previous social systems, are now jointly employed under the system of Soviet socialism? Historical and contemporary data eliminate the last remainders of doubt in this regard. "Nationalization" and expropriation were measures of extra-economic coercion. However, after these measures' implementation, those who lost their property were economically compelled to work "for the benefit of society." The collectivization of agriculture resulted not from economic stimuli but from the application of the most brutal violence. Thus, membership in collective farms, compelled by extra-economic coercion, supplies Soviet agriculture with a labor force, which could not be guaranteed in any other way. Two additional methods have been applied to ensure the continuity of supply of agricultural labor.

On the one hand, bureaucratic control makes it impossible for the children of collective farmers to avoid become members of their farm upon reaching the age of 16.[26] On the other hand, the system of registration of permanent residence, introduced in the USSR in 1933, i.e. immediately after completion of the collectivization of agriculture, has functioned differently in villages than in cities. Urban inhabitants received documents called "passports." Under the passport legislation, all persons in urban areas were required to present identification to the authorities on various occasions and residence permits entered in passports were required for stays of more than a few days in most urban areas. The passports provided city-dwellers with identification and a place for their residence permits. Collective farmers received no passports. They could visit cities briefly with written permission from their collective farm—this permission would serve as identification—but they could not obtain residence permits because they had no passports in which the permits could be entered. In the late 1970's passports were also issued in rural areas. However, in principle, the previous system has suffered no modification because of certain indications included in collective farmers' passports known only to agencies of MVD (Ministry of Internal Affairs), which are responsible for administering the passport and residence permit laws. These indications identify the passport holder as being engaged in an agricultural profession, and therefore the same restrictions with respect to freedom of movement continue to apply to such individuals. Such restrictions, of course, strengthen extra-economic coercion. Extra-economic coercion is supplemented by economic coercion, bearing in mind that the plot of land allocated to each collective-farm family for private farming, the principal source of sustenance for a collective farmer and his family, will be withdrawn immediately if the farmer terminates his membership in a collective farm or ceases to work in the collective farming operations.

In contrast, urban workers have always been economically compelled to sell their labor, because the means of production necessary for engaging in independent economic activity actually are no more available to them today after the "victory of socialism" than they were in the pre-socialist period. But even in this case extra-economic coercion proves to be indispensable. Comparing the official salary paid by state enterprises with the income that one could earn from engaging in individual labor activity, one can imagine the number of workers that would engage only in individual labor, were they not compelled to combine this activity with the status of an employee at a Soviet economic entity or other Soviet organization. Finally, the general prohibition against individual ownership of any means of production, except extremely restricted range of implements (e.g., a violin, a typewriter, a paintbrush), functions as the most substantial form of extra-economic coercion, ensuring "socially useful" labor from those who otherwise could develop their genuine social usefulness. In addition, extra-economic coercion in the USSR includes punitive violence, while economic coercion is almost entirely devoid of economic incentive. Taking into account all these considerations, one can not only ascertain but also explain the weakest points of the Soviet production economy. Generally speaking, its vulnerability stems from the absence of economic interest on the part of the direct producers, whose labor is therefore always forced, regardless of whether economic or extra-economic coercion prevails under any given set of circumstances. This general vulnerability manifests itself in various specific forms, the most important of which have become the scourge of the Soviet economy, and, consequently, these forms are deserving of special analysis.

Fluctuations in the availability of manpower have long since become a permanent problem in the USSR, and the construction industry suffers more than any other industrial branch from such fluctuations. Ultimately, the Soviet government was compelled to establish certain privileges for construction enterprises. They are allowed to recruit workers in rural areas and to guarantee these workers residence permits in the city to which they were recruited, on the condition that they agree to work for no fewer than three years. Continued work for the same employer is rewarded by the allotment of apartments in one of the buildings constructed. Such privileges are very important, taking into consideration that the food supply in industrial cities is far better than in small settlements and that acquisition of the right to use living space in a state apartment building is the dream of a great many individuals in the USSR. Therefore, these special regulations make it possible for building industry enterprises to prevent fluctuations of manpower, or at least to retain employees for several years. Other enterprises, which do not have similar advantages, must overcome their difficulties by means of special inventiveness. Numerous plants in Moscow, Leningrad, and other cities, where issuance of residence permits is severely restricted, hire their workers in September and October, when the draftees are discharged from the Soviet armed services and are free to take any job of their choice not only in the city or another place where they resided at the time they were drafted. The ex-soldiers try to take jobs that will improve their places of residence from the viewpoint of food supply, housing conditions etc. Since, however, the newcomers disperse soon after arrival, the same procedure must be repeated the following September and October. Unilateral termination of labor relations puts workers in a very disadvantageous situation in regard to social insurance and even with respect to the acquisition of a new job (only through a special bureau, in accordance with its recommendation, etc.). But none of these kinds of economic and extra-economic coercion are sufficiently successful. Therefore, the management of enterprises, having just completed the training necessary for one "detachment" of hired workers several months earlier, must begin the training anew after the expiration of this short period of time. Thus, even if the Soviet authorities were to implement the technological renovation of their industry at the promised level, untrained workers could remain as an insurmountable obstacle on the path of technological progress.

Along with fluctuation in manpower, a low level of labor discipline impedes economic progress in the USSR. For instance, several professors from Leningrad University came to the conclusion, on the basis of personal observation, that after subtracting time lost due to starting work late, extending midday meal breaks, overstaying "smoke breaks," quitting for the day early, etc., the actual time worked at the largest Leningrad automobile repair plant was not over two hours and forty minutes, rather than the official eight hours. In order to compare, in this regard, work in industry with work in services, they managed to obtain the necessary information from machine-building and shipbuilding plants. The results were approximately the same.[27] Thus, Andropov had serious reasons to consider the strengthening of labor discipline as the most important source of raising the productivity of labor.[28] Were this source to be fully exploited, Soviet industry could produce far more than produced at the time of Brezhnev's death. However, even Soviet media, accustomed to exaggerate the country's achievements, calculated the actual increase in the productivity of labor as only 3% to 5%. Thus, violations of labor discipline on a massive scale are inseparable from the nature of the Soviet economy, and while extra-economic coercion can compel one to work, it cannot compel one to work well. However, Andropov resorted only to forcible measures, and it apparently did not occur to him that economic stimuli would be more efficient. Therefore, the eventual result could be foreseen from the very beginning: as you saw, you shall know.

In addition, the Soviet economy suffers immense losses on account of drunkenness. There is no need to elaborate upon this open secret. A Soviet governmental decree of May 7, 1985,[29] initiated by Gorbachev and directed primarily against drunkenness during working hours, eloquently explains the actual state of affairs in one of its provisions, which prohibits the sale before 2 p.m. on any work day not only of liquor, as is stated in the published text, but also of Eau de Cologne, as is provided in the unpublished text.

It is quite possible that, as a result, drunkenness during work hours will be if not entirely eliminated, then at least substantially diminished. One must not, however, assume that the decrease which has been mandated in the production of liquor will bear as a part of new legislation to corresponding curtailment of state income. While decreasing production, the Soviet authorities have increased the price of alcoholic beverages to such a level that little income will be lost. In May of 1985, retail liquor prices were increased 25%, and on August 1, 1986, according to *Izvestia*, the prices were increased another 25%. In combining these two measures, Soviet rulers know quite well a fact that might astonish a foreigner but not the country's inhabitants: the average Soviet citizen rarely spends a day off without consuming a bottle of vodka, and no increase in price can prevent the observance of this historically rooted habit. Thus, it is not those who drink but their families who feel the blow from this aspect of Gorbachev's anti-alcohol policy. To appreciate the strength of the blow inflicted, one must bear in mind that with eight days off during a month and with each bottle of vodka costing seven rubles, one third of the average monthly Soviet salary of 180 rubles is consumed in the purchase of alcohol. The real causes of Russian drunkenness stem, however, not from the price of vodka but from pervasive material and spiritual factors, which have never been mentioned by Soviet publications but the functioning of which cannot be concealed. The Soviet rulers understand this quite well, as is shown by the decree mentioned above, which, as part of the battle against drunkeness, provides for the construction of new clubs, sports complexes, and other recreational facilities. Yet, the financing allocated for these goals is so preposterously limited that no one could consider it as a genuine counterbalance to such a widespread evil. The traditional combination of economic and extra-economic coercion in the fight against drunkenness will be no more efficient in maintaining sobriety than it is in maintaining labor discipline.

Now, because the Soviet labor force is primarily made up of the generations born during World War II and in the postwar period, the Soviet economy experiences specific difficulties: the methods traditionally used to effect the extensive development of the national economy collide with the country's shortage of manpower. Therefore, the new Soviet leadership decided to try the method of intensive economic development, by improving the "dead" component of production activity, the means of production, instead of expending its "living" component, human labor. The necessity of such an approach was first proclaimed by Gorbachev on June 11, 1985, at a meeting sponsored by the Central Committee of the Party and dedicated to "means of accelerating scientific/technological progress" in the USSR.[30] In his view, "the concept of acceleration of the social/economic development of the country on the basis of scientific/technological progress" signifies "not simply an increase in the tempo of the growth of the national economy," but "a new quality of development," relying upon intensification, rather than extensiveness, and demanding effective forms of economic management.[31] He argues that "the necessity of accelerating social/economic development is determined by . . . internal demands," and, at the same time, it "results from external circumstances. We must make necessary investments in the country's defense . . . We cannot allow military superiority over us."[32] Thus, the economic undertakings suggested by Gorbachev preclude any change in the distribution of funds earmarked for military and non-military goals. Nevertheless, he knows that the "implementation of a new technological reconstruction . . . will demand enormous investment."[33] He asks: "Where will one get them?," and he asserts: "The answer in principle is as follows: the projected measures accelerating scientific/technological progress must pay for themselves."[34] However, when can this occur? Gorbachev does not avoid this question, and he has the correct answer: "It is necessary to have a certain time for this goal."[35] Well, but what must be done before this "certain time" expires, bearing in mind especially that "resources are immediately necessary"?[36] Unfortunately, in this case the answer is not so definite as the question. "Here," the answer proceeds, "it is impossible to act without manipulation of resources, their concentration in key positions."[37] Such a response is completely inexplicable, remembering that any manipulation of military funding is precluded and that the alternative of manipulation with respect to salary and wages would cause an unbearable economic situation for the Soviet citizenry. The future will show the extent to which Gorbachev's economic policy is practicable, although, judging from his arguments, he himself is not sure that he will be able to find a way out of the dilemma currently faced by the Soviet economy.

In connecting human labor with the means of production by combining economic and extra-economic coercion, the Soviet authorities, since they proclaim the existence of various forms of socialist ownership in their society, must employ, at least in appearance, different forms of establishing the desired links on the basis of state and collective farm/cooperative ownership. To some extent this differentiation is formally observed: enterprises relying upon state ownership execute labor contracts, while membership plays the same role for enterprises based upon collective farm/cooperative ownership. Should socialist ownership really express itself in two different forms, the areas in which labor contracts and membership are employed would be entirely distinguishable, and any overlapping would be completely precluded. In practice, however, it is otherwise.

State ownership has never served as a basis of membership. But workers who have finished professional schools and those who have graduated from universities and institutes must enter into labor contracts with the often geographically remote enterprises or other entities to which they are sent by the competent agencies and where they must work for no less than two or three years depending on the character of their professional training. Consequently, in these cases, labor contracts are as compulsory as is collective farm membership. Children of collective farmers, upon reaching the age of 16, automatically become members of the same collective farm, and even the purely formal procedure of admission to membership at a general meeting of collective farmers, provided for by legal provisions,[38] is not regularly observed in practice. On the other hand, collective farms employ the labor not only of their members but also of those who have been attracted to collective farm production by means of labor contracts. As the Model Collective Farm Charter states in Article 24, "the hiring of specialists and other workers from outside for work is permitted only in those instances when there are no corresponding specialists on the collective farm or when agricultural and other work can not be accomplished within the necessary periods by the efforts of the collective farmers." The latter demand is, in fact, satisfied not so much by means of labor contracts as through the compulsory dispatch to rural areas of urban inhabitants, not only adults but also schoolboys and schoolgirls, in order to help collective farms during the annual harvest, the most important season of agricultural production. And because one master would never send his workers to serve another master without some form of reimbursement, this fact alone is sufficient to prove that the property of collective farms is under state ownership to no less degree than is state property itself. The situation of consumer cooperatives is very peculiar. Inhabitants of rural areas are obliged to be members of consumer cooperatives. But the only duty of the members is to pay monetary dues. The daily work of consumer cooperatives is implemented by salesmen and other officials or workers with whom the cooperatives execute labor contracts. Management officers (chairmen and their deputies), while actually appointed by Party agencies, are formally elected at general meetings or at conferences of cooperative members. Therefore, these officers must also be members of the cooperatives. However, they actually function not as elected members but as appointed managers, and the cooperative form of socialist ownership does not affect their official position. Thus, the unity of state ownership in the USSR, despite the Soviet rulers' statements about different forms of socialist ownership, can be demonstrated not only by analyzing ownership itself but also by examining production as the second component of the Soviet economy.

Distribution

As discussed above,[39] the Soviet economy, organized on the model of "a single national economic complex," is directed by state plans. The centralized planning of the Soviet economy starts with the size of output and then addresses the area of distribution in the relations between the state and separate entities, between these entities themselves, and between each of these entities and their individual workers.

Distribution in the area of relations between the state and separate entities includes, as a rule, monetary resources, and when dealing with collective farms, their agricultural product. Financial distribution moves in two opposites directions: from separate entities to the state, and from the state to the separate entities. The first direction is the principal one with respect to entities that carry out profitable economic activity. Normally, these entities must transfer annual payments for the use of production funds to the state.[40] The larger these funds, the higher the level of payments. A portion of the remaining profit serves as the source for the creation of incentive funds at these economic entities.[41] Beyond these limits, profit in monetary form must be transferred to the state at the end of the economic year, except for that portion required for the performance of the following year's planned tasks.[42] Briefly, then, profit must be transferred to the state after subtracting the deductions listed, while production funds and specially designated portions of profit are retained by economic entities.

The movement of monetary resources in the second, opposite direction, from the state to separate entities, occurs only in cases provided for by the law. The character of these cases can serve as the first illustration of the profitability for the Soviet regime of various managerial methods based upon the legal differentiation of various forms of socialist ownership despite the actual domination of unitary state ownership. The state finances major construction projects undertaken by state entities.[43] Collective farms and consumer cooperatives themselves finance their major construction projects, despite the facts that the farms enrich the state by selling agricultural products to state procurement agencies at prices officially set far below market.[44] and that the cooperatives transfer to the state the lion's share of their profit in the form of turnover taxes. Further, since the state is especially interested in developing military, metallurgical, and certain other branches of production, it establishes for the enterprises in these sectors a privileged regime of planned losses compensated by state subsidies. Collective farms and consumer cooperatives receive from the state, if necessary, loans, not subsidies. Finally, state institutions and other non-profit-making entities are maintained by state financing. But where institutions are connected with cooperative or social organizations, these organizations, not the state, provide the necessary financial resources.

The distribution of agricultural products is subordinated to different regulations with respect to state farms and collective farms. Both state farms and collective farms are obliged to transfer to the state a large portion of their output, a portion determined by the plan and paid for at established prices, which are lower than the cost to the producers.[45] However, state farms are compensated for the resulting deficit by state subsidies, while collective farms must resort to extracting profit from other sources in order to cover their costs (sale of surplus agricultural produce to consumer cooperatives and to individuals, low payment for the labor of collective farmers, etc.). Soviet law does not expressly provide for land rent for the "nationalized" land made available to collective farms. It is clear, however, that the losses incurred by collective farms, which result from the established low prices paid by state procurement agencies for collective farms' agricultural produce, ultimately are borne by collective farmers themselves. Thus the legal fiction that the farms are held in collective farm ownership rather than state ownership serves as the justification for the *de facto* charging of land rent by the Soviet regime.

Distribution in the area of relations between Soviet entities themselves is based upon the centralized planning of distribution of the goods produced. A part of the goods, not very important from the economic point of view, primarily those goods whose production exceeds demand, is left at the disposal of the producer. This part may be sold to any entity as a purchaser. In this case, exchange with no preceding distribution leads to acquisition by one entity of articles produced by another entity. In all other cases, exchange is illegal without planned distribution. From the Soviet point of view, the ideal situation assumes complete congruity between production, trade, and distribution planning. However, such congruity can be established only with regard to production activity. The system of trade receives in the form of distribution only the amount of goods that can be provided by production capacity, regardless of the level of consumer demand. A system of rigidly fixed prices prevents the use of price to match demand to supply. And in the process of planning production activity, true conformity between indices of production and distribution arises only as a rare exception to the general rule. If divergence takes the form of distribution of supplies to a producer exceeding the planned recipients needs, it is more convenient for the intended purchaser to refuse the planned surplus supply than to buy it. The acquisition of surplus production assets funds entails an increase in the annual payment to the state for the use of such assets. At the same time, the organization that has acquired surplus assets may not directly sell them, but is obligated to first try to transfer them to the area of the planned distribution.

If, vice versa, the indices of distribution do not provide the purchaser with resources adequate to meet its production needs, this creates a very complicated situation for the purchaser. Formally, the purchaser is entitled to demand modification either of its production plan or of the supply quota allocated to it by distribution plans. However, because of the notorious Soviet red tape, it can often occur that the modifications needed will be carried out too late, and the purchaser will fail to fulfill its plan, and will suffering all of the negative results of this underfulfillment (reduced transfers to incentive funds, payment of smaller bonuses to officials and workers, etc.). Therefore, economic managers strive to fulfill the established production plan despite any disproportion between it and the plan of distribution. Depending upon the circumstances, this can be achieved either by means of bribery, which "encourages" the supplier of the requisite materials to illegally sell them regardless of the planned distribution, or by padding or other manipulation of accounts concerning the fulfillment of plans. Although both approaches are punished as crimes,[46] economic managers often prefer to appear up to the mark in their professional activity than to yield to legal threats. Furthermore, judicial practice, severe as it is with respect to bribery in general, only rarely deals with bribes employed in inter-official relations, and judicial hearings of cases connected with so-called fakery or eyewash ("*ochkovtiratel'stvo*") are used, apart from special campaigns initiated by new leaders, more as educational show trials than as a method of fighting against violations inseparable from the Soviet system.

Distribution in the area of relations between Soviet entities and their workers is based, in conformity with the Soviet Constitution, on the principle "From each according to his ability, to each according to his labor." Since the level of income of Soviet citizens is also planned, this principle can be implemented only within the limits of plan indices. As a result, the rule "to each according to his labor" does not mean that labor is paid in the USSR according to its value. Even relying upon obviously exaggerated Soviet official data, which has indicated 180 rubles as the average monthly earnings, one can easily believe statistics that after all deductions (income taxes, payment for housing, purchase of clothing, etc.) the typical Soviet family can spend only 3 rubles and 30 kopecks (about 2 dollars and 55 cents) a day for food.[47] Thus, the additional benefits received by the Soviet citizenry (education and medical treatment free of charge, social insurance at the expense of employers, low rent in state apartment buildings, etc.) that serves as a pretext for continual boasting by the Soviet rulers, merely increases individuals' earnings to a level which is at the bottom limit of natural necessities. The rule "to each according to his labor" also does not mean, despite its literal wording, equal pay for equal work. The same job is lower paid in rural areas than in urban areas. Moreover, in rural areas workers at state farms receive higher pay than do members of collective farms. The official explanation for this difference is that salary at state farms is determined by the state, while the income of collective farmers depends on the profitability of their collective farms. In fact, however, this is yet another illustration of the economic advantages derived by the Soviet rulers from the artificial separation of collective farm/cooperative ownership from state ownership. Finally, the rule "to each according to his labor" is not combined with any criteria which would justify differentiation in payment for different kinds of labor. Why does an engineer earn less than his subordinate, a skilled craftsman? Why are scholars of the same level paid differently where their research establishments officially belong to different ranks? Why do writer's fees depend less on the quality than on the length of the published book? No one can satisfactorily answer these questions. At any rate, these phenomena have nothing in common with the Constitutional rule of distribution addressed to individuals.

The Constitutional rule has nothing in common with the actual distribution applicable to the ruling bureaucracy. In monetary form, the salary of a bureaucrat of the lowest rank is approximately twice as large as the average salary in the USSR. Soviet officials of the highest rank are paid approximately five times as much as the lowest ranking members of the bureaucracy. However, salary in monetary form does not constitute all of the income received by the Soviet bureaucracy. Their most important privileges are connected with signs reading "CLOSED": closed shops and restaurants, closed hospitals and drugstores, closed health resorts and country houses, etc. Since such closed establishments provide goods and services to their clients without charge or at prices lower than cost, the formal ratio of two to one of a low-ranking bureaucrat's salary to an average working person's salary must be replaced by a ratio of ten to one of effective income levels. Comparison of the income of top Soviet officials with the salaries of ordinary citizens is meaningless, because these officials, in effect, have unlimited resources at their disposal.[48]

In contrast, the Soviet policy of pricing goods for the consumption of the public at large has moved in the opposite direction,[49] at least if one studies this policy beginning with the early 1960's. At that time Khrushchev, who had previously promised to surpass the USA in the production of meat, butter, and milk, substantially increased the prices of these very items. Since then, modifications in retail prices have been periodically implemented in three principal forms: (1) public increases in the prices of goods which do not qualify as items of mass consumption (gold and fur products under Brezhnev) or the consumption of which is a social evil (vodka and other alcoholic beverages under Gorbachev); (2) public decreases in the prices of articles which are not in demand (clothes made of synthetics under Brezhnev) or the consumption of which, as opposed to a social evil, is not connected with large expenses (nonalcoholic beverages under Gorbachev); (3) concealed increases in almost all other prices disguised by the replacement of withdrawn goods by new goods with different and perhaps fancier labels, but of the same quality (Khrushchev and all his successors, including Gorbachev). The psychological ground for these concealed increases in retail prices of the form described has been cleverly prepared by the Soviet leadership. Most important was Khrushchev's monetary reform of the early 1960's. In appearance, his reform was economically neutral: the value of money and the prices of goods were simultaneously ten times decreased. However, if a price is, for instance, 10 rubles, an increase to 13 rubles would strike one's eye, while the same manipulation performed by the transfer from a price of one ruble to one ruble and thirty kopecks would go almost unnoticed. The results of this "reform" were manifested very soon. With the old money, the price of a tolerable midday meal at a plant cafeteria did not exceed two or three rubles, while with current money, one ruble, formally equivalent to ten old rubles, provides a meal of a far lower quality. Thus, an increase in the average salary from 160 to 180 rubles a month, officially proclaimed by the Soviets several years ago, even if it has really occurred, signifies only nominal progress. Taking into consideration the dynamics of retail prices, the actual situation has worsened rather than improved.

The preposterously small share of national income distributed to the Soviet citizenry neither corresponds to the rule "to each according to his labor" nor stimulates one to follow the rule "from each according to his ability." Nevertheless, there is no hope that the Soviets will, in the foreseeable future, change their economic policy in this area, because it is owing to just this policy that they manage to resolve problems which otherwise would remain insoluble.

First, the traditional principle of distribution in relations with individuals is the most important economic guarantee against unemployment in the USSR. If the workers really received payment according to their labor, they would not miss a minute of their working hours, and, as a result, a smaller staff could achieve the same economic efficiency. This would inevitably lead to unemployment, despite the extensive method of Soviet economic development. In reality, under the system of payment for labor employed in the USSR, unemployment exists as a phenomenn deeply concealed by the payment of salaries lower than the amount paid in the Untied States as welfare benefits and by the habitual alternation of work hours and hours of idleness. Of course, a decrease in the number of hours of idleness as a source of an increase in the number of work hours would be a positive development but only on the condition that salaries remain at the same level. As to a simultaneous increase in salaries, this would be a crushing economic burden, the lightening of which could be obtained exclusively by means of reductions in personnel with unemployment as the final result. Therefore, Soviet rulers, in their struggle to strengthen labor discipline, resort to coercion and avoid encouragement.

Second, the extensive method of economic development assumes that labor is cheap to the extent which renders increase in personnel more profitable than technological renovations. Conversely, fair payment for labor is impossible without a move from extensive to intensive economic methods. The latter, however, would entail an increase in expenses which far exceeds the economic capacity of the USSR as a "closed" country unable to extract material resources on the basis of international cooperation. Thus, the Soviet economy cannot be developed other than by means of unrestrained exploitation of the Soviet people. In this regard, it is very noteworthy that Soviet statistics have never presented a comparison of the salary of producers with the value of the goods produced, because such statistics would reveal the true degree of exploitation in the country whose Constitution contends that "Soviet power . . . has ended forever the exploitation of man by man."[50] The Soviet leaders have invented a more simple and less dangerous interpretation of salary/production ratio: since each individual works for both himself and his society, then, regardless of the labor devoted to each, there is no exploitation in the USSR.

Third, while relying upon extensive development of their economy, the Soviet authorities cannot disregard the necessity of intensive development. This a necessity does not depend merely upon extraordinary circumstances such as the present problems relating to the provision of the Soviet economy with the labor force it needs.[51] There exist more important factors of a permanent nature. Especially significant among them are the social ambitions of a country claimed to be the most progressive in human history and the military ambitions of its rulers to be one of the two world superpowers. However, intensive economic development in the USSR has two peculiar characteristics. On the one hand, technological innovation has never led to the rejection of manual labor. Where the replacement of manual labor with sophisticated machinery is not absolutely essential, the former seems preferable to the latter. On the other hand, though new technology demands the labor of more qualified individuals, this does not, in principle, affect the size of the share of income allocated by "society" for individuals. And it cannot be otherwise, since it is by keeping this share small that society provides the only source of financing the introduction of new technology.

It is true that, along with accelerating social/economic development on the basis of scientific/technological progress,[52] Gorbachev promises the Soviet people that the resources used to satisfy their needs will be doubled during the forthcoming fifteen years.[53] But the same people have been already promised that they would live under communism by 1980, and since this has not occurred, Gorbachev himself considered it necessary to correct the Party Program issued by his voluntaristic predecessor. The future will tell whether or not Gorbachev's predictions also must be corrected. However, under all circumstances, the earmarking of an extremely small portion of distributed resources for individual consumption is the most important feature of the Soviet economic system. Whoever is the Soviet leader, this factor will not be susceptible either to elimination or even to modification.

Exchange

Marxist theory rejected the use under socialism of economic-exchange characterized by goods-money relationships. In accordance with this theory, Lenin abolished exchange and introduced direct distribution of goods, upon his proclamation of War Communism after the Bolsheviks seized political power. Direct distribution, applied to economic and other entities as well as to individuals, was implemented on the meager basis of permanent underproduction. Therefore, it actually developed into rationing, and thus, during War Communism, rationing replaced exchange.

When War Communism turned into an economic disaster, Lenin announced the New Economic Policy. The implementation of this policy involved not merely a limited restoration of private ownership in the Soviet economy, as some Western scholars contend, erroneously following the official interpretation widespread in the USSR.[54] NEP was a universal infusion of goods-money relations into the Soviet economy, regardless of whether the participants in these relations were individual consumers, private enterprises, or states entities. As a result, the introduction of NEP entailed the replacement of rationing by exchange.

The abolition of NEP did not eliminate exchange. But new methods of economic management led to the restoration of rationing in the form of planned distribution for Soviet entities and of direct or concealed rationing for individual consumers.[55] Because of these innovations, goods-money relations lost their traditional features: instead of free decisions exercised by their participants, commands dictated "from above" began to play the determinative role in economic relations. Neither pure rationing nor genuine exchange but exchange governed by rationing has prevailed in the USSR. The new system, introduced by Stalin, has suffered certain fluctuations in favor either of exchange or of rationing, but, in principle, no subsequent leader has ventured to abandon this mixed system, since such a step would undermine the Soviet variant of economic management and, in the final analysis, the Soviet system as a whole. Gorbachev frankly supports this continuity, emphasizing the necessity of simultaneously strengthening "centralized principles of management and planning," on the one hand, and "economic independence and responsibility of associations and enterprises," on the other hand.[56]

In relations between Soviet entities, exchange governed by rationing means that the plan of distribution outlines the highest upper limits for the acquisition of equipment, materials, etc. At the same time, the monetary resources that are at the disposal of the planned recipient must then prove its economic capacity to buy that which the plan allows it to acquire. Thus, the plan of distribution rations purchasing on the basis of the size of output and the scope of demand, and, if, as is usually the case, demand exceeds output, the planning agencies take into account the significance of the economic activities of different purchasers and calculate correspondingly the different quotas for each of them. After that, the purchasing power of an addressee of distribution, evidenced by its monetary resources, allows for an indirect verification of the compiled plan as correct or erroneous. Economic entities (such as factories), acting as purchasers, can take advantage of the opportunities offered by the plan only on the condition that their profitability has provided them with money sufficient to make the requisite payments. Non-economic institutions (such as universities), may spend for the same purpose only specially allocated financing and only on the condition that the required expenses are indicated in their approved budgets. In the area under discussion, the agencies of centralized planning control exchange not only by conducting distribution in kind but also by regulating purchase prices. Raising a price diminishes demand, while decrease of a price increases demand. Conforming to the actual interests of Soviet rulers, economic entities of one group sell their product at artificially high prices, and any surplus profit is transferred to the state along with the greater portion of normal profit, while economic entities of another group sell their product at artificially low prices, and their losses are covered by state subsidies. Manipulation of prices allows the planning agencies to keep exchange within the limits desired, even where it is not preceded by centralized distribution.[57] In addition, all kinds of economic activity auxiliary to exchange also are subject to centralized planning. For instance, a product once sold must be transported from the seller's to the purchaser's place of business by rail, water or other means of transportation, operated by the appropriate independent entities. Of course, an efficient system of centralized planning would ensure the requisite coordination between the plan of distribution and the plan of transportation. Unfortunately, the daily reality is far from the ideal. The backwardness of Soviet transport additionally hampers the normal development of Soviet exchange, and a supplier is relieved of all liability, if distributed and acquired goods have not been delivered on time to the purchaser because of an insufficient allocation of transportation resources in the plan for the given economic relation. Due to all these circumstances and contrary to the dogma that only the negative remnants of the past engender violations of law in the USSR, the Soviet system of exchange employed in relations between Soviet entities, has created its own, purely Soviet types of punishable behavior. Violations of law such as the acquisition of a distributed product by an entity not indicated by the plan, the purchase of this product in a quantity exceeding the planned quota, deviations from the centrally established price structure, delivery of goods contrary to planned transportation, etc.—all of these crimes are incompatible with a market economy. Such violations can be committed only within a socialist economic system of the Soviet type.

In relations where Soviet entities must supply individuals with goods and servicing of various kinds, the subordination of exchange to rationing results from a great number of policies in effect. In addition to direct or concealed rationing,[58] the following methods are the most common in Soviet practice:

(1) Pricing policy. Prices of goods in short supply are systematically increased either by the Government or by the State Committee on Prices. The discretion of the agencies that plan retail prices is especially substantial in respect to imported goods, the amount of which grows year after year. The Soviet consumer cannot estimate the actual value of these goods by comparison with the prices of similar articles of domestic production because of the complete absence of any similarity. At the same time, even at very high prices, the demand for imported goods far exceeds their supply. Therefore, according to a confidential conversation with one of the officials of a planning agency, which deals with the regulation of the prices of imported goods, these officials strive to establish the highest possible prices, taking their maximum level "out of the air." However, because of the incessant lag of supply behind demand, certain members of the Soviet citizenry have accumulated so much money, that even the most expensive goods are immediately bought up. Thus, instead of normalizing exchange, the planned increase of retail prices affects the purchasing capacity of average customers, leaving untouched the same capacity of well-to-do individuals. Nevertheless, the Soviet authorities understand that certain goods must be available to all individuals for the sake of the stability of the regime. They have never forgotten that "bread mutinies" (*khlebnye bunty*) brought about the downfall of Russian tsarism in February 1917. This is why they do not hesitate to spend gold and hard currency to

provide their socialism with the "grain aid" of capitalism, since the required resources cannot be provided by the Soviets' own agriculture. Moreover, in the USSR, as an exception to the rule, the price of bread is lower than cost,[59] and the bread supply, though far from uninterrupted, is incomparably better than is the supply of other goods.

(2) Policy of territorial differentiations. The prices of basic necessities usually are uniform throughout the entire country. Beyond these limits, what are called zonal prices (*poiasnye tseny*) are employed. Such prices would be quite justified, if their variance resulted from different transportation expenses or other costs. Actually, however, these factors are of only minor significance. Other reasons are taken into account: the attraction of manpower to certain districts of the country, the creation of a counterbalance to the increased salaries established for northern areas and certain other parts of the country, the artificial decreases in demand when supply is worse than usual, etc. Along with manipulating prices, the Soviets differentiate between territorial areas by determining different supply levels for different locations. Formally such differentiation is a secret, but in fact it is an open secret. Everybody knows that, in this regard, Moscow is an extraordinary city, while other cities and provinces belong to one of three ranks determined by the Soviet government. Furthermore, different districts of Leningrad or other large cities have their own ranks within the established territorial limits. The higher the rank the better the supply. The inhabitants of Leningrad know that they can buy certain articles on Nevsky Prospect but not at the outskirts of the city. As to provincial inhabitants, they periodically visit the nearest city of supply of the first rank in order to procure needed goods either for themselves or for a group of individuals distributing transportation costs and other expenses among themselves. This tendency disrupts to some extend the efficiency of the territorial policy in the area of supply. But most citizens rely upon the retail-trade system functioning nearest their places of residence. Thus, ultimately the Soviet leadership achieves its goal of creating the appearance of a good or, at least, tolerable supply in the most visited areas at the expense of the population settled in less important districts.

(3) Policy of special rules. There is no need to deal separately with the special rules applicable in the area of "closed" supply for the benefit of the Soviet elite.[60] Receiving goods either without charge or at prices below cost, the Soviet elite in fact enjoys distribution without exchange in the former case and very inexpensive exchange in the latter case. As to the level of supply, it is a direct function of one's position on the hierarchical ladder, and there is no upper limit on supply at the top of this ladder. In contrast, special rules that have everyday significance are established with the purpose of decreasing the purchasing capacity of average citizens in addition to economic limitations. Thus, the quantity of certain kinds of food bought by one purchaser at a state store may not exceed established limits.[61] Automobiles and other scarce articles of durable use are sold on the principle of chronological priority only to persons registered in advance

in the established manner.[62] The principle of registered priority, although it limits citizens' purchasing capacity, is, at any rate, better than the system that prevails, for example, at automobile repair shops where only by spending the previous night outside of such a shop can one expect that his car will be repaired on the following day. The acquisition of prefabricated houses is available to those who have received a plot of land for building purposes, but the land plots are allocated subject to certain conditions (the lack of living premises or their substantial defects) and the fulfillment of complicated formalities (registration at one's workplace, observance of the principle of priority, etc.). These and similar rules also subordinate exchange to distribution, though in a different form than rationing, regardless of whether this subordination is direct or concealed.

In relations between individuals, exchange does not rely upon rationing as a matter of course. This is the only area of the Soviet economy entirely devoid of rationing, putting aside those legal rules that limit the number of certain articles available to individuals.[63] And what is more, exchange between individuals is the other side of the coin with respect to rationing: the stronger the rationing in a given area of the economy, the broader individual exchange. The best proof of this conclusion can be found at so-called collective farm markets.

Although the markets existing in all Soviet cities and the majority of Soviet settlements are called collective farm markets, it is not collective farms but collective farmers and other individuals conducting family farming operations who function there as the principal *dramatis personae.* Data, published in the West and announced in the USSR, differ with regard to the figures expressing the true economic strength of these farming operations. According to information received by one of the authors of this book from reliable sources in 1979, the holders of small plots of land supply thirty-seven percent of all agricultural produce, although they occupy only seven percent of the cultivated land.[64] This economic force is so substantial that the Soviet rulers, hard-pressed by the incessant difficulties of food supply, have decided to move individuals' farming operations onto an "organized" course in the desired direction. Retaining the prohibition on state procurement of individual produce,[65] Soviet law has "allowed" state farms and has "recommended" for collective farms[66] to purchase from collective farmers and other individuals, residing in districts where these organizations are situated, milk as well as cattle and poultry that are bred in accordance with long-term contracts.[67] The decree cited candidly recognizes the economic weakness of the official agricultural system, in providing that such purchased produce after its transfer to state procurement agencies shall be taken into account in computing the size of production of the given state or collective farm for purposes of determining the performance of the state plan of procurement of agricultural produce.[68] This is, however, a form of exchange between Soviet entities and Soviet individuals peculiar inasmuch as, in contrast to the common situation, the former function as purchasers, not sellers, and the latter act as sellers, not purchasers. As to exchanges between individuals themselves, collective farm markets play a dual role.

In cities such as Moscow, Leningrad or Kiev, where the state retail-trade system ensures a supply of the main food necessities, collective farm markets are the place to buy the same goods of better quality, or to purchase certain goods without wasting a number of hours as would be the case in a state store, or to acquire those goods which seldom appear in retail-trade enterprises. In other locations, including not only small settlements but also large cities (Sverdlovsk, Cheliabinsk, Novosibirsk—there is no end to the list), all kinds of foods, except for the barest necessities (and sometimes even certain kinds of the barest necessities) are purchased by those individuals who do not belong to the local elites either at collective farm markets or nowhere.

Restrictions on trade at collective farm markets consist of certain sanitary rules and the payment of relatively small charges. Only in the case of black marketeering, i.e. the resale of purchased goods (another crime engendered by the Soviet system), are penal sanctions applied. Other violations can lead to administrative fines. Contracts at such markets are executed voluntarily, and all of their terms, including price, depend exclusively on the parties' agreement. An attempt to set maximum prices at collective farm markets, once undertaken in Moscow and Leningrad, failed because sellers disappeared entirely and the state retail-trade system could not fill the vacuum thus created. Planned prices employed by state shops affect the market prices of individual produce only when the official supply equals or exceeds the level of demand (which seldom occurs) or if the restricted purchasing capacity of the average customer compels collective market sellers to sell their produce at a reduced price rather than have it rot untouched (which often takes place directly before the market closes for the day). Thus, from the viewpoint of price formation, collective market trade is similar to the underground economy.[69] But, being permitted by law, this kind of economy cannot qualify as underground. As a result, the Soviet authorities' position in this area is very complicated. They can neither prohibit nor tolerate household farming operations. Prohibition would entail the complete collapse of the functioning system of food supply, while tolerance could undermine the Soviet state's economic monopoly and, consequently, the exercise of unlimited political power. The Soviet rulers have managed, however, to find the golden mean. As political monopolists they allow individual agricultural activity within legally outlined limits, but as economic monopolists they maintain the dependence of this activity upon the plots that are granted to collective farmers by the state and that can be withdrawn at any time.

Such is the Soviet economic system examined as a whole and as a complex of the appropriate elements. From both these perspectives the Soviet economy demonstrates its entire conformity with the Soviet system as unlimited political power of those who keep economic monopoly in their grasp. The subsequent legal analysis of each element of this economy, beginning with ownership, continuing with production, and ending with distribution and exchange, must strengthen and enrich the conclusion formulated. However, in order to be prepared to master the analysis suggested, one must be generally informed not only about the economic but also about the legal system operating in the USSR.

Notes

1. Art. 4, 10.
2. Art. 4.
3. Art. 7.
4. Art. 9.
5. For greater detail, see D. M. Genkin, *Pravo sobstvennosti v SSSR* (Moscow: Izd-vo Iuridicheskoi literatury, 1961).
6. Art. 2.
7. Marx i Engels, *Sochineniia*, vol. 4, p. 446.
8. Art. 20.
9. Art. 10.
10. Art. 16.
11. Actually, this is a new program, quite bizarre but not so bizarre as Khrushchev's Program of 1961. The latter had to be replaced not because it was fulfilled, but owing to its utterly fantastic nature. This is why Gorbachev's Program is called a new version and not a new program.
12. *Izvestia*, March 7, 1986.
13. Ibid.
14. *Izvestia*, Dec. 12, 1985.
15. S. Sdobnov, "Obshchestvennaia Sobstvennost' v period razvitogo Sotsialisma," *Kommunist*, 1982, no. 2, p. 16.
16. *Razvitie sotsialisticheskoi obshchestvennoi sobstvennosti* (Sofia, Moscow: 1980) p. 35.
17. N. D. Egorov, "Tipy, vidy i formy sobstvennosti i prava sobstvennosti v SSSR," *SGiP*, 1986, no. 5, p. 65.
18. Above, in the present section.
19. See Chapter 3 ("Ownership and the Law of Ownership").
20. Ibid.
21. Compare Art. 4 of the 1936 Constitution and Art. 14 of the 1977 Constitution.
22. Compare Khrushchev's Program, *Materialy XXII S'ezda KPSS* (Moscow: Gospolitizdat, 1961), p. 441, and Gorbachev's Program, *Izvestia*, March 7, 1986.
23. Art. 40, 60.
24. 1977 Constitution, art. 40.
25. Ibid., art. 60. Soviet criminal law provides for penal punishment for certain forms of such avoidance (*RSFSR Criminal Code*, art. 209).
26. The current Model Collective Farm Charter (*SP SSSR*, 1969, no. 26, item 150) establishes this rule in Art. 3.
27. O.S. Ioffe, *Soviet Law and Soviet Reality* (Dordrecht: Martinus Nijhoff, 1985), p. 95.
28. In accordance with this policy, a number of normative acts was adopted, e.g.: decrees of the Central Committee of the Communist Party, the USSR Council of Ministers and the All-Union Central Council of Trade Unions of July 28, 1983

(*SP SSSR*, 1983, no. 21, items 115–116); edict of the Presidium of the USSR Supreme Soviet of Aug. 12, 1983 (*Ved. SSSR*, 1983, no. 33, item 507).

29. *SP SSSR*, 1985, sect. 1, no. 17, item 82.

30. *Pravda*, June 12, 1985.

31. Ibid.

32. Ibid.

33. Ibid.

34. Ibid.

35. Ibid.

36. Ibid.

37. Ibid.

38. Above, in the present chapter.

39. See the "Introduction."

40. *SP SSSR*, 1979, sect. 1, no. 18, item 118.

41. Ibid.

42. Ibid. Surplus profit resulting from a decrease in planned tasks may be withdrawn during the economic year.

43. Above, note 40.

44. See the section of Chapter 7 ("Distribution and its Legal Forms") on "Planned Distribution."

45. *SP SSSR*. 1981, sect. 1, no. 1, item 1. To give an idea of the difference between actual and official prices in the area of the state procurement, a single reference to Soviet law is sufficient. According to a 1986 decree (*Izvestia*, March 29, 1986), in cases where state farms or collective farms sell to the state more grain than the amount indicated by the plan, they must receive double the regular state procurement prices.

46. RSFSR Criminal Code, art. 152-1, 173, 174.

47. Ioffe, *Soviet Law and Soviet Reality*, pp. 128–129. The author was forced to make his own calculation because of the absence of any other data—either official or unofficial. The result indicated above was obtained despite interpretation of all available figures in the light most favorable for the Soviet system. Bearing in mind these figures, it is no wonder that any Soviet individual who does not belong to the Soviet elite must strive to find some supplemental source of income, even when such a search will involve illicit activity on most occasions.

48. For more details see Mikhail Voslensky, *Nomenklatura—Gospodstvuiushchii klass Sovetskogo Soiuza* (London: Overseas Publication Interchange Ltd., 1985), pp. 281–342.

49. Remote reverberations of this policy can be found, e.g.: U. K. Shedenov, *Sfera obsluzhivaniia* (Alma-Ata: Kazakhstan, 1983).

50. 1977 Constitution, Preamble.

51. See the section on "Production" of the present chapter.

52. Ibid.

53. 1986 Program of the Communist Party of the Soviet Union.

54. Unfortunately, the same erroneous interpretation of NEP was presented at a 1984 Conference on Soviet Law and Economy at the University of Connecticut, by Y. I. Luryi, a former Soviet lawyer, now a professor of law in Canada.

55. Direct rationing, accompanied by official registration in the form of a document that entitled one to acquire a certain amount of goods each month, was employed from 1929 to 1935, during the war, and for the first post-war period (1941–1947). Concealed rationing is employed even now in a great number of Soviet cities and

towns, where certain kinds of goods may be acquired only after producing special coupons distributed at Soviet entities or at places of residence.

56. 1986 Program of the Communist Party of the Soviet Union, *Izvestia*, March 7, 1986.

57. See the section on "Distribution" of the present chapter.

58. Ibid.

59. Because bread is so cheap, and cattle fodder is so hard to find, the Soviets have had to struggle with peasants and other individuals feeding bread to cattle (Art. 151-1 of the RSFSR Criminal Code).

60. See the section on "Distribution" of the present chapter.

61. 1973 Fundamental Rules of Retail Store Operation issued by the USSR Ministry of Trade. *Osnovnye pravila torgovli* (Moscow: Ekonomika, 1981), pp. 48–67.

62. E.g., *Osnovnye pravila torgovli*, p. 245–249.

63. See the section of Chapter 3 ("Ownership and the Law of Ownership") on "The Right of Personal Ownership."

64. Olimpiad S. Ioffe, "Law and Economy in the USSR," *Harvard Law Review* 95 (1982): 1596. Compare Franklin D. Holzman, *The Soviet Economy* (Foreign Policy Association, Headline Series, No. 260, Sept./Oct. 1982) p. 35: "Private plots occupy just 3 percent of the land but produce approximately one fifth of the nation's crops and about one third of its livestock products."

65. Fundamental Principles of Civil Legislation, art. 51.

66. It is no secret that, if necessary, Soviet commands often take the form of permissions and recommendations.

67. *SP SSSR*, 1981, sect. 1, no. 6, item 37.

68. Ibid.

69. See the "Introduction."

2

The Soviet Legal System in Connection with the Soviet Economic System

General Structure of the Soviet Legal System

Soviet legal scholars generally divide the Soviet legal system into branches each with its own subject and method of legal regulation. Like their Western European colleagues,[1] but unlike their counterparts in the United States, Soviet scholars believe that this division is based not on convenience but upon objective, scientific criteria. Because those involved in developing the legal system believe these divisions are important, they in fact become important. Typically these branches serve as the bases for organization of law school courses and for the coverage of textbooks. Often, but not always, the law for given branches is separately codified. The branches of law generally recognized by Soviet scholarship are: State Law, Administrative Law, Finance Law, Civil Law, Civil Procedure Law, Labor Law, Land Law, Collective Farm Law, Family Law, Criminal Law, and Criminal Procedure Law. Essentially this scheme includes the system of law recognized by Western European legal scholars of the nineteenth and early twentieth century and taken over by Russian legal scholars. The traditional legal categories are augmented with the new category of Collective Farm Law to reflect the special features of the organization of Soviet agriculture.

This standard Soviet categorization is not entirely logical. State law, administrative law, civil law, criminal law, civil procedure law, and criminal procedure law are distinguishable by the subject matter (different types of regulated relations—power relations, property relations, etc.) and by the method of legal regulation (subordination, coordination, etc.). Finance law, collective farm law, labor law, and land law are distinguished by subject matter area, rather than method of legal regulation. If law is to be classified by subject matter, the number of possible classifications becomes almost infinite. For instance, the above list does not include environmental law. If environmental law were included, it could be broken down into air pollution law, water pollution law, noise pollution law, etc. The problem becomes worse if the suggestion of many Soviet scholars is adopted that "economic law" be accepted as a branch of Soviet law, since the purposes of economic law are accomplished by various methods of legal regulation, though mainly through administrative and civil law. For most of the period of Soviet power, a debate has gone on between proponents of "economic law," who believe there should be a separately codified branch of law dealing with relations between state economic organizations, and that these relations should be removed from the civil code, and supporters of maintaining a clear division between civil law and administrative law.[2] The latter would continue the practice, begun in the 1920s, of treating horizontal relations between state economic organizations as part of the general civil law.[3] The question is of far more than theoretical significance, since keeping Soviet economic organizations under the civil code provides a legal framework for giving these organizations at least limited independence in their operations, while the creation of an economic code would blur the distinction between the administrative area, where economic organizations are subject to arbitrary commands from above, and the civil law area, where relations are determined by the law of property and contract. Two meetings of Soviet scholars held in 1985 pointed up the difference between these two schools. At one meeting, Professor V.V. Laptev, the leader of the "economic law" proponents, presented a Draft Economic Code of the USSR for consideration.[4] Those invited, obviously selected to be his supporters, received the project enthusiastically, though the members of the audience engaged in practical economic administration pointed to various parts of the proposal that were unrealistic. The other meeting was attended by leading Soviet professors of civil law.[5] They discussed how the civil codes could be further developed to meet the needs of the economy, and proposed that administrative legislation relating to the economy be codified in a separate law, to be called the Fundamental Principles of Legislation on the Management of the National Economy.

Soviet legislation does not follow the orderly pattern of branches developed in Soviet legal theory. The difficulty is that the legislative bodies sometimes pass laws codifying one part of the system of Soviet law, while at other times they pass legislation dealing with a particular social problem by applying the methods of a number of different branches of law. An example of the former approach is the Criminal Procedure Code which provides a comprehensive set of procedural rules for trying criminal cases in court. An example of the latter approach might be a law dealing with water pollution. It might well involve state law, creating new state agencies to deal with pollution; administrative law, putting potential polluters under a duty to obey cleanup orders from these agencies; finance law, providing funds for pollution control; civil law, allowing suits for damages for those injured by pollution; labor law, providing extra job benefits for pollution control workers; and criminal law, making water pollution a crime. Since Soviet legislation thus follows a dual pattern, partly branch-of-law oriented and partly problem oriented, the organizers of the Code of Laws of the USSR (prepared in the late 1970s and early 1980s, and published in the 1980s), faced a task for which there was no perfect solution. They adopted a largely pragmatic approach, generally placing each piece of legislation in a section devoted to the primary social problem dealt with by the legislation, or, where there were several problems, using a system of cross-references.[6] However, they have had to deviate from their scheme to avoid splitting up the codified branches of Soviet law.

Subjects and Methods of Legal Regulation

The Soviet economy is only one of the broad subject matter areas regulated by Soviet law. However, it is regulated, to a greater or lesser extent, by each of the branches of Soviet law. In this chapter, we will look at these branches, but only to the extent that they regulate economic questions. In contrast to the subjects of legal regulation, which are extremely numerous, the methods of legal regulation are relatively few. State law creates institutions with certain powers. For instance, local government has general legislative power over local matters. The courts have the power to decide cases brought before them. (American readers should be aware of a terminological trap. In American usage, "state law" refers to the law of the 50 states, as opposed to "federal law," which refers to the law of the United States. In discussing Soviet law, the term "state" law is used to designate what in American terminology would be a part of "constitutional law." Legislation of the 15 Soviet republics is called "republic" legislation, while legislation of the *Union* of Soviet Socialist Republics is called "All-Union" legislation.) Administrative law works on the basis of subordination to authority and thus may be said to deal with vertical relations, between superiors to subordinates. Civil law involves mainly property-connected rights and treats parties as equals; thus it may be said to deal with horizontal relations. Criminal law, like administrative law involves a vertical relationship, but not that of administrator to subordinate, but of the state to all its citizens, by the definition of general categories of punishable prohibited conduct.

While every economic system has both vertical and horizontal legal relations, the main distinguishing features of the Soviet system are (1) that vertical legal relations predominate over horizontal ones, in contrast to a capitalist system, such as that of the United States, where horizontal relations dominate; and (2) that horizontal legal relations are largely created involuntarily, in contrast to a capitalist system, where most, though not all, horizontal legal relations are voluntary on both sides. However, it would be quite a mistake to think of the Soviet economy as based solely on commands from above, with no voluntary horizontal elements, just as it would be wrong to think of the United States economy as operated without any government regulation. Consider, for instance, the example of aviation law. In both countries, government air safety authorities set standards for airplane maintenance and perform air traffic control functions. In both countries, passengers freely decide whether or not to buy tickets and therefore whether or not to create horizontal legal relations. In both countries, the airline must sell a ticket to a passenger if space is available, so that the airline-passenger relationship is voluntary on the part of the passenger, but not on the part of the airline. However, in the Soviet Union, vertical orders from planners determine which factory builds how many airplanes, who buys them, which jet fuel distributors sells how much fuel to which airline enterprise, which flights go where, the price of airline tickets, in which bank the airline deposits its receipts, and what it pays its employees. In some cases, these vertical orders result in the creation of horizontal relations, such as purchase contracts for airplanes or jet fuel, bank account relationships, or employment contracts. In the case of ticket prices, the vertical orders affect the contract terms, but do not force the conclusion of a contract. In the United States, all of these decisions are made on the basis of horizontal relations negotiated voluntarily between the parties.

The Branches of Law

According to Soviet legal theory, "state law" is the leading branch of the Soviet legal system. State Law regulates the governmental and political structure of the USSR. The Soviet Union is like all other countries in that actual political power structures differ substantially from those described in the Constitution and other legislation on state structures. (The United States Constitution, for instance, mentions neither political parties nor the President's Cabinet.) However, unlike most economically-advanced countries, the Soviet Union does not allow legal scholars, political scientists, or anyone else to publish frank discussions of many of these differences. Thus foreign Sovietologists must try to reconstruct the actual legal and political structure of the state using sources that are full of deliberate omissions and falsehoods. The task is somewhat easier with respect to those institutions that regulate the Soviet economy, because, as compared, for instance, to the laws regulating elections or dissent, these institutions operate in a way that more closely tracks the model provided by the laws expressing them and because speech is considerably more free with respect to economic regulation. The lesser illegality and greater freedom of discussion are largely necessitated by the complexity and rapid pace of change of modern economies. It is essential for those making economic decisions to understand the economic power structure. If the actual power structure differed totally from the picture in written legislation, economic managers would be like pilots flying in the fog with faulty instruments. Instead, the existence of a legal structure buffeted by interference from high administrative agencies and the Party makes the task of the economic manager more like that of flying a normal airplane through a storm. The rapid pace of technological development requires rapid institutional change. To achieve some rationality in this change requires relatively free discussion of alternatives. This discussion aids the Politburo in exercising its function of setting general policies to which all economic decisions must conform. Soviet law provides an important method by which this conformity is achieved. Although the Politburo retains the ultimate power to intervene in any economic decision regardless of the law, the sheer mass of economic decisions to be made in comparison with the few hours a week that the Politburo can meet means that only a very small percentage of decisions will be affected by direct intervention from the very top.

There are three basic types of Soviet government economic administrative agencies: those with general powers, such as the Council of Ministers and the State Planning Committee; those that administer a particular type of subject matter, for instance water quality enforcement agencies; and those that administer a particular area of the economy, for example the Ministry of Ferrous Metallurgy. There is a tension between these agencies, in some ways parallel to the tension between government and business in a capitalist country, though major conflicts of policy are prevented by the fact that the ultimate power rests in the top levels of the Party.

All important economic legislation is approved by the Politburo. However, it is never issued in the name of the Politburo. Formally, it is issued either: (1) in the name of the Supreme Soviet or its Presidium, (2) in the joint names of the Central Committee of the Party and the Council of Ministers of the USSR, or (3) in the name of the Council of Ministers of the USSR alone. In theory, legislation issued by the Supreme Soviet is superior to other legislation. However, in theory also, the Central Committee of the Party is the highest political power in the country. In practice, the fact that all legislation comes ultimately from the Politburo avoids serious conflicts between the formal legislative bodies.

General economic administrative agencies may be divided into a number of groups, on the basis of their respective responsibilities: production and distribution of goods and services, fixing of prices and wages, research in science and technology, audit and supervision.

Planning the production and distribution of goods and services is primarily the responsibility of the State Planning Committee (*Gosplan*), with secondary roles played by the State Committee on Supply (*Gossnab*), the State Committee on Construction (*Gosstroi*), and the Ministry of Trade.[7]

The fixing of prices and wages are the responsibility of the State Committee on Prices and the State Committee on Labor and Social Problems respectively. The decision to allocate the power to set prices and wages to these government agencies rather than allowing them to be set by the operating entities on the basis of market forces explains many of the problems and institutions of the law regulating the Soviet economy. Almost all prices and wages are fixed by the government with the exceptions of food sold at collective farm markets and wages of employees hired by private citizens (e.g., baby-sitters). The setting of rational prices and wages would be an impossibly difficult task for any government. The difficulty is compounded for Soviet economists by the requirement that they purport to follow the Marxist "labor theory of value" and by political pressures that make prices of public transportation, bread, and certain other essentials untouchable. The result is that prices and wages are set in a highly unrealistic manner. Many of the legal institutions regulating the Soviet economy are directly necessitated by the deviations of the price and wage systems from what would prevail if there were a free market.

Prices for consumer goods are set too low for many goods, too high for some. The price of meat in state stores, for instance, is well below the free market price, as can easily be seen by comparing the state store and the collective farm market. The result is reflected in various types of legal problems. State store clerks are tempted to divert meat to the black market. Local authorities have to impose rationing. Citizens have to stand in long lines or sneak away from work when stores are uncrowded. Prices on unfashionable clothes are set too high, with the result that the clothes sit in the store unsold. It takes just as much labor to make unfashionable as fashionable clothes; only the willingness of the authorities to largely ignore the labor theory of value in practice allows price differentiation between the two, but the price differentiation is never enough to allow fashionable clothes to remain in the stores or to sell all the unfashionable clothes. At the industrial level, pricing is even more artificial. If enterprises were set free to make their own decisions, the artificial pricing system would lead to decisions very harmful to the economy. For these reasons, discussions of granting real discretionary powers to enterprises cannot be considered serious unless a proposal to abolish the State Committee on Prices is also included.

There are also many flaws in the setting of wages. Differentials between the wages paid in various cities are not proportional to the relative attractiveness of various cities. As a result, an elaborate residence permit system is necessary to slow immigration to some cities, while an extensive labor recruitment system and job assignment system is needed for other areas.

State law creates the administrative agencies and gives them their powers. Administrative law regulates the exercise of these powers by administrative agencies with respect to subordinate entities and individual citizens. Examples of matters subject to administrative law are: orders to operating entities from planners, environmental protection agencies, and production ministries.

Unlike state law, where there are a number of fictions, such as elections and the power of the Supreme Soviet, the rules of administrative law involving vertical legal relations are almost always real, though they do not always indicate the total extent of control from above. If Soviet legislation grants a certain agency the power to order certain actions by a subordinate entity, this power almost always exists and is used in practice. However, practice goes further. Often an agency at a higher administrative level will issue orders to a lower agency without any clear legal authorization and the lower agency will have to obey. Indeed, in the case of economic entities, higher agencies routinely issue and force obedience to orders that concern matters clearly left by the law to the discretion of these entities. On the other hand, orders from outside the regular chain of command have no legal or political force, unless they come from or are confirmed by Party officials. Thus if, for instance, the Ministry of Education orders a factory subordinate to the Ministry of Light Industry to produce more blackboards, the factory can and will ignore this order with impunity. At the same time, if the Ministry of Light Industry gave the same order to a subordinate factory, that factory would have to obey in practice even if the relevant administrative legislation left the factory the discretion to plan the assortment of goods produced.

Soviet law almost never allows an adversary procedure for settling disputes involving vertical legal relations. This fact has been recognized and frequently criticized by Soviet legal scholars, who have discussed possible reforms, but nothing has been done in practice. In some cases, the need for firm discipline clearly makes an adversary procedure inappropriate. If an air traffic controller tells an airplane not to land on Runway No. 1, the law must require the pilot to obey. However, if the environmental protection authorities tell an airline to adopt a certain fuel-wasting flight path so as to avoid making excessive noise over populated areas, there is no such practical obstacle to allowing litigation over the conformance of this order with environmental legislation. Yet the Soviet system would typically deny any sort of adversary litigation in the second case as well as in the first. The result is that many disputes which would be decided judicially in the United States are decided in the USSR either arbitrarily by the bureaucrats at the top or politically, if the affected organization is powerful enough.

Civil Law regulates "horizontal" relations between citizens, between a citizen on one side and a Soviet organization on the other, and between two Soviet organizations. These relations include such matters of great importance in Soviet law as the legal personality of production and distribution enterprises; their property rights; contracts between enterprises for the sale of goods, for construction, and for transportation; and the rights of authors and inventors. As discussed above, some Soviet theorists argue that relations between Soviet organizations are regulated not by civil law, but by a separate branch of law, Economic Law.

The basic legislative acts in the area of civil law are the Fundamental Principles of Civil Legislation of the USSR and the Union Republics and the civil codes of each republic. The following discussion will concentrate on the civil code of the Russian republic; the codes of the other republics are almost identical. The code is divided into eight parts: (1) General Provisions, (2) Law of Ownership, (3) Obligations (with subparts: General Provisions on Obligations, Individual Types of Obligations), (4) Copyright, (5) the Right to a Discovery, (6) Invention Law, (7) Inheritance Law, and (8) the Legal Capacity of Foreigners and Stateless Persons, the Application of Civil Laws of Foreign States, the Application of International Treaties and Agreements.

Civil law does not regulate all important horizontal relations or all important property relations in the Soviet economy. Labor relations, in particular the respective rights of employer and employee are regulated by labor law. Relations connected with monetary payments for the benefit of the State or with distribution of monetary resources among state entities are regulated by finance law. Property rights on the collective farm are regulated largely by collective farm law. In some of these cases, the relationships are regulated by both civil law and the more specialized branch of the law.

Labor Law regulates employer-employee relationships. With insignificant exceptions (e.g. priests and baby-sitters), the employer is a state agency or an entity that is for practical purposes equivalent to a state agency (e.g., a cooperative or a societal organization). The basic labor legislation is the USSR Fundamental Principles of Labor Legislation and the Codes of Laws on Labor of the individual republics. This legislation is supplemented by a mass of administrative regulations. Labor law regulates employer-employee relations and also the role of what are called "trade unions" but really are government agencies administering various aspects of labor policy. Unlike relations in the industrial supply area, where most contracts are based upon administrative plans, most (but by no means all) employer-employee relations are freely created by contract. Employees are generally free to quit their jobs; however, labor legislation restricts employers in firing them. The details of labor law are discussed in Chapter 6 below.

Land Law regulates relationships involving the ownership and use of land. Basic legal provisions are provided in the Fundamental Principles of Land Legislation of the USSR and the Union Republics. Each republic has a land code. Like means of production and industrial goods, all land is the property of the state, but can be allocated to individual users. However, unlike means of production and industrial goods, land is not bought and sold and has no price attached to it. The result is that land law is largely "vertical" in nature, since decisions on land use are made completely administratively. However, these administrative decisions may affect civil law rights, for instance by transfer of a plot of land from one user to another, a transfer which may be with or without compensation.

Finance Law regulates budgetary income and expenditures, state borrowing, credit, accounting, monetary circulation, and foreign currency exchange. There is no method of legal regulation peculiar to finance law; rather, finance law applies the method of vertical command found in administrative law and the method of horizontal relations found in civil law. In many non-communist countries, control of money and credit is the main means of government intervention in economic affairs. In the Soviet Union, however, the direct physical planning of production, distribution, and construction greatly reduces the importance of finance law. The Soviet government cannot, for instance, encourage the building of factories by making low-cost loans available, since the amount of building is determined by national construction plans. Rather, the main function of Soviet finance law and the institutions that enforce it is to reduce the discretion of operating agencies by depriving them of any funds to operate unplanned programs and by ensuring that all transactions are subject to the scrutiny of financial authorities. This is accomplished through the rulemaking and auditing functions of the Ministry of Finance and the monopoly roles of the State Bank, the Construction Bank, and the Foreign Trade Bank in handling all monetary transactions.

Formal adversary procedures are generally, but not always, available for settling disputes over horizontal legal relations. There are, however, some important exceptions. Typically disputes in the area of banking cannot be taken to court. If a bank refuses to conduct a transaction on the ground that it is illegal, or if it makes a mistake in figuring accounts, the aggrieved enterprise may only complain to higher banking authorities, not to the courts. If management cannot agree with the trade union on one of the minor items left to local discretion in the conclusion of "collective contracts," the dispute must be settled through higher levels of union and management. There is no forum for adjudication, and strikes and lockouts are contrary to Party policy and thus cannot occur except through a serious breach of Party discipline.

The Soviet Union has two separate systems that engage in the adjudication of economic disputes. There is a system of economic agencies called "Arbitrazh" that decides all disputes where neither party is a private citizen or a collective farm. There is a regular court system, which decides only those disputes where at least one party is a private citizen or collective farm. Both systems operate rapidly and inexpensively, though these virtues are achieved at the cost of some lack of depth in the investigation of the facts of the cases brought before them. However, the organization and procedure of the two systems differ radically.

The vast majority of cases of economic significance do not involve private citizens or collective farms, so they are decided in the "Arbitrazh" system. (The Russian word "Arbitrazh" is sometimes translated as "Arbitration," but this translation is misleading, since Arbitrazh, unlike an arbitration organization, has compulsory jurisdiction, permanently-appointed decision-makers, and full enforcement powers.) There are two types of arbitrazh. Disputes between two organizations with a common superior, for instance between two production associations subordinate to the same ministry, are decided by an arbitrazh agency subordinate to this superior agency, in this case the ministry. This type of arbitrazh is called "departmental arbitrazh." Disputes between organizations with different superior agencies are decided by a system of arbitrazh independent of the economic ministries and subordinate only to government agencies at various levels. This system is called "state arbitrazh."[8] Arbiters are generally lawyers with substantial experience in economic matters. They hear cases in a rapid, simplified procedure, basing their decision largely on documentary evidence.[9] Within the system of state arbitrazh, appeals are possible to higher level arbitrazh tribunals. Arbitrazh also has rulemaking powers, under which it issues binding instructions in areas where the law is unclear or lacks detail.

A number of types of economic cases come within the jurisdiction of the ordinary courts. These include labor cases (e.g., unlawful discharge), consumer protection (for citizens who buy faulty goods), accidents (private car and state-owned vehicle collide), farm cases (collective farm sues state agency in contract dispute), and economic crimes. The court procedure in civil cases would not strike a Western observer as unusual.[10] Trial is conducted before a single judge and two laymen. All three theoretically have equal powers, but in practice the laymen are dominated by the judge. Each party may have a lawyer, present evidence, and call witnesses. Adverse decisions may be appealed. The Supreme Court of the USSR and the supreme courts of the republics have the power to issue binding explanations of the law. They use this power to supplement the very general provisions of the codes and other laws with detailed rules for situations that arise frequently.

Collective Farm Law regulates the relationships of members of collective farms with the farms and some aspects of the relations of the farms with state agencies. The degree of fiction and fantasy is substantially higher in collective farm law than in other areas of law related to the economy. Thus, for instance, the Statute on the State Enterprise indicates that director of an enterprise is appointed by the superior organization and that he is in charge of the enterprise. In fact, the director is appointed by the superior organization (on the recommendation or with the approval of the corresponding level of the Party). While his freedom of action is limited by the power of higher government and Party authorities, to a large extent he really does make the decisions governing the operation of the enterprise. The Model Charter of the Collective Farm indicates that the chairman of a collective farm is elected directly or indirectly by the members and that the general meeting of the members or their representatives is the highest authority of the farm. Both these statements are falsehoods, as every Soviet peasant knows. The chairman of the collective farm is in fact appointed jointly by local Party officials and government agricultural administrators. He rules the farm autocratically, as long as the government officials and the Party are satisfied with his work. The organization of the collective farm is formally a cooperative, with the farmers as members. In fact, in terms of power relationships the cooperative-member arrangement is indistinguishable from the employer-employee relationship found at state enterprises, except that in many ways collective farm members have fewer legal rights than do state enterprise employees.

Family Law regulates such matters as marriage, guardianship, child support, parenthood, and adoption. The basic legislative provisions are the Fundamental Principles of Legislation on Marriage and the Family of the USSR and the Codes on Marriage and the Family of the individual republics. The economic significance of this legislation is more in what it does not do than in what it does do. It does not reflect any of the ideas of the more radical Communists of the early 1920s, who called for the replacement of the family with some sort of communal living system. Rather, it is in most respects identical to modern family legislation in those non-communist countries where secularism has replaced religion in determining the family policy of the state. Men and women are given equal rights. Divorce is relatively easy to obtain. Alimony is unavailable to spouses able to work. Earnings during marriage become community property.

Soviet economic planners would like to see a country of stable married couples, each with two or three children. The husband and wife in such stable families tend to be reliable workers and are less subject to alcoholism. The two or three children would guarantee a slow but steady growth of the younger, well-educated population and thus indirectly reduce the percentage of poorly-educated older workers and dependent old people. However, low wages, which force each family to have two full-time wage earners, the lack of labor-saving consumer goods (such as frozen meals, dishwashers, and clothes dryers), and the inadequate availability of housing tend to create social forces which defeat the planners' goals.

Real reforms in these areas could be achieved only through some combination of drastic cuts in the military budgets to provide increased funds for wages and housing and major expansion of genuine private enterprise to provide needed services. Neither type of reform has been attempted because of the threat to the Soviet system involved. Instead, there have been a number of items of legislation adopted, seeking to reduce the pressures on working mothers. This legislation increases maternity leaves and provides extra time off to care for sick children.

Two separate mechanisms are used for the creation and enforcement of general rules for the punishment of conduct dangerous to the Soviet economic system. Criminal law regulates the punishment of those who have committed serious intentional or negligent acts harmful to the interests of the state or of individual citizens. Acts that present only a limited danger to the system are punished under the law on "administrative violations." Note that in the phrase "administrative violations" the word administrative is used in a different manner from that in which we have been using it. In this phrase it does not denote an order from a superior to a subordinate, but rather a procedure for handling minor offenses expeditiously, but without the full safeguards of a formal criminal trial.

Criminal law, the law of administrative violations, and the corresponding procedural branches of law are unusual in that they are fully codified. One might contrast civil law, where, for every rule on a particular type of economic contract in the Civil Code, there are a hundred rules scattered among various administrative regulations outside the Civil Code. All criminal offenses are listed in the Criminal Codes of the respective Soviet Republics. All administrative violations are listed in the Codes on Administrative Violations of the respective republics. The basic principle of human rights, "nulla poena, nullum crimen sine lege," (no act should be criminally punished unless previously defined as a crime), requires for its application that the definitions of crimes be made in some manner accessible to the public. The complete codification of Soviet criminal and administrative violation law appears on the surface to satisfy this requirement. However, in practice, it may be as hard to determine the content of criminal or administrative violation law as it is to determine the content of the civil law of economic contracts. The problems are twofold. First, numerous articles of the Codes of Administrative Violations, and some articles of the Criminal Codes incorporate administrative regulations by reference: "violation of the rules on handling explosive substances," "violation of the rules on foreign currency transactions," etc. Often the rules referred to are unpublished, or if published are in obscure sources that the average member of the public could never hope to find. The second problem involves vague language in the Codes. An important section of the Criminal Code describes the economic offense of "theft of state property on an extremely large scale," and prescribes the death penalty for it. Yet the criminal code contains no definition of what "an extremely large scale" means. This gap and many others have been filled, in the case of the criminal law, by binding instructions issued by the Supreme Court of the USSR and the supreme courts of the republics. However, many vague provisions of the codes remain uninterpreted by the supreme courts.

As pointed out above, usually for vertical legal relationships, and often for horizontal legal relationships, no adversary judicial procedure is available for settling disputes in Soviet law. However, the imposition of criminal punishment without giving the accused the right to a fair trial is repugnant to the most basic principles of human rights. Both the need to maintain at least a minimal international respect for its human rights policies, and the bad memories of the Stalinist practice of massively imposing criminal penalties without trial force the Soviet Union to maintain a system of criminal justice whose rules afford such basic protections as representation by counsel, the right to cross-examine witnesses, and the right of the defendant to be aquitted if his guilt has not been proved in the trial. While the rules of criminal procedure are broken in practice in political trials, and while at times ordinary criminal defendants may be wrongly convicted because of political pressures to "get tough on crime" or wrongly acquitted because of judges who take bribes, the overwhelming majority of those who are tried for economic crimes are in fact guilty, and are found guilty after fair trials.

The Code of Administrative Violations also establishes procedural rules. The number of minor infractions, such as fishing in a prohibited area, is too great to make it practical to offer a full trial to all the offenders. Soviet law, like many other legal systems, treats these minor offenses not as crimes, but as mere administrative violations. Violators are generally subject to a small fine, imposed on the spot by administrative authorities. They then have the right, not to a full-fledged trial, but to a streamlined administrative hearing, in which they may try to show that no offense was committed and that the fine was mistakenly imposed.

Criminal procedure law regulates the court procedure for determining guilt or innocence and for sentencing. The structure of criminal procedure law gives a great advantage to the state in cases involving economic crimes. Often the more complex economic crimes involve a huge conspiracy, in which various officials of an enterprise or a group of enterprises have conspired to defraud the state of its property. The complexity of the crime makes necessary an equally complex investigation. This investigation is performed by an investigator of the procuracy, who has the right to hold suspects incommunicado for months. By isolating the main suspected conspirators, and offering each some leniency if he will confess and implicate the others, the investigator puts them in the classic "prisoner's dilemma" of game theory.

* * *

In this chapter, Soviet law has been examined in accordance with its traditional division into "branches." Those aspects of each branch have been emphasized that are of particular importance to the economy. The remaining chapters will consider particular problems and institutions of the Soviet economy and how they are regulated by the various branches of Soviet law.

Notes

1. See John H. Merryman, *The Civil Law Tradition*, 2nd ed. (Stanford: Stanford University Press, 1985), 90–100.
2. A history of the dispute is found in O. S. Ioffe, *Razvitie tsivilisticheskoi mysli v SSSR*, pt. 1 (Leningrad: Izd-vo LGU, 1975), pp. 39–108. The views in favor of economic law are stated in V. V. Laptev, *Predmet i sistema khoziaistvennogo prava* (Moscow: Gos izd-vo iuridicheskoi literatury, 1969).
3. Views of the civil law school are found in S. N. Bratus', *Predmet i sistema grazhdanskogo prava* (Moscow: Iuridicheskaia literatura, 1963); O.S. Ioffe, *Pravovoe regulirovanie khoziaistvennoi deiatel'nosti v SSSR* (Leningrad: Izd-vo LGU, 1959).
4. V. K. Andreev, "Obsuzhdenie proekta Khoziaistvennogo kodeksa SSSR," *SGiP*, 1985, no. 11, p. 135.
5. L. I. Brycheva, "Konferentsiia 'Grahdanskoe pravo i ekonomika,'" *SGiP*, 1985, no. 12, p. 119.
6. Steven D. Steinmetz, "The U.S.S.R. Digest of Laws: Legal Reform a la russe," *New York University Journal of International Law and Politics*, 17 (1985), 949.
7. For details, see below, Chapters 7 and 8.
8. Law on State Arbitrazh, *Ved. SSSR*, 1979, no. 49, item 844; Statute on State Arbitrazh of the USSR, *SP SSSR*, 1980, No. 16–17, item 104.
9. A. A. Dobrovol'skii, ed., *Arbitrazhnyi protsess v SSSR* (Moscow: Izd-vo MGU, 1983).
10. A standard civil procedure textbook is A. A. Mel'nikov, ed., *Kurs grazhdanskogo protsessual'nogo prava* (Moscow: Nauka, 1981), 2 Vols.

3

Ownership and the Law of Ownership

General Principles

Ownership exists in law and in fact. Ownership in law is the formal recognition of the right to possess, use, and dispose of property. Ownerhsip in fact is the actual opportunity to possess, use, and dispose of property. This distinction is important from two points of view. First, ownership in fact sometimes does not coincide with ownership in law. In these cases, the owner in fact, not the owner in law, functions as the real proprietor. So it was for centuries in ancient Rome: if the complicated procedure established for the purchase and sale of certain things was not observed, the seller continued to be the *de jure* owner, while the purchaser became the *de facto* owner.[1] Second, ownership in fact can be expressed by different forms in law. In the systems based on the civil law tradition, including Soviet law, a sharp distinction is made between the law of ownership and other areas of law, such as the law of contracts. Under the law of ownership, for instance, a proprietor of a house is the owner in law, regardless of whether he himself uses this house, or a tenant is the actual user. However, if the owner uses his own house, this use is regulated by the law of ownership, while, if the house is rented, the landlord-tenant relationship is governed by the law of contracts. While the owner remains formally the legal owner under the law of ownership, his actual rights and duties are substantially altered by the rules of contract law applicable to a contract of lease. If we did not make the distinction between ownership in fact and ownership in law, we would have to say that to the extent the landlord transferred the right of use of the apartment to the tenant, the landlord was no longer the owner. However, it seems more appropriate to say that the landlord is still the owner in law, but the actual practical rights and duties of the landlord, what we call "ownership in fact," are now regulated not only by the law of ownership but also by the law of contracts. Thus, ownership in fact may be regulated not only by the law of ownership, but also by other legal institutions (the law of contracts, the law of inheritance, etc.).

Certain scholars deny this dualism, considering it to be a fabrication of Marxism. Harold H. Berman, a renowned American professor of Soviet law, has assessed the dualist analysis negatively in connection with analysis of state ownership in the USSR. In criticizing an assertion that "state ownership means *de facto* ownership by Soviet leaders viewed collectively,"[2] he contends that such a postulate is rooted in Marxist-Leninist theory,[3] because just according to this theory, "ownership is of two kinds: legal ownership and economic ownership."[4]

Yet such a dualism was known long before the appearance of Marxism, as history of Roman law proves. And what is more peculiar, Professor Berman employs the same postulate himself. When dealing with state ownership in the USSR, he qualifies it as "theoretical ownership, the fictitious ownership of the state as such"[5] (despite the quite definite indications of Soviet law), connecting "the actual benefit of ownership" not with the Soviet state but with state enterprises[6] (despite the definitely opposite Soviet legal provisions). Consequently, the dualism indicated seems quite acceptable to Professor Berman, at least within the limits of cases, where ownership in fact does not coincide with ownership in law. He ignores, however, another, not less important, effect of this dualism: the expression of economic ownership not only in the form of legal ownership but also in various other legal forms, and thus his position renders inexplicable the system of ownership established in the USSR.

The Soviet Constitution provides that state ownership is one of the two (or more than two?) forms of socialist ownership.[7] At this point, let us disregard the issue of who is the rightholder.[8] A certain real phenomenon exists under the designation of "state ownership," regardless of whether one has one's own interpretation of this phenomenon or shares Professor Berman's view that the state is the theoretical owner, the Soviet elite the postulated owner, and each of the Soviet enterprises an actual owner.[9] As soon as the appropriate interpretation has been presented, one can employ the Soviet official terminology "state ownership" without risk of being misunderstood. Should ownership in fact be inseparable from ownership in law, the transformation occurring with state ownership in process of the transitions from production to distribution and then to exchange[10] would be completely incomprehensible. At the stage of production, the owner's activity is governed by law of ownership. But even here fact differs from law, because the owner cannot productively exploit his property without hiring a labor force, and the labor force connected with the owner's property is hired on the basis of labor contracts, not on the basis of the law of ownership. At the stage of distribution between the state and its workers, the law of ownership functions insofar as the state in its capacity as a producer may include as an object of its ownership all that is produced. But a certain portion of the producer's property must be distributed in the form of salary to the producer's hired workers. Although the object of distribution is state property in this instance as well, not the law of ownership but labor contracts serve as the legal basis for this distribution process. At the stage of exchange, goods-money relations acquire contractual forms (sale, delivery, etc.), and it is according to the law of contracts that the dynamics of ownership operate in general, including the dynamics of state ownership. And so, once more, at the final point of the economic cycle, the identity of ownership in fact and in law demonstrates its incompatibility with actual circumstances. The assumption that there is a difference between the law of ownership and ownership disproves the conclusions just mentioned. This is the best argument in favor of the assumption. Thus, if one equates ownership in fact with ownership in law, the conclusions would be unavoidable that in the USSR: (1) state ownership exists until production is begun, and, as a result, only the law of ownership must be employed; but (2) from the moment that production is initiated until the full completion of the distribution process, state ownership disappears to the degree that the law of ownership must be combined with labor law; and (3) at the stage of exchange state ownership vanishes completely, since the law of contracts, not the law of ownership, governs goods-money relations. The fact that an assumption of the identity of the law of ownership and ownership leads to such conclusions is the best argument against the assumption. On the contrary, if one adopts the distinction between ownership and the law of ownership, neither the shift from one economic stage to another nor the resulting change of legal forms will affect the existence of actual ownership, and, consequently, Soviet state ownership will be retained, despite transitions from production to distribution or exchange, and notwithstanding the alternation of the law of ownership, labor law, and the law of contracts.

The difference between the law of ownership and ownership is important not only for Soviet state ownership. Soviet law would be the object of ridicule, if, having proclaimed the domination of state ownership, it admitted the diminishment or disappearance of this domination as a function of the economic cycle and the various legal forms applicable at each economic stage. Therefore, the illustration chosen seems especially striking and quite convenient. But the Soviet system aside, in any society ownership and the law of ownership are different, though interdependent, phenomena. Ownership pertains to the economy, while the law of ownership is a legal institution. Ownership determines economic capacity, while the law of ownership outlines the latter's permissible limits. Ownership can lead to the necessity of active cooperation on the part of other persons (as workers, purchasers, lessees, etc.), while the law of ownership guarantees only these persons' passive conduct (non-interference in others' ownership, abstention from its violation, etc.). Consequently, the law of ownership is necessary but it is not sufficient for full-blown exercise of ownership. This goal also requires other forms of legal regulation. Therefore, the reduction of ownership to the law of ownership impoverishes the former and distorts the latter.

There are other circumstances that in this regard must be taken into account. Ownership should be correctly mirrored by law of ownership. To assume the identity of ownership and the law of ownership is to disregard the historical distinction between the two. Roman law was not limited by an abstract definition of ownership as *plena in re potestas* (full power over a thing),[11] but it also distinguished between legal rules addressed to things of different economic importance, for instance, to slaves and to less significant objects. The downfall of the slave-owning society rendered this distinction useless. However, the Roman distinctions between immovables (land and buildings) and movables (other things) are still extant in capitalist and even in certain "socialist" countries. The Soviet law of ownership includes the appropriate abstract definition, but the core of this law is embodied in the differentiations of various kinds and even various cases of ownership according to their economic significance.

The abstract legal definition of the rights of an owner states that "an owner has the right to possess, use and dispose of property within the limits established by the law."[12] To possess is to keep property in the owner's power, to use is to extract all useful qualities from the owned thing—physical as well as economic, and to dispose is to determine the actual or the legal fate of property by sale, donation, consumption, or even destruction. The owner's rights are not unlimited. He is obliged not to exceed the limits established by the law, though, as a matter of course, legal limitations are differently expressed with regard to individuals subordinate to the law and to the Soviet state as an owner and the lawmaker at the same time.[13] In formulating these limitations, the Soviet legislator least of all meant to bind the Soviet state. There was another problem to resolve. Possession, use, and disposition can be exercised by others than owners. Tenants, depositaries, agents, carriers, etc. each have one or several of these rights. Therefore, along with listing the rights of an owner it was necessary to indicate their peculiarities in cases where the holder of these rights is in fact an owner. The words "within the limits established by the law" were included in order to a classificatory goal. These words establish that the power of an owner is far stronger than the power of other rightholders with respect to the same object: an owner must only observe those restrictions provided by the law, while other possessors are also subject to commands made by the owner.

In any country with a free economy, an abstract formula like that given above would be sufficient as a legal definition of the right of ownership. In the USSR, where political power is based upon the economic monopoly of its political rulers, the abstract definition of the right of ownership in general has had to be supplemented by a specific outline of the different kinds of this right in order to ensure the domination of one type of ownership and the subordination of other types. The 1977 Constitution provides for two types of ownership: socialist and personal. State ownership, collective farm/cooperative ownership, and the ownership of trade unions and other social organizations qualify not as different types of ownership but as different forms of the same type of ownership—socialist ownership.[14] But as soon as Soviet legislation turns from ownership to the law of ownership, the official position changes substantially. The Fundamental Principles of Civil Legislation distinguish four kinds of ownership rights: (1) of the state, (2) of collective farms and other cooperatives, (3) of trade unions and other societal organizations, and (4) of individuals.[15] It will be demonstrated later that in the USSR just as with ownership, which consists of two types—state ownership and personal ownership—despite those constitutional provisions defining socialist ownership as a type and state, collective farm/cooperative and social organization ownership as three forms of this type,[16] there really exist only two kinds of ownership rights—of the state and of individuals—despite those constitutional and civil law provisions listing four types of ownership rights.[17] It is important to emphasize, however, that Soviet legislation distinguishes between four kinds of ownership rights without considering three of them only as different forms of the same right. This is in contrast to ownership which is classified by Soviet legislation as having two types, there being three forms of the first type. This signifies that Soviet law sanctions socialist ownership but it does not provide for socialist ownership rights. According to Soviet law, one can consider the three forms of socialist ownership as being of the same economic type but one cannot view the ownership rights of state, collective farm/cooperative, and social organization ownership as three forms of a single legal institution. Does this divergence stem from the Soviets' practical demands or from the "Marxist invention" of economic ownership in contrast to legal ownership?

The actual (not invented) difference between ownership and the law of ownership is in this case important as the justification for the above ascertained divergence: since ownership does not coincide with the law of ownership, the latter cannot repeat the former. However, there are also pragmatic reasons for the distinction. If the right of socialist ownership were to be legally provided for, the different kinds of this right would have to be independent from one another and subordinated only to established general rules. In contrast, in the absence of general socialist ownership rights, Soviet law can determine the right of state ownership in conformity with the model of the right of ownership and the rights of collective farm/cooperative and of social organization ownership on the model of the property right allocated by the Soviet state to state entities. As has been mentioned[18] and as will be explained in detail,[19] state entities hold not the right of ownership but the right of operative administration of property which belongs to the state. Correspondingly, the state must qualify as the owner of the property of collective farms, cooperative and social organizations, if under the title of "the rights of property" these organizations in fact possess the right of operative administration.[20] This is the principal reason for the construction of three different rights of ownership which correspond to the three forms of socialist ownership and which at the same time are not supplemented by a legal institution correlating with socialist ownership as a whole.

Further, legal ownership as a combination of possession, use, and disposition is neutral toward the economic differentiation of property rights.

This combination remains the same, regardless of whether the object of ownership is a coat, a house, a factory or a bank. In any country having a free economy, the independence of such a legal abstraction from economic differentiation would be limited only by rules that, without entailing a corresponding legal differentiation, are required to strengthen owners' positions with respect to the most economically important objects (registration of the acquisition of immovables, a special form of sale for automobiles, etc.). However, despite these additional rules, the freedom of goods-money relations would not be restricted in the least. In the USSR there also exist similar rules, connected if not with immovables (because land as the property of the state can be neither sold nor purchased), then with certain other objects (houses, automobiles, etc.). But the Soviet system requires more substantial special rules in order to ensure the economic monopoly of those who keep political power in their grasp. Therefore, not only different formalities but different legal regulations are established for different cases of ownership depending on the economic importance of the different objects of ownership. Ownership of means of production is subordinated to a legal regime other than that governing ownership of consumer goods; instruments of production require legal rules that differ from those dealing with objects of production; land occupies a special legal status in comparison with other estates, etc. Do these phenomena stem more from the "Marxist invention" of economic ownership in contrast to legal ownership than from practical demands?

The actual (not invented) difference between ownership and law of ownership is important in this case because law can only take into account but not create economic differentiation. The latter exists objectively, in the economy, not in law. However, the economy cannot by itself control goods-money relations. Only law is equal to such a task, and practical demands necessitate the desired solution. Should goods-money relations be legally uncontrolled in the USSR, any kind of ownership would become available to anyone—at least formally if not economically. As a result, the political rulers would lose their economic monopoly, and unlimited power would slip from their grasp. To prevent such undesirable consequences, Soviet law defines ownership in accordance with its subject (the state, collective farms and cooperatives, trade unions and other social organizations, and individuals)[21] and also outlines rights of ownership in accordance with their objects unlimited for the state, not quite so unlimited for collective farms and cooperatives, trade unions, and social organizations, and extremely restricted for individuals.[22] The mere fact that an individual possesses an object exceeding by its character the limits of the right of personal ownership renders his possession illegal and the object owned transferable to the state by means of confiscation. If the appropriate limits are violated by collective farms or cooperatives, or by trade unions or other social organizations, the withdrawal of the illicit objects by the state from their illegal possession actually is identical to the withdrawal from state entities of goods that may not be objects of these entities' operative administration. Such withdrawal is not confiscation, because the ownership remains with the state (in fact or even formally), but withdrawal of the illicit possessions acts as a measure that prevents the entities which are punished from becoming more independent than the state wishes to allow. This is the principal reason for the supplementation of the abstract definition of the right of ownership with specific definitions of the rights of state, collective farm/cooperative, social organization, and personal ownership.

Finally, the legally unlimited right of ownership evidenced in the ancient Roman or Napoleonic code interpretation is incompatible with the present epoch of intensive human interdependence. Therefore not only Soviet legislation with its words "within the limits established by the law," but also any legislation redrafted in the twentieth century in any country provides for limitations in one form or another. In countries having a free economy, a general provision on ownership, accompanied by specific rules to protect the public interest (e.g. environmental legislation and urban zoning), is considered to be both necessary and sufficient. Soviet law also combines general and special provisions. However, while the former are similar to those established throughout the world, the latter must serve the specific purposes of a system where unlimited political power must be maintained by the leadership's economic monopoly. There are, for instance, two similar rules dedicated to the achievement of the same purpose but from obviously different sides. The 1977 Constitution states: "No one shall have the right to use socialist ownership for the purposes of personal gain or other mercenary purposes."[23] This legal prohibition is addressed not to the owner, as is evident from the text cited and from the fact that Soviet law employs the terminology "socialist ownership" only in an economic sense, but to each individual obliged not use for purposes of private gain property formally designated for either all-the-people's or collective interests. In contrast, the Fundamental Principles of Civil Legislation are directed toward the owner, establishing that "property in the personal ownership of citizens may not be used to derive non-labor income."[24] What "non-labor income" signifies is neither explained by the law itself nor unanimously interpreted in Soviet doctrine.[25] But the genuine goal of its prohibition is common knowledge: to preclude any forms of personal enrichment, except for those directly provided for by the law. The identical goal can be ascertained in legal rules forbidding Soviet citizens to have more than one dwelling house,[26] determining the maximum number of cattle that may be individually owned,[27] etc. The right of ownership of collective farms and cooperatives, trade unions and other social organizations, also suffers legal limitations, because Soviet law distinguishes between different objects of this right and dictates, according to their economic significance, which actions may or may not be taken.[28] It is, however, noteworthy that, dealing with these organizations as alleged owners, the legislator dictates that they may be governed by either the same or similar restrictive rules as those binding for the state entities, though the latter possess no right of ownership.[29] At the same time, the right of state ownership is free from any limitations, and therefore it can be exercised without restrictions. Here, does the "Marxist invention" of the difference between economic and legal ownership prevail over Soviet practical demands?

The actual (not invented) difference between ownership and the law of ownership is important also in this case, because the material significance of property objects pertains to economy, not to law. However, the purposes pursued by the policy described are achievable only through law, not through economy. In restricting the right of ownership in the areas indicated and by the means indicated, the Soviets pursue three purposes: (1) to ensure the all-embracing domination of state ownership, regardless of whether the latter exists under its own title or under the pseudonym of ownership of collective farms and consumer cooperatives or trade unions and other social organizations; (2) to retain only one exception to the domination of state ownership, and personal ownership is the only allowed exception regardless of whether the latter exists in its proper sense or in a modified form such as ownership of housing, garage, and other analogous cooperatives or social organizations; (3) to prevent the transformation of personal ownership into a source of individuals' economic independence by restricting its size, objects etc., and to maintain individuals' economic dependence on state ownership by eliminating all of the obstacles in the path of the state's, in principle, limitless expansion.

The analysis of ownership and law of ownership in the USSR has produced several general conclusions. First, a difference between ownership and the law of ownership objectively exists, and this difference permeates Soviet law of ownership. Second, in defining the different kinds of the right of ownership, Soviet law deviates from its definitions of the different types of ownership and their different forms. Third, the purpose of this deviation is to strengthen legally the economic monopoly of the holders of unlimited political power and to maintain the economic dependence of the dominated individuals upon the dominating elite. Fourth, in discovering the substance of Soviet law that lies beneath its verbal form, one can ascertain that only two rights of ownership exist under the Soviet system: one belongs to the state personified by the ruling bureaucracy, and the other belongs to individuals, who, in such cases, are called personal owners by Soviet law. These rights will be the direct object of the discussion which follows.

The State's Right of Ownership

In defining the rights of ownership that belong to the state, Soviet law distinguishes between two groups of objects. The first group consists of things that may be owned only by the state: land, its minerals, water, and forests.[30] The law calls these the objects of exclusive state ownership, and they may not be purchased or sold. Individuals, collective farms, cooperatives, and trade unions or other societal organizations may act as users of plots of land, not as owners. However, despite the categorical terms of the Constitutional provision cited, the same Constitution establishes that "the land occupied by collective farms shall be allocated to them free of charge and in perpetuity."[31] In dealing with Soviet law, one must not trust its general declarations until these declarations are verified by legal practice and, not infrequently, by other legal rules. In the relevant legislation, one will find a provision that reads as follows: "The withdrawal of land plots used by collective farms . . . shall be permitted only in instances of special need."[32] It is also interesting that the same rule mentions, along with collective farms, also state agricultural entities, as if there were no difference between the former and the latter. This can occur only because the Soviet legislator does not act in earnest, providing collective farms with perpetual use of land plots as well as delimiting collective farms in their capacity as owners from state entities, which do not have the same capacity. A similar line of Soviet legislative activity can be ascertained in a number of other areas. Thus, on the one hand, a state monopoly of foreign trade is proclaimed,[33] and its implementation assumes that only certain state entities directly entitled by the law may execute foreign trade transactions. Yet, on the other hand, consumer cooperatives, beginning with their provincial, or more often republican links, have the right to take part in foreign trade relations, although formally these cooperatives are separated from the state and its entities. This is only one illustration of numerous cases where the Soviet legislature itself acts as if no distinctions existed between state and non-state organizations. The second group of objects of state ownership, which is not designated as "exclusive" by the law, comprises "the basic means of production in industry, construction, and agriculture, means of transport and communications, banks, property of trade, municipal, and other enterprises organized by the state, the basic city housing fund, and also other property needed to carry out the tasks of the state."[34] These objects do not pertain to the state's exclusive ownership because some of them can belong to non-state entities, which formally represent other subjects of ownership, and even to individuals who legally and actually are owners independent from the state. Nevertheless, the overwhelming majority of the objects enumerated are also in the state's grasp, and by means of production and reproduction the state ensures further enlargement of their number. It is, however, quite noteworthy that, even according to Soviet official data, plans for the production of means of production have always been overfulfilled, while plans for the production of consumer goods usually have been underfulfilled.[35] A Soviet principle of "primary development of producing the means of production," maintained by plans and strengthened in practice, relies not so much upon the goal of technological development as upon the clear understanding of a simple truth that the means of production are retained by the state, in contrast to consumer goods, which ultimately must be transferred to individuals. Therefore not one Soviet leader has deviated from this principle, and Gorbachev is no exception, judging from the Fundamental Directions of Economic and Social Development of the USSR for 1986–1990 and for the Period up to the year 2000 promulgated by the Twenty-Seventh Congress of the Communist Party of the Soviet Union.[36] These Fundamental Directions make it a primary goal "to steadily strengthen heavy industry—the basis of the country's economic development," and "to develop at an accelerated tempo those branches of industry that determine scientific/technological progress."[37]

In referring to certain details of its legal regulation, the right of state ownership can be typified as unrestricted as to its objects, the methods of acquisition, and the means of protection.

The objects of state ownership are listed by the rules cited only for the purpose of outlining those which entirely or paramountly belong to the state. But the listing is not exhaustive, as the concluding words of this list show: "and also other property needed to carry out the tasks of the state."[38] In its capacity as a sovereign, the state itself may determine what qualify as "state" tasks and the "property needed" for their implementation. In addition, not one special rule addressed to state ownership formulates a restriction on what may be owned, while all other kinds of ownership that are formally or actually recognized by Soviet law are limited by countless special rules. As a result, the state may own anything. Therefore, at least from this viewpoint, there is no obstacle to transfer of any property to state ownership, in contrast to the transfer of any property from the state to other persons, which can occur only in cases provided for by law.

Acquisition of property by the state may be implemented by all of the methods available to other subjects of Soviet law: contracts, unilateral transactions, etc. At the same time, there are methods of property acquisition especially established for the state and unavailable to anyone except for the state: nationalization, foreign trade contracts, inheritance of escheated property, etc. Among these specific methods, "confiscation of property," i.e. withdrawal of other persons' property for the benefit of the state as a sanction for certain legal violations, deserves special mention. Confiscation may be applied as a punishment for a crime,[39] as a negative consequence of an administrative misdemeanor,[40] and as a civil law sanction for engaging in illegal transactions,[41] etc. And what is more peculiar, Article 473 of the RSFSR Civil Code states that "property obtained at the expense of another person, not pursuant to any transaction but as a result of other acts knowingly contradicting the interests of the socialist state and society, if not subject to confiscation, shall be recovered for the benefit of the state." For example, such a characterization is applicable in the USSR if a person's action can be deemed "begging," and therefore, under the title of "unjust enrichment," even alms can become income for the Soviet state. Moreover, Soviet law establishes the following general rule: objects that belong to no one must belong to the state.[42] The latent idea behind this rule is sufficiently clear: the state is the owner, unless the law provides otherwise.

Protection of state ownership is restricted neither by the rights of good faith purchasers nor by statutes of limitations. The state may recover its property that has been unlawfully alienated by whatever means and that has been unlawfully received by any acquirer.[43] However, collective farms and other cooperative and social organizations enjoy the same privilege.

Restrictions are formulated only for personal owners who may recover their unlawfully alienated property only where an acquirer has acted in bad faith, because he knew or should have known of the illegality of his acquisition, or where a good-faith acquirer unlawfully receives another person's property without charge or, even if not without charge, where such property has been lost, stolen, etc.[44] No statute of limitations may be applied with regard to actions brought by state organizations for the return of state property that is in the illegal possession of collective farms or other cooperative and social organizations or citizens.[45] In other words, regardless of the time that has passed from the moment of the violation of the state's right of ownership, the protection of this right nevertheless will be ensured. The same legislation denies this advantage not only to individuals but also to collective farms and other cooperative or social organizations. But what happens to their property after the expiration of the period of limitations? The property is considered ownerless at that time and therefore must be transferred to the state. As a result, the state enriches itself at the expense of individuals and of those social organizations that constitute individual ownership in a modified form.[46] As to collective farms and other cooperative or social organizations which actually exercise state ownership in disguise, the Soviet state loses nothing by refusing to apply in these cases a privilege established for state ownership in its proper meaning. The expiration of the period of limitation simply results in a change of label: that which actually has been an object of state ownership becomes legally recognized as such because the property of collective farms, cooperatives and social organizations may be protected only within the limits of established periods. There also is no obstacle for the state to return disputed property to its former "owner" despite the expiration of the period of limitation; however, this can be done not on the basis of judicial or Arbitrazh decisions, but in the form of administrative distribution. Bearing in mind such opportunities, one can hardly ascertain substantial distinctions between the protection of state and other forms of "socialist" ownership. As discussed above, only in property disputes between state entities and individuals or non-state entities does the statute of limitations not apply with respect to ownership of the state. On the contrary, this statute is binding where both the plaintiff and the defendant are state entities. When the statute is applied, the legal consequences are identical to those arising for non-state entities as a result of the expiration of the period of limitation: the previous possessor loses its property in a dispute resolved by Arbitrazh. However, this property can be returned in the form of administrative distribution.

In characterizing state ownership, Soviet theory proclaims, in accordance with Soviet law, the principle of the "unity of the fund" (*edinstvo fonda*) of this ownership. The 1982 commentary to the RSFSR Civil Code states in this regard:

"The Soviet state is the unitary and the only owner of all state property, whatever its embodiment and whoever its possessor. All state property without any exception constitutes the unitary fund of state ownership. The Soviet state, combining in its grasp comprehensive political power with all owner's rights, itself determines the legal regime of its property."[47]

As can be seen, Soviet scholars, in contrast to some Western Sovietologists accept the idea of political monopoly based upon economic monopoly. Subsequently, we shall try to determine if "the unity of the fund" is peculiar only to state ownership or if it has any applicability to other forms of "socialist" ownership.[48] At present, it seems important to clarify the principle of "unity" within the limits recognized by Soviet law and Soviet doctrine.

There are Soviet entities that act in behalf of the state in the area of property relations (for instance, the Ministry of Finance in administering sources of the state budget) or which function in their own behalf (for instance, all state entities possessing the rights of legal entities [juridical persons] when these engage in their proper functions). Any Soviet entity of either of these types uses a certain amount of state property. However, the property used by entities of the first type, acting in behalf of the state, is undistributed state property administered by the state in the person of the authorized agency. The property used by entities of the second type, functioning in their own behalf, is distributed state property, and the legal title under which it is held by these state entities is called "operative administration." What does "operative administration" mean and to what extent does it differ from "ownership"?

Soviet law dedicates a special rule, Article 26–1 of the Fundamental Principles of Civil Legislation, to the legal definition of operative administration. According to this definition, operative administration as well as ownership in its legal interpretation includes "possession, use, and disposition of property." Thus, in this respect both legal phenomena seem identical. However, the holder of ownership is restricted only "within the limits established by the law,"[49] while the holder of operative administration is also subject to other restrictions. This holder must function not only "within the limits established by the law" but simultaneously in accordance with the following:

(1) *The Purpose of Its Activity.* The state, in creating each state entity, connects its activity with certain purposes. Industrial entities may not engage in retail trade; trade entities may not grow crops; a steel mill may not produce candy; a pharmacy may not sell postcards; etc. Deviating from the purposes determined by the state as the owner means that a state entity exceeds the limits of operative administration.

(2) *Planned Tasks.* These tasks are also determined by the state as the owner through its appropriate planning agencies. State plants and factories must produce their products in conformity with the planned number and types of goods; state department stores and other state shops may not sell articles not designated by the relevant plan indicators; etc. Economic activity contradicting planned tasks is generally illegal. Violation of the limits of operative administration is one of the most significant forms of such illegal activity.

(3) *The Purpose of the Property.* A portion of the state property allocated to any state entity is divided among different funds. Each fund must be employed in accordance with its purpose, and, except in cases and by procedures specially established, no fund may be replenished at the expense of another. Employment of one fund for purposes related to another fund or a shift of resources between different funds without special legal authorization is not a permitted activity for a holder of operative administration.

Because of the separation of different funds one must examine more closely the rule stating that possession, use, and disposition constitute the legal components of operative administration. This rule is abstractly correct, since, taking together all of the property funds employed on the basis of operative administration, one finds possession, use, and disposition as actually exercised by the rightholder. However, a separate analysis of the different funds proves that in each case at least one of the opportunities enumerated is lacking: either disposition, or use, or even possession. To clearly establish this fact let us consider the property rights of those state entities, such as production associations or independent production enterprises, that carry out production activity. Such entities possess various property funds under the title of operative administration.[50]

The first fund consists of buildings and installations. Economic entities possess and use these objects, but disposition is extremely restricted. Buildings and installations that have been left unused for less than one year may be leased to other organizations by the possessing entity. All other forms of disposal of such property (including withdrawal of buildings and installations left unused for more than one year) are subject to the jurisdiction of superior agencies, not to the holder of the right of operative administration.

The second fund, called the charter fund, consists of basic assets and circulating assets. Basic assets include all kinds of equipment and means of transportation that both have a value of more than one hundred rubles and can be productively used for more than one year.[51] When basic assets are in use for production, no right of disposition belongs to the economic entity, and only planning agencies may implement their redistribution. But if some basic assets become completely unnecessary, and planning agencies, after being informed of this fact, adopt no decision during the period of time fixed by law, then the economic entity itself may sell them to any Soviet organization. It must include the amounts received in its production development fund.

Circulating assets, as the other component of the charter fund, consist of raw materials, other supplies, fuels, and money earmarked for current economic activity. Physical assets are classified as circulating assets if they are worth less than one hundred rubles or have a useful life of less than one year. While these physical circulating assets are necessary for production activity, the economic entity has no rights other than the use and possession of this property. Only the money for production use is at its disposal. But money included in circulating assets must be deposited in the State Bank (*Gosbank*), thus leaving the economic entity's possession, and no payment can be made other than through the bank and under its supervision. Any surplus of circulating assets in kind is subject to redistribution by a superior agency or to sale by agencies of supply. Only in instances where these agencies fail to exercise such opportunities may sales be effected by the economic entity itself, on condition that the amounts obtained through such sales will be transferred to the monetary part of circulating assets.

Monetary funds are rather numerous, but each of them is designated for a specific goal and may be spent only in furtherance of this goal under the strict observance of the relevant regulations. With the exception of the monetary part of circulating assets, which is a component of the charter fund, all other monetary resources of the economic entity can qualify as various species of a third type of fund.

The capital investment fund is not a permanent fund. It is created only in cases where a plan issued by the appropriate governing agency provides for new construction. In accordance with the plan, the economic entity receives from the Treasury and keeps in the bank the required monetary resources. The money thus received may be used only to pay for construction work and not for the replenishment of circulating assets, just as circulating assets may not be used to replenish the capital investment fund.

The amortization fund is a permanent fund created and replenished by regular amortization transfers during a period and in the manner provided by law. A portion of these transfers must be put at the disposal of the entity's superior agency. The other part may be used by the economic entity for financing major repairs or for the acquisition of new equipment to replace obsolete machinery.

Incentive funds are created for the purpose of stimulating increased economic productivity. There are three kinds of incentive funds: (1) the production development fund, earmarked for the introduction of new technology, the modernization of equipment, etc.; (2) the fund for social-cultural measures and housing construction, which must be employed by the economic entity in the erection of new apartment buildings, the reconstruction of old apartment buildings, the acquisition or building of health or vacation facilities, etc.; and (3) the material incentive fund, which serves as the source for bonuses paid to workers and officials according to their personal achievements, etc. All incentive funds are created and replenished by periodic deductions depending on the fulfillment and overfulfillment of plans. However, the legal treatment of these funds is not entirely clear. The 1965 economic reform prohibited their withdrawal from economic entities, even at the end of the economic year. The economic experiment ordered by Andropov in 1983 adopted the same rule only with respect to the material incentive fund and exclusively for economic entities participating in this experiment.[52] Gorbachev enlarged the scale of the experiment but did not introduce new rules concerning the fate of incentive funds after the expiration of the economic year. At any rate, any economic entity, regardless of whether or not it is among those included in the economic experiment, has the right to dispose of incentive funds for the purposes listed during the economic year through the bank that keeps these monetary resources in its possession.

An examination of the legal provisions established for goods produced, goods which are the result of production rather than a fund for production, is useful for a full comprehension of the operative administration exercised by a producing economic entity. In this case, the rightholder has the rights of possession and disposition, but not the right of use. To use its own product, the economic entity must transfer the requisite portion of it from goods produced to production or other funds. If the goods produced are subject to planned distribution, then, in order to acquire its own product, the producer must be included in the plan of distribution issued by planning agencies. Violations of this rule lead to legal sanctions.[53] If the goods produced are excluded from planned distribution, then, in order to acquire its own product, the producer must have adequate resources in a monetary fund that may be employed for such an acquisition, and when part of the entity's product becomes a part of its fund of physical goods, the price of the product thus obtained must be deducted from the appropriate monetary fund and added to the amount of gain resulting from the sale of the product.

Thus, in comparison with the right of ownership, personified by the Soviet state, operative administration, personified by state entities, is an essentially restricted property right. Now, that this has been shown, we must once more return to Professor Berman's work where he compares state ownership as a "theoretical" or "fictitious" phenomenon[54] with operative administration as a "legal invention" the "genius" of which is the ensuring of "the actual benefit of ownership . . . to the enterprises."[55] As emphasized, this is the only instance where Professor Berman deviates from his negation, in principle, of any difference between ownership *de jure* and ownership *de facto*.[56] Yet, because operative administration does not contain as its "gist" the right of ownership, while in the USSR state ownership plays a more essential than purely "theoretical" or "fictitious" role, the author could avoid even such a deviation from his original point of view. However, if the holder of operative administration is not an owner, in such case who is the owner of the property distributed among the state entities in the USSR? "The Soviet state," answers Soviet law. Well! But ownership cannot belong to an abstract phenomenon. Which persons specifically or collectively act as the owner where the owner is deemed to be the Soviet state? This problem also entails no difficulty for Soviet law: "all the Soviet people," it proclaims. However, it is impossible to prove such a declaration, because even the restricted property rights encompassed by operative administration are unavailable to the Soviet people as a whole, and, in addition, Soviet law itself includes its own limitations in this regard. Dealing with the fiction of the all-the-people's state, Article 2 of the 1977 Constitution indicates that "the people exercise state power through the Soviets of people's deputies." But who acts as an intermediary in the people's exercise of possession, use and disposition of state property? One would look in vain for the necessary indications in Soviet law, which recognizes, except in the declaration mentioned above, neither direct nor indirect participation of the people in the exercise of the right of state ownership. Soviet propaganda also must capitulate in this case. Unlike strikes, which have been declared unimaginable as a protest of Soviet citizens against themselves,[57] the stealing of state property has never been denied as a senseless appropriation of one's own estate.

In contrast to Soviet law and Soviet propaganda, certain critics of the Soviet regime, including the authors of this book,[58] identify the Soviet state with the ruling elite of this country. Critics diverge as to the specific outlines of ruling elite—a new class, the "nomenklatura," the Party bureaucracy, or the Party summit—but they agree that a comparatively limited collective body maintains a political and economic monopoly. Counter-criticism of these critics includes a number of arguments which, insofar as they do not relate to the topic of our research, need not be addressed. However, one critic argues in such a peculiar way that a large extract from his work deserves to be cited. He writes:

> The state is defined by Professor Ioffe, according to Marxist-Leninist theory, in two different ways. Legally the Soviet state consists of such agencies as the Soviets, the councils of ministers, and the like—agencies that exercise legislative, administrative, and judicial powers. But *de facto* the state consists of the people who control those agencies. In Lenin's definition, the state—he was referring, of course, to the bourgeois state—is "the executive committee of the ruling class." Professor Ioffe therefore identifies the Soviet state with the leadership of the Communist Party of the Soviet Union. . . ."[59]

According to Ioffe, the critic continues,

> [T]he employees and officials of the state—not only the plant managers but also the heads of agencies that administer branches of the economy, including the economic ministers themselves, have interests that may conflict with those of the state. Here the terminology is the reverse of the official Soviet terminology. In official Soviet terminology, the Party leadership is *not* the state; in Professor Ioffe's it is precisely the party leadership that *is* the state, and that *is* referred to *in fact* when it is said that under Soviet socialism there is 'state ownership' of the means of production. In official Soviet terminology, the heads of ministries—including, say, the minister of the automobile industry, the minister of the oil industry, and other economic ministers—exercise state power; in Professor Ioffe's terminology, they are merely servants of the Party leadership, to whom the Party leadership reluctantly gives whatever limited power is necessary to carry out its orders."[60]

Is it not truly peculiar that a critic of the Soviet regime allegedly relies upon Marxist-Leninist theory, while a critic of this critic protects the Soviet regime by criticizing Marxism-Leninism? Can criticism of the Soviet system be persuasive if it contradicts official Soviet terminology? If it can, then what is proved by emphasizing such terminological divergence? If it can not, then how, for example, contrary to the same terminology, can Gorbachev, the leader of the Party, negotiate on behalf of the state with French President Mitterrand and American President Reagan? But *quad licet Jovi non licet bovi*: as the first person among Soviet rulers Gorbachev may disregard official formalities, in contrast to critics of these rulers, who must observe Soviet terminology as binding. Can economic ministers and other economic managers have interests conflicting with those of the state, since they themselves are state officials? And if they are state officials, how can it occur that the state is in the grasp of the Party leadership, while economic ministers and economic managers are only this leadership's servants? Consider one more argument: members of the Politburo publicly call themselves "servants of the state"; so, how can they have their own servants? Is there any reason to suspect that the Party leadership reluctantly gives limited power to economic ministers and to economic managers? Unfortunately, it is well known that the power given to them at one moment is often withdrawn at another moment. Does not this occur because the former act expresses the leadership's true desires and the latter act is done only with reluctance?

We do not think that the questions stated above entirely exhaust the available arguments and counter-arguments, and it is not our goal to pursue the matter further. At present, there is only one problem: who holds the right of state ownership in the USSR? Since the owner and the state must be the same person, a group of persons or an organized collective body, the identity of the state will be discovered as soon as the identity of the owner is ascertained.

The author of the passage quoted above contends that Soviet entities as holders of operative administration retain state property in their "actual ownership."[61] As an analysis of the components of operative administration demonstrates, however, such an idea does not stand the test. In addition, the author's view contradicts his own negation of Marxism-Leninism (actual and legal ownership!) and his attitude toward Soviet terminology (state ownership is all-the-people's ownership).

Certain Soviet scholars, maintaining the fiction of all-the-people's ownership, try to employ the idea of divided ownership borrowed from medieval jurists—postglossators.[62] However, divided ownership signifies that none of its participants has supremacy over any other, and the right of each is restricted by the rights of the others. Soviet economic entities do not occupy such a position in relations with the Soviet state, because the latter's power is in no way limited by the former's rights.[63]

We think that the problem under discussion must be solved in accordance with the nature of the right of ownership itself. Although the right of ownership includes three kinds of power ("a triad," in the terminology of Soviet legal theory)—possession, use, and disposition, the owner retains ownership even in cases where the entire "triad" is transferred to another person on condition that as soon as such a person exhausts the legal opportunities acquired the rights must be restored automatically to the owner. This phenomenon, called in Roman jurisprudence *jus recadentiae* or elasticity of the right of ownership, is not unknown with respect to the right of state ownership. For instance, a tenant in a state apartment building has the right to possess and use the occupied apartment, and the state may not evict him as a general rule. However, eviction in cases provided for by the law or unilateral cancellation of the contract by the tenant terminates his rights and automatically returns these rights to the state. Meanwhile, with respect to operative administration, the state needs no *jus recadentiae* in order to obtain the same result: any property may be withdrawn at any moment from any holder of operative management on the basis of an order issued by a sufficiently high state agency. This renders indisputable the conclusion that even if in cases of *jus recadentiae* the right of ownership is not lost, it is all the more evident that the right of state ownership is retained where the rights of operative administration are delegated, since the owner may withdraw these rights at any time without waiting for their exhaustion and without relying upon the elasticity of ownership. Therefore operative administration provides its holders with neither "actual" nor "divided" ownership, and, consequently, state ownership is not supplanted by operative administration.

Along with *jus recadentiae*, there exists another indicator proving that the right of ownership is retained despite the transfer to another person of the rights of possession, use, and/or even disposition. The rightholder remains the owner, if, notwithstanding the implemented transfer, he is entitled to interfere with the transferee's activity connected with the received property. Such a phenomenon also is not unknown with respect to the right of state ownership. Let us again use the example of a tenant in a state-apartment building. Although an apartment is possessed and used by the tenant, nevertheless, the state exercises control by mandating strict observance of the rules of housing laws, not in the capacity of the lawmaker but in that of the owner. With respect to the transfer of state property to the operative administration of state entities, the nature and principal goal of such a transfer create for the state far more substantial opportunities "to interfere" than do any other types of property transfer carried out by the state. One must not forget that operative administration is implemented by state entities not so much in their own interests as in the interests of the state. Conflicts between both kinds of interests, in fact, do exist, despite the ironical astonishment of those who think that state officials by definition cannot have conflicts with the state rulers,[64] and, that consequently (such might be the logical conclusion) no conflict can arise between the state and its entities. Even authors who see operative administration as actually embodying the rights of ownership have been compelled to recognized that the 1965 reform, which strengthened the initiative and economic independence of state enterprises, was reduced almost to nothingness by "unpublished regulations of the highest administrative authorities."[65] They neglect to explain, however, why this has occurred. But in the USSR it is an open secret: exercising greater independence, state economic entities began to produce primarily articles that were of little use to the state but that were quite profitable for the producers. Such and other similar conflicts have always been resolved in favor of the state and to the detriment of state entities. As the owner, whose right of interference is retained under operative administration to an even greater degree than under lease or other forms of property transfer, the state has unlimited opportunities to manipulate the situation to its liking by means of new plans, modified regulations in regard to the rights of economic entities, and, if necessary, by specific orders countermanding these entities' own decisions. This is why operative administration does not hinder the state's enjoyment of the full right of state ownership.

However, both *jus recadentiae* and the right of interference only confirm that, despite operative administration, the state retains its rights of ownership. These phenomena do not expose the personal substratum of state ownership, i.e., they do not answer the question: who personifies the state as owner? In order to resolve this problem, one must separate from all other forms of disposition the supreme disposition of the given property. The owners are those who implement the supreme disposition, the disposition in the final instance, which no one may modify, repeal or otherwise affect. Since, according to the Soviets themselves, their state combines completeness of political power with the right of ownership,[66] owners are those who have in their grasp unlimited political power. In search of the holders of political power, it is again very important to prevent the confusion of political domination with the distribution of ruling functions.[67] From the viewpoint of ruling functions, political power is carried out by a great number of agencies and by an even greater number of officials. In contrast, political domination is a privilege held only by a certain agency personified by a limited circle of officials. This occurs because political domination assumes that (1) power is real, rather than symbolic (as, for instance, the power of the USSR Supreme Soviet); (2) power is all-embracing, rather than partial (as, for instance, the power of ministries); (3) power is supreme, rather than subordinate (as, for instance, the power of the USSR Council of Ministers); (4) power is unlimited, rather than in some way restricted (as, for instance, the power of KGB). In our opinion, only one agency, the Politburo, combines all of these features, and thus only this body can exercise true political domination. Certain other authors think that the top of the Soviet regime consists not only of the Politburo but also of the Secretariat of the Party Central Committee.[68] It would be inappropriate to deal with this debate on politics in this book on law. In order to avoid unnecessary deviations from our topic, we shall employ the words "the Party summit," instead of the Politburo separately from or together with the Sectetariat. And since the Party summit keeps in its grasp political domination in the Soviet state, the same summit must also be the holder of the supreme disposition of state property. This conclusion can be verified by the same criteria that have already been employed to ascertain those who implement political domination in the USSR.

First, supreme disposition expresses the right of ownership, if such disposition is real, not symbolic. Symbolically, the state plan and the state budget, these most important forms of the supreme disposition of state property, are issued by the USSR Supreme Soviet. However, those who know planning and budgeting practice in the USSR can attest to the fact that without the Politburo's approval drafts of the plan and budget cannot become issues of discussion in the USSR Supreme Soviet and, whenever subsequent modifications in a plan or budget are needed, the special sanction of the Politburo is required. The well-known fact that the USSR Supreme Soviet has always made unimportant modifications in drafts presented to it is no enigma for the informed: the Politburo approves two drafts of the plan and of the budget in advance—one for public discussion and the other for official promulgation. Therefore, within the limits of the first feature, the supreme disposition is a privilege of the Party summit.

Second, the supreme disposition available only to an owner must be all-embracing, not partial. Disposition concerning a certain part of state property is often implemented even by the lowest links of the Soviet system. In contrast, only the Party summit has at its disposal state property as a whole and in every respect. This does not, of course, mean that the Politburo or the Secretariat will itself undertake the activities of separate entities acting in the areas of trade or service. Such an interpretation of supreme disposition would distort and vulgarize its substance. An owner need not act directly to be an owner. However, taking into consideration all intermediary links, one can always discern a connection between the acts of the lowest and the supreme disposition. Sometimes, this connection encompasses even trifles. During wartime, Stalin's signature was necessary to sell oranges for the Moscow children's New Year's tree decorations. Under normal circumstances, such extremes hardly occur. However, even in the early 1960's, Ill'ichev, then a nonvoting member of the Politburo, describing the activity of this body in his speech at the meeting of the chiefs of the humanities departments of universities and institutes in Leningrad,[69] told the audience that at nearly every session the Politburo struggled for hours to find several million additional rubles for demands that had suddenly arisen. Thus, the second feature of supreme disposition, the all-embracing nature of the power, also proves that the Party summit is its actual holder.

Third, supreme disposition is not subordinate, by definition. Any Soviet agency, carrying out property acts, relies either upon the law or upon special permission. For the Party summit, even the law is not binding. It is no secret that the state budget, as embodied in the law adopted by the USSR Supreme Soviet, undergoes a number of modifications during the economic year. However, the USSR Supreme Soviet has never modified such a law in the entire history of this body's activity. Who allows these actual modifications? Everyone knows that Soviet military expenditures, in fact, immensely exceed the formal budget indices. Who sanctions such substantial deviations? Not one Soviet budget allocates monetary resources for the activities of the Soviet and foreign Communist parties, although their maintenance depends not so much on their own income as on state "subsidies." Who orders the granting of the required "subsidies"? The answer is annoyingly monotonous: the Politburo. Consequently, the supreme nature of the power of the Party summit further indicates that this summit possesses the third feature typical for the holder of the supreme disposition.

Fourth, supreme disposition in the area of state ownership is unlimited, not in any way restricted. This conclusion follows from the fact that, generally speaking, an owner must exercise possession, use, and disposition within the limits of the law,[70] but because the state simultaneously is the lawmaker, the scope of the right of state ownership depends on the state itself. However, similar to any state, the Soviet state is a hierarchical system, and a hierarchy assumes that restrictions are loosened in proportion to one's distance from the bottom of the system and that they are entirely eliminated at the totalitarian top. Under the Soviet regime only the Party summit enjoys such freedom from restrictions and only this summit may unrestrictedly exercise the right of state ownership. This can be ascertained both in the most significant and in the most trifling matters. The fact that not a single large construction project is undertaken without a "directive" from the summit is commonly known these days, insofar as weekly summaries of Politburo meetings are regularly published. However, there are only a few persons who can attest to the fact that it was the Politburo whose command caused all of the major Leningrad hotels to remain uninhabited during the 1980 Olympic Games, because Soviet citizens were prevented from registering in these hotels by an order of the Politburo. This order remained in effect even though the number of foreign vistors was greatly reduced as a result of President Carter's boycott. And so, the fourth feature of supreme disposition, its unlimited nature, also justifies considering this disposition as an attribute of the Party summit.

The previous arguments lead only to one final conclusion: both the unlimited political power and the economic monopoly of the Soviet regime reside with the Party summit, which simultaneously personifies the Soviet state and the holder of the right of state ownership. What, however, about the second and third forms of socialist ownership which, though constituting a palpable economic force, are not included in state ownership according to the literal language of Soviet law?

Let us begin with collective farm/cooperative ownership insofar as, in our opinion, it is state ownership in a disguised form, directly personified by collective farms and consumer cooperatives.[71] This ownership formally is personified by each collective farm and by each link in the consumer cooperative system. However, there are what are called centralized funds created by all collective farms and all links in the consumer cooperatives system for special purposes (social security, construction, etc.). Soviet law categorizes these funds as the common property of the farms and cooperatives. But collective farms do not have their own administrative system, and in this case the centralized funds are administered by the appropriate governmental bodies (for instance, by the Ministry of Social Security), while consumer cooperatives transfer payments for centralized funds to *Tsentrosoiuz*, which is the highest link in the cooperative chain and which is subordinated in turn to the Soviet government through *Gosagroprom* of the USSR. As a result, even formally centralized funds belong not so much to collective farms or consumer cooperatives as to the Soviet state.[72] Soviet law restricts the objects of collective farm/cooperative ownership by reference to the "charter tasks," respectively, of collective farms and consumer cooperatives. Such a restriction, however, is typical not of ownership but of operative administration.[73] In addition, the property of each collective farm and of each consumer cooperative consists of various funds both monetary and in kind, and all of these funds (production and non-production, basic and circulating, current and insurance) must be replenished regularly and employed only in accordance with their purposes. This restriction is also characteristic of operative administration, not the right of ownership. Finally, collective farms and consumer cooperatives must employ their property in conformity with the planned tasks formulated by the Soviet state. To demonstrate this conclusion, one can point to the legal description of the rights of *Gosagroprom*, the government agency which implements the administration of collective farms and consumer cooperatives. The appropriate decree states that *Gosagroprom* "is the central agency of state administration of the agricultural-industrial complex of the country, and it bears, along with the Councils of Ministers of the Union Republics, full responsibility for increasing production, the performance of plans of procurement of agricultural produce and ensuring its safekeeping, high-quality processing and substantial enlargement of assortment of consumer goods. For these purposes *Gosagroprom* has the appropriate rights and powers in the areas of planning, financing and supplying the agricultural—industrial complex with material—technical resources. The decisions adopted by USSR *Gosagroprom* within the limits of its jurisdiction are binding upon and must be performed by all ministries and departments, institutions, associations, enterprises, and organizations."[74] As is known, the subordination of property rights to plan tasks, similar to the other restrictions enumerated above, is not characteristic of the right of ownership but of operative administration. Thus, the phenomenon officially called "the right of collective farm/cooperative ownership" lacks all of the qualities essential for true ownership, and at the same time possesses all of the attributes of operative administration as the latter is defined by Art. 26–1 of the Fundamental Principles of Civil Legislation. Because collective farms and consumer cooperatives have only the rights of operative administration, there must be another entity that holds the right of ownership with respect to the same property. As a matter of course, it is only the Soviet state that can be this "other entity," since it is the state itself that establishes those restrictions on property rights which may be established only by the owner and, in addition, by a specific owner capable of creating, on the basis of its ownership, the right of operative administration. Should it be otherwise, a number of important events would remain inexplicable. How can the Soviet state transform, when it deems this necessary, collective farms into state farms without compensating the previous owners? How could the Soviet state liquidate consumer cooperatives in urban areas in 1935 and transfer their property to the state trade system without reimbursement of the cooperative members? How was the Soviet state able to liquidate trade cooperatives in the late 1950's and to transfer their estate to state industrial enterprises without reimbursement as well? Were these measures confiscation of property? Not at all. Confiscation is a punitive sanction only assessed against individuals or entities as a result of violations of law. However, neither the collective farms transformed into state farms nor the consumer and trade cooperatives liquidated in part or (in certain republics) completely had committed any violations. Moreover, the members of these farms and cooperatives did not even notice what had happened, though the actual deprivation of ownership of a genuine collective body could not help but impinge upon the interests of its members. In fact, no such impingement resulted because there was no transferal of ownership. The state was the owner beforehand, and it at no time relinquished its ownership. Only the "outer shell" was removed: state ownership disguised as collective farm/cooperative ownership was deprived of this "outer shell" and appeared in undisguised form as state ownership.

The same situation can be seen with respect to ownership by trade unions and other social organizations, putting aside those few voluntary societies which personify transformed individual (not state) ownership.[75] Among the proprietors of the so-called third form of socialist ownership trade unions are the most numerous organizations, since their membership includes the entire working population with the exception of collective farmers and military personnel.[76] In the USSR, trade unions are organized in a unified system spread across the entire country and consisting of lower, higher and central links. Each of these links has the rights of a subject of law, but the trade unions as a whole do not enjoy the same rights. Therefore, Soviet law provides for ownership by trade unions without determining the owner,[77] while Soviet theory proclaims the trade union system to be the only owner of trade union property,[78] though this is legally impossible because such an organization simply does not exist as a legal entity. All of the links of trade unions have a certain amount of property sufficient only for the fulfillment of their tasks. However, the Statute of Trade Unions[79] categorizes these rightholders not as owners but as entities that may dispose, in conformity with established rules, of various amounts of trade union property. This is indicative, of course, not of the right of ownership but of operative administration.

The identical conclusion follows from the fact that the law, after listing the property purportedly available to trade unions as objects of their ownership (membership dues, cultural-educational and sports establishments, subsidiary enterprises etc.), establishes general restrictions which stem from the "charter tasks" or from the "purposes of activity" of trade unions in the USSR.[80] Restrictions of this character are incompatible with the right of ownership, which can be limited only by the law, not by other demands. In comparison, Article 26–1 of the Fundamental Principles of Civil Legislation refers to the "purposes of activity" limitation as the primary feature of operative administration. The legal provisions regulating the exercise of trade unions' property rights reveal two other features of operative administration.[81] On the one hand, the law mandates that these organizations maintain basic assets, cultural-educational and other funds and employ each type of these funds exclusively in accordance with its purpose. On the other hand, trade unions also have their own plans, prepared on the basis of the state planning tasks, though formally confirmed by the appropriate agencies of the trade unions themselves. It must be clear, since trade unions are restricted in their property rights by the objectives of their activity, planning tasks, and the purposes of the property, as determined by the state directly or ultimately, that the right of ownership belongs to the state, and that trade unions hold only the right of operative administration.

Thus, to summarize our analysis of Soviet ownership in its predominant type and proclaimed forms, as these are outlined by Soviet law but are implemented differently in Soviet practice, we can conclude the following.

First, from the economic point of view,[82] despite the broad pronouncements of Soviet legislation, neither socialist ownership nor any of its three forms (state ownership, collective farm/cooperative ownership, and trade union or other organization ownership) exists in the USSR. Actually, the Soviet authorities have established the absolute domination of state ownership, calling it by its proper name or disguising it with euphemistic terminology. In fact, Soviet law itself indirectly recognizes the contradiction between Soviet legal provisions and Soviet reality when, dealing with legal as opposed to economic phenomena, it does not formulate the right of socialist ownership as a general type and simultaneously avoids qualifying as subordinate species the right of state ownership, the right of collective farm/cooperative ownership, and the right of ownership of trade unions and other social organization.

Second, Soviet law distinguishes in connection with state ownership between the right of ownership, which belongs to the state, and the right of operative administration, which is allocated to each state entity in its status as an independent subject of law. The right of operative administration is derivative from and subordinate to the right of state ownership. This ensures an analogous subordination of state entities to the Soviet state. The property rights of state entities are protected to some extent from violation by higher agencies. However, the ruling summit is not restricted in this regard either actually or even by law. Therefore the leadership's economic monopoly within the limits officially called "the right of state ownership" is also formally, let alone factually, beyond doubt.

Third, the property rights of collective farms and consumer cooperatives, trade unions, and other social organizations are declaratively called rights of ownership in the general provisions of Soviet legislation. However, these same provisions, and especially those rules which deal directly with the specifics of the rightholder's activities, characterize the rights of ownership mentioned above exactly as they do with respect to the rights of operative administration allocated to state entities. Similar to the interests of the state entities, the interests of collective farms and the other organizations discussed are, at least formally, protected against interference from certain state agencies but not with regard to the Soviet leadership. The right of state ownership actually also includes ownership of non-state organizations, and, as a result, the economic monopoly of the ruling summit encompasses so-called socialist ownership in all of its forms and ramifications.

Accordingly, the final conclusion must be that the USSR is a country in which the right of state ownership is dominant, and all Soviet entities (state, collective farm, consumer cooperative, and social organizations) are holders not of the right of ownership but of operative administration. Because the right of state ownership is so broadly extended, the Soviet leadership can keep an economic monopoly in its grasp and exercise on this basis unlimited political power.

The Right of Personal Ownership

Along with the dominant right of state ownership, examined in its basic and disguised forms, there also exists the right of personal ownership, as the Soviets call ownership by individuals. Although the latter is unavoidable, because individuals may freely dispose of the payment received for their labor from Soviet entities, the legal recognition of the right of personal ownership affects neither the all-embracing domination of the right of state ownership nor the economic monopoly of the Soviet leadership. In order to maintain one's economic monopoly one must be the monopolist in the area of production. As to the right of personal ownership in the USSR, it is attached by Soviet law to the area of consumption. Therefore, individuals' property rights are quite compatible with the state's economic monopoly. It is true that the 1977 Constitution permits individual labor activity to an extent far beyond that allowed by the 1936 Constitution.[83] This, however, provides no basis for the unqualified contention that "the provisions of the new Constitution are laying the legal foundation for the use of objects of personal property in all spheres of the economy" and that "these spheres include not only consumption (as always) but also production and exchange."[84] A Soviet scholar A. A. Rubanov to whom K. Malfiet, the author of the lines cited, refers in this connection formulates his thoughts more carefully and with a number of reservations.[85] In addition, authors of recent Soviet publications have in no way adopted such a viewpoint. As a 1985 publication emphasizes, property may be an object of personal ownership only so long as it "has a labor origin and bears a consumer character."[86] To some extent individual production activity was permitted prior to the 1977 Constitution, and this document enlarged but did not establish such an opportunity.[87] However, similar to its predecessor, the Constitution in force limits individual economic activity, allowing it to include only the labor of the owner and members of his family, precluding aquisition by individuals of any means of production except for minor implements, and introducing a new rule, according to which "the state shall regulate individual labor activity, ensuring its use in the interests of society."[88] Of course, however individual labor activity may be restricted, since it has been legally implemented, such activity can be found in all spheres of Soviet economy to some extent. But, bearing in mind the limits outlined by law, one cannot typify the Soviet economy simply as a combination of state and individual components. The Soviet state, incapable of properly supplying the Soviet population with even the barest necessities, is forced to allow individual labor activity on a larger scale than it might desire[89] but at a lower level than necessary for normal supply. In addition, it is entirely a matter within the state's discretion whether the permission promulgated to engage in such activity will be retained, restricted, or abrogated because, according to its officially recognized definition, the right of personal ownership must serve consumer purposes, while certain production goals can be either tolerated or prohibited. Therefore, the economic monopoly of the Soviet state exists, despite the modified scope of the right of personal ownership.

In order to maintain the state's economic monopoly, the Constitution limits in Art. 13 the objects available for personal ownership to the following: articles of everyday use, personal consumption, convenience, and subsidiary household husbandry, a dwelling house, and savings from labor earnings.[90] In this list, the means of production are not mentioned at all. Only civil legislation mentions "minor agricultural implements" with reference to collective farm household ownership.[91] At the same time, admitting the existence of subsidiary household farming operations and the implementation of individual labor activity, the Constitution cannot help implying, while not admitting directly, the availability to individuals of certain means of production required for these farming operation and for such activity. However, that which is only implied must not go beyond that which is provided *expressis verbis*. Since collective farm households may include only "minor agricultural implements," the same restriction is applicable to subsidiary household farming operations and, except for the word "agricultural," to other types of individual labor activity.

Thus, in principle, the means of production, at any rate those which affect the economic structure of any society, are not included in the class of objects of personal ownership, and this approach, confirmed by Soviet law, is intended primarily as a method of ensuring the economic dependence of the Soviet citizenry on the Soviet state. In order to strengthen this dependence, Soviet law provides for a number of other restrictions with respect to these objects which, generally speaking, can be owned by individuals. We have already indicated that a Soviet family may have not more than one house.[92] Now it is appropriate to emphasize that, as a rule, this house must not contain more than 60 square meters, and the payment received if it is rented to others must not exceed limits established by law.[93] A second house illegally acquired (by purchase, for example) is subject to confiscation, and in cases of legal acquisition (by inheritance, for example) all houses but one must be sold or they will be withdrawn.[94] Violations of the limits on payments for the rental of a house or a part of a house, lead to the same sanctions as are applicable with respect to the extraction of non-labor income.[95] The Soviet family has the right to sell a house no more than once every three years.[96] Otherwise the contract will be void, and its object will be confiscated. Moreover, the acquisition of houses for permanent residence depends on the passport regulations which are in force in a given city or other settlement. Should these regulations preclude the registration for residence of a prospective purchaser, the latter may not buy a house in that location. The acquisition of country houses ("dachas") is even more strictly regulated. The law in force prohibits individual construction of country houses anywhere in the country,[97] and unpublished instructions render the purchase of country houses extremely complicated: the purchaser must receive special permission from the appropriate local executive committee, and on the outskirts of cities such as Moscow or Leningrad, only persons who have been registered for residence in these cities may buy country houses—and these individuals must be willing either to forego their right to eventual distribution of state living premises on the principle of priority or, if they live in state apartment buildings, to cancel their lease for the benefit of the state. Individuals may lend money or other property only without charging interest.[98] Even the 2% or 3% interest which may be paid by saving banks is not allowed in relations between citizens. At the same time, Soviet banks extend credit to citizens only in cases provided for by the law for the construction of individual houses, or to create funds for participation in housing cooperative construction of apartment buildings, on the condition that a set of extremely complicated rules are strictly observed. Beyond these limits, an individual can either obtain a loan from a close friend in accordance with law, or from one who charges interest, in contravention of the law. However, in the former case the borrower feels awkward, knowing that the lender is sacrificing interest income by not having the money on deposit in a savings bank, and in the latter case the borrower will lose the interest he has paid and the lender will be forced to pay the sum of the loan to the state, if the performance of the illegal contract is discovered by the appropriate agencies.

With respect to individual labor activity, the actual situation is not so simple as some scholars would have us believe. The Constitution generally proclaims in Art. 17 that it permits individual labor activity in the sphere of handicrafts, agriculture, and domestic service. However, in order to fully understand the meaning of this permission, one must consult the relevant special rules. The most important of these rules are embodied in a new law of November 19, 1986, "On Individual Labor Activity."[99] This law does not take effect until May 1, 1987. The details of the application of this law are to be given by yet-to-be promulgated administrative regulations.

Therefore, we are not now in a position to make a detailed analysis of this legislation. Instead we offer a general characterization of it in the Afterword to this book.[100] However, the principal thrust of the new law is quite clear: to enlarge the area of individual labor activity because of the incapacity of the state to satisfy various urgent economic needs. The law also calls for strengthening state supervision over this labor activity. And in the USSR it could not be otherwise. Considering the significant gap between supply and demand, individual labor activity, should it be remain without state control, enrich the individuals engaging in this work to an extent incompatible with the principle of their economic dependence on the state. The same factor induces the Soviet authorities to maintain all other restrictions on the right of personal ownership, even where the problem of unavailability of means of production does not actually arise.

The limits on the permissible size of individual houses were established not because of considerations connected with architectural requirements or with the specifics of land-use planning. The legislator's goal was to preclude the execution of leases of dwelling premises in citizens' houses on a large scale, because such activity, considering the housing situation in the country, would substantially increase lessors' "non-labor income" by evasion of the legal restrictions on the rent that may be charged for individual apartments. Almost unlimited income could be extracted from the unrestricted sale and purchase of living premises. As a judicial case proves, by means of two sales in one year, a seller earned four thousand rubles, i.e., approximately twice as much as the average annual salary in the USSR. Such persons would hardly work at state entities, were there no fear of punishment for violations of the rules that forbid the sale of more than one house in any three year period. Measures directed against the acquisition of country houses by citizens, designed with the same goal in mind, also take into account certain psychological factors. A country house is an attribute of membership in the Soviet elite, and this attribute is forfeited as soon as an official loses his privileged position. In possessing a country house of his own, the man in the street shockingly renders himself equal to the Soviet elite, at least in this respect, and, what is worse, once obtained, this form of equality is not affected by the owner's social status, in contrast to privileges which belong only to Soviet bureaucrats. Ruling bureaucrats cannot, of course, confiscate all individual country houses and thus strengthen the social barriers. Therefore, comparatively milder, and purely restrictive measures are employed, owing to which representatives of the elite have country houses as a rule and the man in the street may acquire this object only as an exception to the rule.

In referring to the preceding outline, one can compare two rights of ownership actually existing in the USSR: that of the state and that of citizens. For scholars who qualify ownership as an exclusively legal phenomenon,[101] the similarities and distinctions between both rights must be reduced to the following: (1) the state and the individual as owners are entitled to possess, use, and dispose of their property within the limits provided for by law; (2) these limits are broader for the state and more restricted for the individual. In developing the latter conclusion, one can present additional qualifications. The right of state ownership is unrestricted as to its objects. In contrast, the class of objects that may be owned by individuals is restrictively predetermined by law. Further, the methods of acquisition of the right of state ownership also are unrestricted, and, what is more, certain methods connected with such a purpose may be employed solely by the state. In contrast, only common methods (contracts, other transactions, inheritance, etc.) can lead to the acquisition of the right of personal ownership. Finally, the right of state ownership is unrestrictedly protected. In contrast, protection of the right of personal ownership, when the owner sues an unlawful acquirer, depends on the latter's good or bad faith and other circumstances irrelevant to the protection of the state's property interests.[102] No other information can be deduced from a purely legal comparison of state and personal ownership, and therefore the most significant distinctions are invisible to scholars ignoring the economic substance of the analyzed issue. Yet principal importance must be attributed not to the abstract fact of restriction on personal ownership, but to the exclusion from its objects of the means of production, as the general rule, to the prevention of the enlargement of this ownership beyond limits compatible with the nature of the Soviet system, and to the perpetuation in such a way of the economic dependence of Soviet individuals on the Soviet state. Conformingly, state ownership is not simply unrestricted, but it also embodies monopolistic possession of the means of production admitting only insignificant deviations, and precluding, as a result, the transformation of personal ownership into a component of production activity except in accordance with special rules and, consequently, rendering invulnerable the economic dominance of the state over its citizenry. These economic distinctions create the grounds for the very different legal regulations, and to fully understand the latter relying upon comprehension of the former, one must examine ownership not only as a legal but also as an economic phenomenon.

An analogous conclusion stems from a comparison of the right of personal ownership not with the right of state ownership but with its "derivative"—the right of operative administration, at least insofar as this "derivative" is recognized by Soviet law itself.[103] We have already seen that operative administration is a separate phenomenon and not a factual embodiment of state ownership as a purely theoretical fiction.[104] Bearing in mind the subordination of the property rights of state entities to the state's right of ownership,[105] one could hardly deviate further from Soviet reality than do those who proclaim the entity that has absolute control over property only a theoretical property owner, and who consider the actual proprietor to be the organizations, the rights of which are severely restricted in favor of the genuine owner. But this extraordinary viewpoint aside, what conclusions can be formulated as a result of a comparative analysis of the right of personal ownership and the right of operative administration?

To deny that there is a difference between economic and legal phenomena of the same name is senseless also in this case, and such an approach can lead only to a distortion of the real situation. For adherents of such a negation, the similarities and distinctions between both rights must be reduced to the following: (1) the individual owner and the holder of operative administration may possess, use and dispose of their property; (2) these opportunities are broader for the individual owner (limited only by law) and more restricted for the holder of operative administration (limited, not only by law, but also by the objectives of its activity, established planned tasks, and designation of different property funds). In developing the latter conclusion, one can present additional qualifications. The right of personal ownership includes the rights of possession, use, and disposition without exception. In contrast, the right of operative administration can lack one or two of these rights with respect to specific types of property funds. The right of personal ownership may be withdrawn only as a punitive sanction for illegal behavior. In contrast, withdrawal of the right of operative administration can result from the redistribution of state property in cases where planning agencies consider this expedient. The right of personal ownership is legally protected against any person and all entities. In contrast, the right of operative administration is legally unprotected from intervention by the owner in the rightholder's affairs. No other information can be deduced from a purely legal comparison of the rights of personal ownership and operative administration, and therefore the former seems stronger than the latter. Yet principal importance must be attributed not to the fact that the right of ownership is more complete than the right of operative administration in the abstract but to other, economic aspects of the right of personal ownership in comparison with the right of operative administration. Possession as a component of operative administration is a prerequisite of economic activity, while possession based upon the right of personal ownership may be used only to satisfy the rightholder's individual demands. Use in the aspect of operative administration primarily involves production activity, while for the holder of the right of personal ownership use is nothing but individual consumption. Disposition by the holder of operative administration is the systematic start and the natural end of each cycle of the production process, while the holder of the right of personal ownership disposes of his property sporadically and within restricted limits. If one ignores the difference between ownership as a legal and an economic phenomenon, the true substance of the right of personal ownership will be concealed, regardless of whether it is analyzed separately or in comparison with other property rights regulated by Soviet law.

As a rule, the right of personal ownership is exercised in its basic form. In rare cases ownership by cooperative and social organizations represents a modified form of personal ownership. The degree of modification depends on the peculiarities of the collective entity.

Thus, there are mutual aid funds that can be established by members of the trade unions of Soviet entities and by members of collective farms.[106]

The resources of these funds are accumulated by collecting dues from individual members and are employed to extend small loans carrying low interest rates. It may seem strange, but Soviet citizens, while generally finding it difficult to obtain loans,[107] seldom participate in mutual aid funds. However, in cases where such funds exist, the money transferred by their members belongs to the appropriate fund as a social organization and, consequently, its ownership is viewed as an example of the "third" form of socialist ownership, according to the official Soviet terminology. Nevertheless, a member of a mutual aid fund may leave it at any time and be entitled to the return of his monetary contributions. The same consequences result when a majority of the members of a mutual aid fund decide to liquidate it. Only in cases where a deficit has been entailed by the improper conduct of those members who have failed to repay their loans does a mutual aid fund have the right to proportionally decrease the sums due to its other members. This one rule aside, personal ownership retains all its features, despite the creation of a social organization and regardless of the formal shift of individual property to the area of "socialist" ownership.

The right of personal ownership undergoes a more substantial transformation as a result of the creation of such cooperative organizations as gardening societies.[108] These societies can be created by workers of a Soviet entity (other than a collective farm) in order to implement "collective" gardening, as the Model Statute states.[109] However, each member possesses a separate plot of land and may engage not only in gardening but also in cattle and poultry breeding within established limits, disposing of his product as an owner independent from the society. A member himself may build a small house, the permissible size of which is outlined by the Model Statute,[110] and may treat it as his own property, though its alienation is prohibited. In the case of a member's death one of his heirs who is eligible to replace the decedent as a society member receives the testator's share in kind on condition that he must monetarily reimburse the decedent's other heirs. In contrast, should a member leave his society or should he lose his membership because of violations committed, not the property in kind but its monetary equivalent is repaid after deduction of the society's expenses distributed among all members in accordance with their shares. Therefore, one can qualify these property rights neither as purely "socialist" nor as strictly personal ownership. Personal ownership in its proper meaning remains, despite the creation of a gardening society, but to a certain degree it is modified by virtue of membership in a society created by a group of individuals.

The most palpable modification of the right of personal ownership is entailed by the creation of a housing cooperative.[111] At the same time, housing cooperatives must be given special attention, since they serve as an important means of combatting the Soviet housing shortage, one of the country's greatest problems, and since a decree of the Central Committee of the Communist Party and the USSR Council of Ministers of April 17,

1986, considered citizens' participation in cooperative housing construction as an extremely substantial contribution to the solution of the country's housing problem.

The apartment buildings of housing cooperatives created in the early period of the Soviet regime were transferred by Stalin to the state without compensation in the late-1930s. To some extent the cooperative members won as a result of this arbitrary action: payments for the use of a state apartment are smaller than the contributions made by members of a housing cooperative for its expenses, and after the withdrawal of the cooperative apartment buildings, the duty of major repairs became the duty of the appropriate state entities, etc. But the advantages were outweighed by disadvantages, because in state apartment buildings the size of tenants' living premises could not exceed the limits established by the law, and a so-called surplus of space in such premises might be withdrawn, resulting in the transformation of a single unit into a several-family apartment, etc. The resurrection of housing cooperatives in the USSR was one of Khrushchev's innovations, closely connected with his groundless promise that by 1980 each Soviet family would reside in a separate apartment. Owing to such an innovation, the Soviets managed to shift a great percentage of the expenses required for housing construction from the state to the citizenry, and this proportion has been systematically modified to the detriment of citizens and in favor of the state. Gorbachev "reedited" Khrushchev's Program of the Communist Party in order "to more precisely . . . determine the perspectives of development of the Soviet society," and, accordingly, the performance of Khrushchev's promise was postponed until the year 2000.[112] Relying upon previous experience, and taking into account the new program's directive to develop cooperative housing construction more broadly,[113] one can predict that the proportion of construction expenses borne by the citizenry will continue to grow, at least for the remaining part of the current century.

Housing cooperatives' apartment buildings are constructed at the expense of the members of each cooperative organization. The state provides credit, the sum lent, as a rule, being 60% of the amount that each cooperative member must pay for his apartment. Interest is charged on this loan, and the borrower is obliged to repay his debt within 10 to 15 years after the completion of construction. An individual must pay the remaining 40% to be admitted to the cooperative. Besides economic difficulties, there are a number of formal obstacles to the acquisition of cooperative membership. Because of the housing crisis dominating in the country, only those individuals who are registered as residents in the given city, but who have no housing or insufficient housing may become cooperative members. Moreover, even under such circumstances, in accordance with the system of priority, one must wait for several years for one's opportunity to become a member of a cooperative.

The completed apartment building belongs to the cooperative and is, consequently, an object of cooperative property held under a form of "socialist" ownership. No single member of the cooperative is the owner but rather is a user of a cooperative apartment. However, so long as he has performed all of his membership duties, his rights as a user cannot be restricted. This renders a member similar to an owner. Such similarity also appears in the fact that expulsion from a cooperative or voluntary termination of cooperative membership entails the right to the return of the individual's membership share in monetary form, taking into account a deduction for the depreciation of the apartment's value as a result of its previous use. The member's share becomes an object of inheritance upon a member's death. Should the heir also be a relative of the member who has the right to acquire cooperative membership after the testator's death, he will assume all of the testator's rights and duties in respect of the cooperative relationship. This further indicates the similarity of the property rights of housing cooperative members with the rights of personal ownership of the same individuals. On the other hand, although the right of cooperative membership is in almost all respects individual, certain features transform it to some extent into a common family right. Should a member of a cooperative give up his membership or be expelled from the cooperative, the members of his family who have been residing in the same apartment do not lose their right of residence so long as one of them joins the cooperative and pays a membership share. This payment is used to repay the departing member. Often the initial payment made on behalf of one family member represents contributions made by entire family. This, however, is a matter of internal family relations, and has no bearing on relations between the cooperative and its members. Only spouses enjoy a special privilege. The monetary share paid in the name of one spouse pertains to both spouses under the title of common ownership based upon the principle of equality. Therefore, termination of cooperative membership by one spouse entails the repayment by the cooperative of a half share to the departing spouse, leaving membership available to the other spouse on condition that he or she pays an additional half share to the cooperative.

Thus, the legal regulation of housing cooperatives ensures ownership in kind to cooperatives and monetary ownership to cooperative members, if one considers this situation from the economic point of view. From the legal point of view, each cooperative is an owner, and each cooperative member is a potential creditor of the owner. However, the debtor in this case is obliged to return the creditor's share only after the latter is replaced by a new member and this new member has presented his own share. The situation, sufficiently intricate in and of itself, is made even more complex by the regulatory system directed toward cooperative apartment buildings. The creation of any housing cooperative must be sanctioned by the state acting through the executive committee of the given location. The local executive committee also issues a list of the initial members of a new cooperative, making sure that only individuals previously registered with the same agency as entitled to join a housing cooperative in accordance with the rule of priority are included on this list. Only after this procedure is completed are the members of the ruling bodies of the cooperative elected, in conformity, as a matter of course, with a "recommendation" from above. At this stage the list of members of the cooperative prepared by the executive committee may be rubberstamped by the cooperative itself. Distribution of apartments among the cooperative members, implemented by the cooperative, must be confirmed by the local executive committee, and only upon receipt of the latter's orders issued in writing may the cooperative members settle in the allocated apartments. An apartment left vacant by a cooperative member and his family may be presented to a new member, if he is admitted to the cooperative in accordance with the "recommendation" of the local executive committee.

These and other rules demonstrate that the expenses connected with the construction and maintenance of cooperative apartment buildings are paid by cooperatives and, in the final analysis, by the cooperative members. However, ultimate disposition of these same buildings belongs to the state and is implemented by local executive committees. This signifies that the property of housing cooperatives, on the one hand, is held under personal ownership in a modified form, and, on the other hand, constitutes state ownership of a type that involves no property duty but only significant property rights. Thus, neither cooperative and social organizations, which involve disguised ownership by the state, nor those collective entities, the creation of which leads to modified personal ownership, disprove the assertion that only state and personal ownership exist in the USSR.

Despite the common title "ownership," the right of the state and the rights of individuals are unequal in their legal form and in their economic content. As shown, legally the right of personal ownership is extremely restricted in comparison with the unlimited right of state ownership, and economically the right of state ownership, encompassing the means of production, prevails over the right of personal ownership, the objects of which are limited to consumer goods. However, to adequately discern the most significant features of the distinctions discussed, one must supplement legal and economic analyses with political considerations. The Soviet state is not only an owner. It combines the right of ownership with political power, and this additionally affects the correlation between state and personal ownership.

As the 1977 Constitution proclaims, "labor income comprises the basis of personal ownership."[114] This income for the most part is in the form of the salary paid individuals by Soviet entities. The size of payment depends on the appropriate indices of state plans, not those which are published to achieve propaganda goals, but those which are actually binding planning commands. Thus, the Fundamental Directions[115] promulgated by the Twenty-Seventh Congress of the Communist Party of the Soviet Union provide for an increase in individual income of 60–80% by the year 2000. Since the Soviet leaders have not discarded their dogma to the effect that the "productivity of labor must surpass increases in labor payment," this level of individual income is achievable only assuming that the annual increase in the productivity of labor will be on the average of 6–8% over the next fifteen years. Considering the present 3–3.5% annual increase,[116] one must have a vivid imagination to predict such achievements, and any observer must be completely naive to believe this prediction.[117] However, real and fanciful data aside, because individual income is planned, the state can ultimately determine the extent to which ownership by the state will prevail over ownership by its citizens. In addition, the state determines not only the size of monetary payments for labor but also the prices of the goods that can be bought with the salary received. If the average salary really is 180 rubles a month, as Soviet sources officially contend, this would demonstrate nothing without a comparison with the level of prices, and because prices are continually rising,[118] the domination of state ownership over individual ownership will remain intact, despite any increases in salary that may be granted.

No less important for a proper appreciation of individuals' income is the degree of "goods coverage" of the monetary resources that are at a citizen's disposal. In cases where an individual cannot buy all of the objects he requires, including certain bare necessities, the real level of his income is actually lower than a comparison of his salary and the prices of goods might suggest. It is true that the Fundamental Directions plan "to more fully satisfy the growing demands of the Soviet people with respect to high quality and varied goods and services."[119] However, this dictum, included without fail in all Soviet economic plans, has never been realized, and Gorbachev's fifteen year economic program obviously proves that the Fundamental Directions were not serious. The Fundamental Directions predicted an increase in retail trade commodity turnover of 80%, i.e., equal to the highest predicted increase in individual income in the year 2000. But at present the supply of goods for retail trade lags far behind individual income. Thus, if both are equally increased, the gap between the supply of goods and the citizens' demand will remain unchanged. The actual situation must be even worse, bearing in mind the degree of practicability of the adopted plan. Therefore, however poor the average salary in the USSR may be because of the growing gap between production of consumer goods and citizens' labor income, the Soviet population, taken as a whole, regardless of the financial position of persons in different social strata, cannot help but accumulate monetary savings of tremendous proportions over the course of several decades of insufficient supply. According to the cautious calculations presented by a well-known economist I. Birman, in 1983, the monetary resources kept by the citizenry in saving banks, in the form of state bonds (according to official data), and in cash ("*v kubishkakh*," accordingly to I. Birman) are in excess of 200 billion rubles.[120] This situation aggravates the commodity deficit: production and trade plans are compared with plans of individual income, while true monetary demand must be reckoned with respect to previously accumulated savings. This is why in the USSR all goods with the possible exception of those hideous suits of Soviet manufacture that fill to overflowing the racks of Moscow and Leningrad department stores are sold like hotcakes. Yet credulous foreigners, unaware of or ignoring the actual situation, are overjoyed by the Soviet people's wellbeing. "How the living standard of these people has been increased," they exclaim,[121] bringing to mind the foreigners described by A. Solzhenitsyn, who, unaware that trucks marked with a sign "food" were being used to transport prisoners around Moscow, earnestly contended: "Say what you will, but the food supply of the Soviet capital has been substantially improved." A realistic, not fanciful, assessment of the phenomenon of the tremendous accumulation of monetary resources in the citizenry's possession reveals its only, or at least its most important, significance: the level of payment for labor in the USSR is diminished to the extent to which monetary income is not matched by goods coverage, and prices in the USSR are not as flexible as they are in free market countries where the relation between supply and demand plays the decisive role in this regard. And because the level of production of consumer goods is predetermined by plans, the principal form of Soviet economic policy, this factor affects the adequacy of the actual correlation between the demands of the citizenry and the planning of salary and prices by means of which the Soviet state strives politically to establish the desired proportion between state and personal ownership in the ruled country.

All of the factors discussed seriously decrease the value of Soviet money in the domestic market. In the international market this money, as non-convertible currency, has no official value at all. As a result, Soviet citizens cannot sufficiently insure their property interests by depositing monetary resources in savings banks or by retaining cash "*v kubishkakh.*" Therefore they often strive (and this is quite natural) to insure themselves through the acquisition of commodities or currencies more stable than Soviet rubles. However, here they must contend with restrictive or prohibitive rules of Soviet law.

Freely convertible foreign currency is one of the objects the acquisition of which could solve the problem. But Soviet law prohibits such acquisition.[122] Even those who have legally received foreign currency (in the form of royalties, inheritance, etc.) are obliged to exchange it at a bank agency either for Soviet rubles at an artificially low official rate or for special coupons (certificates, or checks, in Soviet terminology) the possession of which entitles the bearer to purchase goods in special shops where these goods are not so scarce as they are in ordinary enterprises of retail trade and where prices are lower, bearing in mind that there is a higher rate of exchange for certificates than for Soviet rubles. The sale and purchase of foreign currency on the black market is a crime which can be punished by death under certain circumstances.[123] Soviet law also prohibits individual possession of precious metals in ingots, pay dirt, nuggets, semi-finished articles or finished articles for production or laboratory purposes, and diamonds. Should such objects be discovered in an individual's possession as a result of a search connected with a criminal accusation or owing to other circumstances, they will be confiscated if they have been illegally acquired, or if no violation of law has been committed, the possessor will receive an arbitrarily established monetary equivalent.[124]

The second group of objects attracting the interest of those who have sufficient monetary savings includes gold articles and high-priced furs or fur products. In order to "squeeze" out the money accumulated by the Soviet populace, the prices of these objects are periodically doubled. Nevertheless, early in the morning, long before the opening of jewelry and fur shops, large crowds besiege their entrances, and only food shops can be found surrounded at this time by crowds of the same, or larger, size. Despite the rulers' wish that the tremendous sums of individual savings be liquidated, they cannot increase the production of these articles to the level required for the achievement of this goal. A similar situation prevails with respect to other objects of high demand: automobiles, carpets, high-quality furniture, etc. As to houses and country houses as objects of investment for citizens, the restrictions described above actually preclude this means of transforming monetary savings into another economic form.

The third object sought by citizens could be very efficient in this regard: foreign tourism. Living in a hermetically sealed country, anyone who has surplus money would not think twice before spending it if an opportunity to travel abroad were available. However, owing to political and economic factors, the Soviet authorities restrict foreign tourism, instead of fostering it. Politically such tourism is dangerous, because the more broadly it is allowed, the more defectors will leave the USSR and the more citizens will return "corrupted" by capitalist influences. Economically this peculiar form of individual rest and entertainment is detrimental, because simultaneously with the extraction of citizens' money the Soviets must lose incomparably more important foreign currency. In contrast, domestic tourism is not so attractive to Soviet citizens as is foreign tourism, and, moreover, Soviet economic mismanagement precludes the exploitation even of this quite acceptable method to the extent of its availability. Thus, not one of the more or less substantial approaches that could help the Soviet authorities to cope with the immense accumulation of individual monetary resources are or may be employed under the political regime established in their country.

The situation to which this gives rise presents a threat to the Soviet system. On the one hand, depositors need only simultaneously demand their money from saving banks, and an economic crash would be unavoidable. However, such a run on the banks, while theoretically imaginable, is impossible in fact. One also must not forget that the savings banks are enterprises of the Soviet state, which as a holder of unlimited political power not only may diminish this threat by means of monetary reforms, such as have been employed in the USSR more than once, but also can act quickly to prevent such an activity, should it become an actual threat. On the other hand, accumulated money represents demand, and the Soviets must, in order to fill the market with consumer goods or, using their favorite expression, in order to fully satisfy the people's demand, produce these goods in a quantity and quality corresponding not only to the planned increase in individual income but also to the actual level of individual savings. The impossibility of solving this problem in the foreseeable future is so obvious that it can be predicted without prophets. The right of personal ownership is even more affected by these circumstances than the Soviet system as a whole. Being incomparably weaker in fact than in law, this right depends on the state's economic monopoly more completely than the law euphemistically recognizes, in proclaiming that, first and foremost, "the labor of the Soviet people . . . shall be the source for the growth of social wealth," and only in the final analysis this will ensure "the wellbeing of . . . every Soviet person."[125]

Notes

1. In order to spare the reader from having to consult Roman sources or special textbooks on Roman Law, we recommend Adolf Berger, *Encyclopedic Dictionary of Roman Law*, (Philadelphia: American Philosophical Society, 1953), pp. 344, 495, 601–602.

2. Harold J. Berman, "The Possibility and Limits of Soviet Economic Reform," in *Soviet Law and Economy*, ed. Olimpiad S. Ioffe and Mark W. Janis (Dordrecht: Martinus Nijhoff, 1986), p. 62.

3. Ibid., pp. 62–63.

4. Ibid., p. 62. As an honest scholar, Professor Berman simultaneously points out, in order to prevent political rebukes based upon his own postulate: "I should stress that one may accept all of these postulates without being a Marxist-Leninist, and indeed, all of the postulates are accepted among a great many Western Europeans and Americans who would be shocked to be told that they are Marxists (let alone Leninists)." (Ibid., p. 63).

5. Ibid., p. 66.

6. Ibid.

7. 1977 Constitution, art. 10.

8. This issue will be discussed below, in the section of the present chapter on "The State's Right of Ownership."

9. In formulating such an assumption, it is psychologically impossible to imagine that managers of Soviet entities could consider themselves as representatives of genuine owners, in contrast to the Soviet state (whose officials they are) as the fictitious owner and differently from Soviet elite (upon whom they actually depend) as a postulated owner. Nevertheless, at the present stage of our analysis we may accept any of the above indicated assumptions, since they are irrelevant to the ascertainment of the distinctions between ownership and law of ownership.

10. See above, in same section.

11. Berger, *Encyclopedic Dictionary*, p. 441.

12. Fundamental Principles of Civil Legislation, art. 19.

13. See the section on "The State's Right of Ownership" in the present chapter.

14. See the section of Chapter 1 ("The Fundamental Structure Elements of the Soviet Economic System") on "Ownership."

15. Articles 21–25.

16. See note 14.

17. See note 13.

18. See above, in the present section.

19. See note 13.

20. For additional arguments see note 13.

21. See note 14.
22. Fundamental Principles of Civil Legislation, art. 21–25.
23. Art. 10.
24. Art. 25.
25. For a review of various conceptions, see V. P. Gribanov, *Predeli osushestvleniia i zashchiti grazhdanskikh prav* (Moscow: Izd-vo MGU, 1972), pp. 121–122.
26. Fundamental Principles of Civil Legislation, art. 25.
27. RSFSR Civil Code, art. 112.
28. See note 13.
29. Ibid.
30. 1977 Constitution, art. 11, Fundamental Principles of Civil Legislation, art. 21.
31. 1977 Constitution, art. 12.
32. Fundamental Principles of Land Legislation, art. 16.
33. The 1977 Constitution, art. 73.
34. Above, note 30.
35. These data, relating to the Soviet five-year plans, are reproduced in Mikhail Voslensky, *Nomenklatura—Gospodstvuiushchii klass Sovetskogo Soiuza* (London: Overseas Publication Interchange Ltd., 1985) pp. 239–242.
36. *Izvestia*, March 9, 1986. The fact that the same Fundamental Directions provide for 1986–1989 an increase in the production of means of production of 20–23% and an increase in the production of consumer goods of 22–25% simply camouflages the principle mentioned, and it cannot be taken as a departure from this principle.
37. Ibid.
38. Above, note 30.
39. Fundamental Principles of Criminal Legislation, art. 21.
40. E.g., Fundamental Principles of the USSR and Union Republics on Administrative Violations, art. 16.
41. Fundamental Principles of Civil Legislation, art. 14.
42. RSFSR Civil Code, art. 143. Furthermore, dwelling houses and cultural treasures, even if these have owners, are to be transferred to the state if the owners fail to take proper care of them. Compensation is paid in the latter case but not in the former (art. 141–142 of the same code).
43. Fundamental Principles of Civil legislation, art. 28.
44. Ibid.
45. Fundamental Principles of Civil Legislation, art. 17.
46. See the section on "The Right of Personal Ownership" in the present chapter.
47. *Kommentarii k Grazhdanskomu kodeksu RSFSR*, ed. S. N. Bratus and O. N. Sadikov (Moscow: Izd-vo "Iuridicheskaia literatura," 1982) p. 121.
48. See below, in the present section.
49. Fundamental Principles of Civil Legislation, art. 19.
50. Articles 38–53 of the Statute of the Production Association, *SP SSSR*, 1974, no. 8, item 38.
51. *SP SSSR*, 1979, no. 26, item 172.
52. For details, see O. S. Ioffe, "Soviet Law and the Economic Experiment," in Olimpiad S. Ioffe and Mark W. Janis, ed., *Soviet Law and Economy*, pp. 5–58.
53. *SP SSSR*, sect. 1, 1981, no. 9–10, item 62.
54. Note 2.
55. Ibid.
56. Ibid.

57. Insisting that such events are unimaginable, Soviet propaganda disregards both foreign (for instance, the Polish) experience and well-known Soviet facts (strikes in Leningrad, Tagliotti, etc.).

58. Olimpiad S. Ioffe, "Law and Economy in the USSR," *Harvard Law Review*, 95 (1982), 1591; Olimpiad S. Ioffe and Peter B. Maggs, *Soviet Law in Theory and Practice* (New York: Oceana, 1983).

59. Harold J. Berman, "The Possibilities and Limits," p. 62.

60. Ibid. p. 64–65.

61. See above, in the present section.

62. E.g., V. P. Shkredov, *Ekonomika i pravo* (Moscow: Ekonomika, 1967) pp. 102–105.

63. Including incentive funds which Soviet law sometimes protects against interference from certain higher agencies but not from the Soviet state.

64. See above, in the present section.

65. Harold J. Berman, "The Possibilities and Limits," p. 60.

66. See above, in the present section.

67. See the "Introduction."

68. Voslensky, *Nomenklatura—gospodstvuiushchii klass Sovetskogo Soiuza*, pp. 375–378. The author is even inclined to consider the Secretariat stronger than the Politburo, contending that in cases of conflicts between these agencies the former vanquishes the latter (ibid.). However, on the one hand, a series of inaccuracies has been admitted. Thus, Khrushchev's victory in 1957 resulted not from a fight between the Politburo and the Secretariat, but from the interference of Marshal Zhukov who gathered together the members of the Central Committee of the Communist Party, and for the first and only time in Soviet history these members overrode the Politburo's decision. On the other hand, the genuine victory of any political contingent never has been secured until the moment when this contingent acquires a majority in the Politburo. Therefore, contrary to M. Voslensky's assertion, Stalin's personal dictatorship was established not after he ousted the majority of the Politburo (Trotsky, Kamenev, Zinoviev, Bukharin, Rykov) but at the time when, by means of the purges initiated in 1937, the Politburo was filled by Stalin's minions.

69. Ioffe, "Law and Economy in the USSR," 1605.

70. Above, note 12.

71. 1977 Constitution, art. 11; Fundamental Principles of Civil Legislation, art. 23; RSFSR Civil Code, art. 99–101; Model Collective Farm Charter (1969), modified by the Presidium of the USSR Supreme Soviet on July 10, 1980; Model Charters of all links of consumer cooperatives *Sbornik normativnykh aktov po grazhdanskomu zakonodatel'stvu*, 1, 130–159.

72. See note 14.

73. See above, in the present section.

74. *Izvestia*, November 23, 1985.

75. See the section on "The Right of Personal Ownership" in the present chapter. As to the nature of Party ownership, see above.

76. The legal status of trade-union ownership is established by the Fundamental Principles of Civil Legislation, art. 24, the civil codes of Union Republics (the RSFSR Civil Code, art. 102–104), and the Statute of Trade Unions of the USSR. See *Grazhdanzkoe zakonodatel'stvo*, (Moscow: Iuridicheskaia literatura, 1974), pp. 248, 343–344.

77. Fundamental Principles of Civil Legislation, art. 24.

78. E.g., A. I. Masliaev, *Pravo sobst'vennosti profsoiuzov v SSSR* (Moscow: Iuridicheskaia literatura, 1975), p. 72–82.

79. Art. 54, 57.
80. Fundamental Principles of Civil Legislation, art. 24.
81. Above, note 76.
82. See note 14.
83. Ibid.
84. K. Malfiet, "The Economic Function and Purpose of Personal Property and Its Legal Implementation," in Olimpiad S. Ioffe and Mark Janis, ed., *Soviet Law and Economy*, p. 173.
85. A. A. Rubanov, "Konstitutsionnye osnovy prava lichnoi sobst'vennosti v SSSR," *SGiP*, 1981, no 4, pp. 33–36.
86. N. D. Egorov, Typy, Vidy i Formy Sobst'vennosti i prava sobst'vennosti v SSSR, p. 62.
87. See note 14.
88. The 1977 Constitution, art 17. This position was essentially strengthened by decrees of May 28, 1986 published by Izvestia on the same day and separately adopted by the Central Committee of the Communist Party, Council of Ministers of the USSR, and the Presidium of the USSR Supreme Soviet with the purpose of "eradicating" so-called non-labor income of citizens.
89. Decrees: (1) of September 14, 1977, "O lichnikh podsobnikh khoziaistvakh kolkhoznikov, rabochikh, sluzhashchikh i drugikh grazhdan i kollectivnom sadovodstve i ogorodnichestve," *Resheniia Partii i Pravitel'stva po khoziaistvennim voprosam*, (Moscow: 1979), vol. 12, pp. 104–112; (2) of January 8, 1981 "O Dopolnitelnikh merakh po uvelicheniiu proizvodstva selskokhoziaistvennoi produktsii v lichnikh podsobnikh khoziaistvakh grazhdan," *SP SSSR*, 1981, no. 6, item 37.
90. Because the Constitution deals generally with subsidiary household farming, without specifically addressing collective farm households, certain Soviet legal scholars suggest abrogation of the special regulation of the latter and the establishment of unified regulation in this area. E.g., V. V. Ustukova, "Sovershenstvovanie pravovogo regima imushchestva lichnogo podsobnogo khoziaistva," *SGiP*, 1985, no. 10, p. 116–120. However, the civil codes and current legislation retain and, in our opinion, will retain special rules addressed to collective farm households.
91. Fundamental Principles of Civil Legislation, art. 27.
92. See the section on "The State's Right of Ownership" in the present chapter.
93. RSFSR Civil Code, art. 106; RSFSR Housing Code, art. 131.
94. RSFSR Civil Code, art 107.
95. RSFSR Housing Code, art. 131.
96. RSFSR Civil Code, art. 238.
97. *SP SSSR*, 1961, no. 1, item 2.
98. RSFSR Civil Code, art. 270.
99. Izvestia, November 21, 1986.
100. See the "Afterword."
101. Above, note 2.
102. See note 13.
103. Ibid.
104. Ibid.
105. Ibid.
106. *Grazhdanskoe zakonodatel'stvo*, p. 253–256.
107. See above, in the present section.
108. *Sbornik normativnykh aktov po grazhdanskomu zakonodatel'stvu*, p. 171–181.
109. Ibid, art. 2.
110. Ibid, art. 8.

111. *SP SSSR*, 1982, no. 23, item 120; *SP RSFSR*, 1960, no. 33, item 160 and 1979, no. 11, item 69.

112. *Izvestia*, February 26, 1986.

113. *Izvestia*, March 7, 1986.

114. Art. 13.

115. *Izvestia*, March 9, 1986.

116. In 1986 Soviet media began to employ the figure 6.7% (e.g. *Izvestia*, April 20, 1986). But such a miraculous "jump" always occurs in the USSR as soon as one leadership is replaced by another.

117. The Fundamental Directions plan a 200% increase in industrial production for the same time-period (ibid.). However, the fulfillment of this equally fantastic plan could ensure the predicted increase in individual income, if during the same period the Soviet population diminishes in size.

118. See the section of Chapter 1 ("The Fundamental Structural Elements of the Soviet Economic System") on "Distribution."

119. *Izvestia*, March 9, 1968.

120. I. Birman, *Ekonomika nedostach,* pp. 70–71.

121. E.g. *Newsweek*, 1983, no. 9, p. 8.

122. RSFSR Civil Code, art. 175.

123. RSFSR Criminal Code, art. 88.

124. RSFSR Civil Code, art. 150.

125. 1977 Constitution, art. 14.

4

Production: Its Legal Organization

General Principles

Each economic cycle starts with production. It is customary to distinguish between industrial production and agricultural production. Legal analysis of the Soviet economic system would be impossible without this distinction, because, along with common features, there are significant differences in the legal organization of industrial and agricultural production in the USSR. At the same time, the general principles of the Soviet economy also operate in all areas of production, despite the special features of various branches.

Officially, the leading principle of the Soviet system as a whole, including the economic system, is the principle of democratic centralism as a combination of "unified direction with initiative and creative activity."[1] All Soviet rulers, without exception, have made use of this principle in speeches and directives, employing almost the same expression verbatim. Gorbachev's Program uses in this regard the following formula directly addressed to economic administration: democratic centralism signifies the combination of two requirements, i.e. "an increase in the efficiency of centralized management as well as the substantial enlargement of the economic independence and responsibility of associations and enterprises."[2] Similar definitions are developed by Soviet legal theory: "the correlation between centralized and democratic principles in the management of the economy is primarily a combination of the centralized administration of the economy and the economic independence of the lowest links."[3]

Speaking abstractly, such a combination does in fact exist. The problem, however, is which of these two principles—centralism or democracy, i.e. decentralization, is the dominant one? Political declarations and official doctrine refer to both as equal. But this cannot be true. Economic monopoly, as the source of unlimited political power, absolutely requires centralism, and only the economic stagnation bred by strict centralization compels the introduction of limited economic decentralization. Thus, centralism dominates, while decentralization is subordinate. In addition, the cyclical development of the Soviet economy, in the form of periodic shifts from rigid centralism to relative decentralization and then back from such decentralization to strong centralism, is incompatible with Gorbachev's appeal for the "substantial enlargement of the economic independence" of the lowest economic links. Such economic freedom cannot endure for long periods of time under such a cyclical system. To adhere to the truth, one must recognize that, for the Soviet economy, centralism is the principle and decentralization is a deviation from this principle.

Centralism as a principle assumes that economic entities functioning as producers and, consequently, representing the lowest links of Soviet economy are subordinated to higher agencies and that these "vertical" relations ultimately are locked into the very top of the centralized pyramid. Previously, such a system was formally comprehensive in the realm of industry and partially, with regard to state farms, applicable to agriculture. Production entities were subordinated directly or indirectly to the appropriate economic ministries or equivalent agencies and through their ministries or other higher bodies to the ruling center of the entire Soviet system. Since the creation of *Gosagroprom*[4] as the body to which collective farms are also subordinated, the formal situation of agriculture does not differ, with respect to centralism, from that of industry.

For decades, the lowest links of industry were enterprises. This situation was changed by Brezhnev's reform of 1973-1974.[5] Only the largest enterprises retained their independence. These exceptions aside, production associations, which were created in the process of the Brezhnev reform, replaced enterprises as the lowest links of industry, and enterprises, having lost their independence, were transformed into departments of these associations under the title of "production units."[6] The agencies superior to production associations are industrial associations, which were also created as a result of the reform. The latter exercise administrative functions, and their economic activity is permitted to encompass only certain specific actions concerning supply, technological research, etc. Gorbachev is of the opinion that industrial associations should be liquidated,[7] and, as Ryzhkov informed the 1986 Congress of the Communist Party, almost 80% of these agencies have already ceased to exist.[8] To the extent that they continue to function, industrial associations are either All-Union (i.e., subordinate to an agency of the USSR government) or republican (i.e., subordinate to an agency of one of the fifteen constituent republics of the USSR), and usually production associations are subordinated either to one or to another industrial association, but sometimes republican industrial associations are in turn subordinated to All-Union industrial associations. Each branch of the economy is assigned to production and industrial associations of a specific profile, and has at its top an economic ministry or other central agency of the same level as a ministry. The new Soviet leadership, initiating the process of liquidation of the intermediate administrative agencies—industrial associations—is resorting at the same time to the creation of administrative bodies higher than economic ministries—bureaus of machine building, of energy etc., which will run the appropriate groups of ministries.[9] In other words, centralism will be eliminated at the middle level, i.e., at the level of industrial associations, and at the same time it will be strengthened at a higher level, i.e., at the level above economic ministries. The nature of the highest bodies in this "vertical" structure (the Council of Ministers, the Presidium of the Supreme Soviet, and the Supreme Soviet itself) as well as the relations between various links of an economic branch and the Communist Party agencies are the same in this area as in other public activity in the USSR.

The lowest links in agriculture are state and collective farms. Retaining the status of independent entities, state and collective farms are, nevertheless, included in district agricultural-industrial complexes. These complexes also include certain other state and non-state entities connected with agricultural activities.[10] District agricultural-industrial complexes are under provincial complexes also called agricultural-industrial complexes,[11] and *Gosagropromy* of the union republics are subordinated to *Gosagroprom* of the USSR, which is at the top of the administration of Soviet agriculture. Here, too, the highest bodies of the "vertical" structure as well as the relations between its links and party agencies require no special analysis. It is significant, however, that collective farms, formally voluntary non-state organizations, have been subordinated to *Gosagroprom* without even a ritual reference to their consent to be subordinated in this way.

In contrast to centralism, decentralization assumes that economic entities functioning as producers, and consequently constituting the lowest links of the Soviet economy, are relatively independent from higher agencies and adopt their own decisions in conducting economic activities. Because, however, of the peculiarities of Soviet economic development, this independence cannot be stable. It fluctuates in accordance with the specific stage of the Soviet economic cycle. In the period of War Communism (1917–1920), centralism was so extreme that production entities were deprived of any independence, and, conversely, during the New Economic Policy, i.e., NEP (1921–1928), there was such a high degree of decentralization that the same entities acquired the greatest economic independence ever permitted under the Soviet system. Stalin (1929–1953) did not restore War Communism, but his centralism did not retain much of the previous independence of the lowest economic links. In comparison, Khrushchev and Kosygin (1953–1965) did not restore NEP, but their decentralization revived the independence of the lowest links to a significant degree. As discussed above, Brezhnev, with the proclamation of the 1973-1974 reform, initiated a drastic return to centralism, and, as a result, enterprises lost their independence, while production associations, created at that time, shared their independence with industrial associations. Only the future will show the ultimate direction that Gorbachev's plans will take, because the measures that he already has managed to carry out combine components of both centralism and decentralization.[12] Logically speaking, decentralization, as a phase that follows periods of centralized economic development in the USSR, seems more probable than centralism. However, bearing in mind that Brezhnev's centralism was comparatively restricted, and taking into account that Andropov and Chernenko did not have sufficient time to implement significant economic changes, Gorbachev may consider himself the direct successor of Brezhnev, matching the latter's limited centralization with equally limited decentralization.

The principle of democratic centralism, actually representing the changeable correlation between centralism and decentralization, is referred to by Soviet leaders and Soviet theorists not only in characterizing the Soviet economy as a system of governing and subordinate links. The identical principle, as a combination of one-man management and collegiality, is employed with respect to the lowest links of the Soviet economy—production associations and independent enterprises. One-man management signifies that the chief of an economic entity personally resolves all problems in the entity's daily activity, except for those whose solution is within the jurisdiction of higher agencies. Actually, however, the higher agencies may intervene in the settlement of any problem, and though sometimes this violates certain legal provisions, one cannot find a single instance in Soviet practice of a legal dispute initiated by lower officials in connection with their superiors' illegal conduct. Collegiality means that the manager of an economic entity must discuss certain problems with the entity's labor collective before any final decision can be adopted. Dealing with these collectives, the 1977 Constitution uses an alluring formula: collectives of workers of each establishment "shall participate in the discussion and decision of state and social affairs, in the planning of production and social development, in the training and placing of cadres, and in the discussion of questions of the management of enterprises and institutions, the improvement of labor and domestic conditions, the use of assets earmarked for production development, and also for socio-cultural measures and material incentives."[13] However, the Constitution itself provides for only one such right: the nomination of candidates for deputies to all Soviets, both supreme and local.[14] In all other regards Brezhnev took no risks such as investing labor collectives not only with "the right to discuss," but also with "the right to decide." The latter right could not become effective without the promulgation of a specific regulation. Brezhnev himself, however, avoided doing this. He left that task to his successors. Yuri Andropov addressed this issue in a special law on labor collectives,[15] which, not surprisingly, provided only "the right to discuss," and not "the rights to discuss and decide." Neither Chernenko nor Gorbachev considered it necessary to adopt a new law or to modify the one promulgated by Andropov. And this is nothing extraordinary, bearing in mind the Soviet experience. During all of Soviet history, the regulation of the organizational structure either of political or economic power has proceeded from the principle that the larger a collective body, the less it can actually wield real power (the Soviet people, for example), but the more it must be given titular power. And vice versa, the smaller a collective body and the more capable it is of governing politically or economically (collectives of associations or enterprises, for example), the less titular power it must be given. Only at a certain point—to use dialectical jargon—does a transition from quantity to quality occur: those extremely small collective bodies of high personalities that keep a firm hand on political and economic domination have always managed to find direct or, more frequently, roundabout ways of confirming their powerful position through law-making and still more though application of law in the USSR.

Thus, the fictitious combination of one-man management and collegiality is, in principle, of the same nature as the more substantial combination of centralism and decentralization. However one appreciates their genuine significance and purely propagandistic content, both centralism and decentralization are methods of economic administration in the USSR. These methods are employed in the daily activities of two types of Soviet establishments: agencies of economic planning and entities of industrial and agricultural production. Both are analyzed below.

Agencies of Planning

Centralism in the Soviet economy is implemented not only in the form of planning. In practice, the interference of party and governmental agencies in the daily activities of economic entities is no less substantial and, to some extent, it is even more palpable. However, while such interference involves for the most part extra-legal methods of economic administration, except in the few cases enumerated by the law,[16] planning has comprehensive legal force sanctioned by the Soviet Constitution itself. "The direction of the economy," reads the Constitution, "shall be carried out on the basis of state plans."[17]

At the same time, the constitutional principle cited has not been developed extensively by current legislation. The legislature has shown absolute indifference toward numerous suggestions of Soviet scholars to adopt a law on planning.[18] The legal rules addressed to economic planning are dispersed among a number of legislative acts.[19] Sometimes, these legislative acts are of general significance, for instance the decree of the Central Committee of the Communist Party and the USSR Council of Ministers of July 12, 1979, "On the Improvement of Planning and the Strengthening of the Influence of the Economic Mechanism upon the Efficiency of Production and the Quality of Work."[20] More often, various normative acts include legal provisions concerning certain specific issues of economic planning, as can be illustrated by the decree of the Central Committee of the Communist Party and the USSR Council of Ministers of October 28, 1983, "On the Improvement of the Planning . . . of the Transportation of Economic Goods. . . ."[21] As to the planning of production in the proper meaning of the word, only the statutes of state enterprises, economic and industrial associations[22] contain relevant rules, which, however, do not go beyond regulation of the internal activities of these entities.

Thus, the USSR, officially and actually based upon a planned economy, has not created and even is avoiding the creation of unified planning legislation encompassing the whole economy or at least its different components (production, distribution, exchange). This could not, of course, be accidental. Even a dictatorial regime, which itself may disregard its own law, would be to a greater or lesser degree fettered by comprehensive regulations of this sort. And the Soviet authorities would least of all want to restrict themselves in an area such as the administration of the economy, bearing in mind its importance for the maintenance of unlimited political power. Therefore, dispersed provisions relating to economic planning are preferable to systematized and comprehensive legal regulation. In appearance, such a preference entails a great number of gaps in Soviet legislation. However, in fact, there are no gaps, because of the goal of the Soviet rulers: the fewer regulations in the realm of economic planning the more freedom for those who implement this planning in practice. Therefore, the planning of Soviet production cannot be understood by looking only to Soviet law. One must know Soviet practice in order to present an adequate picture of Soviet planning.

In contrast to distribution and exchange,[23] production is comprehensively planned by the central agencies of economic administration. The distribution and exchange of goods produced can remain partially unplanned, and, within certain very restricted limits, a producing entity may itself select its own purchasers and determine the portion of the entity's output that must be sold by means of separately executed contracts. As to production, independent enterprises and economic associations also have their own plans, drafted not at their discretion but dictated by plans promulgated centrally. A producer may overfulfill the planning task assigned from "above." But, the overfulfillment of a production plan may be prohibited (for instance, where production exceeds demand, e.g., black and white television sets; or for social reasons, e.g. vodka) or, in the absence of prohibitions, overfulfillment may depend on planning in connected areas of the economy (for instance, in the area of supply of materials, fuel, etc.). This signifies the unrestricted subordination of producers to planners in the area of production.

The agencies that deal with the planning of Soviet production are multifarious, and the process of planning varies, insofar as this process leads to the issuance of different forms of planning acts. Depending on to whom they are addressed, planning acts are either *general* or *direct.* General acts establish planned tasks for the entire economy (for instance, the task of increasing the productivity of labor), and in cases concerning a distinct branch of the economy (for instance, the task of increasing the productivity of light industry), a general plan is addressed not to its performers (production associations and independent enterprises) but to the organizer of its performance (for instance, the Ministry of Light Industry). Direct planning acts are addressed not to the organizer of performance (a ministry, for instance) but to the performers themselves (production associations and independent enterprises), and therefore the planned indicators must be more detailed than under general planning. Depending on the time-periods involved, planning acts are either *perspective* or *current.*

Perspective planning is calculated for several years, as a rule, for five years, and sometimes even for longer periods of time. Thus, Gorbachev's "Principal Directions of Economic and Social Development of the USSR" encompass, on the one hand, a five year period (1986–1990), and, on the other hand, a fifteen year period (1986–2000). General perspective plans cannot, of course, direct economic activities without supplementation by detailed planning tasks geared for shorter periods of time. This goal is ensured by current planning, earmarked for periods of not more than one year and broken down into quarterly and monthly periods.

Depending on the planned objects, planning acts are either *comprehensive* or governing a *particular branch.* Comprehensive plans regulate the economy of the entire country. Such are, for example, the "Principal Directions" mentioned above. Plans governing particular branches are applicable only with respect to those parts of the Soviet economy (machine building, metallurgy, etc.) which constitute the direct objects of their regulation. These two types of planning acts were recently supplemented by acts of *complex planning,* which serve to avoid mutual isolation of actually connected branches of the Soviet economy. At present, complex planning is applicable nationwide in connection with certain branches of economic activity (for instance, those enumerated by the 1982 Food Products Program of the USSR[24]), territorially with regard to different groups of interdependent economic entities (for instance, those included in the same territorial-industrial complex according to a 1982 governmental decree[25]), and organizationally toward inter-branch scientific-technical complexes (for instance, those created in conformity with a 1986 governmental decree[26]). Finally, in their planning practice, the Soviet authorities distinguish between acts of *planning administration,* by means of which superior agencies govern subordinate entities, and acts of *operative planning* (or self-regulation), compiled by subordinate entities in accordance with the commands of the superior agencies.

The planning of the Soviet economy relies upon such a great number of different acts, that their preliminary drafting and subsequent confirmation is a complicated process involving a very long chain of participants. This process begins with the issuance of general directives by the Politburo, sometimes also rubber-stamped by the Plenum (session of all the members) of the Party's Central Committee. Such directives precede the compilation of all perspective and annual current plans. The Soviet media briefly outline the Politburo's position while party and governmental agencies instruct the participants of the planning process in all of the necessary details. After this, all information required for the drafting of plans begins to move from the bottom to the top of the Soviet system. In industry, production associations and independent enterprises inform their governing agencies up to economic ministries or equivalent government establishments about the production capacity at the entity's disposal and about the output that can be expected under these circumstances. In the area of agriculture, the same information is sent by state and collective farms through the local and republican *agropromy* (agricultural production administration agencies) to the *Gosagroprom* of the USSR, which also receives similar reports from other subordinate economic entities.[27] As a matter of course, these lower-level organizations are required not only to adjust their suggestions to the Politburo directives, but also include in their reports data that genuinely reflect their economic position. However, in contrast to the former command which is never violated, the latter demand is far from being strictly observed. Associations and enterprises, state and collective farms strive, as a rule, to minimize their stated production capacities and to thus avoid the necessity of working on the basis of demanding production plans. Although these entities' reports have no binding force, the planning agencies cannot, nevertheless, disregard the information received, in drafting each entity's planning tasks. In order to stimulate the lowest links of the Soviet economy to work under demanding plans, Soviet law has, since the 1965 reform, called for the payment of larger bonuses for the fulfillment of production plans than for their overfulfillment. But these stimuli do not work, because the difference between the two kinds of bonuses is insignificant, while a demanding plan, once adopted, threatens to be an eternal burden, since plan targets always move up each year.

Such an attitude on the part of associations and enterprises, of state and collective farms at the stage of providing planning information becomes entirely comprehensible, if one takes into account that their reports serve at the same time as production plans voluntarily suggested by the potential performers. Yet the voluntary suggestions concerning upcoming plans are summarized at various levels, when reports are sent along the informational chain: industrial associations and economic ministries, local and republican *agropromy*, and *Gosagroprom* of the USSR. What, however, if the information forwarded by a higher agency differs from that received from a lower link? In the aspect of centralism, this is a trite situation. But how can the problem be solved with respect to the officially proclaimed democratic centralism? The law in force is silent in this regard. As to practice, it varies from one economic branch to another. Certain ministries have incorporated into the process of planning a procedure of "protection." This procedure entitles associations and enterprises to send representatives to the higher industrial associations, and it also permits industrial associations to send their representatives to the appropriate economic ministry. In both cases the planning department of the respective agency adopts its final decision on the basis of the discussions held with these representatives.[28] In general, however, the right of "protection" is not available to lower economic links, and they either are simply informed of differences between their data and the summarized reports, or such preliminary information may be withheld, and they receive notice of their production tasks after the confirmation of the plan. This latter method renders further objections impossible.

On the basis of all of the aggregated reports concerning industry and agriculture, the USSR State Committee on Planning (*Gosplan*) compiles the drafts of all perspective and annual current economic plans.[29] After the completion of this task the drafts prepared by *Gosplan* are forwarded for approval to the USSR Councils of Ministers. Usually, such approval is given only after *Gosplan* incorporates a number of changes in accordance with governmental instructions. Once the *Gosplan* drafts are approved by the government, the most significant phase of Soviet planning begins: the Council of Ministers presents its drafts to the Politburo. This holder of absolute power may adopt any decision, and there have been several cases in Soviet practice where the Council of Ministers' plans have had to be completely overhauled because of a new economic policy formulated by the Politburo. The draft is transformed into an adopted plan from the time of its approval by the Politburo. In substance, the planning process is thus complete, and without the Politburo's sanction not a single indicator and not one word subsequently can be modified. However, a purely ceremonial stage of the planning procedure begins directly after the Politburo's adoption of this final substantive decision.

Perspective plans always have been discussed by Congresses of the Communist Party, while annual current plans usually have been considered by plena of the Party's Central Committee. The end result of all of this ceremonial loquacity is that the plans are unconditionally approved. Meanwhile, before this formalistic ritual begins, two documents take immediate and irrevocable force upon endorsement by the Politburo: the draft of the law on the plan for economic and social development of the USSR (accompanied by the draft of the law on the state budget, if the plan is annual rather than perspective), and the draft of the decree of the USSR Council of Ministers on the plan of the same name (accompanied by the draft of the decree dedicated to problems of the annual budget). Both laws, which are comparatively brief, must be adopted by the USSR Supreme Soviet verbatim, although sometimes certain changes, sanctioned beforehand by the Politburo, are permitted in order to pay tribute to the demands of democracy. Governmental decrees contain all of the requisite details, and therefore either these decrees are withheld from publication or parts of them, only remotely informative, are released to the public. The secrecy of these governmental decrees, in contrast to the publicity of the corresponding laws, ensures yet another advantage for the Soviet rulers. Should it become necessary to modify the plans and budgets, the corresponding laws can be left intact as if nothing has occurred, while the required changes can be incorporated into the appropriate governmental decrees without publicity, behind closed doors.

So it is with Soviet economic planning considered within the process of movement of information from the bottom to the top. After the completion of this phase, the process of movement of directives from the top to the bottom must begin. This means that *Gosplan* informs, in writing, each economic ministry or equal agency, and *Gosagroprom* of the USSR of the planned tasks established for the branches of the economy that are subordinate to these bodies. The tasks determined must be then apportioned among the lower links of the same economic branch, and the distribution thus initiated continues until the specific indicators of the plan reach the actual performers of planned tasks: production associations, independent enterprises, and state and collective farms. Strictly observing the planned tasks assigned to them, the performers elaborate their own operative plans with the details required for daily economic activity that the higher-level planners lacked the information to supply. One must also bear in mind that just as perspective plans are turned into detailed annual current plans through the actual and ceremonial activities of the governing bodies, the annual plans themselves are more precisely specified with respect to quarters, months, or other short periods by means either of planning administration implemented by higher agency or of operative planning carried out by the lowest economic links.

In describing the process of economic planning firmly established in Soviet practice, we have dealt exclusively with industry of All-Union importance. There also exist industrial entities of republican significance subordinate to the economic ministries of union republics, and certain enterprises or associations of local industry, which are administered by the appropriate departments of local executive committees. The production activities of both republican and local associations or enterprises are planned, in principle, by the same methods employed with respect to the lowest links of the all-union economic system. Only the following distinctions must be taken into account. Informative data connected with local and republican industry are summarized before they are passed on to *Gosplan* of the USSR, not by All-Union economic ministries but by republican *Gosplan*'s, and, in the final analysis, by republican councils of ministers. All-Union plans, within the limits of economic tasks addressed to local and republican industry, are apportioned to the union republics, not directly to republican ministries or local executives committees. Each union republic adopts its own plans and budgets for the republic, relying upon the appropriate All-Union documents and apportioning planned tasks among the ministries and provinces of the republic. Similar plans and budgets are issued by provinces, districts, cities, and certain other territorial subdivisions. The specific planned tasks of the actual performing entities are assigned them, respectively, by republican ministries, departments of local executive committees, or by the local executive committees themselves, should these have no departments or none of the appropriate competence. After receiving the data determining their planned tasks, economic entities of republican and local importance draft and adopt their own plans of operation.

This system of economic planning, based in all respects upon administrative subordination, leaves almost no room for the democratic component of Soviet centralism. In transmitting the required information from the bottom to the top, lower links really are performing their duties to their higher agencies, rather than developing their own initiative, as Soviet scholars usually contend.[30] Since this information has no binding effect on its addressees, one cannot speak of a combination of centralism and democracy, but, at most, about a system premised upon the strictest observance of subordination allowing for modest suggestions on the part of subordinates. By the same token, in transmitting planned tasks from the top to the bottom, the higher agencies really are exercising their administrative rights, rather than supporting the lower links' initiative, even in those rare cases where a confirmed plan coincides with the information received. Since these tasks are the commands of the rulers, and not offers that may be accepted or rejected, one can speak in cases of such coincidence not about democracy preceding centralism, but, at the most, about the astute predictions of subordinates anticipating the final managerial decision.

The administrative nature of Soviet planning creates a great number of specific problems, economic in character and legal in form.

First of all, plans must be balanced, i.e. their indicators must be mutually coordinated. In the area of production, this means the appropriate correlation between the planned tasks of the myriad of interdependent production entities. The idea of complex planning[31] resulted from efforts to enhance the degree of achievable coordination. These same efforts led to the development of territorial planning in addition to planning in regard to particular branches. Along with union republics and provinces, the objects of territorial planning include economic regions, formed by Khrushchev in the late–1950's as areas administered by regional economic councils (*sovnarkhozy*)[32] and retained, with certain modifications, by Khrushchev's successors, despite the replacement of *sovnarkhozy* by economic ministries. In 1982, the USSR Council of Ministers created special planning agencies for each economic region: plenipotentiaries of USSR *Gosplan* as heads of each of the regional planning organizations.[33] The principal responsibility of each such organization is the preparation of suggestions concerning plans for the development of the economic region and the territorial-industrial complexes situated within the region. To ensure balanced plans, a number of other measures have been undertaken from time to time. Nevertheless, none of these measures has been successful to any significant degree. Extremely centralized planning in such a large country as the USSR makes balanced planning virtually impossible. As a result, the scope of "unfinished production" is growing year after year, because not all producers participating in the manufacture of complicated objects are obliged by their plans to present the requisite components in the necessary quantity and at a convenient time. "Unfinished production" transferred from one year to another causes tremendous damage to the Soviet economy, and the Soviet leadership is aware of this disastrous situation. Its awareness can be proven by reference to a 1967 governmental decree[34] which provides for the creation of reserve funds by economic ministries to be used for the provision of monetary assistance to enterprises and associations in cases where these suffer damage as a consequence of planning errors. This decree takes into account all planning defects, not only those resulting from the absence of the required coordination. It is quite noteworthy that, in contrast to the 1965 reform, which first introduced financial liability for planning agencies for damage caused by planning errors to planned entities, the 1967 decree only empowered economic ministries to pay compensation for such damage at their discretion and not on the basis of the victim's claims. Such a principle might seem unjust, but it is indisputably reasonable. Mistakes of planning result for the most part not from planners' fault but from the backbreaking character of centralized planning itself. At the same time, within the limits of the Soviet system, the rejection of centralized planning is impossible, as already has been emphasized more than once.[35] Thus, liability based upon fault would be senseless with respect to planning agencies. Strict liability of planning agencies would be no more sensible, because one cannot stimulate the improvement of planning activity by means of property sanctions in cases where the planners are not to blame. Therefore, the only acceptable option is to ensure compensation for damages from the monetary resources of the state. This method actually has been chosen, taking into consideration that the economic ministries' reserve funds are financed by the state and that payment of compensation depends not on legal prerequisites but exclusively on factors of economic expediency.

Further, a plan must be not only balanced but also prepared in a timely fashion. However, timely plans are beyond human capacity to an even greater degree than are balanced plans. Given the difficulties of obtaining accurate data, the backwardness of Soviet computer hardware and software, and the flaws of dogmatic Marxism in Soviet economic theory, *Gosplan* would have to start processing the numerical data collected from all over the USSR several decades before the planned economic year in order to produce the desired plan at the appointed time. The fact that, nevertheless, annual plans appear after a delay of no more than three or four months is a miracle in itself. Of course, this miracle occurs because numerous mistakes are completely disregarded. But from the Soviets' point of view, it is better to have a centralized plan containing mistakes but issued after a short delay, than to await irreproachable centralized plans that could be obtained only after the expiration of the planned period. Yet, even the short delay in the issuance of the plan actually adopted gives rise to a unique problem. Not only must the inevitable mistakes in the plan, resulting from haste and inefficiency, be contended with, but also, because the associations and enterprises are left without a plan for the first few months of each economic year, there is the problem of how these entities can continue their production activities during this period. The legal provisions addressed to production planning contain no solution for such a situation. However, normative acts dealing with distribution and exchange, regulate the consequences of planning delays in these areas.[36] According to the established rules, the previous year's plan regarding the supply of materials and other objects must be looked to, and supply must be continued in conformity with that plan until the new annual plan is ready, at which point the parties will be able to carry out the necessary adjustments not only prospectively, but also retroactively on the basis of the indicators of the new plan. Because distribution and exchange depend on production and simultaneously determine its desired scope, the same principle is employed for production, though it acts as a rule of practice, not as a provision of law. In this way, the problem of ensuring continuity in production has been solved, despite the inevitable interruption in the planning process. However, there is another predicament with which one cannot cope and which constantly occurs in the Soviet economy as a known but irremediable scourge: "*shturmovshchina*," as it is called in Russia. A well-informed Soviet purchaser will never buy an article designed for long-term use without checking the date of its production. If this date is toward the end of a month, quarter, or year, the purchase will be avoided at all costs. This occurs because of the knowledge that as the end of each planning period (month, quarter, year) approaches, production entities strive to make up for lost time, sacrificing quality for quantity. This phenomenon has been nicknamed "*shturmovshchina*," ["storming"] and is the result of a number of factors, including purely psychological ones: not until the ultimate deadline approaches do the entities (and their workers) begin to motivate themselves to complete their planned tasks. But, in fact, this scourge is inherent in the nature of Soviet planning. As a matter of course, each new plan provides higher indicators than did the previous one. In working for at least three or four months in accordance with the previous plan, production entities knowingly produce less than their output will be retroactively planned. And in order to fill the gap that has arisen because of the delay in planning, the producers have no other option but to engage in "*shturmovshchina*," despite all of its negative consequences.

Finally, a plan should be not only balanced and adopted in a timely fashion but also stable and, in principle, unalterable. We have already expressed the view that, because of defects in Soviet planning, frequent modifications of adopted plans are a lesser evil than would be rigid stability.[37] However, the nature of planning assumes stability as the general rule and admits modifications only as rare exceptions. At any rate, such is the official Soviet position. "Planning tasks confirmed for a production association should be stable and may be changed by a superior agency only in exceptional instances,"[38] states the 1974 Statute on the Production Association. But what if this rule is violated? The question remains unanswered by the Statute cited. Its only requirement is that confirmed tasks be changed by a superior agency "after preliminary discussion of such changes with the administration of the association according to the procedure and within the periods established by the USSR Council of Ministers."[39] The fact that more than ten years after the promulgation of the 1974 Statute this "procedure" and these "periods" have not yet been "established" illustrates the degree of seriousness with which the requirement of "preliminary discussion" has been formulated. And what will occur if such preliminary discussion does not take place? This question too remains unanswered by the statute. As a result, the official position actually is reduced to mere precatory language, sounding more like an admonition to planners than a guarantee of protection for the performers of plans. And it cannot be otherwise. Since coordinated and timely plannning is impossible, only subsequent modifications can provide for the correction of unavoidable planning mistakes, at least to the extent that the latter can be discovered while there is still time to prevent economic disaster. Therefore, in this regard, the realities of economic practice bear no relation to the verbiage of the statute. Planning tasks, confirmed by a higher agency in accordance with the procedure described, are modified by the same agency or by an even higher body not in "exceptional instances" but a number of times during annual, or even shorter, periods of current planning. And no legal remedy against this illegal practice is at the disposal of production associations and independent enterprises. The reserve funds of the economic ministries serve as these entities' only recourse, though the availability of such funds depends not upon the right "to demand" but upon the opportunity "to request."

In discussing the economic and legal problems that arise in connection with Soviet planning, we have intentionally omitted the issue of the correlation between binding planning indicators and free economic initiative. The principal features of this correlation were explained by a description of the cyclical development of the Soviet economy from centralism to decentralization and back from decentralization to centralism.[40] It seems, however, quite appropriate to cite at this juncture a general rule of Soviet law that regulates the permissible level of independent initiative, bearing in mind especially the very peculiar approach taken to this matter. "The superior agency," states the 1974 Statute, "shall confirm the five year and annual planned tasks according to the established system of indicators . . . All remaining indicators of the plans of the association shall not be confirmed, but shall be elaborated by the association."[41] In appearance, this formula restricts centralism and promotes democracy: all production indicators depend on the producers themselves, except those which are to be confirmed by the superior agency. However, instead of listing the indicators included in the jurisdiction of the superior agency, the 1974 Statute refers to the "established system of indicators." As is known, such a system does not exist in a stable and unified form. Producers of different goods are subordinated to different systems, which, in addition, undergo substantial modification depending on whether the economy is in a phase of centralism, relative decentralization, or somewhere in between. But regardless of what the actual situation may be, the formula cited from the 1974 Statute will be always convenient as a *carte blanche* for the higher agencies. No matter whether decentralization is broadened or centralism absolutely prevails, this legal provision will always be retained, since it states: the superior agency confirms those indicators which the established system of planning provides for, while all the rest are to be determined by the subordinate entities. What this "all the rest" means will be shown in the subsequent discussion.

Agencies of Production

The lowest links of the Soviet economic system are the agencies of production in the USSR. Production is carried out by production associations and independent enterprises in industry and by state and collective farms in agriculture. These entities may be considered the lowest links of the Soviet economy because it is only at this level that some degree of economic and legal independence is retained. Each of these links has its own subordinates: production units in associations, shops in enterprises, departments in state farms, and brigades in collective farms. However, these subordinates are not economically separate, and, instead of being legally independent, they function as internal subdivisions of the respective entities. Therefore the link structure of Soviet production ends at production associations and independent enterprises as well as at state and collective farms, without descending to production units, shops, departments, and brigades.

The economic independence of production entities is differently characterized in official doctrine with respect to state producers and collective farms. The latter personify collective farm ownership, and, as an owner, each collective farm is thereby economically independent. The former are not owners, because only the Soviet state as a whole may personify state ownership. Therefore, as the indicator of the economic independence of state producers one employs not personification of ownership but a specific Soviet phenomenon—economic accountability, or in Russian, *khozraschet.* This differentiation is no less fictitious than is the delimitation of state and collective farm ownership.[42] Actually, neither state nor collective producers function as owners, and in both cases it would be more correct to speak of *khozraschet* rather than of other economic prerequisites of production activity. Sometimes, even the compilers of Soviet laws forget the official terminology (it is artificial to such a degree), and, as a result, references to *khozraschet* (economic accountability) appear in legal documents where they are absolutely inappropriate from the view point of Soviet dogmata. The 1969 Model Collective Farm Charter provides the most striking illustration. "The social ownership of a collective farm shall be . . . the economic basis of a collective farm," states Article 11 of the 1969 Charter. Nevertheless, according to Article 15 of the same Charter, "the production and financial activity of a collective farm shall be carried out on the basis of economic accountability." If a collective farm is an owner, why should it need economic accountability, applicable only to economic entities that do not qualify as owners? And vice versa, if a collective farm is to carry out its production activity on the basis of economic accountability, does this not mean that ownership, which should be more effective than economic accountability, actually is unavailable to collective farms? In coming across such questions, Soviet authorities must either abandon their dogmata, which is entirely precluded, or completely ignore the problems that arise, which they actually do. But such conduct does not help. The problems that have arisen exist, regardless of whether they are studied or ignored, and only a comparative analysis of economic accountability and Soviet ownership will indicate the circumstances inducing the Soviet authorities to supplement ownership with economic accountability.

Speaking generally, economic accountability (let us call it by its Russian name, *khozraschet*) signifies property autonomy from the Soviet state and from other entities. Such autonomy results from the fact that the state, creating an economic organization, provides it with the necessary resources: buildings, equipment, raw materials, and monetary funds. These resources do not cease to be objects of the state's ownership, and, consequently, any newly-created organization acquires only the right of operative administration.[43] At the same time, the right of operative administration is sufficient to ensure that degree of autonomy to economic entities which seems desired and expedient from the viewpoint of the Soviet rulers. As demonstrated,[44] collective farms also exercise the right of operative administration, albeit under the disguised title of collective farm ownership. Therefore, the application of *khozraschet* to collective farms meets no substantial obstacles, colliding only with terminological barriers. However, considering the original source of collective farm property, one objection can be advanced. At the time of the creation of collective farms in the late–1920's—early–1930's it was not the Soviet state but the Soviet peasants, compelled to become collective farmers, who transferred their property to the newly established organizations. In assessing this objection, one must remember that: (1) the principal means of agricultural production, the land, belongs to the state and only its use is permitted to collective farms just as only use is allowed to all state entities; (2) the socialized property of the collective farmers would not have been sufficient to initiate even the original economic activities of the collective farms, were other property objects not transferred to these farms by the state without charge; and (3) at present, new members' property never has been socialized, while the property originally socialized no longer exists, either in kind or in monetary form. Thus, the 1969 Charter is not far from the truth, in speaking of collective farm *khozraschet* rather than of collective farm ownership.

The property autonomy of *khozraschet* economic entities has as its goal the inclusion of the output of Soviet production in goods-money relations. The Soviet state had occasion to experience economic management without goods-money relations during the period of war communism.[45] This experience proved that the distribution of goods, free of monetary equivalents, entirely eliminated economic incentive on the part of producers and ultimately could lead to the collapse of the entire economic system. In contrast, a producer, obliged to pay for equipment, materials, fuel, etc., must strive to produce at least as much as is necessary to receive the required money from customers for its production output. Along with creating economic incentive, the introduction of monetary equivalents into the area of economic activity in the USSR provides an efficient method of supervision over state entities: *kontrol' rublem* (supervision by means of the ruble), as this is called in official jargon. The worse an entity works, the less money it will have, and the more restricted its capacity as a purchaser will be. Conversely, this capacity will be broader, the better an entity works and the more money it can earn. All these advantages of goods-money relations in comparison with direct distribution became clear to the Soviet rulers long ago, at the time when they replaced War Communism with NEP in the early 1920s. However, they could not develop monetary exchange solely through the restoration of private ownership which was admitted by NEP only within very restricted limits. The problem of how to retain state ownership as the economic source of political power and simultaneously to use goods-money relations, recognized as unavoidable prerequisite of economic efficiency, was solved by *khozraschet*, a purely Bolshevik economic invention. State ownership was retained, because economic entities acquired only the right of operative administration, and goods-money relations were developed, because economic autonomy could not function without monetary exchange. Later, private ownership of means of production was liquidated, but *khozraschet* remained, and therefore goods-money relations did not disappear.

As the principal form of governmental organization of the Soviet economy, *khozraschet* comprises three equally important and closely interdependent features. If even one of these features is absent, there is no genuine *khozraschet*. First, all economic entities working on the basis of *khozraschet* must cover their expenses with their own income. For instance, Soviet communications enterprises (post, telegraph, telephone) transfer all their income to the state budget and cover all their expenses by means of budget financing. As a result, the organizational form of their economic activities is called not *khozraschet* but "budget estimate financing." Second, *khozraschet* assumes equivalence, i.e. payments for all acquisitions and repayments for all alienations. For instance, Soviet hospitals, as a rule, are not paid for medical treatment, and therefore *khozraschet* is inapplicable, though it is applicable to a few hospitals that do employ *khozraschet* because their patients are required to pay a charge. Third, *khozraschet* requires profitability, inducing economic entities to generate income in excess of their expenses. For instance, although Soviet museums usually charge an entrance fee, the monetary sums collected in this form fall so far short of expenses as to preclude entirely the application of *khozraschet*.

The economic independence embodied in *khozraschet* requires a corresponding legal independence expressed by the rights of legal entities or, using the terminology of the civil law system, the rights of juridical persons. These rights belong to all "state enterprises and other state organizations which are on economic accountability," provides Article 11 of Fundamental Principles of Civil Legislation. Similar to *khozraschet*, the status of being a juridical person also has indispensable features. First, a juridical person must have its "separate" property. The word "separate" (not "own") is used by Soviet legislation in order to make it clear that even the right of operative administration is sufficient for an entity to possess the status of a juridical person. However, if an entity (for instance, a church community) does not possess separate property on the title of ownership or operative administration, it is only a group of individuals but not an organization, or even possibly an organization but not a juridical person. Second, a juridical person may acquire property and other ("non-property") rights as well as bear property and other ("non-property") duties in its own name. "In its own name," a verbatim expression of Soviet law, means in its own behalf. If an entity functions in the legal area only in behalf of other subjects of law (for instance, Soviet trade representations abroad may act only in behalf of the Soviet state), it can possess different legal capacities, but not that of a juridical person. Third, a juridical person bears "independent" property liability for all of its actions, and therefore it possesses the legal capacity to act as plaintiff or defendant in court, arbitration tribunal, or arbitrazh.[46] The word "independent" signifies that neither the higher nor lower agencies of a juridical person may be sued for the latter's actions, except in cases where these agencies are obliged to be liable on the basis of a suretyship or guarantee established by contract or by law. If an entity cannot be independently liable (for instance, one may not sue an enterprise included in a production association), it does not have the status of a juridical person.

The combination of *khozraschet*, as an expression of economic independence, and the status of a juridical person, as an expression of legal independence, provides all that is required of an economic entity for participation in goods-money relationships. This leads to the following very important conclusions. On the one hand, the inability to take part in goods-money relations proves that neither *khozraschet* nor the status of a juridical person are available to the given entity. For instance, previously independent enterprises lost their independence upon inclusion in production associations, and their capacity to participate in goods-money relations disappeared as well. Therefore neither *khozraschet* nor the status of a juridical person are compatible with such enterprises. On the other hand, an entity recognized as a juridical person, although it does not directly engage in economic activities, may take part in goods-money relations, relying not upon *khozraschet* but upon other prerequisites provided for by law. For instance, state institutions fulfill not economic but administrative or cultural functions. Nevertheless, a great number of these institutions possess the rights of a juridical person. This occurs, however, owing not to *khozraschet* but to other prerequisites. As Article 11 of Fundamental Principles of Civil Legislation establishes, the right of juridical personality belongs to those "institutions . . . which are on the state budget[47] and have an independent estimate[48] and whose managers enjoy the rights of disposing of credits."[49] All of these circumstances deserve special attention, if one wishes to recognize the distortions of *khozraschet* and to understand the causes of its distortion in Soviet practice, Soviet law, and Soviet theory.

Distortions in practice primarily stem from the preference for planning over *khozraschet*, indicative of the general desire to ensure the domination of centralism over decentralization. Thus, although *khozraschet* assumes an economic entity's duty to independently cover all its expenses, this principle is completely abrogated for certain privileged organizations which, functioning in military, metallurgical, and certain other areas, operate under a regime of planned losses and state subsidies.[50] Conversely, the ability of other organizations to cover their expenses is frequently undermined by the withdrawal of certain portions of their funds for roadbuilding or for other "societal" needs. Local Party agencies, ignoring legal restrictions, often finance the construction of theaters, sports buildings, or convention halls by squeezing money from organizations under their "supervision." The ability of economic entities to meet their expenses is also undermined in a number of cases by the mandatory priority of sudden governmental orders disrupting the routine process of organizations' production. The rule of equivalence undergoes substantial curtailment too. This is true with respect not only to subsidized entities but also to numerous other organizations. Enterprises, buildings, and installations, even those constructed with the resources of production associations, may be withdrawn in accordance with a decision of the appropriate governmental agency at any time and without compensation. The monetary equivalent received for products sold at established prices is actually drained off as well, because all surplus financial resources exceeding an entity's requirements for the next year's plan are redistributed by its higher agency on the basis of an entity's annual account. The state is, in addition, the ultimate beneficiary of compensation for damages received by economic entities from their contractual partners as a consequence of breaches of contractual duties. Although such compensation serves as a substitute for the exchange equivalent, money paid by offenders must be transferred to the state treasury at the end of each economic year since its payment results not from an entity's own activity but from violations committed by its partners. As to profitability, the situation does not seem much better. By definition, the command of profitability cannot apply to subsidized enterprises. The withdrawal for the benefit of the state of surplus resources and compensatory payments in accordance with bookkeeping data ascertained at the end of each economic year can hardly stimulate a special striving to extract of profit on the part of economic managers. Moreover, the greater the profit earned, the larger an entity's production capacity is judged to be, and the larger this capacity, the higher will be the planned indicators for the following year. Such a possibility is extremely dangerous, and economic managers would prefer to reduce profits rather than to receive a more demanding planned task. Thus, *khozraschet* in theory differs from *khozraschet* in practice. In addition, the Soviet leadership has managed to narrow the sphere of *khozraschet* even in this curtailed form. After the reform of 1973-1974 all of the previously independent enterprises lost all *khozraschet* capabilities owing to their transformation into internal subdivisions of production associations. Certain vestiges of this former independence have nothing in common with the substance of *khozraschet*.[51] And it cannot be otherwise under a system whose rulers, praising this organizational form in theory, assess it in practice not so much as a rational approach but as an inevitable evil.

Not only distorted in practice, *khozraschet* has also been severely misstated by law. This trend of Soviet legislation was started by Khrushchev. In creating *sovnarkhozy* to replace economic ministries,[52] Khrushchev hoped to achieve a personnel reduction in the area of state administration. However, reality destroyed these hopes. After a short time the personnel of *sovnarkhozy* were more numerous than those of the liquidated ministries. In order to conceal this failure, Khrushchev decided to defray the expenses connected with the maintenance of *sovnarkhozy* not with funds from the state budget but with money from other, less conspicuous sources. These sources were found among the monetary funds of state enterprises administered by *sovnarkhozy*. Each enterprise was obliged to periodically transfer certain sums to the *sovnarkhozy* for maintenance of the latter's department to which the payor was subordinate. This system was called *khozraschet*, and the departments of the *sovnarkhozy* were proclaimed to be working upon the basis of *khozraschet*.[53]

As a matter of course, *khozraschet* in its proper meaning is absolutely inapplicable to administrative agencies. These agencies neither produce nor sell anything, and where they do make purchases the monetary resources used for this purpose are provided by monetary transfers from subordinate entities, not from the economic activities of the administrative agencies. Then, how can such organs rely upon their own *khozraschet*?[54] Although any reasonable answer to this question is entirely precluded, Soviet legislation, instead of rejecting such an obvious absurdity, continues to develop "administrative *khozraschet*." At first, The 1973 General Statute on All-Union and Republican Industrial Associations[55] established that these associations, though administrative agencies in nature, should function on the principle of *khozraschet*. Then, in the form of an experiment, *khozraschet* was introduced for several economic ministries. Finally, a decree of July 12, 1979, known in Soviet literature as the decree on the economic mechanism, ordered its addressees "to improve the *khozraschet* methods of activity of All-Union (republican) associations and to gradually introduce these methods in the area of activity of industrial and construction ministries."[56] In implementing this order, the State Committee of Planning, the USSR Ministry of Finance, the State Bank, and the Construction Bank issued, in conjunction with the All-Union Central Council of Trade Unions, "Instructions on Procedure for the Transition of the Industrial Ministry to the Khozraschet Methods of Activity."[57] In judging from the content of these regulations and from theoretical analyses of actual practice, the real idea behind the adoption of ministerial *khozraschet* is to establish an organizational form by which each branch of the economy, headed by the appropriate ministry, will be able to ensure complete recovery of all of its costs. In principle, this measure is fruitless. From the economic point of view, the situation remains identical, regardless of whether economic entities transfer monetary resources only to the state treasury, from which the requisite part will be retransfered to the economic ministries for their maintenance, or the same entities divide resources transferred into two parts earmarked respectively for the maintenance of their ministry and for the state treasury. From a political point of view, however, the new system is of significance, because the imposition of a duty to maintain ministries upon the subordinate economic entities leads to the exclusion of the appropriate sums from the state budget, and this creates the purely propagandistic appearance that the Soviet rulers have managed to decrease administrative expenses. At the same time, such a propagandistic gain leads to certain psychological disadvantages negatively affecting economic management. Real *khozraschet*, assuming economic autonomy, stimulates, or at least can stimulate, the desire to achieve the highest possible economic efficiency. However, if every type of property segregation is *khozraschet*, even in cases where the agencies whose property is segregated are not directly engaged in economic activity, then the *khozraschet* of economic entities also can be reduced to property segregation accompanied by either total or substantial disregard for economic incentives, the most significant effects of genuine *khozraschet*. It is also very important to ascertain whether the *khozraschet* of economic ministries can lead to any positive results of an economic character.

The maintenance of economic ministries by subordinate producers involves monetary payments to economic ministries covered by a portion of the purchase prices that are established for the producers' product. Since prices are planned in the USSR, the producers have no right to increase their prices in proportions equal to money transferred for the ministry's maintenance. These transfers only increase the costs and decrease the profits of producing entities. In addition, the amount of the transfers does not depend on the economic efficiency of separate payors or of the economic branch headed by a ministry. Legislative acts determine this amount as a fixed quantity. Economize as ministries might with respect to their administrative expenses, the producing entities would still not bear a lessened burden, because lower administrative expenses affect neither the established prices nor the amount of transfer payments demanded of entities. Even ministries themselves cannot use the accumulated savings: at the end of each year these savings must be transferred to the state treasury. The only imaginable way in which ministerial *khozraschet* might positively affect the administered economic branch would be the following: after reducing of its administrative expenses, a ministry could apply for a decrease in the transfer payments made in its favor in order to provide a corresponding decrease in wholesale and, consequently, also retail prices. However, what would ever prompt a ministry to act in such a strange way? Its own economic situation would be adversely affected as a result of decreasing the payments from the subordinate producers. The subordinate producers would, at best, remain in the same situation economically, should the prices of their products be decreased in proportion to the diminishment of their payments. Furthermore, the ministry's request concerning a decrease in prices that ought to be implemented would not be binding on the appropriate governmental agencies. And it might be that these agencies would prefer the annual transfer to the state treasury of such surplus resources by the ministry making the appeal to a decrease in prices and transfer payments. However, even if the ministry's request concerning the level of prices and the amount of transfer payments were approved by the decision-making bodies, what positive effect would it have on the ministry itself or its subordinates? Neither bonuses nor other encouragements are provided for by the law in force for such indicators. One would have to be, therefore, very naive to believe that ministerial *khozraschet* is in any way similar to genuine *khozraschet*. Meanwhile the Soviet rulers may be accused of many shortcomings but not of naivete. Since, nevertheless, they proclaimed ministerial *khozraschet*, this could occur only because of one purpose: to disguise the Soviet budget even more than it has already been disguised by creating the appearance of a decrease in administrative expenses despite their increase in fact.

Along with practice and law, Soviet theory also plays a substantial role in distorting the meaning of *khozraschet*. To understand this role, one must know that in the USSR the word "*khozraschet*" is employed in three different types of cases concerning, respectively, the lowest economic entities, the higher agencies administering economic activity, and the internal subdivisions of economic associations and independent enterprises. As discussed above,[58] in the first case there exists or can exist genuine *khozraschet*, while in the second case *khozraschet* bears a fictitious character. As to the third case, it must be specially examined. Among the internal subdivisions of economic associations and independent enterprises there are such ones that deal with governing activities (the administration of economic entities) or with specific other functions (a department of supply, department of planning, etc.) of a non-production character. These subdivisions are encompassed by *khozraschet* not separately but only insofar as *khozraschet* of the whole entity is implemented. Looking to other subdivisions which directly carry out production activities (for instance, shops of enterprises or units of associations), one must bear in mind that external relations of any kind, including goods-money exchange, are precluded in this case, and, as a result, here too it is not separate *khozraschet* but the comprehensive *khozraschet* of the entity as a whole that operates or, at least, can operate. However, production subdivisions differ from other subdivisions in one very important respect: in contrast to the latter, the former engage in activity whose results can be expressed in monetary terms. This fact allows for the use of economic stimulation with respect to these subdivisions. At the beginning of each economic year, quarter, or month, each such subdivision receives planned tasks determining the quantity of goods that must be produced and setting the highest allowable cost for the production of these goods. At the end of each month, quarter, and year the objects actually produced and the actual costs of their production are compared with the corresponding planning indicators. If the real achievements are equal to the planning indicators or if the former exceed the latter, the appropriate subdivision receives, respectively, the usual or an increased amount of money for its incentive funds. In the opposite situation, the same subdivision will receive either no incentive resources or funding at a lower level than is standard. Such a method of economic encouragement is called "internal economic accountability" (*vnutrennii khozraschet*).

Thus, although the designation is the same, the substance differs from one context to another. The *khozraschet* of economic entities clears the path for participation in goods-money relations. Neither administrative nor internal *khozraschet* involves the same consequences. Economic ministries may establish goods-money relations within the limits of their budgets regardless of whether their financing is provided by the state budget or by the subordinate producers, while subdivisions of associations or enterprises are deprived of this capacity, regardless of the application or non-application of economic encouragement on the basis of a comparison between their planning indicators and actual achievements. On the other hand, administrative *khozraschet* is a specific method of financing administrative activities. Neither the *khozraschet* of economic entities nor that of their subdivisions has any connection with such a purpose. Economic entities themselves support their current activities, and within these limits the problem of special financing does not arise at all (if economic accountability is strictly observed). Economic entities' subdivisions cannot be separately financed whether or not it is found expedient to employ internal *khozraschet*. In addition, internal *khozraschet* only separates a producer's subdivisions from a bookkeeping point of view, and in no way makes for economic autonomy. Both the *khozraschet* of economic entities and administrative *khozraschet* are different from internal *khozraschet*. In both cases, the results are more substantial, entailing economic autonomy, though this means economic self-sufficiency for the *khozraschet* of economic entities, but only special financing for administrative *khozraschet*.

These numerous distinctions point out the obvious fact that the three kinds of *khozraschet* have absolutely nothing in common, except for their name. One would not, therefore, expect any attempt at making generalizations about these separate phenomena to be successful. Yet certain Soviet scholars have tried to work out a general definition of *khozraschet*, finding it, for instance, to be "an instrument of the economic policy of the state, created consciously but in accordance with the demands of objective economic laws . . . as a general principle of socialist economy, which allows for use in the socialist economy of notions of exchange values and the material interests of the labor collectives of *khozraschet* links for the purpose of achieving from these collectives the best production results."[59] A more detailed classification than the three-part analysis above has also appeared, but it treats as different certain phenomena which in fact are identical in substance. Actually, however, the author quoted above basically directs his analysis toward three types of *khozraschet*: that of administrative agencies, that of economic entities, and that of these entities' internal subdivisions.

At any rate, for adequate comprehension of the described conception without an excessive broadening of "the field of discussion," reducing the author's list of *khozraschet* types to three seems appropriate.

The theoretical generalization of *khozraschet*, put forth not only in legal but also in economic literature,[60] is far from a purely theoretical construction. It results from political demands and is subordinated to practical purposes. As has already been emphasized,[61] *khozraschet* is in substance a method of including state property in the economic sphere of goods-money relations. This was the goal of its invention in the early–1920's, and, though there have been curtailments of its use from time to time, this goal has always determined the limits of the use of *khozraschet*. However, the Soviet authorities, in recognizing the inseparability of monetary exchange from economic efficiency, assess such exchange as, in principle, a vestige of capitalism, in contrast to planning, which is proclaimed to be an exclusively socialist phenomenon. They strive to refrain from development of monetary exchange at the expense of centralized planning. Their apprehension of another path of development attained its zenith when, in the late–1960's, the events in Czechoslovakia known as the "Prague Spring" were accompanied by a call for "socialism with a human face," whose economic designation was "market socialism." Because of the growing apprehension of the ruling elite, all of the supporters of the liberal tendencies in Soviet doctrine, resulting from the 1965 economic reform, underwent ideological persecution. For example, a talented economist, G. S. Lisichkin, who insisted upon the subordination of planning indicators to market demands,[62] vanished from the pages of economic literature. Furthermore, one can generally contend that the failure of the 1965 economic reform, predetermined by the threat to the rulers' economic monopoly, was politically prepared by dissemination of the idea that "market socialism" was incompatible with socialism of the Soviet type.

Under these economic and political circumstance, it was very important for the Soviet regime to revise certain deep-rooted theoretical dogmata in view of the threat that such dogmata could present if interpreted in the traditional fashion. Because "market socialism" was deemed to be especially dangerous, it was hardly surprising that the "obsolete" interpretation of *khozraschet* became one of the first objects of the desired revision. The *khozraschet* of producers, analyzed separately from administrative and internal *khozraschet*, can only be explained as the principal prerequisite of goods-money relations. However, internal *khozraschet* entails no such relations, and administrative agencies engaging in goods-money relations do not establish these relations on the basis of administrative *khozraschet*. Therefore, *khozraschet* as a general notion has no direct connection with monetary exchange, since this notion encompasses all "types" of *khozraschet*: internal and administrative to the same extent as that of the lowest link of the Soviet economic system. As a result, one can proclaim that *khozraschet* does not preclude the establishment of goods-money relations, but that these relations must not be viewed as the unavoidable consequences of *khozraschet*.

Adherents of the interpretation of *khozraschet* outlined above act with absolute consistency, in simultaneously denying the applicability of the status of juridical persons with respect to the functioning and ruling agencies of the Soviet economy. As indicated above,[63] juridical persons may, according to Article 11 of Fundamental Principles of Civil Legislation, acquire property rights and bear property duties in their own behalf. Translated from legal into economic language this means that juridical persons are potential or actual participants of goods-money relations. However, if a political task determined by the Soviet regime and conscientiously fulfilled by its servants is to eliminate an insurmountable chain of causation between any of the instruments employed and goods-money relations, then the status of juridical persons must be abrogated in the first place insofar as one deals with the legal situation of different links of the Soviet economy. In analyzing economic activity, the authors of the same book, which generalizes all of the "types" of *khozraschet*, speak not about juridical persons but about economic organizations (*khoziaistvennye organy*) and their subdivisions.[64] Economic organizations comprise, as a general notion, "enterprises, production associations and organizations of economic administration."[65] Each organization has its jurisdiction (*kompetentsiia*), and within the limits of this jurisdiction it carries out economic functions of various kinds: planning, producing, supplying, purchasing, etc.[66] The establishment of goods-money relations is not mentioned at all. But the fate of the status of juridical person with regard to the different links of the Soviet economy is predicted in no uncertain terms: "The need to employ the institution of the juridical person" will disappear in the future, once Soviet economic legislation has been "put in order,"[67] contend the authors cited. And in this case they are extremely candid: "The uselessness of the institution of the juridical person in economic law is connected with the fact that it [this institution] determines the legal personality of socialist organizations one-sidedly, only from the viewpoint of their participation in property relations [i.e. in goods-money relations]. Meanwhile, economic relations indissolubly combine property and planning organizational elements [i.e. such goods-money elements which are admitted by planning (administrative) ruling]. . . . Therefore, in economic law the institution of the juridical person must be replaced by the notion of the economic organization looking to the participation of the subjects of economic law in horizontal and vertical economic relations [regardless of whether these are or are not relations of monetary exchange] and expressing a unified approach to the definition of the economic legal personality in all of these relations."[68] To be brief, generalization of *khozraschet* accompanied by the suggestion that the notion of the juridical person be replaced by the notion of the economic organization has as its ultimate goal the strengthening of the centralized administration of the Soviet economy and simultaneously the undermining of the relative independence of the lowest economic links. What degree of independence, however, is enjoyed by the entities under present legislation? Let us consult two legislative acts: the Statute of Production Associations with regard to industry and the Model Collective Farm Charter in connection with agriculture.

In addressing production associations, one must ascertain the degree of their independence from higher agencies, on the one hand, and the strength of their power toward their internal subdivisions, on the other hand.

In relations with higher agencies, production associations have different rights and duties. Putting aside those connected with property and described above,[69] these rights and duties, states the Statute on Production Associations, lie in the domains of planning, scientific and technological progress, capital construction, material-technical supply, cadres, labor and wages, finances, credit, records, and reports. Problems of scientific and technological progress as well as labor relations are the subjects of other chapters of this book.[70] Issues such as records and reports are not substantial for the characterization of the legal status of production associations. Therefore we will restrict our analysis here to rights and duties in the areas of planning, capital construction, material-technical supply, finances and credit.

In the areas of planning, the production association drafts five year and annual plans, proceeding, however, from planned tasks formulated by its superior agency. The superior agency also confirms these plans within a system of indicators differently established for different industrial branches. In accordance with the confirmed planned tasks and with executed contracts, the production association must work out technical/industrial and financial plans (*tekhpromfinplany*) for each year and also for each quarter and month. However, in contrast to confirmed planned tasks which have inviolable force, executed contracts may be taken into consideration only to the extent that they are consistent with the superior agency's planning order. As a rule, the modification of plans is a prerogative of superior agencies. Amendments of the production plan may be effected by production associations only where these result from justified changes in the orders of trade enterprises for consumer goods, on the condition that the associations observe the limits set by the confirmed plans with respect to the volume of consumer goods and certain other indicators. Unless special prohibitions preclude overfulfillment of the planned task, production associations may manufacture a product in excess of the established plan, if the eventual sale of the additional product is guaranteed beyond doubt.

For capital construction, the confirmation of the construction plans is entirely outside the jurisdiction of production associations. The latter may work out only certain prerequisites of the prospective construction project on the basis of the confirmed plan, and the number of such prerequisites is broader in cases where an association finances the project itself, using its own incentive funds, rather than state budget resources. Beyond these very narrow limits, production associations are performers of construction plans issued by superior agencies. In the area of capital repairs, financed by amortization funds, the associations' planning rights are more substantial than in the area of capital construction. The manager of the association himself confirms the work plans for capital repairs and related support plans.

In the area of material-technical supply, associations must strictly observe distribution plans, regardless of whether they act as sellers or purchasers. Only the sale and purchase of objects whose distribution is not planned or which are surplus because of the refusal of planned purchasers to buy these objects depend upon the discretion of a production association. Even under such circumstances, however, there are a few special rules that must be observed. In addition, production associations may modify, by agreement with their partners, assortment and certain other terms of material-technical supply called for by the plan, on the condition that the appropriate planning agency is timely informed of any such modifications. In accordance with the established procedure, a production association may refuse entirely or in part to buy objects of material-technical supply allocated by a plan of material distribution. In the case of a divergence between an association's production plan and the distribution plan of its product, the producer may abstain from sale until both indicators are coordinated by the planning agencies.

In the area of finances and credit, production associations are subordinated not only to their superior agencies but also to bank establishments as organs of financial control. Similar to other Soviet entities, these associations must deposit their money in and conduct monetary payments through the bank. Unsupervised maintenance and disposal of cash can occur only in very limited cases specifically provided for by law. Bank credit is extended to the production associations in accordance with properly confirmed credit plans. Therefore, although the amount of circulating assets is established by an entity's superior agency, a production association may itself determine the portion of these assets that must be procured by means of bank credit, presenting to a bank establishment a timely application with respect to its credit needs for the following year. Certain financial and estimate calculations are implemented by the production associations themselves in accordance with established normative standards.

As is obvious, production associations do have a degree of independence from their superior agencies, but even in law this independence is more restricted than *khozraschet*, literally interpreted, would mandate. Another situation characterizes relations between production associations and their subdivisions, where the latter function as subordinate units and the former as administering agencies.

Production associations may include independent enterprises. The rights and duties of such enterprises toward production associations are the same as the rights and duties of production associations toward their superior agencies. However, for the most part, enterprises as subdivisions of associations lose their independence, being transformed from production entities into production units. Similar to shops, as subdivisions of enterprises, production units, as subdivisions of associations, function on the basis of internal *khozraschet*,[71] without participating in goods-money relations and only receiving a portion of the association's incentive fund for the rewarding of the unit's workers in conformity with this unit's production achievements. At the same time, production units differ from enterprises' shops. Production units receive from production associations a portion of the basic and circulating assets required for current production activities, independently dispose of these assets in their production process, execute economic contracts in behalf of the production association but within the jurisdiction of the production units, and open current accounts with the bank from which money is paid and to which it is transferred on the basis of contracts entered into by production association through production units. As a result, despite their withdrawal from direct activities in the goods-money economic sphere, production units are close to this sphere, if not as participants, then at least as the participants' representatives.

As to relations between production units as subdivisions and the production association as a whole, which includes these subdivisions and administers their activities, the following legal rules are in force. The production association allocates the required basic and circulating assets to the production units, retaining the right to redistribute these resources in conformity with changing economic demands. Basic indicators of the five year, annual, quarterly, and monthly plans of the production units are established by the production association, and, relying upon these indicators, production units work out their own plans specified with regard to these units' shops and other subdivisions. For capital construction, production units possess no rights at all, except for the right to have a special account with a bank, if capital investments are allocated to the given unit. The position of the units is different with regard to material-technical supply. A production unit situated in a location different from that of the association receives from the association allocation certificates (*fondy*)[72] for material resources distributed in the planning procedure and executes in behalf of the association all of the contracts requisite for the realization of these allocations. In the area of finances and credit, the production association functions only as a single whole. Exceptions are presented by the mentioned bank accounts, which may be opened by production units for their disposal in behalf of the production associations.

Thus, the replacement of independent enterprises by production units signifies: (1) economically, the establishment of internal *khozraschet*, instead of the *khozraschet* of an economic entity, and (2) legally, the creation of a subordinate subdivision, instead of an independent juridical person. It is true that production units possess certain rights unavailable to shops and other production subdivisions. However, this demonstrates the transition to dependence from independence rather than organizational movement in the opposite direction.

So it is with industry organized into production associations and their internal subdivisions. In agriculture, collective farms are the most important production entities. Because Soviet law qualifies collective farms as independent owners, the Model Collective Farm Charter is based on principles designed to lead readers of Soviet laws to the conclusion that collective farms are independent in all of their economic activities. Each collective farm generates its own property funds and is the only holder of the rights of use, possession, and disposal of its property. As an economic entity, a collective farm operates on the basis of *khozraschet*, while its internal subdivisions (departments, brigades, etc.) are governed by internal *khozraschet* similar to that used with respect to subdivisions of state enterprises and associations. Production plans are confirmed by collective farm members at their general meetings, and the goal of these plans is to determine the production activities of the collective farm as a whole and of each of its subdivisions. Collective farms also have independence in the area of finance and credits (opening accounts with a bank, disposing of money deposited, receiving bank credit in cases where this is specially requested, maintaining monetary accounts with contractual parties and with the state budget through the appropriate bank agency, etc.). Material-technical supply requires that applications from collective farms for such supply be approved by distribution plans. The size and character of capital investments also depends on decisions adopted by the collective farms.

The first suspicion arising upon reading the Model Collective Farm Charter results from the fact that this Charter has been confirmed by the Central Committee of the Communist Party of the Soviet Union and the USSR Council of Ministers, and that, consequently, it belongs to the class of Soviet statutory rules binding upon their addressees. Therefore, collective farms not only have the rights to create and replenish the property funds enumerated by the Charter but also are obliged to do so just as they are obliged to observe all of its other provisions concerning bank accounts, prerequisites of supply and credit, monetary accounts with contractual partners and the state budget, etc. The size and character of capital investments, depending in appearance on collective farms' own decisions, are predetermined by the state plan for construction work, as well as by the subordinate plans of inter-state-collective-farm construction organizations, the ultimate contractors, without which no construction for a collective farm can be effected. Moreover, the autonomy of collective farms in production planning is formulated in such a way that actually almost nothing remains of this autonomy in practice. As Article 14 of the Charter states, "when working out plans, a collective farm shall proceed from the need for expanded reproduction of the social economy, fulfillment of the state procurement plan, procurement contracts for agricultural produce and the sale of grain and other products needed by the state in excess of plan, and the satisfaction of the material and cultural requirements of collective farmers." As to the material and cultural requirements of collective farmers, these must, of course, be satisfied but only after the fulfillment of collective farms' duties toward the state and exclusively to the extent that such fulfillment is not negatively affected. Moreover, the predetermination of collective farms' production plans by state procurement plans and even by state demands exceeding planned procurement eliminates collective farm autonomy in planning to the same degree as this autonomy has been eliminated for production associations. The truth of this proposition becomes indisputable if one looks not only to the provisions of the Model Collective

Farm Charter but also to the legislative rules addressed to agricultural-industrial associations.

District agricultural-industrial associations are created by decisions of the local executive committees, and the collective farms of each district must be included in the association not upon their application but "in the established procedure."[73] The plans for district associations include the principal indicators of plans which will be worked out by the subordinate collective farms.[74] In turn, district associations are included in provincial agricultural-industrial associations.[75] The principal indicators of perspective and annual plans of the subordinated collective farms must be determined by district association in accordance with directives of provincial associations.[76] A similar correlation is established for provincial associations and republican *gosagropromy*.[77] Finally, the *Gosagroprom* of the USSR, as has been indicated already,[78] adopts decisions concerning agricultural activities that have binding force for all subordinate entities, including the collective farms throughout the country. Consequently, one can only speak about the economic autonomy of collective farms insofar as certain remainders of such autonomy are preserved despite the strict observance of legally binding rules and the severe enforcement of planned tasks consecutively established by the tremendous mechanism of ruling bureaucracy.

Taking into account such similarities between industrial and agricultural administration, based upon the domination of centralized planning and the subordination of producers' initiative, when planners may issue any orders except for those directly prohibited, while performers may take only those actions specifically allowed, the Soviet authorities have every reason to contend that their economy constitutes a single complex directed from one center and retaining its unity despite its multifarious ramification. Neither proclaiming the existence of various forms of socialist ownership nor distinguishing between governmental and cooperative entities can affect the creation of such a complex in a country where the ruling elite feels itself free to direct economic activities, regardless of whether the law qualifies these activities as personified by different collective bodies or by the state itself. Legal provisions may express the highest respect and maintain exquisite politeness toward those who formally are called proprietors. But since the entities so designated may not dispose of their property at their discretion, and because, in the final analysis, the required decisions must be adopted by other bodies, then the state and not the collective bodies is the proprietor in the genuine meaning of this word. At any rate, an analysis of the legal forms acting in the area of production, assessed on the side of planning agencies as well as on that of the directly producing organizations, eliminates all doubt in answering the question: who is the owner of the economic complex in the USSR? The Soviet state personified by the Soviet rulers is the actual owner. Subsequent discussion will demonstrate whether or not the identical answer follows from an analysis of distribution and exchange, taken in their economic substance and legal forms.

However, before addressing distribution and exchange, one should exhaust the problems connected with production. Its organizations both at the planning and acting stages has already been outlined. But production as a process involves the interaction of two factors: the means of production and the labor force. The means of production will be considered with respect to their development as a result of scientific and technical research, while the labor force must be examined as a component of labor relationships.

Notes

1. 1977 Constitution, art. 3.
2. *Izvestia*, March 7, 1986.
3. V. V. Laptev, ed. *Khoziaistvennoe pravo* (Moscow: Nauka, 1983), p. 28.
4. See the section of Chapter 3 ("Ownership and the Law of Ownership") on "The State's Right of Ownership."
5. *SP SSSR*, 1974, no. 8, item 38, and 1973, no. 7, item 32.
6. A few enterprises did retain their status as enterprises despite their inclusion in associations.
7. *Izvestia*, June 12, 1985.
8. *Izvestia*, March, 4, 1986.
9. Ibid.
10. *SP SSSR*, 1983, part 1, no. 1, item 1.
11. *SP SSSR*, 1983, part 1, no. 1, item 2.
12. See above, in the present section.
13. 1977 Constitution, art. 8.
14. Ibid., art. 100.
15. *Ved. SSSR*, 1983, no. 25, item 382.
16. In addition, the appropriate laws mention only governmental, not Party agencies. Primary Party organizations, i.e. those created at all establishments of which three or more workers are members of the Communist Party, exercise the function of supervision over these establishments in accordance with Rules of the Communist Party of the Soviet Union (the Rules in force were adopted by the Twenty-Seventh Congress of the Communist Party of the Soviet Union in 1986, *Izvestia*, March 8, 1986). However, the Party's Rules are not law, and even these Rules deal with primary Party organizations, although in practice the higher the Party agency the broader its opportunity to interfere in the daily activities of economic entities.
17. Art. 16.
18. Such suggestions, first appearing in the early 1960's (e.g. R. O. Khalfina, *Pravovoe regulirovanie postavki v narodnom khoziaistve*, (Moscow: Nauka, 1963), p. 111, have been and continue to be repeated incessantly (e.g. *Sovetskoe zakonodatel'stvo i khoziaistvennyi mekhanism*, (Moscow: Iuridicheskaia literatura, 1984), p. 74.
19. For greater detail, see, e.g., A. F. Nozdrachev, *Gosudarstvennoe planirovanie i pravovoe regulirovanie* (Moscow: Ekonomika, 1982).
20. *SP SSSR*, 1979, no. 18, item 118.
21. *SP SSSR*, 1983, part 1, no. 13, item 64.
22. *SP SSSR*, 1965, no. 19–20, item 155; 1974, no. 8, item 38; 1973, no. 7, item 32.

23. See Chapters 7 and 8.

24. *Prodovol'stvennaia programma. Normativnye akty* (Moscow: Iuridicheskaia literatura 1985).

25. *SP SSSR*, 1982, part 1, no. 28, item 145.

26. *Izvestia*, January 23, 1986.

27. Above, in the present section.

28. Subsequent complaints addressed to the minister or his deputies are not precluded; however, these are actions exercised beyond the procedure of "protection."

29. Officially, these plans are called "plans for economic and social development" (1977 Constitution, art. 16). However, we prefer to use the terms "economic plans" not only because of the limits of our analysis, which does not comprise "social development," but also taking into consideration the minimal value of Soviet "social plans" (predicting decrease of criminal activity, the improvement of the morality of the Soviet citizenry, etc.).

30. E.g. above, note 18.

31. Above, in the present section.

32. See the "Introduction."

33. *SP SSSR*, 1982, part 1, no. 28, item 145.

34. *SP SSSR*, 1967, no. 2–3, item 9.

35. Above, the section on "General Principles", in the present chapter.

36. *SP SSSR*, 1981, part 1, no. 9–10, item 62.

37. Above, in the present section.

38. *SP SSSR*, 1974, no. 8, item 38.

39. Ibid.

40. See note 35.

41. See note 35.

42. See note 4.

43. Ibid.

44. Ibid.

45. See the section of Chapter 1 ("The Principal Structural Elements of the Soviet Economic System") on "Exchange."

46. Arbitrazh is a special Soviet agency which hears and resolves property disputes between Soviet organizations, except for disputes to which a collective farm is a party.

47. To be "on the state budget" means to receive the requisite financing from the state treasury.

48. To have "an independent estimate" means to be separated with regard to monetary resources from the estimate of the higher agency.

49. To enjoy "the rights of disposing of credits" means to be empowered to issue orders, connected with monetary expenses, that are binding on those bank establishments to which the budget financing resources of state institution have been transferred.

50. See note 45.

51. Below, in the present section.

52. See note 32.

53. *Ved. SSSR*, 1957, no. 11, item 275. See also A. V. Venediktov and O. S. Ioffe, "O grazhdansko-pravovikh voprosakh sviazannykh s reorganizatsiei upravleniia promishlennost'iu," *Vestnik Leningradskogo Universiteta*, 1957, No. 17, p. 131–144.

54. These arguments against "administrative *khozraschet*" have been presented even by certain Soviet scholars. E.g. V. A. Rakhmilovich, *Pravovye formy kho-*

ziaistvennogo rascheta v promyshlennykh ob"edineniiakh, (Moscow: Iuridicheskaia literatura, 1977) p. 37–46.

55. *SP SSSR*, 1973, no. 7, item 32.
56. *SP SSSR*, 1979, no. 18, item 118, art. 46.
57. *BNA*, 1979, no. 1, p. 19–26.
58. Above, in the present section.
59. V. V. Laptev, ed. *Khoziaistvennoe pravo*, p. 134.
60. E.g. G. S. Merzelov, *Khozraschet v systeme upravleniia otrasl'iu* (Moscow: Ekonomika, 1980).
61. Above, in the present section.
62. G. S. Lisichkin, *Plan i rynok*, (Moscow: Ekonomika 1966).
63. Above, in the present section.
64. V. V. Laptev, ed. *Khoziaistvennoe pravo*, p. 55.
65. Ibid.
66. Ibid., p. 51.
67. Ibid., p. 61.
68. Ibid.
69. See note 4.
70. Chapters 5 and 6.
71. Above, in the present section.
72. These documents certify the right to receive material resources distributed by the plan.
73. *SP SSSR*, 1983, part 1, no. 1, item 1.
74. Ibid.
75. *SP SSSR*, 1983, part 1, no. 1, item 1.
76. Ibid.
77. *Ved. RSFSR*, 1985, no. 48, item 1649.
78. Above, in the present section.

5

Production: Research and Development

General Principles

Lenin, like his predecessor Peter the Great and like his successors in the Soviet leadership, tried to force the Russian and Soviet people into modernization. His methods, like Peter's before him, were centralizing planning of modernization, and commanding subordinates to perform the necessary tasks. Both leaders realized that modernization was a necessity if their country was to be a major economic and military power. But history has shown that Soviet modernization by command from above has produced results far inferior to those achieved through capitalist modernization by initiative and competition from below.

During the next twenty years, the Soviet Union will have to try to achieve economic growth while its labor force is diminishing in size and natural resources are becoming more expensive to attract. The only avenues open to sustained growth are economic reorganization, reduction of military expenditures, and technological advance. Technological advance is attractive because, unlike economic reform or reduction of military expenditures, it offers little threat to the Soviet system. However, there are a number of fundamental political policies that seriously limit Soviet ability to encourage advances in applied technology. These include the policy against unplanned increases in institutional wealth and power, the policy of limits on individual wealth, the policy of job security, and the policy of tight planning of resources. The numerous legislative reforms discussed above and below fall into two categories: attempts to achieve an optimum technological policy within the restraints of these policies and modification of the policies themselves where modification does not threaten essential political principles.

The greatest policy barriers to technological innovation are, on the one hand, the policy against the uncontrolled creation of institutional wealth and power and the related policy of limitation on individual income and wealth, and, on the other hand, the reluctance to close factories or unemploy workers. The problem is that the experience of the countries most successful in applied technology clearly demonstrates that the best way to stimulate this technology is through a combination of high rewards for those who overcome the high risks involved in innovation with severe penalties for those who fail to modernize. Creating a climate for innovation without major rewards for innovation or major penalties for failure to modernize is a truly challenging task. The policy against high rewards, whose effects will be discussed in detail below, effectively removes incentives to take risks to innovate. The lack of market competition and of its concomitants—bankruptcy for enterprises that fail to mondernize and unemployment for their staff—removes the risks of non-modernization.

Because these policies make it impossible to rely primarily upon innovation inspired from below, the Soviet leadership must instead order innovation from above and supervise lower-level organizations to see that innovation in fact takes place. The difficulties this system faces are of two types: (1) how can government bureaucrats, distant from actual suppliers and customers, know what innovation is needed; (2) how can these bureaucrats be sure that they are getting real and not simulated innovation. The saving factor is the fact that Soviet technology lags substantially behind the technology of the United States, Japan, and the most advanced countries of Western Europe, and indeed often falls short of the level of the more successful developing countries such as South Korea. The result is that the planners, and the agencies that implement their plans, can see where to go by observing where others have gone before them. They can determine the level of plan performance by comparing the results with those in Western countries.

The most important area of Soviet law affecting research and development is that which governs the making and implementation of plans for technological progress on the basis of policy decisions taken at the highest levels of the Party. In addition to this system for planned innovation, the Soviet Union has a system which on paper appears quite similar to the patent system of capitalist countries. However, in practice, this system plays a relatively limited, though still important role, functioning mainly as a means for collection and distribution of information and of providing bonuses for outstanding employee effort.

The Soviet attempt to modernize by planning from above has resulted in the creation of a complex legal system related to technological innovation. Unlike free market countries, which provide basic protection for patents, trademarks, trade secrets, and other forms of intellectual property, and then leave modernization to the forces of the marketplace, the Soviet Union governs every aspect of the modernization process either by law or by legally binding administrative commands. This law and these commands deal with: planning of research and development; financing of research and development; organization of research and development; import of technology; and distribution of information.

Planning, Financing, and Organization of Research and Development

The planning of research and development and of the implementation of its results must be more flexible than ordinary planning of ordinary industrial production, because new scientific and technical discoveries may make even the best plans obsolete. The longest term of planning is the "Complex Program for Scientific and Technical Progress" for a 20-year period.[1] More specific details on planned research and development are included in the "Fundamental Directions of Economic and Social Development of the USSR," which have a five- and a fifteen-year perspective. Still more details are supplied in separate five-year plans. Not everything can be foreseen in advance. Therefore the five-year plans include some unallocated reserves of materials and production capacities. These can be used to take advantage of new scientific discoveries or to deal with unexpected needs.

Long-term plans are based on goal-oriented scientific and technical programs, for instance a program to create a microcomputer industry. Once the broad policy decisions on these programs have been made by the leadership, relying upon the advice of leading scientists, the planning agencies have the task of providing the necessary resources. Because the leadership now especially emphasizes the crucial importance of scientific and technical progress to maintaining the economic and military power of the Soviet Union, planners can be expected to divert the necessary resources from lower-priority programs to allow for the fulfillment of scientific and technical goals. In accordance with decrees of 1979, 1983, and 1985, these programs are drafted for the State Planning Committee (*Gosplan*) by the State Committee on Science and Technology and the State Committee on Construction jointly with the Academy of Sciences of the USSR.[2] The programs are comprehensive, starting with the scientific and technical research to be done, and continuing through the initial stages of production. They define the ministries and departments responsible for the programs, and they nominate actual persons to head the programs. Lower level organizations (USSR ministries and departments and councils of ministers of the union republics) are also required by the same decree to draft plans for the creation and implementation of new technology within their respective areas of jurisdiction.

The five-year plans developed on the basis of the expert input of State Committee on Science and Technology, and the feasibility estimates of the State Committee on Construction and the various USSR and republic administrative agencies, are quite detailed, leaving relatively little to the discretion of lower links in the system. Still further details are introduced in the one-year breakdowns of the five-year plans.[3] There are at least three fundamental reasons for this detail. The first is a desire to maintain central political control over key decisions affecting the future of the whole Soviet economy. The second is a distrust of the technical qualifications of provincial industrial management. The third is the lack of an incentive system structured to ensure that decisions made locally will be in the national interest.

Details of planning methods are found in a 1980 *Gosplan* order, entitled "Basic Methodological Provisions for the Development of Goal-Oriented Systematic National Economic Programs."[4] This order provides for various types of programs. In many cases, science and technology constitute only one component of a program which also calls for such matters as organizational reform and construction of expanded production facilities. In other cases, science and technology are the main purposes of the program. As is true in other areas of Soviet planning, lower levels have considerable input in the planning process, but final decisions are made at the top and in great detail.

All planning of research and development must be supported by a cost/benefit evaluation in accordance with criteria stated in 1977 legislation.[5] The criteria set up by this important legislation are used for multiple purposes: picking the best alternative research direction; setting indicators for measuring research performance; determining the actual effectiveness of research that has been done; calculating the bonuses for research results; and improving price formation. The methodology requires the comparison of the results of the research and development proposed or undertaken by a Soviet organization against the base of the best alternative planned Soviet technology and the best available foreign technology. The useful effect of the base technology and the new technology are each calculated according to the following formula:

$$Z = C + E_n K$$

where Z = total cost per unit
C = variable production cost per unit
E_n = Normative coefficient of effectiveness of capital investment (set at 0.15 for all branches of the economy except automated systems)

In applying the formula, future expenses and income are reduced to current value using a discount rate of 10%. The difference between this figure and the 15% return on capital in the above formula presumably represents an allowance for amortization of capital.

The formula is obviously based on very arbitrary assumptions as far as rate of return, discount rate, and amortization rate are concerned. Nevertheless, it appears to be a useful approach to the evaluation of planned and completed research aimed at lowering production costs. It provides no guidance where the result of research is a new and different product, rather than a better way to make an existing product, unless that new product in turn is designed to save money in production. This shortcoming is recognized in the legislation, which creates different procedures for decisions with respect to the introduction of new productions, as appropriate, by the respective ministry or department or union republic council of ministers by agreement with Gosplan and the State Committee on Science and Technology. Such new product decisions are apparently made on the basis of subjetive judgment, without the application of a formula.[6]

In areas where the Soviet Union is substantially behind the capitalist world, for instance consumer products, rational decision making is relatively easy. Those consumer products that have been a clear success in foreign markets can be copied, while those that have failed can be avoided. The situation is much more difficult in areas where the Soviet Union is attempting to keep up with advanced foreign technology. Here, it can easily identify major new technology programs, and start its own to copy them. However, this mode of operation condemns it to repeat the mistakes of the rest of the world. It has led to such mistakes as the Soviet decision to design a supersonic passenger airplane.

In analyzing the legislation on the financing of research and development, it is important to distinguish two questions. The first is the location of the power to decide how much will be spent and on what kind of research. The second is the actual source of money to pay the costs of doing the research. As will be shown, there is substantial decentralization in the sources of money for research, but very little decentralization in decision-making on research funding.

There are three essential types of financing for research and development: (1) budgetary financing; (2) organizational financing; and (3) contract financing.[7] Over the past two decades, the percentage of budgetary financing has declined; however, it still amounts to almost 50% of research financing. Budgetary financing tends to be used for basic research. Organizational financing is used for research within the confines of a single ministry, production association, or independent enterprise. Contract financing is used both as a means of payment for work done by an organization subordinate to one ministry for an organization subordinate to another, and as a means of bookkeeping for transfers between two organizations subject to the same superior agency.

Budgetary financing remains by far the most important source of funds for research and development. Even though the proportion of budgetary financing has declined substantially in the last two decades, it still remains the source of almost half of all research funding. It is generally used for basic research, research of value to many different branches of the economy, and for very expensive research projects. Budget estimates are prepared by organizations engaged in research and development and are consolidated by the superior organizations for presentation to the State Committee on Science and Technology and *Gosplan*, which are responsible for making the detailed budgetary decisions necessary to implement the research and development policies set by the top leadership.

The next major source of funding is the unified fund created at the ministerial level for the financing of research and development.[8] The unified fund is used for financing research and development work and for startup expenses of new production. Amounts in the fund remain with the ministry, rather than reverting to the treasury at the end of the plan year. Part of the fund may be transferred by ministries for distribution at the discretion of industrial organizations, and of major production and scientific-production associations, to finance planned research and development measures.

The fund is formed primarily from transfers of a certain amount of the planned profits of organizations subordinate to a ministry. The amount is set in the five year plan, with an annual breakdown. Usually it is expressed as a percentage of net (i.e. value-added) production, but in some branches of the economy it is fixed as a percentage of goods production. The decision on the percentage to be transferred is made jointly by *Gosplan*, the USSR Ministry of Finances, and the State Committee on Science and Technology. Thus, the individual ministry has no real discretion in determining its own level of research and development expenditures. Successful ministries will, however, have higher transfers to the unified fund from another source. Half of the extra profits from the higher prices set for new products and products awarded the state seal of quality goes to the unified fund. The other half goes to the incentive funds of the organizations producing the product.

A variety of research expenditures are covered by the unified fund: (1) planned and supplementary expenses for research and development for the branch, including both work done by organizations subordinate to the ministry and work done under contract with organizations outside the ministry; (2) expenses connected with preparation for the production of new products and the introduction of new production processes; (3) expenditures for raising the quality and durability of products above that required by state standards; (4) extra expenses connected with the initial production of new or modernized products (unless these expenses are compensated by temporary high wholesale prices for types of products entirely new to the USSR); (5) other expenses related to the implementation of new technology; and (6) repayment of loans incurred for the development of new technology.

Up to 20% of the assets of the unified fund of the ministry may be allotted to organizations subordinate to the ministry, for basic research and for funding of research proposals initiated by staff of these subordinate organizations.

The introduction of new products entails substantial costs for Soviet enterprises. Inevitably there is an interruption of the production process and relatively low productivity for a period of time as the enterprise masters the production of the new product. In a country with a free market, this problem would be met in a number of different ways. A better product would naturally command a higher price. Patents could be used to give exclusive rights for a length of time sufficient to enable the manufacturer to recoup the costs of introducing a new product. In the Soviet Union, almost all prices of industrial goods are fixed by the State Committee on Prices, so that a manufacturer cannot unilaterally raise prices for a superior product. Nor can the manufacturer expect to be the exclusive producer of a new product for long. As explained below, Soviet enterprises cannot have exclusive patent rights or keep trade secrets from one another. Legislation providing increased prices for new products is designed to establish a formal mechanism for overcoming the economic disincentives to putting new products into production.[9] Because the amounts allowed have tended to be inadequate, changes have gone in the direction of continually increasing the price allowance. A 1979 Decree called for the establishment of higher prices on new high-quality products, with corresponding price reductions for old, low-quality products. This decree was implemented by a 1979 decision of the State Committee on Prices. It provided for setting prices for new products for industrial use on the basis of their annual economic effect, with up to 70% of the positive effect going to the manufacturing enterprise during the first year of production. Higher prices may be charged for several years for products that have been awarded the State Seal of Quality. The economic effect was to be calculated in accordance with detailed rules adopted in 1977. Regulations adopted in 1980 provided for sales of limited quantities of new and high fashion goods at retail at prices agreed upon between the Ministry of Trade of the USSR, wholesale organizations of the republics, and industrial associations. The industrial association manufacturing the goods would keep 50% of the increased profits, and 30% of this 50% would go for bonuses. Because, as indicated above, industrial associations are being abolished, the same rights will probably be transferred to the economic ministries. The idea of prices set by contract was extended in a decree of March 1983, which allowed agreement between buyer and seller within relatively narrow guidelines (planned cost plus 10% to 20%) on new types of industrial materials and components. In what appeared to be a recentralization of the power to raise prices, an August 1983 decree gave the State Committee on Science and Technology power to allow price increases of up to 30% for products incorporating new technology.

At the level of the production units there is a fund for the development of production, formed from transfers to cover amortization of equipment, transfers from profits, and sales of unneeded equipment. This fund provides a substantial portion of the assets needed for investment in new higher-technology production equipment. A similar fund, the organization development fund, is formed in scientific production organizations from contract earnings, profits, sales of licenses, wholesale price surcharges, and sales of surplus equipment.[10]

The regulation of planning and financing is supplemented by a system of supervision of research and development. This function is a duty of ministries and production associations with respect to the organizations subordinate to them. However, there has been a steady growth in the supervisory powers of the State Committee on Science and Technology, which has the staff with the technical expertise to evaluate the performance of ministries and lower level organizations, and apparently is highly trusted by top Party decision makers.[11]

Because the typical major scientific and technical program involves the cooperation of organizations subordinate to a number of different ministries, a coordinating body must be set up at a rather high level so that its decisions can be binding upon the respective ministries. A number of mechanisms are in use.[12] For particularly important programs, an ad hoc coordinating committee may be set up to deal with scientific and technological matters. Thus, for instance, for a major agricultural program, a Commission of the Council of Ministers on the Agroindustrial System was created, and eventually absorbed into *Gosagroprom.*[13] It is responsible for supervising the agricultural research and development work of a number of bodies, including the State Committee on Science and Technology, the Academy of Sciences of the USSR, the academies of sciences of the union republics, and the Academy of Agricultural Sciences.[14] For programs of somewhat lower priority, management is placed in a commission attached to *Gosplan* rather than the Council of Ministers. An example is the Interdepartmental Commission on the Use of Renewable Energy Sources in the National Economy, now absorbed into the Bureau of Energy of the USSR Council of Ministers. It was created as an expert commission of specialists and scientists from *Gosplan*, the State Committee on Science and Technology, the State Committee on Supply, and various ministries, departments, research institutes and enterprises. It was given broad powers to develop and manage projects in the areas of solar, geothermal, and wind energy.[15]

A special role in the fulfillment of research and development plans is assigned to scientific-production associations. They are meant to combine research and development with start-up production of new products. They are subordinate directly to ministries and serve as the research departments of the ministries. Soviet authors have reported some conflict between their research and production roles, because of pressures toward expansion of production at the expense of research. Their work is planned in such detail, that they cannot be considered to be entrepreneurial organizations. A scientific-production association has essentially the same legal structure as does an ordinary production association. The difference is found in extra planning indicators and extra powers and financing in the area of research.[16]

The scientific-production association is subordinate to a ministry and serves as a research center of the ministry, providing research services for the production associations subordinate to the ministry. Detailed plans cover tasks for the whole process from research to production, starting with basic research, followed by design, experimental models, and actual industrial production. The plans also include tasks involving the transfer of this technology to production associations.

The scientific-production association has as its central unit a scientific research institute and various production units that are supposed to provide support in turning the results of the research done by the institute into practical products. A Soviet commentator lists two potential problems: the situation where production units have far more capacity than is needed, so that their energy is directed at commercial rather than experimental production, and the opposite situation where production units have too little capacity to carry out the task of putting prototypes into production.[17]

A substantial amount of research is also conducted in the research departments of larger enterprises. This research is included in the enterprise plan.

The Soviet Academy of Sciences retains an important role in applied research. Even though past reorganizations have moved many applied research institutes away from the Academy to the jurisdiction of the ministries, applied industrial research remains an important function of the Academy of Sciences system. The Academy is organized into the Academy of Sciences of the USSR (for the USSR and the Russian Republic), and academies for the union republics (except the Russian Republic). In addition, the USSR Academy has some coordinating role for specialized academies, such as the Academy of Medical Sciences. The Academy has a research plan and supervises performance of this plan by institutes subordinate to it. Often research is conducted by contract with outside organizations, usually in accordance with plan, but in some cases without a basis in plan, where an Academy Institute has excess research capability.

In contrast to the Academy of Sciences, higher educational institutions have played a much smaller role in research and development in the Soviet Union than in the United States. There have been a number of reasons for this difference. Probably the most important has been the long tradition of channeling government support for research through the Academy of Sciences. The underutilization of the human resources of higher educational institutions for research has led to the underfunding of their laboratories, making it impossible for many types of research to be done at these institutions. A series of decrees starting in the late 1970s have been aimed at remedying some of these problems, so that better use could be made of the research potential of the intellectual capital in higher education. Many of these decrees seemed aimed at duplicating in the Soviet Union the type of university scientific research environment found in the United States. By the late 1970s, many leading Soviet scientists had studied at universities in the United States and were well aware of the American system of government financing of research through universities. A 1978 decree established a list of "leading higher educational institutions" (unfortunately not published with the decree). It provided for organization of research departments within universities.[18] Capital was to be provided by the State Committee on Science and Technology and the Ministry of Finances, while the State Committee on Supply (*Gossnab*) was to provide allocations of the necessary equipment. Faculty members engaged in research were to be given lower teaching loads. Experiments were to be conducted with research organizations connected with higher educational institutions, financed on a *khozraschet* basis from research contracts. A 1979 Order of the Ministry of Higher and Secondary Specialized Education provided for setting up a system of research planning and support in leading higher educational institutions similar to that found in research institutes.[19] It also provided for setting up cooperative research centers joining the resources of several higher educational institutions. Other decrees improved the organizational structure for coordination of the research done by higher educational institutions.[20]

Some Soviet authors have argued for the creation of a "fourth system" of scientific research institutions (in addition to those of the industrial ministries, the Academy of Sciences, and the Ministry of Higher Education).[21] They argue that there is a gap between the very basic research done by the Academy and the very applied research done by the ministries. In addition, they argue that the present system is poorly suited to applied research whose conduct and benefits cuts across the jurisdiction of ministries. They suggest the creation of additional research institutes to bridge these gaps, with the additional institutes to be subordinate to the State Committee on Science and Technology. A few such institutes do exist and are pointed to as models by the proponents of this scheme.

A major reorganization has been the transfer of a great deal of research and development to a system of economic accountability, either full or internal *khozraschet* as defined in Chapter 4.[22] Before the reorganization, research institutions generally had a research plan, which served as the basis for a research budget. The plan was expressed largely in terms of expenditure of man-hours and equipment rather than in terms of results achieved. Budgetary resources were doled out on a periodic schedule, in time to meet payroll and equipment needs as expressed in the plan. The reorganization instituted a system of accounting and payment similar to that used for organizations engaged in construction contracting. Instead of planning man-hours to be spent, the planners specify results to be achieved. A rewards system similar to that in other branches of the Soviet economy was introduced, with bonus funds whose size depends upon success in meeting planners' targets. In many cases, these results are to be achieved not in the abstract, but for specific customers, with whom the research organizations are to make contracts. Interim financing of personnel and equipment costs during contract performance is effected through bank loans made on the basis of these contracts. This reorganization appears to have had a number of aims. The most important was probably to channel research in directions most needed for the solution of problems related to programs approved by the Soviet leadership. The commission in charge of one of these programs would in the course of planning discover many research subgoals that would have to be reached in order to achieve the main goal of the program. The use of the tried and tested plan and contract method could help aim the work of research organizations directly at these problems. The reorganization also improved financial control over the activity of research organizations. By segregating costs among various projects, it became easier both to judge the cost/benefit ratios of these projects, and the effectiveness of the research organizations in performing the projects. Finally, and undoubtedly least important was the fact that a mechanism was created for unplanned research and development. To the extent that its full capacity was not utilized by planned contracts, a research and development organization could negotiate research contracts with various customers to meet their needs.

Contract research by higher educational institutions is much less developed in the Soviet Union than in the United States. Largely this is caused by the fact that the Academy of Sciences has under its jurisdiction a high percentage of both the physical academic research facilities and scientific talent. However, in recent years, some efforts have been made to bring universities more into research on the United States model. Legislation provides for conclusion of research contracts by universities with outside customers.[23] Both planned and unplanned contracts are allowed, but planned contracts have priority. Contracts are to be concluded with first priority given to the fulfillment of work provided for by plan, orders of higher agencies, scientific-technical programs, and coordination plans of the Academy of Sciences and the Ministry of Higher and Specialized Secondary Education. The type of work done, the annual volume of expenditures, and the maximum total wage payments are subject to the approval of the Ministry to which the higher educational institution is subordinate. The overall direction of scientific work engaged in by institutions officially classified as "leading" requires in addition the agreement of the USSR Ministry of Higher and Specialized Secondary Education. Regulation of contract research was updated by a 1984 Ministry order. This established that the contracts were to be concluded with top priority given to work provided for by economic plans, coordination plans of the Academy of Sciences and orders of the Ministry. To the extent that research capacity remained after these contracts were concluded, other contracts could be made at the discretion of the higher educational institution. There are direct incentives for both the institution and its staff. Faculty members can earn up to 50% extra pay by participating in research projects.[24] The institution gets a 20% overhead markup. It must use at least 70% of this markup for modernizing equipment, but can use up to 30% for sports. Up to 1.5% may be used for publications and for the organization of patent-licensing and scientific-technical information.

Enforcement and Encouragement

Performance of plans for research, development, and implementation of technical innovations is carefully monitored. Procedures are specified by *Gosplan* and the Central Statistical Administration.[25] Evaluation is made with respect to the fulfillment of the basic tasks of the scientific and technical programs, the development and implementation of new technological processes, the technical level of production and products, and the economic effect from the implementation of scientific and technical measures.

The State Committee on Science and Technology, in addition to its role in planning projects for development of new technology, has a general watchdog role in checking on how the new technology is being developed. It sets up state commissions to verify the activity of research organizations. These commissions obtain information on the progress of projects from the All-Union Scientific Information Center. The commissions report to the State Committee on Science and Technology, which then sends resolutions to ministries requesting appropriate action to remedy any problems uncovered.[26] The State Committee on Construction (*Gostroi*) has similar powers for ensuring the conformance to technological standards of new plant facilities under construction.

Another formal mechanism for ensuring technological progress is attestation. Because the Soviet Union lacks a free market mechanism, it cannot count on poor quality or obsolete goods being forced off the market by more modern goods. Furthermore, enterprises cling to the production of old models of goods because their long experience in producing them makes it easy to fulfill production plans. As will be discussed, there are price incentives designed to overcome the reluctance of enterprises to produce new, modernized products. Unfortunately, these incentives often fail of their purpose, either because they are too small in amount, or because increased profits do not adequately offset the risk of failure to fulfill output plans under the de facto incentive scheme. Therefore, direct pressures are necessary to try to end production of outdated goods. One such method is formal attestation.[27] Goods are rated by quality categories. Products that repeatedly fail to meet the quality requirements are supposed to be ordered withdrawn from production. In practice, the lack of substitutes may prevent implementation of this requirement.

Economic incentive funds similar to those found in ordinary production organizations are found at scientific research institutions.[28] These funds are designed to tie incentives to the results of the work of the organizations. Incentive funds are formed from a number of sources. The first is transfer payments from additional profits realized by enterprises due to cost savings traceable to results achieved by the research organization. These transfer payments are made according to a percentage set for the branch of industry involved and extend for three years from the date of implementation of the new technology. The payments in the first year are based upon the economic effect of introducing the innovation, those in the second and third years on any further economic effect occurring in those years above and beyond that of the previous year. A second source is the increased profits received by economic entities in the respective branch of the economy from higher prices allowed under price-setting legislation as an incentive for introducing new products. Special rules provide for payments into the incentive funds where the economic effect of the innovation is not directly measurable in terms of reduced costs and increased profitability. Other special rules deal with research done for purposes other than direct economic benefit to the Soviet economy, including design of unique prototypes, design for export, development of standards, feasibility studies, environmental work, safety research, development of information services, improvements in reliability, and automation. Where economic effect is relevant, it is calculated in accordance with 1977 regulations.[29]

In addition to these bonus funds at the research organization level, there are bonus funds at the Ministry level.[30] These funds are formed by transfers of up to 20% of the bonus funds formed at lower levels. They are used by the ministries to reward outstanding work by employees at lower levels that would not receive sufficient recognition through the fixed bonus formulas employed by lower-level organizations. In particular, bonus funds may be used to reward the following: (1) basic scientific research; (2) development of technology having social or other useful effects, not measurable in economic terms; (3) development of technology that reduces labor requirements, particularly requirements for labor under difficult or dangerous conditions; (4) development of technology for export or for import substitution; (5) and other achievements, at the Ministry's discretion.

In the Soviet Union the vast majority of inventions and innovations are made by employees in the course of their employment. The legal system of rewards for inventors thus amounts essentially to an employee bonus scheme. In its economic essence it differs substantially from the patent system in countries such as the United States, where the prospect of profits from the patent monopoly serves as a guide to companies in investing research and development funds. In the Soviet Union, investment decisions are made as part of the planning process, and the potential availability of intellectual property protection is not a factor in investment decision-making. In addition to establishing bonuses for outstanding employees, the Soviet intellectual property system provides an important means for technical information distribution, as will be discussed below.

The primary means of protection under Soviet intellectual property law is the "inventor's certificate." The issuance of an inventor's certificate provides recognition, fringe benefits, and cash rewards to the inventor, but it does not give him a monopoly on the invention. Soviet law does provide for patents, but these are hardly ever used by Soviet citizens and only rarely by foreign companies and individuals.

The procedure for obtaining an inventor's certificate is similar to that for obtaining a patent in most other countries. The inventor submits an application in a form corresponding to Soviet and international standards. (The Soviet Union is a party to the Patent Cooperation Treaty, which sets a standard form for patent applications worldwide.) The inventor's employer is required to help the inventor in the preparation of the application. While this involves paperwork and clerical time for the employer, the fact that inventions are made looks good in reports of fulfillment of plans for research and development. The application is sent to the State Committee on Matters of Inventions and Discoveries for examination. The employee pays no fees for preparation or for examination. The application is checked to see that it meets formal requirements and, if it does, technical experts examine it in the light of the Committee's collection of world patent and technical literature to see if the invention is really new. If the application is rejected in whole or in part, the inventor has the right to administrative appeal within the Committee, but no right to contest the rejection in court.[31] Disputes between Soviet citizens as to who really made an invention are subject to court jurisdiction.[32] If the application is approved (by no means a certainty—a high percentage are rejected, since the Committee sometimes is overvigilant in exercising its quality control functions), an inventor's certificate is issued and a summary of the invention is published. However, special rules apply if, in the course of an examination, it appears that the invention should be classified as a military secret.

The holder of an inventor's certificate is entitled to a number of legal rights. The first is the moral right of authorship. The inventor and only the inventor may list the invention on his resume; the inventor may name the invention as he pleases, subject to the approval of the State Committee on Inventions and Discoveries. These moral rights are not unimportant since an engineer with a large number of inventor's certificates on his resume may expect to advance much more rapidly in his career. The inventor also obtains a number of rights related to personal status, particularly important in Soviet society, where personal status can often obtain what money cannot buy. He has the right to participate in work aimed at implementing his invention, the right to have information on his invention entered into his work record book, the right to preference in research-related travel, and, in the case of major inventions, the right to use the invention in place of a thesis for obtaining an advanced academic degree. Finally, he has the right to payment if his invention is used. Payment is calculated on a complex formula, based largely on the economic savings realized from the use of an invention.[33] The inventor receives a token award of 20 to 50 rubles upon issuance of the inventor's certificates, and more substantial rewards if the invention is widely used in practice. The maximum total amount that may be received for one invention is 20,000 rubles, but few inventors indeed receive anything close to this limit. In practice the system works, but not perfectly. There are problems with the highly subjective process of conducting an economic analysis, and problems with enforcement against enterprises that use an invention covered by an inventor's certificate but do not pay the compensation required by law.[34]

There is a second legal scheme of rewards for employee suggestions (called "rationalization proposals" in Soviet legislation), similar to the employee suggestion scheme used by many companies in free market economies. This scheme of reward for ideas that fall short of being inventions differs from similar schemes used by private companies in capitalist countries, in that details of the Soviet suggestion reward system are specified by USSR legislation rather than by individual enterprise policies. The procedures for obtaining these rewards are considerably simpler than those for obtaining inventor's certificates and the rewards are correspondingly smaller, with a maximum size of 5000 rubles per suggestion.[35]

Individuals who make innovations that are not job-connected also have the right to take advantage of the invention protection system. Nearly always such individuals seek inventor's certificates rather than patents. There are several reasons for this. First, inventor's certificates are issued without charge, while large fees must be paid for patents. Second, inventor's certificates entitle the holder to payment whenever the invention is used by state industry, while a patent gives an exclusive right which is essentially worthless in a system where private manufacturing operations are illegal. Third, inventor's certificates add substantially to the reputation and earning power of the holder, while patents mark the holder as outside the mainstream of Soviet society. In the past, some Soviet inventors have been asked by the authorities to obtain patents, because there was some doubt about whether or not inventor's certificates would be recognized for priority purposes under the international treaty governing patent rights. That treaty, the Paris Convention for the Protection of Industrial Property, has now been revised to provide equal treatment for patents and inventor's certificates on an international basis; thus international patent law no longer provides a reason for Soviet inventors to obtain Soviet patents. Since foreign countries outside Eastern Europe generally have only patents and not inventor's certificates, it is quite common for Soviet inventors to get patents abroad, in the United States for instance. They assign these patents to a Soviet foreign trade organization which licenses them to foreign companies, and pays the Soviet inventors royalties, in the form of coveted hard currency certificates that can be spent in special well-stocked stores.

On very rare occasions, a Soviet inventor will obtain a patent. For instance, a circus performer with a unique apparatus that he uses in his act may patent the apparatus to protect his act from competition by other circus performers.

Other Legal Forms of Modernization of Technology

Because the Soviet Union lags substantially behind foreign countries in most areas of technology, the planned import of technology is an essential part of the Soviet drive for technological modernization. This import occurs in three different ways—the import of technological information and prototype products, the import of assembly lines, and the import of total Soviet needs of particular products. Each of these modes of importing is governed by extensive legal regulations.

Soviet law provides an elaborate system for the planned import of technical information and for the distribution of such information to end users. This import is effected through a network of libraries of technical and patent literature. At present legal and practical measures are being set up for direct access to foreign technical data banks and for the creation of technical data banks and data networks within the Soviet Union. Since thése operations are relatively low cost in terms of foreign exchange, the main efforts are directed at the improvement of the internal organization of information distribution within the USSR. Because the information is technical and largely devoid of political content, the censorship system does not present a barrier to its distribution.

A high percentage of Soviet foreign exchange earnings have always gone for the import of complete assembly lines from abroad. Two notable examples are the major automobile factory built by Fiat and a truck factory built by joint efforts of various foreign contractors. However, these are but a few examples of the large number of turnkey contracts that have been made for the import of assembly lines. While expensive in terms of foreign exchange, these contracts have provided instant modernization for various areas of Soviet industry.

There are two limits on their more widespread use. The first is the net quantity of foreign exchange available to the Soviet Union. Since most Soviet foreign exchange earnings come from international oil and gas and much of these earnings must be spent on food in years with bad harvests, the Soviet Union's ability to import assembly lines depends upon oil and gas prices and upon the weather, both factors beyond government control.

A way to avoid the whole problem of technological modernization is the import of total Soviet needs of particular products. This approach is found in two areas. Within the Council for Economic Mutual Assistance, there are elaborate legal mechanisms for planning specialization in production. The Soviet military, unable to wait until the Soviet Union has the ability to produce high quality weapons components, may import the needed components from Western countries through clandestine channels. For instance, if each of 300 Soviet medium-range ballistic missiles needs a particular high-quality bubble memory chip to carry its computer code, it may be much cheaper and quicker to smuggle the memory chips out of the United States than to set up a bubble memory production facility. The Soviet Union has long been reluctant to become totally dependent upon sources of supply outside Eastern Europe for any type of product in widespread use, because of both the foreign exchange costs and the danger that political developments could cut off the source of supply.

There is a dual system for the planning of technology imports. Imports for civilian purposes, and imports of production equipment for both civilian and military purposes are planned on the basis of requests submitted by individual production associations, consolidated by their ministries, and evaluated by the State Committee on Science and Technology and *Gosplan*. Requests are also made for technology for special, project-oriented organizations set up to create modern manufacturing plants for high priority areas of the Soviet economy. Planning for the import of prototypes of and documentation for military equipment is done by the Military Industrial Commission on the basis of requests submitted by the various military manufacturing industries.[36]

The methods used for importing vary depending upon whether or not the source country has export restrictions on the goods or information desired. If there are no export restrictions, appropriate foreign trade organizations work with the respective ministries in purchasing the ministries' import needs in accordance with plans approved by the planning authorities. Legislation adopted in September 1986 would allow some 70 ministries and economic entities to engage in direct foreign trade and technology transfer arrangements with foreign firms, bypassing specialized foreign trade organizations.[37] This change could provide better exposure to foreign technology, but may face problems in implementation, since it goes contrary to the longstanding policy of limitation of foreign contacts of Soviet citizens and Soviet organizations.

Scientific information is gathered openly by the Academy of Sciences and the State Committee on Science and Technology. If there are export controls, more clandestine means are used. The KGB and the Main Intelligence Administration of the Ministry of Defense appear to have about equal roles in such clandestine imports, with a much smaller role being played, either alone or in cooperation with these intelligence agencies, by the Ministry of Foreign Trade, the State Committee on Science and Technology, the State Committee for Foreign Economic Relations and the Academy of Sciences.[38]

In an effort to avoid duplication of research already done, what Russians call "inventing the bicycle," an All-Union Scientific-Technical Information Center has been created. Organizations engaged in research and development work are required to report the results of their work to this Center.[39] Within 30 days after approval of a plan, conclusion of a contract, or execution of some other document as a basis for research and development work, the organization involved is required to send a registration card describing the work contemplated to the Information Center. The Center then gives the work a registration number which must be used in all further reports on the project. Upon completion of each independent stage of the work and of the work as a whole, detailed reports must be provided to the Information Center. As a means of enforcement, it is provided that research work shall not be completed until a final report has been filed with the Information Center.

The Information Center in turn distributes information from its files to outside organizations, charging appropriate fees for its bibliographic search and photocopying services. If the recipient needs more detailed information, for instance detailed blueprints, it must obtain the information directly from the research organization, using the contract procedure described below. The Information Center does not function as a public library. There are restrictions on distribution designed to protect national security, guard trade secrets from foreign eyes, and protect the intellectual property interests of organizations engaged in research. National security is served by exempting secret research (which constitutes a very high percentage of all Soviet applied research) from reporting requirements. In addition, if a research project originally made public is reclassified as secret during the course of research, the research organization is obliged to notify the Information Center at once so that its file on the project can be made secret. To protect potential international patent rights, a file may be temporarily closed at the request of the State Committee on Matters of Inventions and Discoveries. While Soviet organizations may not keep trade secrets from one another, Soviet policy is to use trade secrecy and knowhow licensing as a means of obtaining foreign currency earnings. Therefore, the services of the Information Center are not available to private citizens and are only available to foreign organizations on the basis of special agreements.

There is also a system for the distribution of patent information (including information on inventor's certificates).[40] The main purpose of this system is to provide Soviet engineers with access to foreign technology, though it also serves to distribute Soviet technology. Copies of patents are collected from all major industrial countries. The most important patents are selected for translation, and translation services are available on request. Abstracts of patents are sent to regional centers, which function in cooperation with the All-Union Society of Inventors and Innovators. Work is now under way on computerizing this valuable information.[41] Since very few foreign companies obtain Soviet patents, and since the legal force of patent protection under international patent law is limited to the territory of the country where the patent is obtained, Soviet engineers may quite legally incorporate the latest patented foreign technology in their designs. Problems may arise if the products designed are to be exported, since if, for instance, they violate French patents, they may not be sent to France without the risk of a lawsuit. Therefore procedures exist for preclearance of export products to prevent inadvertent patent violation.

While Soviet law forbids one Soviet organization to keep a trade secret from another, it does provide for some compensation for transfer of technical information. This compensation is provided under a model contract adopted by *Gosplan*, the USSR Ministry of Finances, and the USSR Ministry of Justice.[42] Under the model contract, the party that has developed the information agrees to transfer it to another party in return for the latter's agreement to pay the actual out-of-pocket expenses of transfer, plus a small payment, based upon the economic effect of the information transferred. The out-of-pocket expenses are reimbursed to the transferring enterprise, while the payment for economic effect goes as bonuses to the employees who developed the technology. However, the payments required by law are not enough to provide an incentive for an organization with superior technology to aggressively seek out users for that technology.

The system of scientific research and development has consistently been able to meet a large number of goals of the Soviet leadership, but at the cost of a 10 to 15 year lag in technology behind the most advanced capitalist countries. These goals appear to include: limiting individual wealth; guaranteeing job security; restricting migration to large cities; keeping central control of prices; maintaining tight centralized planning of research activity; minimizing expenditures; and also minimizing contacts with foreigners and foreign ideology. The legislation of the late 1970s and of the 1980s shows continual attempts to fine tune the existing system to make better use of available resources, without abandoning any of the listed goals. There has been a mobilization of underutilized resources, such as university faculty personnel, an increased sophistication in evading foreign export controls, and a slight relaxation of the tightness of planning, allowing some negotiation of free contracts at lower levels, and leaving some funds free to support worthy projects suggested from below. Connections between production and research have been improved by the integration of research institutes into production associations. These incremental improvements, which will presumably continue, do nothing to shorten the time lag of Soviet technology behind Western technology, because organizational improvements are also taking place in capitalist countries at about the same pace. If the Soviet leadership were to be satisfied with the country's 10 to 15 year technology lag, it would appear that the present system of legal regulation of research and development could be continued indefinitely. However, the increasingly rapid pace of the scientific and technical revolution makes this lag far less tolerable than it was in the past. With, for instance, the average capacity of computer memory chips doubling every two or three years, a 10 to 15 year technology lag leads to intolerable backwardness in every branch of technology, civilian and particularly military. This means that, without some radical change in policy, the Soviet Union can anticipate a steady decrease in its relative military power, as well as continued difficulty in selling manufactured products as exports in the quality-conscious world market. The consequences of handicaps imposed by political policies on the Soviet system of innovation thus include lower productivity from factories and construction organizations using older technologies, delays in the appearance of new consumer products, backwardness in military hardware, and loss of export earnings. The first two consequences are tolerable—they merely result in a somewhat lower standard of living for the Soviet people and the need to devote somewhat more capital and manpower to military production. The third raises increasingly serious problems as modern military might comes to depend more on the level of technology than on the number of soldiers and guns, and to depend more on the level of technological achievement of the country as a whole than on parity with potential adversaries in a few narrow engineering disciplines. The days are gone when the Soviet government could find a small number of brilliant mechanical engineers, reward them well for designing high-quality tanks for the Soviet army, and then pay large numbers of master mechanics high wages to build the tanks properly, substituting the cream of Soviet manpower for sophisticated manufacturing machinery. The coming generation of tanks are part of the electronic battlefield. Their quality will depend upon the overall quality of the Soviet electronics and computer industry. No matter how clever they are or what they are paid, skilled technicians alone cannot produce the necessary computer chips and other exotic electronic components. While at one time the Soviet Union could produce poor quality buses for civilians and good quality tanks for the military, there is no such possibility for computer components. A typical computer chip contains a million memory elements. If any memory element fails, the chip is worthless, whether for civilian or military application.

Military technology needs to place two types of limits on the extent to which Soviet planners can rely upon copying or importing foreign technological developments. The increasing interdependence of military and civilian technology means that no area of civilian technology can be allowed to lag far behind the level of the same technology in the United States, if the Soviet Union is to remain a competitive military power. With respect to purely military technology, areas such as rocket design, the Soviet Union must maintain an extensive research and development effort, since foreign military secrecy and export controls make it impossible to rely entirely upon copying or licensing.

Notes

1. M. P. Ring, *Khozraschetnaia sistema sozdaniia i vnedreniia novoi tekhniki: Pravovye problemy* (M.: Nauka, 1982); A. A. Zvorykin and D. D. Raikov, ed., *Planirovanie i upravlenie v nauchnykh kollektivakh* (Moscow: Nauka, 1981); Louvan E. Nolting, *The Planning of Research, Development, and Innovation in the U.S.S.R.*, U.S. Department of Commerce, Bureau of the Census, *Foreign Economic Report* no. 14, (Washington, D.C.: U.S. Government Printing Office, 1978); Berliner, Joseph S., *The Innovation Decision in Soviet Industry* (Cambridge, Mass.: MIT Press, 1976).

2. O shirokom rasprostanenii novykh metodov khoziaistvovaniia i usilenii ikh vozdeistviia na uskorenie nauchno-tekhnicheskogo progressa [summary], *SP SSSR*, 1985, no. 23, item 403. O merakh po uskoreniiu nauchno-tekhnicheskogo progressa v narodnom khoziaistve, [summary] *SP SSSR*, 1983, no. 24, p. 419. Ob uluchshenii planirovaniia i usilenii vozdeistviia khoziaistvennogo mekhanizma na povyshenie effektivnosti proizvodstva i kachestva raboty, *SP SSSR*, 1979, no. 18, item 118.

3. *SP SSSR*, 1979, no. 18, item 118, Para. 7.

4. M. P. Ring, *Khozraschetnaia sistema*, p. 215.

5. Metodika (osnovnye polozheniia) opredeleniia ekonomicheskoi effektivnosti ispol'zovaniia v narodnom khoziaistve novoi tekhniki, izobretenii i ratsionalizatorskikh predlozhenii, *Voprosy izobretatel'stva*, 1977, no. 7, p. 46; D. S. L'vov, "Edinye printsipy opredeleniia ekonomicheskoi effektivnosti novoi tekhniki," *Izvestiia Akademii nauk SSSR, Seriia ekon.*, 1984, no. 5, p. 13; N. V. Beilina, "Ekonomicheskaia otsenka tselesoobraznosti priobreteniia litsenzii," *Voprosy izobretatel'stva*, 1981, no. 3, p. 57.

6. M. P. Ring, *Khozraschetnaia sistema*, p. 215.

7. Louvan E. Nolting, *Financing of Research, Development, and Innovation in the U.S.S.R.*, U.S. Department of Commerce, Bureau of the Census, *Foreign Economic Report* no. 22, (Washington, D.C.: U.S. Government Printing Office, 1985); M. A. Lupachev, "Uluchshat' usloviia proizvodstva novoi tekhniki /O kompleksnom plane finansirovaniia osvoeniia novoi tekhniki/," *Finansy SSSR*, 1983, no. 5, p. 25.

8. Metodicheskie ukazaniia o poriadke obrazovaniia i ispol'zovaniia edinogo fonda razvitiia nauki i tekhniki, *BNA*, 1980, no. 1, p. 3. Ukazaniia o poriadke planirovaniia, finansirovaniia i ucheta zatrat, proizvodimykh za schet sredstv edinogo fonda razvitiia nauki i tekhniki, *BNA*, 1981, no. 5, p. 12.

9. Instruktivnye ukazaniia o poriadke ustanovleniia optovykh tsen i normativov chistoi produktsii na opytnye obraztsy (partii) novoi produktsii proizvodstvenno-tekhnicheskogo naznacheniia, *BNA*, 1984, no. 4, p. 9. Polozhenie o poriadke ustanovleniia dogovornykh tsen na pervye opytnye partii tovarov i osobo modnye izdeliia i differentsiatsii torgovykh skidok, *BNA*, 1981, no. 2, p. 30. Ukazaniia o

poriadke ustanovleniia pooshchritel'nykh nadbavok k optovym tsenam na novuiu vysokoeffektivnuiu produktsiiu proizvodstvenno-tekhnicheskogo naznacheniia i skidok s optovykh tsen po produktsii vtoroi kategorii kachestva, a takzhe po produktsii, kotoraia v ustanovlennyi srok ne attestovana, *BNA*, 1980, no. 3, p. 3.

10. Nolting, *Financing*, p. 35.

11. Louvan E. Nolting, *The Structure and Functions of the U.S.S.R. State Committee for Science and Technology*, U.S. Department of Commerce, Bureau of the Census, *Foreign Economic Report* no. 16 (Washington, D.C.: U.S. Government Printing Office, 1979).

12. M. P. Ring, *Khozraschetnaia sistema*, p. 215; V. A. Rassudovskii and V. P. Rassokhin, ed., *Pravo i upravlenie nauchnymi organizatsiiami* (Moscow: Nauka, 1980).

13. Ob uluchshenii upraveleniia sel'skim khoziastvom i drugimi otrasliami agropromyshlennogo kompleksa, *SP SSSR*, 1982, no. 17, item 89.

14. M. P. Ring, *Khozraschetnaia sistema*, p. 215.

15. Polozhenie o mezhduvedomstvennoi komissii po ispol'zovaniiu vozobnovliaemykh istochnikov energii v narodnom khoziaistve pri Gosplane SSSR, *BNA* 1982, no. 2, p. 3.

16. Polozhenie o nauchno-proizvodstvennom ob"edinenii, *SP SSSR*, 1976, no. 2, item 13.

17. *Pravo i upravlenie nauchnymi organizatsiiami*, ed. B. A. Rassudovskii and V. P. Rassokhin (Moscow: Nauka, 1980), pp. 132–133.

18. O povyshenii effektivnosti nauchno-issledovatel'skoi raboty v vysshikh uchebnykh zavedeniiakh, *SP SSSR*, 1978, no. 10, item 66.

19. Polozhenie o poriadke provedeniia nauchno-issledovatel'skikh rabot v vysshykh uchebnykh zavedeniiakh, *BNA*, 1980, no. 4, p. 29.

20. Polozhenie o mezhvuzovskikh tsentrakh obsluzhivaniia nauchnykh issledovanii, (mentioned in *BNA*, 1985, no. 2, p. 23). Decree on the Scientific and Technical Council of the Ministry of Higher and Secondary Specialized Education of the USSR, *Biulleten' Ministerstva vysshego i srednego spetsial'nogo obrazovaniia SSSR*, 1978, no. 12.

21. V. P. Rassokhin, " 'Za' i 'protiv' chetvertoi sistemy nauchnykh uchrezhdenii," *SGiP*, 1985, no. 3, p. 67.

22. M. P. Ring, *Khozraschetnaia sistema*, Metodicheskie ukazaniia o perevode ob"edinenii, predpriiatii i organizatsii stroitel'stva, transporta, sviazi, geologii, sel'skogo khoziaistva i material'no-tekhnicheskogo snabzheniia na khozraschetnuiu sistemu organizatsii rabot po sozdaniiu, osvoeniiu i vnedreniiu novoi tekhniki, *BNA*, 1985, no. 4, p. 3; Ch. N. Azimov, "Pravovoi rezhim nauchno-tekhnicheskikh reszul'tatov, poluchennykh po dogovoram," *Problemy sotsialisticheskoi zakonnosti*, 1981, no. 8, pp. 89–95.

23. Instruktsiia o poriadke vypolneniia vysshimi uchebnymi zavedeniiami nauchno-issledovatel'skikh rabot po khoziaistvennym dogovoram s zakazchikami, *BNA*, 1985, no. 2, p. 22.

24. Ibid.

25. *BNA*, 1981, no. 9, p. 10, Para. 5; "Effektivnost' zakonodatel'stva reguliruiushchego otnosheniia v sfere nauchno-tekhnicheskogo progressa," in V. P. Gribanov, ed., *Effektivnost' grazhdanskogo zakonodatel'stva (aktual'nye voprosy)*, (Moscow: Izdatel'stvo Moskovskogo Universiteta, 1984): p. 156; E. V. Reunenko and A. N. Emel'ianov, "Novaia forma gosudarstvennoi statistichekoi otchetnosti o postuplenii i ispol'zovanii izobretenii i ratstionalizatorskikh predlozhenii," *Voprosy izo-*

bretatel'stva, 1981, no. 7, p. 58; A. S. Borodkin, *Uchet novoi tekhniki v ob"edinenii* (Kiev: Tekhnika, 1981).

26. Poriadok osushchestvleniia gosudarstvennoi proverki deiatel'nosti nauchno-issledovatel'skikh, konstruktorskikh, proektnykh, proektno-konstruktorskikh i tekhnologicheskikh organizatsii, *BNA*, 1985, no. 5, p. 45.

27. O dal'neishem usilenii roli attestatsii promyshelnnoi produktsii v povyshenii ee tekhnicheskogo urovnia i kachestva, *SP SSSR*, 1980, no. 2, item 11.

28. Polozhenie o poriadke obrazovaniia i ispol'zovaniia fondov ekonomicheskogo stimulirovaniia v nauchno-issledovatel'skikh, konstruktorskikh organizatsiiakh, proiszvodstvennykh ob"edineniiakh i predpriiatiiakh, perevedennykh na khozraschetnuiu sistemu organizatsii rabot po sozdaniiu, osvoeniiu i vnedreniiu novoi tekhniki na osnove zakazov-nariadov (dogovorov), *BNA*, 1981, no. 3, p. 5; Metodicheskie ukazaniia o perevode ob"edinenii, predpriiatii i organizatsii stroitel'stva, transporta, aviazi, geologii, sel'skogo khoziaistva i material'no-tekhnicheskogo snabzheniia na khozraschetnuiu sistemu organizatsii rabot po sozdaniiu, osvoeniiu i vnedreniiu novoi tekhniki, *BNA*, 1985, no. 4, p. 3.

29. Metodika (osnovnye polozheniia) opredeleniia ekonomicheskoi effektivnosti ispol'zovaniia v narodnom khoziaistve novoi tekhniki, izobretenii i ratsionalizatorskikh predlozhenii, *Voprosy izobretatel'stva*, 1977, no. 7, p. 46. Raziasnenie po primeneniu otdel'nykh polozhenii Metodiki opredeleniia ekonomicheskoi effektivnosti ispol'zovaniia v narodnom khoziaistve novoi tekhniki, izobretenii i ratsionalizatorskikh predlozhenii, utverzhdennoe postanovleniem Gosudarstvennogo komiteta Soveta Ministrov SSSR po nauke i tekhnike, Gosplana SSSR, Akademii nauk SSSR i Gosudarstvennogo komiteta Soveta Ministrov SSSR po delam izobretenii i otkrytii ot 14 fevralia 1977 g. no. 48/16/13/3, *Voprosy izobretatel'stva*, 1983, no. 12, p. 57. Tipovoe polozhenie o premirovanii rabotnikov nauchno-issledovatel'skikh, konstruktorskikh, proektno-konstruktorskikh i tekhnologicheskikh organizatsii, proizvodstvennykh ob"edinenii i predpriiatii, perevedennykh na novuiu sistemu planirovaniia, finansirovaniia i ekonomicheskogo stimulirovaniia rabot po novoi tekhnike, *BNA*, 1978, no. 6, p. 4.

30. Polozhenie o poriadke obrazovaniia i ispol'zovania fondov ekonomicheskogo stimulirovaniia v nauchno-issledovatel'skikh, konstruktorskikh organizatsiiakh, proiszvodstvennkh ob"edineniiakh i predpreiiatiiakh, perevedennykh na khozraschetnuiu sistemu organizatsii rabot po sozdaniiu, osvoeniiu i vnedreniiu novoi tekhniki na osnove zakazov-nariadov (dogovorov), *BNA*, 1981, no. 3, p. 5.

31. Instruktsiia o poriadke rassmotreniia zhalob i protestov Kontrol'nym sovetom nauchno-tekhnicheskoi ekspertizy Gosudarstvennogo komiteta SSSR po delam izobretenii i otkrytii, *Voprosy izobretatel'stva*, 1980, no. 5, p. 59; N. P. Levchenko and N. S. Khromushkina, "Sovershenstvovanie normativnykh aktov v oblasti ekspertizy izobretenii," *Voprosy izobretatel'stva*, 1979, no. 1, p. 14.

32. O primenenii sudami zakonodatel'stva reguliruiushchego otnosheniia, voznikaiushchie v sviazi s otkrytiiami, izobreteniiami, ratsionalizatorskimi predlozheniiami i promyshlennymi obratsami, Decree of the Plenum of the Supreme Court of the USSR of November 15, 1984, no. 22. *Biulleten' Verkhovnogo Suda SSSR*, 1985, no. 1, p. 13; F. Aisina, "Zashchita prava avtorstva izobretatelei i ratsionalizatorov v sudebnom poriadke," *Sovetskaia iustitsiia*, 1983, no. 9, p. 8; Ia. Ostrat, "Ekspertiza v sudebnykh delakh izobretatelei i ratsionalizatorov," *SGiP*, 1983, no. 2, p. 115.

33. O dopolnenii Instruktsii po opredeleniiu razmera voznagrazhdeniia za izobreteniia i ratsionalizatorskie predlozheniia, ne sozdaiushchie ekonomii, *Voprosy izobretatel'stva*, 1978, no. 1, p. 63; V. Kolosok, "Trudovye prava avtorov izobretenii i ratsionalizatorskikh predlozhenii," *Sovetskie profsoiuzy*, 1983, no. 8, p. 46.

34. E. Z. Bunatian and T. N. Frolova, "Strogo sobliudat' zakonodatel'stvo pri vyplate voznagrazhdeniia za izobreteniia i ratsionalizatorskie predlozheniia," *Voprosy izobretatel'stva*, 1985, no. 8, p. 35; E. Abramov, "Prokurorskie proverki ispolneniia zakonodatel'stva po izobretatel'stvu i ratsionalizatsii," *Sotsialisticheskaia zakonnost'*, 1985, no. 1, p. 50.

35. Ukazaniia o poriadke sostavleniia, podachi i rassmotreniia zaiavleniia na ratsionalizatorskoe predlozhenie, *BNA*, 1984, no. 8, p. 16.

36. *Soviet Acquisition of Militarily Significant Western Technology: An Update*, September, 1985. This document indicates no author or publisher, but was obviously prepared by a United States government intelligence agency. It appears to be based largely upon data from a Soviet citizen named "Farewell" who spied for France. Thierry Wolton, *Le KGB en France* (Paris, 1985).

37. Serge Schmemann, "Trade Rights Expanded for Soviet Enterprises," *New York Times*, Sept. 25, 1986, pp. 29–30.

38. *Soviet Acquisition of Military Significant Western Technology.*

39. Instruktsiia o poriadke gosudarstvennoi registratsii i ucheta otkrytykh nauchno-issledovatel'skikh i opytno-konstruktorskikh rabot, predstavleniia po nim otchetov i informatsionnykh materialov vo Vsesoiznyi nauchno-teckhnicheskii informatsionnyi tsentr i vydachi informatsii etim tsentrom, *BNA*, 1982, no. 8, p. 16; A. S. Sherstovitov, "Effektivnost' pravovogo regulirovaniia dogovorov na informatsionnoe obsluzhivanie," in *Effektivnost' grazhdanskogo zakonodatel'stva (aktual'nye voprosy)*, ed. V. P. Gribanov (Moscow: Izdatel'stvo Moskovskogo Universiteta 1984).

40. Polozhenie o gosudarstvennoi sisteme patentnoi informatsii, *Voprosy izobretatel'stva*, 1980, no. 2, p. 57.

41. Polozhenie o mezhvedomstvennom Sovete pol'zovatelei patentnoi informatsii na mashinochitaemykh nositeliakh, *Voprosy izobretatel'stva*, 1980, no. 6, p. 60.

42. Tipovoi dogovor na peredachu predpriiatiiami i organizatsiiami svoikh nauchno-tekhnicheskikh dostizhenii drugim predpriiatiiam i organizatsiiam i na okazanie im pomoshchi v ispol'zovanii zaimstvovannogo peredovogo opyta, *BNA*, 1983, no. 4, p. 18; Instruktsiia o poriadke vypolneniia vyschimi uchebnymi zavedeniiami nauchno-issledovatel'skikh rabot po khoziaistvennym dogovoram s zakazchikami, *BNA*, 1985, no. 2, p. 22, at p. 23.

6

Production: Labor Force and Labor Law

General Principles

Soviet labor law involves a combination of detailed government planning of labor allocation, including assignment of workers to specific jobs, with a considerable amount of freedom of individuals in choosing jobs and of employers in choosing employees. Because of the ideological importance of labor in the "workers state," the labor law includes a much higher percentage of rules that are ideological fictions instead of operative law than would be found in areas such as industrial supply contract legislation, where a much higher percentage of the published rules are in fact operative law.

The sources of Soviet labor law are numerous. At the USSR level, there are "Fundamental Principles of Labor Legislation." Each republic has its own "Code of Laws on Labor." In addition, there are a huge number of administrative regulations dealing with labor matters. A recently published collection of these administrative regulations amounted to three volumes of 600 pages each.[1] This collection did not include any of the detailed regulations on wages, which would have required many more volumes. It also did not include the many important regulations dealing with labor planning. In addition, the Supreme Court of the USSR and the supreme courts of the republics have published many decisions and instructions dealing with the most litigated parts of labor law.

The major government agencies regulating labor are the State Committee on Labor and Social Problems and the All-Union Central Council of Trade Unions. Despite the words "trade unions" in the title of the latter and despite the fact that it is formally classified as a nongovernmental body by Soviet legislation, it is really a governmental agency performing functions that might be done by a Ministry of Labor in many countries. This organization and subordinate bodies that exist in the Soviet Union called "profsoiuzy" in Russian (a term usually translated as "trade unions" in English) have nothing in common with real trade unions as found in Western countries. Workers would have to be crazy to try to organize a real trade union. Indeed, a number of workers who tried just this a few years ago were put in psychiatric hospitals by the government.[2] Soviet "trade unions" today perform important legislative and administrative functions in the area of labor and social insurance. During the course of Soviet legal history, many governmental functions have shifted back and forth between government agencies and the "trade unions." We will refer to Soviet "trade unions" in quotes to reflect the fact that they are not actually trade unions.

The creation of an organizational structure for coordinated labor planning came relatively recently in Soviet history. Many of the functions of the Tsarist and Provisional Government labor agencies were continued by the RSFSR People's Commissariat of Labor founded in 1917 and the USSR People's Commissariat of Labor created upon the formation of the USSR in 1923.[3] Before the start of the five year plans, neither the People's Commissariat of Labor nor the All-Union Central Council of Trade Unions had important economic planning functions. Like the prerevolutionary government labor agencies they were mainly concerned with protecting certain rights of workers in areas such as labor safety, and with providing benefits for retirement and job-connected injuries.[4] During the late 1920s, the People's Commissariat of Labor took part in the negotiation of "general collective contracts" which set certain industry-wide labor conditions, until these contracts were abolished in 1931. The People's Commissariat of Labor itself was abolished in 1933 and its functions were transferred to the All-Union Central Council of Trade Unions.[5] This transfer may have reflected a de facto lowering of priority of protection of labor rights at the start of the five year plans. One of the results of the lack of a central state agency specifically devoted to labor was the movement of some of the responsibility for labor policy upward to Gosplan, and some downward to the industrial ministries, which achieved substantial labor policy-making powers. It was not until 1955 that a central government labor planning agency was revived, with the creation of the State Committee on Labor and Wages. However, the labor planning powers of this committee were limited. In 1976, the decision was taken to expand the powers of this state committee, which was renamed the State Committee of the USSR on Labor and Social Matters.[6] At present this committee, along with its branches in the republics, constitutes the main specialized agency for manpower planning in the Soviet Union.

Unlike the State Committee on Labor and Social Matters, which exists only at the All-Union level, as a centralized policy-making organization, the "trade union" structure is an extensive administrative organization, with branches at the level of the republics and primary organizations in economic entities. In the economic entities, the trade union committee performs many functions of a personnel department, severely limiting the discretion of entity's management. Governmental functions performed by lower level "trade union" agencies include distribution of social insurance payments and settlement of labor disputes.

Since the 1930s Gosplan, the central state planning committee, has been responsible for overall planning of the coordination of manpower resources with production plans. Because Soviet ministries have had to function within strict limits on wages and numbers of personnel set by Gosplan, and because they lack the legal power to force employees to move from one city to another under threat of dismissal, these ministries have had only a limited role in labor planning. Their main function is to allocate the wages fund and personnel limits set for them among various subordinate organizations, and to put pressure upon Gosplan and other high authorities to securing the labor needed to perform production and operational tasks.

The Labor Force Planning Process

At the most general level, the labor planning process tries to achieve two goals: that every citizen is working for the benefit of the Soviet system and that each enterprise and farm has sufficient manpower to perform its assigned tasks. There are a number of constraints upon the planning process. In the short run, the total number of able-bodied workers is limited. In the medium term, this number can be influenced by educational policy, to create more prospective employees with particular skills.[7] In the longer term, it can be influenced by population policy. Allowing large-scale immigration is not politically feasible. Labor mobility is limited by the policy of pricing urban housing well below cost, a policy which means that no housing is available for new migrants to major cities, and that unneeded workers are unlikely to give up urban comforts, since they will receive no reduction in rent for moving to the provinces. Planners are also limited in what can be offered in wage differentials (but the law allows substantially higher pay for workers in isolated parts of Siberia, the Extreme North, and the Far East). Many Soviet citizens receive wages so low that they can hardly be reduced. Increasing wages on any substantial scale would introduce serious inflationary pressures into the Soviet economy. To prevent these inflationary pressures and to block individual enterprises from defeating general labor force policy, there are strict limits on enterprise discretion in the areas of total number of employees and total payroll, limits which will be discussed below.

The planned distribution of manpower depends upon and simultaneously affects the planning of population movement in the USSR. The distribution process is complicated by the fact that many natural resources lie far from centers of population, as well as by the policies of full employment and low urban housing rents and prices. The full employment policy tends to attract population to localities with urban amenities and/or a warm climate. The need to exploit natural resources causes a need for labor in places with neither amenities nor a warm climate. Further difficulties are caused by technological change, which may reduce the need for labor in sectors such as agriculture, despite the fact that the rural birth rate exceeds the urban birth rate. In a classical capitalist economy, these problems would be solved by the indirect pressures of such economic factors as unemployment and housing costs. Unemployment would cause workers to move from low employment areas to high employment areas. Housing costs would rise in areas with amenities and climate, e.g. Southern California, to the point where the number of arriving migrants would be limited.

These problems have been attacked in the USSR both by indirect economic means and by direct legal compulsion. The indirect economic means, such as siting factories in towns with growing populations, building more urban housing, or offering higher wages in cold climates, are of great importance, but are beyond the scope of this chapter, which will look instead at the legal measures used directly to prevent or to compel movement to or from jobs in particular areas. Measures of legal compulsion are directed both at employers and at prospective employees. A variety of rules limit the number of employees each employing organization can hire. Other rules, however, restrict employers from discharging existing employees. Employees are prevented by residence permit and housing allocation systems from migrating to many areas. Forced migration of labor has been a significant factor in Soviet history, though it is of much less importance today.

The Russian state grew up as a collection of semi-independent cities under the suzerainty of the prince of the most powerful city. Full freedom to change one's residence from one city of Russia to another never existed. In Tsarist times, population movement was controlled by a passport system, similar to that used to control international population movement in Western countries. Each resident of an urban area had to have a passport and a police residence permit for the city where he lived. The Tsarist passport system was abolished after the revolution, but was restored in 1932.[8] It plays a major role in controlling population movement, by providing a legal barrier to the population shifts that would otherwise occur because of economic forces. Soviet authors are embarrassed about the residence permit system, and tend to underplay its importance in Soviet society or to engage in outright lies about its operation. A standard Soviet administrative law text, for instance, states:

> Under the conditions of a developed socialist society, the improvement of accounting and statistics of the population has important significance for the improvement of the management of the national economy.
>
> Annually in our country many millions of persons change their residence. The interests of Soviet society require a certain regulation of such movement. It is completely obvious that excessive, unaccounted for, and random overpopulation of individual populated points and localities, mainly large cities, could cause, although temporary, nevertheless undesirable consequences, such as difficulties in supply, providing housing, finding work, etc. Without hindering the realization of freedom of movement, the passport system makes these processes orderly by the introduction of special records and registration of citizens living in certain localities.[9]

Law, Plan, and the Formation of the Employment Contract

There are seven possible types of relationship among law, plan, and the formation of the employment contract under Soviet law: (1) the employer is obligated to hire a specific employee who is obligated to work for the specific employer; (2) the employer is obligated to hire a specific employee who is obligated by law to work, but not obligated to work for the specific employer; (3) the employer is obligated to hire a specific employee who is under no obligation to work at all; (4) the employer is indirectly compelled by its production plan to hire a certain number of employees to meet production targets and hires an individual who is obligated by law to work, but not for that employer; (5) the employer is indirectly compelled by its production plan and hires an individual who is under no obligation to work; (6) the employer is under no obligation to hire, but the individual is under a legal obligation to work; (7) the employer is under no obligation to hire, and the individual is under no obligation to work.

The first type of contract is fully planned—a specific employer and a specific employee are legally required to create an employment relationship. The total number of such specifically planned employment contracts is quite large. Such contracts serve the important function of providing a way for the planners to fill essential jobs which cannot be filled through economic incentives to employers and employees. In general these jobs fall into two categories: those where the wage rate has been set by law below the market price; those where the individual is being forced to work for punishment or rehabilitation.

There is no general system for requiring the mass of ordinary citizens to work at specific jobs, though there have been such systems at various points in Soviet history. A civilian work obligation was introduced soon after the revolution.[10] It it was soon replaced by a tax.[11] Compulsory labor reappeared as a World War II emergency measure.[12]

The Soviet Union maintains a large standing military force, with the lower ranks staffed largely by draftees. In some cases the military serves as a flexible source of manpower for economic planners, since soldiers not needed for military duties may be assigned to civilian projects.

Students in full-time day divisions of higher and secondary specialized educational institutions have the obligation to work for prescribed periods of time for the government upon graduation. This obligation is viewed as being in exchange for the free education they have received.[13] In some cases students are supported for study under a contract with a specific organization and have a contractual obligation to work for that organization when they finish their studies.[14]

Convict labor has an honorable Marxist heritage. Karl Marx, in his Critique of the Gotha Program, criticized the following provision from the program of the Socialist Workers' Party of Germany: "5. Regulation of Prison Labor." Marx commented: "A petty demand in a general worker's program. In any case it should have been clearly stated that there is no intention from fear of competition to allow ordinary criminals to be treated like beasts, and especially that there is no desire to deprive them of their sole means of betterment, productive labor. This was surely the least one might have expected from Socialists."[15]

Marx's idea of the importance of labor in the rehabilitation of criminals was adopted wholeheartedly as a principle of Soviet penology. However, it was given new content under Stalin, who combined the obligation of prisoners to work with national economic planning. The Soviet national economic plan for 1941, which was captured by the Germans and later fell into the hands of the United States Army, included very substantial tasks for the national economy envisioning the use of convict labor.[16] A careful study by Dr. Ger P. van den Berg suggests that while the population of labor camps was over 4.0 million in 1950, in recent years the population of labor camps has been somewhere between 1.0 and 1.7 million.[17] Additional persons work at localities to which they have been exiled or at specific jobs to which they have been assigned as criminal punishment.[18]

Following Marx's theory on the moral and educational value of labor, the Soviet Union makes compulsory labor a significant component of therapeutic and educational programs. Labor therapy is a regular part of the prescribed regime in mental health institutions. Alcoholics and drug addicts may be sent to special centers for cures involving a heavy dose of compulsory labor.[19] Recent educational reform legislation has called for a major expansion of the requirement that school children engage in regular, planned, socially-useful labor.[20]

The second type of law-plan-contract relation involves the situation where a prospective employee is under a general obligation to work, but not for a specific employer, while a specific employer is obligated to offer the prospective employee a job. This category includes such favored categories of prospective employees as returning draftees and young entrants into the labor force.

Such persons, like all able-bodied Soviet adults below retirement age, have a legal duty to have a job. Article 60 of the Soviet Constitution provides for a duty to work. Professor Harold Berman has traced this duty back to the universal obligation to serve the state that was a feature of the Mongol conquest of Russia, and which later found its way into feudal obligations under the Tsars.[21] Labor planning is based upon the idea that all citizens able to work should be working. For a person to remain unemployed and to fail to take a job when warned to do so by the local authorities is a criminal offense.[22] The punishment of "parasitism" has roots that reach far into Russian history.[23]

While all able-bodied Soviet citizens are expected to work, only a few categories of citizens have the right to be offered specific jobs. Draftees discharged after their term of service have the right to take their old jobs back.[24] Up to two percent of jobs in each branch of the economy are reserved for disabled veterans.[25] Certain places must be reserved to be filled with young entrants into the labor force; these places are assigned by the Commissions on Affairs of Minors.[26] Young people growing up on a collective farm have a right to joint the collective farm. Article II(3) of the Model Collective farm charter provides:

> Citizens who have reached the age of 16 and have shown a desire by their labor to take part in the social economy of the collective farm may be collective farm members.
>
> Members of a collective farm shall be admitted by the general meeting of the collective farmers on the recommendation of the board of the collective farm in the presence of the person who has submitted the application.[27]

In actual practice members' children who reach the age of 16 are admitted without question. Outsiders are generally admitted only if they marry farm members or their additional labor is needed by the farm.

The third category is that of an employer obligated to hire a specific employee who is under no obligation to work at all. This category is a small one, including, for instance, a returning draftee so severely wounded that he could retire on his military pension, but who nevertheless insists upon working.

The fourth category is by far the largest; the majority of employment contracts in the Soviet Union fall within this category. Here, the employer is indirectly compelled by its production plan to hire a certain number of employees to meet production targets and hires an individual who is obligated by law to work, but not for that particular employer. The employer, typically an enterprise or production association, is caught between conflicting legal pressures. On the one hand, he is pushed to hire more employees to meet the production goals set by the plan. On the other hand, the plan restricts the total amount he can pay for wages and the total size of the workforce. Even if funds are available to hire employees, it may be impossible to find persons with permanent residence permits in the given locality who want to work for the wages the employer can offer. Hiring of employees from other localities is restricted by passport legislation. Legislation limits the giving of incentives to employees to change jobs.

Legislation calls for the setting of three types of labor-related plan indicators for production associations and enterprises. These are (1) a target for the growth of productivity of labor; (2) a maximum limit on the numbers of workers and office workers; (3) a maximum total amount that may be paid for wages ("the wages fund"). The wages fund is to be specified only in branches of the economy for which there is no norm for wages per ruble of production.[28] Such a norm indirectly fixes the maximum total wages. Limits on total wages have long been a feature of Soviet law. These limits serve to restrict employment indirectly, while leaving the employer with some choice as to whether, for instance, to use more lower-paid employees and fewer high-paid employees or more part-time employees and fewer full time employees.[29] Wages paid to various categories have also been restricted since the early days of Soviet power.[30] Economic legislation passed in 1971 omitted limits on total number of employees from the list of plan indicators that could be set by superior organizations.[31] However, legislation later in the 1970s provided for limits upon the numbers of employees to be established by Gosplan for ministries, and by ministries for associations and enterprises.[32] These limits are maxima, not minima, and are set on average, not peak employment. Ministries are authorized to maintain a reserve for allocation to enterprises that have sudden manpower needs in the course of the year. The reinstatement of this system of limits marks a major step toward the recentralization of manpower planning.

If insufficient workers are available locally at the wages the enterprise is allowed to pay, it may be able to obtain temporary residence permits for workers from other localities.[33] Such workers constitute a major portion of the total flow of labor to Soviet cities. For instance, in 1971 about 220,000 persons obtained residence permits in Moscow of whom one-fourth, or 55,000, came with temporary residence permits.[34] Such workers are called "*limitchiki.*" The term apparently derives from the practice of the authorities in limiting both the number of such temporary residence permits for the city and the number made available to any one enterprise for assignment to its workers.

To prevent employing organizations from bidding against one another for workers, there are limits upon what can be offered to induce an employee to change employers. In general, these limits allow very few incentives to be offered to attract employees from other enterprises.[35] Thus they tend to force enterprises to train their own skilled work force.

The fifth type of contract, where the employer is under indirect plan compulsion to hire, but the prospective employee is under no compulsion to work, is similar to the fourth type in all respects, except that it involves a prospective employee under no legal compulsion to work, for instance, an old age pensioner.

The sixth and seventh types, involving an employer that is under no obligation either direct or indirect to hire occur only in the relatively infrequent cases where the employer is a private citizen or a foreign embassy or business. With the exception of writers, who may hire secretaries, private citizens may only hire servants, and not productive employees. No private citizen is ever under a legal obligation or plan pressure to hire anyone. Any private citizen who can afford it is perfectly free to hire personal servants for himself or his family. Such private contracts are governed by special legislation, providing obligations upon the private employee to make social insurance payments. Foreign businesses and embassies in the USSR often have Soviet employees. These must be hired through a special agency, the Administration for Services to the Diplomatic Corps. This organization sets the terms of the employment contract. Unlike Soviet citizens, foreign capitalists may employ Soviet employees in money-making business operations.

As indicated above, the vast majority of employment contracts are created by the voluntary decision of the prospective employee. Despite the existence of a "full employment" policy, carried out by restrictions on migration to cities and by planning to avoid layoffs and plant closings, a "matchmaking" function is needed to get prospective employers and employees together. In major cities there are labor placement offices subordinate to the state committee on labor of the council of ministers of the republic. These offices not only link prospective employees with local job openings, but also recruit workers for other locations, for instance, for major construction projects in distant areas.[36] While at one time there was a great deal of recruitment from farms for urban work, the situation has changed. Urban work now requires higher skill levels that farm youths are less likely to have and there is a shortage of farm labor. As a result, recruiting for urban work is largely done from the urban population.

Uneven birth rates and uneven agricultural productivity have led to an excess population of farm families in some areas of the Soviet Union and to shortages of farm families in other areas. As mentioned above, it is difficult or impossible for the typical farm family to move to a city. Few urban families would want to move to a farm. Thus, the only solution to these problems would appear to be the movement of families from one farm to another. Such movement has occurred in substantial numbers in recent years, both on an unplanned and a planned basis. The wide availability of land in rural areas and the willingness of farm families to accept log cabins without modern facilities has allowed farms to overcome the housing barrier that has prevented urban organizations from recruiting families. The planned program for farm family movement is based upon legislation of 1968 and 1973. The program is under the supervision of the State Committee on Labor and Social Matters of the USSR. Farm families that volunteer for this program are given substantial benefits.[37]

Party members can obtain assistance in finding jobs through Party organizations. At times they may come under pressure from the Party to take particular jobs.

Soviet labor law deals not only with individual employees, but also with "labor collectives." The "labor collective" consists of all the employees at an enterprise, including the management. Soviet law glorifies the labor collective and exhorts it to greater efforts, while giving it no significant legal rights. This propaganda effort is enshrined in the "Law on Labor Collectives," a legislative act much praised by Soviet writers, despite the fact that it entails no real legal consequences, creating no enforceable rights or duties.[38] A similar propaganda effort is the practice of making "collective contracts" each year at each enterprise between the "trade union" and the management.[39] Since all important terms of the contract are dictated by legislation and the economic plan indicators, there is nothing to negotiate in these contract negotiations. Once made, these "contracts" are not enforceable in court. The whole process serves a dual propaganda purpose. One is part of the whole pretense that the Soviet Union has real trade unions. Since real trade unions negotiate collective bargaining agreements, Soviet trade unions should do the same, just as the Supreme Soviet carries out the charade of functioning like a real parliament. The other is the exhortatory function of stating clearly in writing the tasks that are to be achieved under the plan, as a step in "trade union"/management cooperation to perform these planned tasks.

The Labor Contract and Its Terms

The Labor Code provides that there is an individual "labor contract" between each employee and his employer. This contract is not a civil law contract, and its provisions are governed by labor law, not civil law.[40] However, unlike the propagandistic "collective contract," the individual labor contract is a real contract in the sense that it imposes very definite rights and duties on each party that can be enforced in court. In the cases listed above where an employee is compelled to take a specific job, it is a planned contract, or, more precisely, a contract based on administrative commands. In most cases, however, it is planned only in the sense that the enterprise is authorized, but not required, to hire a particular number of employees.

The main types of labor contract are those for an indefinite term, those for a definite term, and those for the performance of specific work.[41] Contracts for an indefinite term are the most common. Indefinite term contracts are not concluded in writing, because the Labor Code specifies all of their terms. Instead, the employee merely begins work and is listed in the records of the employer as an employee.[42] The employment contract, in combination with the labor legislation, gives the employee definite rights with respect to job assignment, working time, time off, and salary, and the employer definite rights with respect to labor discipline.

The labor contract is for a specific job. A person hired to operate a drill press cannot be transferred to sweeping floors, even at the same pay, without his consent. Nor can he be transferred to a different plant in a different city. Normally the only change in job assignment permissible without the employee's consent is to another identical job in the same location.[43] In cases of production necessity, for instance, bailing out water from a flood, workers may be transferred temporarily to another job without their consent.[44]

The work day, work week, and vacation lengths are set by legislation. The normal work week is a 5-day, 41 hour week. Special work weeks are set up for factories that run continuously on shifts, for public service enterprises that must run on weekends, and for other organizations with special needs. Overtime work is discouraged by labor legislation and must be paid at a higher rate. Workers earn annual vacation credit, with longer vacation times for workers with a long unbroken work record. Extra time off is given to persons combining work and study.

The labor contract provides the employee with guaranteed pay for his work. Wages are set under a complex system approved by the State

Committee on Labor and Social Matters. Ordinary workers are classified by skill level. They are paid according to wage-rate handbooks. There are general handbooks covering the whole economy, supplemented by special handbooks for certain branches of the economy. The wage rate specified by the handbook is adjusted for geographical location—for instance, a percentage is added to the handbook wage for workers in the Far North. Production workers are typically paid a guaranteed base wage rate plus a piecework or performance-based supplement. Depending upon production conditions this supplement may be based upon the results of the work of the individual worker or of the group of workers with whom he performs a joint task. Office workers are paid a salary, also set on the basis of uniform handbooks. This salary may be supplemented with bonuses based upon the results of the work of the enterprise. In addition to these systems of pay in accordance with work done, various fringe benefits may be provided from incentive funds based upon enterprise profits.

In ordinary enterprises discipline is governed by "Rules of Internal Labor Order." These are based upon Model Rules of Internal Labor Order approved for the whole country, and upon branch rules, based upon the model rules, and adapted to particular areas of the economy. As an exception, transportation, and communications organizations have "Discipline Charters" providing for stricter discipline, for instance, the kind of discipline a ship's captain has over the crew on an ocean voyage. To a large extent the Rules of Internal Labor Order paraphrase the labor code in somewhat less legalistic language.

A number of provisions of the Model Rules are hortatory, telling workers to work well and management to manage well. The most important part of the Model Rules is the chapter on Responsibility for Violating Labor Discipline, which is based upon the corresponding chapter of the Labor Code. The Rules provide a series of different penalties which may be imposed upon employees who violate disciplinary requirements. These include a warning, a reprimand, a severe reprimand, transfer to lower paid work or an inferior position for up to three months, discharge, reduction of seniority supplement for up to three months, reduction of annual leave, and deprivation of bonus payments.

Labor discipline is also maintained by so-called "Comrades' Courts." The Comrade's Court is an institution that traces its roots back to the early days of Soviet power. The Comrades' Courts are theoretically non-governmental institutions, whose function is to bring social pressure to bear on wrongdoers. Comrades' Courts are organized both at factories and places of residence. The main function of these courts at factories is to bring pressure to bear upon violators of labor discipline. These courts are entitled to hear cases involving absenteeism, drunkenness, tardiness, and other violations of labor discipline. The sanctions they can impose in labor cases are very limited: demanding a public apology, giving a comradely warning, imposing a social censure, making a social reprimand. In addition, they can propose to management that the employee be moved to a lower-paid position temporarily as a punishment, propose discharge of an employee who, under the labor law, can be fired for loss of trust, or propose that, in accordance with the labor code, the employee be deprived of benefits because of his disciplinary infraction. However, in these cases, the employer can only impose sanctions that would be allowed in any event under the labor code. A sanction, even just a "comradely warning," by a Comrades' Court does have one important legal effect. It can serve as the prior disciplinary offense that is required for discharge under the Labor Code provision allowing discharge for repeated disciplinary infractions.

A rather elaborate legal structure exists governing the financial responsibility of the employee for damages caused to the employer. The cause of these damages may be intentional, as in the case of theft by the employee, negligent, as in the case of careless breakage of equipment, or unknown, as in the case of shortage in a cash register. Because of the relatively strong guarantees of job security in the labor code, discharge, which might be the common remedy for employee theft or negligence in many countries, is not so readily available in the Soviet Union. The planning system also discourages discharge. As long as a worker is contributing something to the fulfillment of the plan and no better workers are available, it is worthwhile for the enterprise to continue to employ him even if he is not very competent. Given the limited financial resources of most Soviet citizens, full financial responsibility could be ruinous or uncollectible in many cases. Therefore, the law, with some important exceptions, limits recovery by the enterprise to a fraction of one month's pay, regardless of the amount of damage caused. The seriousness of the effect of a damage claim upon an employee calls for some protection of his rights. The law therefore provides procedural safeguards for the employee to contest his liability in court or through factory dispute settlement procedures.

All employees are financially responsible for damages they cause at least to the extent of one-third of their average earnings for one month. If physical damage is done to materials, goods, or instruments, they are liable up to a maximum of two-thirds of one month's earnings. Managers guilty of allowing losses due to excess payments, improper accounting procedures, or poor protection of valuables are liable up to one whole month's earning. Managers who have improperly discharged or transferred an employee in clear violation of labor legislation or who have disobeyed a court order to reinstate an improperly discharged employee are liable up to a limit of three month's pay (to reimburse the enterprise for what it has had to reimburse the improperly discharged employee for lost wages).

In a number of cases, employees, including managers, are liable without limit. Employees who have signed a written contract to undertake such full liability are fully liable. A list is provided by legislation of those jobs for which such contracts are required. Contracts providing for full liability of employees in jobs not on this list are void. Employees may also be fully liable for items entrusted to them for which they have signed a specific receipt and full liability agreement. Employees are fully liable in cases where they have committed criminal acts resulting in harm to the enterprise. When a procurator brings a criminal case against an employee for stealing from an enterprise, he also usually includes a civil claim on behalf of the enterprise for restitution of the amount stolen. Employees are also fully responsible for damage caused when they are drunk. This provision was added as part of the labor discipline and antidrunkenness campaign of 1983. Full responsibility also applies in cases where the damage was caused by intentional conduct on the part of the employees. It also applies where the damage was done outside the course of the employee's duties (for instance, if an employee, on his day off, drove his car into a truck belonging to his enterprise).

An alternative to individual responsibility under contract for full responsibility is brigade responsibility. Often it is very difficult to tell who is responsible for damage where a group of employees work together. By getting all the members of the group or "brigade" to sign a contract for full responsibility, the employing enterprise avoids the problem of having to decide exactly who is liable. In addition, it creates social pressures within the brigade for members to prevent one another from causing damage.

A problem is caused by the fact that the prices at which Soviet enterprises buy goods are often less than retail prices for the same goods. To avoid temptations for employee theft, the law provides that in case of theft or intentional damage the employee must make reimbursement at the retail price.

At one time all enforcement proceedings for employee financial responsibility had to be brought through the courts. The result was that the vast majority of labor cases in the courts involved financial responsibility enforcement. The 1983 "Andropov" reforms aimed at tightening labor discipline provide that the employer can merely deduct damages from an employee's pay if the amount was less than one-third of one month's average earnings. The employee may object to the deduction, but he must exhaust his remedies within the enterprise with the labor disputes commission and the local committee of the "trade union" before he can go to court. Undoubtedly this reform has greatly reduced the number of court cases involving damage recovery.

Termination of the Labor Contract

With some important exceptions, an employee is free to terminate his labor contract at his discretion, by giving two months' notice to the employer (one month's notice or less is allowed where the employee has a "compelling reason" for quitting, e.g., where he has just been admitted to the day program of a university.[45] Jobs for a fixed term, including those of students assigned to work after graduation cannot be terminated unilaterally by the employee.

Even where an employee is free to quit, voluntarily leaving a job may have serious negative legal consequences. Under certain circumstances moving from job to job may cause a substantial loss of pension rights.[46] If an employee's housing is supplied by the employer, the employee may lose the right to live in the housing if he quits his job.[47] As mentioned above, many men are employed with temporary residence permits to do jobs such as heavy construction labor.[48] Such workers are typically supplied with accommodations in a dormitory belonging to their employer. If a worker with such a temporary permit quits his job, he will lose both his room and his residence permit. Presumably such a worker could return to the farm or village from which he came. However, he cannot stay in the city in which he was working, unless he can immediately obtain another job that provides a residence permit. Thus, temporary workers are effectively barred from taking the vast majority of jobs in the city where they live.

Persons in yet another category face residence permit difficulties as a sanction for quitting; merchant seamen, whose work involves constant movement, are in this category. Secret legislation governs their residence permits.[49] The fact that this secret legislation was coordinated by the issuing authority with two dozen industrial and transport ministries suggests that employees subject to the legislation are found in a large number of industries. The secret legislation creates a category of persons without a permanent residence permit anywhere, for instance, merchant seamen without a home port. Such persons would face highly limited options if they wished to quit their present jobs. Before quitting, they would have to plan carefully, either to line up employment that carried with it at least a temporary residence permit, or to go to some town where they could buy or rent private housing and thus obtain a residence permit—something impossible to do in a major city. Otherwise, they could neither remain legally in the city where they left their ship or their job nor move legally anywhere else.

Collective farmers who stop working on the collective farm lose their collective farm membership and with it their right to the plot of land allocated to them as members for private farming operations.

Employers are less free to discharge workers than workers are to quit. Employers may only terminate a contract on one of the grounds listed in the labor code.[50] Employees may be divided into three groups with respect to the substantive grounds upon which they may be discharged: ordinary employees, those with special protection against discharge, and employees with special responsibilities who may be discharged on special grounds in addition to the ordinary grounds for discharge. As will be seen below, the procedural remedies for employer violations of discharge regulations also differ, depending upon the class of employee, with ordinary employees having the best procedural remedies.

The grounds of discharge available with respect both to ordinary employees and to employees with special responsibilities are the following and no others: liquidation of the enterprise or reduction in staff; a finding that the employee is unsuited to the position held; systematic violation of duties by a worker previously disciplined; unexcused absence; disability for longer than four months; reinstatement of a worker who previously held the same job; and appearing at work drunk.[51] The USSR Supreme Court has provided extensive guidance on the application of these criteria.

One of these grounds is "reduction in staff." However, there is substantial political pressure upon employers not to use this ground in a manner that would create any significant number of unemployed workers in a given locality. In the case of a reduction in staff, the court must determine whether or not the employee's discharge was caused by an actual reduction. If it was, the court must determine whether or not it was in fact impossible to transfer the employee to other work within the same enterprise. In addition, the law provides an order of priorities for remaining at work where a reduction in staff affects some but not all employees. Employees with high productivity, with a large number of dependents, with disabilities, members of the family of military service personnel, and certain other categories are supposed to be favored.[52]

The category of unsuitability for the position held covers at least three distinct grounds for firing: (1) an employee unable to meet the minimum performance requirements for the job held; (2) an employee whose state of health makes it dangerous for himself to continue work; and (3) an employee in certain occupations (e.g. food service, medical care) who has an infectious illness dangerous to others.[53]

Systematic violation of duties by a worker previously disciplined is a ground for discharge. It does not matter whether the systematic violation is negligent or intentional. The previous disciplinary measures include both those imposed by formal disciplinary procedure and by comrades' courts and nongovernmental organizations. Disciplinary sanctions that have expired in accordance with time limits specified by law are not considered.

Unexcused absence has long been a ground for discharge under Soviet law. Until 1983, the absence had to be for a complete working day. Legislation passed in 1983 to strengthen labor discipline provided that absence of 3 hours or more constituted a basis for discharge.[54] The most common excuse for absence is illness. Doctors are given a quota of "sick certificates" that they can issue to patients. These certificates automatically excuse absences. An employee can, however, prove in court that he was ill and therefore should be excused, even though he does not have a "sick certificate."[55] Absence from work for over four months as a result of temporary disability is a ground for discharge. Pregnancy and maternity leaves are not counted in the four months. Absence as a result of job-connected temporary disability is not a ground for discharge no matter how long the disability lasts.[56]

An employee may be discharged on the basis of reinstatement of a worker who previously held the position only if it is impossible to transfer the employee with his consent to another position.

Certain categories of workers have greater job security, except in cases of complete liquidation of the enterprise where they have been working. Temporarily disabled workers may be discharged only under the four-month disability provision. Workers on annual vacation leave may not be discharged. Pregnant women, nursing mothers, and mothers with children up to one year old cannot be discharged, except in case of liquidation of the enterprise, and even then other jobs must be found for them. Personnel summoned to military training meetings cannot be discharged from the time they receive the call until the meeting is over. Men subject to the military draft cannot be discharged, except for systematic violation of labor discipline, during the year in which they are to be drafted. Special rules protect young people, and persons suffering from war or job-related disabilities.

Certain categories of workers are subject to additional grounds for discharge. These include: a single gross violation of labor obligations by an employee subject to discipline by superior authority; guilty actions by one caring for money or valuable goods, if these actions cause a loss of faith on the part of the administration; commission of an amoral act by one having educational responsibilities; sending by a court of an employee to a labor-treatment institution, for instance, for narcotics addiction.

In general, an employee may be discharged only with the consent of the local committee of the "trade union." There are, however, a number of important exceptions. Executives may be fired without the consent of the local committee; the same is true of research scholars discharged for failure to achieve "reattestation." Teaching professors must qualify for reappointment at regular intervals. Complaints may be taken to court by a person who considers that he is an ordinary employee, but has wrongly been treated by management as an executive or scholar. The courts have generally interpreted the list of executive jobs narrowly, in borderline cases giving the employee the benefit of the more favored ordinary employee status. Nevertheless, the steady increase in the average educational level and the growth in the number of scholars will gradually increase the number of persons in the categories that do not have access to the normal dispute resolution procedures. From an examination of the lists of occupations where consent of the local committee of the "trade union" is not required for discharge, it appears that two factors are at work: professional and political. Some of those included on the list have such important managerial positions that it is clearly necessary from an operational point of view for higher management to be able to replace them if they cease to perform well. In addition it is politically necessary that that management be able to replace these employees on the basis of published or secret guidelines or specific orders from higher Party or state authorities. These managerial employees include persons with such jobs as heads of enterprises, institutions, and organizations, head engineers, and chief accountants. The other category consists of persons with politically sensitive positions, whether or not the jobs involve true executive work. Such persons include, for instance: police investigators, elected officials, Intourist guides, and diplomatic couriers.

Other categories of employees subject to discharge by management without "trade union" consent include employees who got their position through a competition, but who have lost in a competition for a new term in the same position; those who have been employed for a fixed term, which has expired; part-time employees who hold another job full time; and probationary employees failing to meet the necessary standards.

In a few cases third parties have the legal right to cause termination of a labor contract. Officially these third parties include "trade union" bodies at the district or higher level, courts (imposing punishment), and a military committee in cases where the employee is drafted or volunteers for the armed forces. Unofficially, Party or KGB agencies may bring about the discharge of employees.[57] Under Article 37 of the Labor Code, a "trade union" body at the district or higher level may require the administration to discharge or transfer a managerial employee if he violates labor legislation, fails to fulfill obligations under the collective contract, or acts in a bureaucratic manner. The employee may complain to a higher "trade union body," but not to the courts. The People's Control Committee may suspend an employee, but removal must come through regular procedures. If someone is employed illegally, he must be discharged at the demand of the Procuracy or other appropriate authority. Typical cases involve the employment of minors and the employment of recent graduates by organizations other than those at which they were assigned to work. If women or young people are employed at jobs restricted to males or adults, they must be offered a transfer before being discharged.

There are a number of crimes listed in the criminal code for which convicted persons may be removed from their occupation. These include such crimes as production of substandard goods (Art. 130) and abuse of authority (Art. 170). In addition, a person may lose his job if he is deprived by court sentence of the permission to engage in a particular occupation, is sent to a labor camp or an alcohol or drug treatment center.

Finally, though there is no clearly applicable provision in published legislation, anyone in the Soviet Union may be fired for political reasons such as retaliation against the distribution for dissident writings. If the target of a political firing is an executive or scholar, he may be fired using the expedited procedures that apply to these categories of employees. If he is an ordinary employee, the procedure is more difficult, because of the limited number of grounds for discharge provided by the labor code and because of the right to court review. Typically, the tactics used are similar to those used by management to rid itself of an undesired employee. The employee will be carefully watched, and the most severe possible penalty will be given for the violation of any rule. A contrived "reduction in staff" may be arranged, to eliminate the employee's job. Evidence of "unsuitability" for the job may be gathered or fabricated as necessary. If the employee takes the case to court, the court, realizing that it is dealing with a political discharge, will not examine closely the purported grounds for discharge.

Procedures for Deciding Employer/Employee Disputes

Employee morale is an important factor in labor productivity. The availability of procedures that seem fair for resolving employer/employee disputes is an important factor in maintaining employee morale. Consequently, the provision of such procedures is an important function of Soviet labor law. In general, the procedures are fairly administered in ordinary labor disputes involving ordinary employees. Executives have no effective procedural guarantees of job security. In the relatively small minority of cases where an employee is discharged for political reasons, the formalities of the procedures may be followed to the letter, but the employee is sure to lose. Over the past three decades, a series of reforms have moved the vast majority of disputes from the courts to "trade union"/management bodies within the enterprise. There are two basic types of employee/employer disputes that find their way to court. These are damage claims brought by the employer against the employee and grievance claims brought by the employee against the employer (usually claiming wrongful discharge or improper calculation of wages).[58] The number of damage claims was 200,000 in 1963 and was 200,000 in 1982. While this was no change in absolute numbers, it represented a substantial drop in claims per employee, because of growth in the labor force. As will be explained below, reforms enacted in 1983 undoubtedly have substantially reduced this number. Court cases involving other types of employer/employee disputes have fallen from 633 per 100,000 employees in 1956 to 42 per 100,000 employees in 1982. In addition to procedural reforms, improved legal work at enterprises probably explains some of the drop in the number of cases. There has been a substantial increase in the number of enterprise legal counsel and in the average educational level of these counsel over the past 30 years. This means that today, when an enterprise fires an employee, it is much more likely to succeed in complying with the formalities provided by law, and therefore the employee is much less likely to have any hope of overturning his discharge in court.

Labor disputes may be divided into three categories, those that may be taken directly to court, those which must first be considered by dispute resolution bodies within the enterprise, and those decided administratively by higher agencies. Claims by the administration to recover damages greater than one-third of an employee's average monthly earnings must be taken directly to court. Also, ordinary employees must take wrongful discharge claims directly to court. Other disputes involving ordinary employees go first to the commission on labor disputes at the enterprise, a body made up of 50% "trade union" and 50% management representatives. Disputes involving the discharge of, or certain bonus payments to executive-level employees are decided administratively. If there is a tie vote in that Commission, the dispute is decided by the local committee of the "trade union." If the employee loses in the commission, he may appeal to the local committee. If the employer loses in the commission, it has no appeal.

If the case does go to the local committee, either because of a tie vote or on employee appeal, the decision of the local committee may be appealed to the courts by the losing party. The procedures are specified by the 1974 Statute on the Procedure for Consideration of Labor Disputes, as amended. There are three further ways the local committee can obtain jurisdiction over a dispute. It may consider the substance of a decision by the commission on labor disputes when asked to issue an execution order because the employer has not voluntarily complied; it may take up a case considered by the commission and consider the substance of its own accord; or it may consider the substance on the basis of a protest by the Procuracy.

Very short statutes of limitations and requirements of speedy decision-making are designed to ensure speedy resolution of labor disputes. A 1983 law reduced the time limit for employees to bring complaints before the Commission on Labor Disputes to three months. The employer has only 10 days to appeal an adverse decision of the Commission to the Local Committee. The employee and employer each have only 10 days to appeal a decision of the local committee in court. If a labor dispute is brought to court, under Article 99 of the Civil Procedure Code it is supposed to be heard within 10 days of the time the complaint is filed.

If the administration does not voluntarily carry out a decision of the Commission on Labor Disputes or the Local Committee in favor of the employee, the employee has the right to receive an execution order from the Local Committee. This order may be presented to the court, where it will be executed in the same manner as a court judgment.

Quite different rules prevail for executives and scholars. Those on the two lists discussed above can appeal to higher administrative agencies (or the Procuracy) only if they believe they have been wrongfully discharged. Such persons have no right to obtain reinstatement through the courts.

Notes

1. *Sbornik normativnykh aktov o trude* (Moscow: Iuridicheskaia literatura, 1984–1985).

2. T. Merov, "Violations of ILO Conventions by the USSR and Czechoslovakia," *American Journal of International Law*, 74 (1980): 206–211.

3. A fascinating account of the transition period by the head of the Department of Social Insurance in the Provisional Government's Ministry of Labor is S. M. Shvartz [S. M. Schwarz], *Sotsial'noe strakhovanie v Rossii v 1917–1919 godakh* (New York: Columbia University Russian Institute, 1968).

4. Originally, the powers and role of the People's Commissariat of Labor were determined by the provisions of "Obshchee polozhenie o narodnykh komissariatakh SSSR," *SU RSFSR*, 1923, No. 106, item 1031. A revised statute of the People's Commissariat of Labor was adopted in 1928: "Polozhenie o Narodnom Komissariate truda," [Statute on the People's Commissariat of Labor], *SZ SSSR*, 1928, no. 62, item 563.

5. *SZ SSSR*, 1933, No. 40, item 238.

6. *SP SSSR*, 1976, no. 26, item 170.

7. Yurii Luryi, "Economic Modernization and Legal Problems of Professional Training of Workers in the USSR," in Peter B. Maggs, Gordon B. Smith, and George Ginsburgs, eds., *Law and Economic Development in the Soviet Union* (Boulder: Westview, 1982), p. 55; Michael Swafford, "The Socialization and Training of the Soviet Industrial Labor Force," in Arcadius Kahan and Blair Ruble, ed., *Industrial Labor in the U.S.S.R.* (New York: Pergamon, 1979), p. 19.

8. "Ob ustanovlenii edinoi pasportnoi systemy po Soiuzu SSR i obiazatel'noi propiske pasportov," *SZ SSSR*, 1932, no. 84, item 516. A decree of Sept. 10, 1940, extended the system to territories annexed under the Hitler-Stalin pact and made new rules for major population centers, border areas, and rail centers. *SP SSSR*, 1940, no. 24, item 591. Further important legislation was adopted in 1974: *SP SSSR*, 1974, no. 19, item 109, 110. See Viktor Zaslavsky and Yuri Luryi, "The Passport System and Changes in Soviet Society," *Soviet Union/Union Sovietique* 6 (1979): 137–53; L. Boim, "The Passport System in the USSR, with Special Reference to the Status of Jews," *Review of Socialist Law* 2 (1976): 15; Kronid Liubarskii, "Istoriia razvitiia pasportnoi sistemy v SSSR i ogranicheniia prava na svobodnyi vybor mesta zhitel'stva vnutri strany," in Leon Lipson and Valery Chalidze, eds., *Papers on Soviet Law*, No. 3 (New York: Institute on Socialist Law, 1981), 40–64.

9. Iu. M. Kozlov, B. M. Lazarev, A. E. Lunev, M. I. Piskotin, ed., *Sovetskoe administrativnoe pravo: Upravlenie v oblasti administrativno-politicheskoi deiatel'-nosti* (M. Iuridicheskaia literatura, 1979).

10. "Trudguzhnalog," *SU RSFSR*, 1921, no. 78, item 658; "Trudovaia povinnost'," 1922 Code of Laws on Labor, Arts. 11–14.

11. *SU RSFSR*, 1923, no. 42, item 451; no. 114–115, item 1053.

12. Edicts of the Supreme Soviet of the USSR of Feb. 13, 1942, *Ved. SSSR*, 1942, No. 6; of Sept. 29, 1942, *Ved. SSSR*, 1942, No. 38; of April 15, 1943, *Ved. SSSR*, 1943, No. 14. Decree of April 13, 1942, *SP SSSR*, 1942, No. 4, item 60.

13. "Polozhenie o personal'nom raspredelenii molodykh spetsialistov, okanchivaiushchikh vysshie i srednie spetsial'nye uchebnye zavedeniia SSSR," (*Normativny akty*, p. 417); "O srokakh personal'nogo raspredeleniia molodykh spetsialistov okanchivaiushchikh dnevnye vysshie i srednie spetsial'nye uchebnye zavedeniia," *SP SSSR*, 1967, no. 15, item 100; "O raspredelenii lits, okanchivaiushchikh aspiranturu s otryvom ot proizvodstva," *SP SSSR*, 1969, no. 22, item 129; "Polozhenie o raspredelenii lits okanchivaiushchikh aspiranturu s otryvom ot proizvodstva," (*Normativnye akty*, p. 461).

14. *SP SSSR*, 1959, no. 17, item 139.

15. "Critique of the Gotha Programme," in Karl Marx and Frederick Engels, *Selected Works in Two Volumes* (Moscow: Foreign Languages Publishing House, 1962), II, 13, 36–37.

16. Naum Jasny, "Labor and Output in Soviet Concentration Camps," *Journal of Political Economy*, 59 (1951): 405–419.

17. Ger P. van den Berg, *The Soviet System of Justice: Figures and Policy* (Dordrecht: Martinus Nijhoff, 1985), p. 109–136.

18. Corrective Labor Code, Art. 83.

19. "O prinuditel'nom lechenii i trudovom perevospitanni zlostnykh p'ianits (alkogolikov)," *Ved. RSFSR*, 1967, no. 15, item 333.

20. "Ob Osnovykh napravleniiakh reformy obshcheobrazovatel'noi i professional'noi shkoly," *Ved. SSSR*, 1984, no. 16, item 237, Ch. IV, "Trudovoe vospitanie, obuchenie, professional'naia orientatsiia."

21. Harold J. Berman, *Justice in the USSR; An Interpretation of Soviet Law* (Rev. ed., enl., 1963: Vintage Books, New York), pp. 196–199.

22. RSFSR Criminal Code, Art. 209. For a detailed interpretation of this crime (under slightly different earlier legislation) see *Biulleten' Verkhovnogo suda SSSR*, 1976, no. 5, pp. 11–13.

23. R. Beerman "Soviet and Russian Anti-Parasite Laws," *Soviet Studies* (1960): 453.

24. Zakon o vseobshchei voinskoi obiazannosti [Law on the Universal Military Obligation], Oct. 12, 1967, *Ved. SSSR*, 1967, no. 42, item 552; as amended, *Ved. SSSR*, 1971, no. 47, item 453; 1973, no. 20, item 267; 1973, no. 28, item 369; 1974, no. 45, item 748; 1977, no. 9, item 158; 1980, no. 52, item 1121.

25. *SP SSSR*, 1965, no. 4, item 22., *SP SSSR*, 1965, item 96.

26. Fundamental Principles of Labor Legislation, Art. 80.

27. *Resheniia partii i pravitel'stva po sel'skomu khoziaistvu (1965–1971gg) (Moscow, 1971), p. 419.*

28. *SP SSSR*, 1979, no. 18, item 118, Para. 8(b).

29. *BNA*, 1973, no. 4, p. 16.

30. "Obshchee normal'noe polozhenie o tarife," *Tarifny biulleten'*, 1919, Issue 7. "Obshchee polozhenie o tarife," *SU RSFSR*, 1920, no. 61–62, item 276.

31. *SP SSSR*, 1971, no. 13, item 91.

32. *SP SSSR*, 1974, no. 8, item 38.

33. D. A. Loeber, "*Limitchiki*: On the Legal Status of Migrant Workers in Large Soviet Cities," *Soviet Union/Union Sovietique*, 11 (1984), 301.

34. *Migratsionnaia podvizhnost' naseleniia v SSSR* (Moscow: Statistika, 1974), 148–153.

35. "O garantiiakh i kompensatsiiakh pri pereezde na rabotu v druguiu mestnost'," *SP SSSR*, 1981, no. 21, item 123.

36. "Tipovaia instruktsiia o poriadke provedeniia organizovannogo nabora rabochikh," *Biulleten' Goskomtruda*, 1980, no. 4, p. 8.

37. The relevant legislation is collected in *Normativnye akty po ispol'zovaniiu trudovykh resursov* (Moscow: 1972), pp. 816–830.

38. *Ved. SSSR*, 1983, part 1, no. 15, item 78.

39. "O zakliuchenii kollektivnykh dogovorov na predpriiatiiakh," *SP SSSR*, 1966, no. 5, item 51; as amended, *SP SSSR*, 1976, no. 24, item 123, *SP SSSR*, 1984, part 1, no. 21, item 114.

40. RSFSR Code of Laws on Labor, ch. III.

41. RSFSR Code of Laws on Labor, art. 17.

42. RSFSR Code of Laws on Labor, art. 18.

43. RSFSR Code of Laws on Labor, arts. 25, 26, 27, 135.

44. RSFSR Code of Laws on Labor, art. 26.

45. "O dopolnitel'nykh merakh po ukrepleniiu trudovoi distsipliny," *SP SSSR*, 1983, part 1, no. 21, item 116, Para. 9. RSFSR Code of Laws on Labor, art. 31.

46. "Ob uvelichenii razmera nadbavki k pensii po starosti za neprerivnyi stazh raboty na odnom predpriiatii, v uchrezhdenii, organizatsii," *Ved. SSSR*, 1980, no. 13, item 40, as amended, 1983, no. 18, item 9.

47. Fundamentals of Housing Legislation, arts. 39–41.

48. B. S. Khorev and V. M. Moiseenko, ed., *Migratsionnaia podvizhnost' naseleniia v SSSR* (Moscow: Statistika, 1974).

49. Instruktsiia o poriadke propiski i vypiski lits, sviazannykh po rodu zaniatii s postoiannym peredvizheniem, Approved by Order of the Ministry of Internal Affairs of the USSR of March 31, 1970, no. 96, agreed upon by the Ministry of

the Gas Industry, the Ministry of the Navy, the Ministry of Transportation, the Ministry of the Shipbuilding Industry, the Ministry of Transport Construction, the Ministry of the Chemical and Oil Industry, the Central Statistical Administration attached to the Council of Ministers of the USSR, the Ministry of Melioration and Waterworks of the USSR, the Ministry of Forests and the Wood Processing Industry of the USSR, the Ministry of the Oil Extraction Industry, the Ministry of the Oil Refining and Oil Chemical Industry of the USSR, the Ministry of Defense of the USSR, the Ministry of Industrial Construction of the USSR, the Ministry of the Construction Materials Industry of the USSR, the Ministry of Fisheries of the USSR, the Ministry of Communications of the USSR, the Ministry of Rural Construction of the USSR, the Ministry of Agriculture of the USSR, the Ministry of Construction of the USSR, the Ministry of Heavy Industry Construction of the USSR, the Ministry of the Coal Industry of the USSR, the Ministry of the Chemical Industry of the USSR, the Ministry of Ferrous Metallurgy of the USSR, the Ministry of Energetics and Electrification of the USSR, the Main Administration of Geodesy and Cartography attached to the Council of Ministers of the USSR, the Ministry of River Shipping of RSFSR, *Spravochnik po zakonodatel'stvu dlia rabotnikov organov prokuratury, suda i ministerstva vnutrennikh del* (Moscow: Iuridicheskaia literatura, 1972). p. 374.

50. RSFSR Code of Laws on Labor, art. 29.

51. RSFSR Code of Laws on Labor, art. 33.

52. RSFSR Code of Laws on Labor, art. 35.

53. *Kommentarii k zakonodatel'stvu o trude* (Moscow: Iuridicheskaia literatura, 1981), pp. 61–62.

54. *Ved. RSFSR*, 1983, no. 51, item 1782.

55. *Kommentarii k zakonodatel'stvu o trude*, pp. 65–67.

56. RSFSR Code of Laws on Labor, art. 33, para 5.

57. Ger P. van den Berg, "The Right to Work and Politically Motivated Discrimination in Soviet Labor Law," *Review of Socialist Law*, 5 (1979), 251.

58. Ger P. van den Berg, *The Soviet System of Justice: Figures and Policy* (Dordrecht: Martinus Nijhoff, 1985), p. 221.

7

Distribution and Its Legal Forms

General Principles

Each Soviet economic entity distributes compensation to its employees for their labor and makes payment in some form to the state for its capital. With this labor and capital it produces goods or services, which must be distributed to other economic entities or to private citizens. Compensation for labor in the Soviet Union, as in other countries, is in the form of wages and fringe benefits. Collective farmers may be paid for their labor, at least in part, not with money but with agricultural products,[1] and, in turn, collective farmers are forced by this distribution in kind to engage in sales operations if they desire to transform their share into money.[2] Sharecropping is found in many countries, so this aspect of compensation also is not peculiarly Soviet. Payments by enterprises to financing agencies for the use of capital and transfer of profits to their owners are also common to socialist and capitalists economies. A purely Soviet phenomenon can be found not in the forms of distribution between producing entities and these entities' employees and owners, but in the regulation of the distribution of the producers' output to other economic entities. The planning of production, though of primary economic significance, is only the first stage of planning addressed to producers themselves. The plan also determines those entities that may acquire the producers' output, the quantity of products available to each potential acquirer, and the identity of the producer that will deal with each acquirer designated by the planning agencies. This kind of distribution is not a common phenomenon in most economic systems. It is found only in a planned economy, and, specifically, in connection with the form of economic planning adopted in the USSR. This chapter will concentrate upon the legal aspects of planned distribution.

The planning of distribution has certain features in common with the planning of production. In both cases planning is centralized, based on non-binding information received from the bottom of the economic system, and determined by mandatory directives emanating from the top. The interdependence of the two forms of planning is obvious. Without planning production one could not plan distribution, and, vice versa, without planning distribution, one could not ensure the appropriateness of the plan indicators established for production. Therefore, mutual coordination as a general prerequisite of comprehensive mandatory planning is especially important where production correlates with distribution. And one can predict what will be discussed in more detail below: since the Soviet authorities are incapable of achieving full coordination of planning for production, one can hardly expect optimum coordination in the plans connecting production and distribution. In Chapter 4, we discussed the problem of the instability of production plans. It must be clear that any modification of a production plan affects distribution plans. In turn, insofar as distribution is mandatorily planned, any modification of a distribution plan must affect a plan of production. There is one more feature common to these two types of Soviet planning. Plans of distribution create, to the same extent as do plans of production, administrative ("vertical") relations: the performance of both may be demanded by planning agencies and must be carried out by the addressees of planning tasks. However, the similarities between the planning of production and the planning of distribution end at this point, and the distinctions are no less important than the similarities.

First, production planning is comprehensive. In contrast, the planning of distribution is limited in a number of respects. Articles that are not important from the economic point of view or those which, as exceptions to the general rule, are not scarce in the USSR, nevertheless must be produced in accordance with production plans. Yet the sale of such goods does not rely upon plans of distribution and depends exclusively on agreements between producers themselves and their economic partners. Later on, we will see that this rule is subject to several restrictions, and that under certain circumstances the producer's discretion is not so unlimited as it might seem at first glance. Nevertheless, freedom from planning, completely unavailable in the production area, can be encountered in the area of distribution.

Second, production planning is unconditionally mandatory. In contrast, the planning of distribution sometimes does not have absolutely mandatory force: though producers are almost always bound by distribution plans, their partners frequently are not. Under certain circumstances and in accordance with the procedure established by the law, customers may at their discretion decline to take goods or services allocated to them by distribution plans, and neither planning agencies nor other agencies have the right to compel them to act otherwise. Details as to why, when, and under what circumstances opportunities for refusal arise and can be employed will be given below. It should be kept in mind that a refusal to follow planning commands, while entirely probihited in the sphere of production, may occur in the area of distribution.

Third, production planning creates only administrative ("vertical") relations. In contrast, the planning of distribution also leads to the creation of civil-law ("horizontal") relations. This occurs because distribution plans are addressed not only to producers but at the same time to the producers' trading partners. Planning agencies maintain administrative ("vertical") relations with producers, on the one hand, and with customers, on the other hand, and are empowered to require the fulfillment of distribution plans by both the former and the latter. Yet in addition, each producer and each of its customers indicated by distribution plans are involved in civil law ("horizontal") relations with one another: each of them is obliged to perform and is entitled to demand performance from the other of the economic tasks assigned by distribution plans. Details as to the correlation between "vertical" and "horizontal" relations resulting from distribution plans will be given below. It should be kept in mind that the combination of these opposite types of relations, while natural in the sphere of distribution, cannot be found in the area of production.

These are the most important differences between distribution and production plans. Distribution planning, however, is not identical in all areas of economic activity. It varies according to the type of production whose output is to be distributed. From this viewpoint, one must distinguish the production of goods, the construction of buildings, and the provision of services.

Production of goods is implemented by separate entities as holders of operative administration with respect to property previously allocated to them by the state as the owner. Of course, the less detailed their plans, the more freely these entities may make their own economic decisions. However, in the final analysis, their economic freedom is predetermined from above by the limited allocation of material resources as well as by the designation of the specific purposes of production activity and the volume of output. This is so regardless of whether the planned indicators are extremely specific or only outlined in general terms. And the Soviet leadership cannot allow the system of production of goods as a whole to be subject to a less stringent regime of centralized planning than is the standard model, despite varying approaches in individual cases. Without ensuring the regular development of the production of goods in accordance with the demands of the system they have established, the Soviet rulers could retain neither their economic monopoly nor the resulting political domination. Therefore production planning is comprehensive, regardless of whether the distribution of its output is planned or unplanned. Relying on such a degree of production planning, the Soviet leadership can take the liberty of allowing relatively flexible planning of the distribution of goods produced, and, in some cases, can entirely refrain from planning distribution.

Building construction is a different type of productive activity. It leads to the enlargement of existing production entities or to the creation of new enterprises. But this would be impossible without the movement of material and monetary resources from one economic entity to another and even between different branches of the Soviet economy. The specific method by which the resources necessary for building production move is of little consequence. Regardless of whether an economic entity may retain money that it otherwise would be obliged to transfer to the state or receives financing from the state for the new construction, under all circumstances building production relies upon the movement of capital. An economic entity, holding the right of operative administration, may not initiate these capital movements on its own. Such a decision can be made only by the authority that exercises the rights of ownership, not merely those of operative administration. And because it is the state that is the owner, building construction is entirely centrally planned. In contrast to the production of goods, which can be carried out before the consumers are identified or even if these consumers are not determined at all, building construction must be designated for specific customers from the very beginning, from the moment when it is first projected, long before it is started. Thus, one cannot plan building construction without at the same time planning the distribution of what is to be constructed. Both processes of planning, encompassing production and distribution, must be simultaneous and congruent in this case. Furthermore, because building construction can rely only upon centralized planning of a comprehensive character, the distribution of the output of building construction production also must be comprehensively planned on the same centralized level. Consequently, cases of the absence of planned distribution may be encountered in the area of production of goods, but never in the area of construction.

The provision of transportation services is also productive activity. The product is the movement of goods or passengers from one point to another. The technical peculiarity of transport activity is that its product (transportation) can be consumed only during the process of its production. But insofar as the transportation of goods is assumed, consumption of the output of transport activity is implemented during the process of exchange, when goods have already been sold and must be delivered by the seller or when purchaser itself must provide for the transportation of goods previously bought. Thus, transportation of goods, though involving a kind of production, is implemented in the area of exchange. Neither exchange nor goods production nor building construction are possible without transportation. Since, however, production ultimately leading to exchange and distribution directly preceding exchange are planned, then transport activity must be planned as well by means of indicators coordinated with the plans of production and distribution. The planned volume of transport services must correspond to the quantity of transportation necessitated by plans for the distribution of the output of ordinary and building production. This volume is also distributed by the plan in order to provide for the demands of all economic entities functioning in other areas of production activity. Thus, not only the production of goods and the construction of buildings but also the provision of transportation services are subordinated to a plan of distribution. However, planned distribution of transport services differs substantially from other types of planned distribution. There is no need, and it would be impossible, to plan transport services as comprehensively as the output of building production is planned. The transportation of goods does not involve the movement of capital; therefore, extremely centralized interference by the state as the owner is unnecessary. On the other hand, transport activity cannot be predetermined as precisely as is building construction: the overall demand for transportation is actually unpredictable. Therefore, a certain amount of transport activity must remain beyond planned distribution, and in this regard transport services are more similar to the production of goods than to building construction. The similarity is not, however, identity. As discussed above, if articles produced are plentiful or economically unimportant, the planning of distribution may be unnecessary. For transportation services, comprehensive planned distribution is impossible because of a number of possible unforseen circumstances: the overfulfillment of plans by entities engaged in production of goods or building construction, unexpected situations in which additional or immediate transportation is required, etc. Thus, in any event, centralized planning addressed to the transportation of goods does not completely preclude carriage of freight implemented without planned distribution.

As a matter of course, along with the areas discussed, there are other sectors of economic activity subordinate to general plans and subject to planned distribution. These include bank credit extended to economic entities and freight handling as an activity related to transportation. Special legislation governs some types of transportation, such as carriage of goods by sea and barge towing. We shall refer to the law regulating these areas of the economy for illustrative purposes and sometimes for substantive discussions. However, the production of goods, construction, and ordinary transportation services will be the principal objects of the analysis which follows. At the same time, planned distribution is supplemented to some extent by unplanned distribution, based, however, on certain administrative prerequisites. Each type of organized distribution relies upon its own legal bases, and therefore both planned and unplanned distribution deserve special examination.

Planned Distribution

The planning of distribution is implemented by different agencies depending on its objects and its goals. The legal provisions connected with this planning are dispersed among a great number of the same legislative acts governing production planning, as discussed in Chapter 4. Bearing in mind the significant incompleteness of the legislation itself, one must look not only to these provisions but also to established practice in order to determine the realities of distribution planning. Some change in this area has taken place as a result of Gorbachev's "concept of accelerating the social/economic development of the country on the basis of scientific/technological progress,"[3] which has led to a number of new decrees, among these the decree of the Central Committee of the Communist Party of the Soviet Union and the USSR Council of Ministers of July 12, 1985, "On the Broad Expansion of New Methods of Economic Activity and Strengthening their Influence on the Acceleration of Scientific/Technological Progress."[4] This decree relaxed centralized planning and broadened the discretion of the lowest links of the Soviet economic system, but was, however, applicable only to undertakings relating to the area of "scientific/technological progress" and exclusively where such undertakings were financed by the incentive funds of economic entities. Yet the role of incentive funds in Soviet economic development is so inconsequential that new methods of planning, financially restricted to these funds, actually cannot have a great effect on the dominant system of planning administration. Therefore, only this dominant system will be taken into consideration.

The distribution of the output of the production of goods is, in principle, a function of three agencies: the State Committee of Planning (*Gosplan*), the State Committee on Supply (*Gossnab*), and the USSR Ministry of Trade (*Mintorg*). We say "in principle" because sometimes higher or even lower agencies administer this process as well. For instance, distribution of the most important and extremely scarce objects must be approved by the USSR Council of Ministers. At the same time, republican agencies or local executive committees deal with the distribution of products produced by associations and enterprises of republican and local significance. However, the great preponderance of distribution planning is carried out by *Gosplan*, *Gossnab*, and *Mintorg*.

Gosplan does not have the planning of distribution as its main function. This agency deals primarily with the planning of production. However, the most important objects, included by the Soviet government on a special list, belong to what is called the "nomenclature" of *Gosplan*, and for output within this nomenclature *Gosplan* works out plans of distribution, usually binding, but sometimes subject to further government approval. The nomenclature of *Gosplan* determines its jurisdiction over distribution planning, regardless of whether the distributed objects are to be used in production or are consumer goods.

As an agency of production planning, *Gosplan* has all the data concerning the output of objects included in *Gosplan*'s nomenclature. All economic entities that have need of goods distributed by *Gosplan* must prepare the appropriate applications (*zaiavki*) and present these applications to their superior agencies by specified deadlines. The latter proceed in the same manner until an economic ministry or other central agency heading a separate branch of the Soviet economy at the All-Union level has the opportunity to work out a composite application (*svodnaia zaiavka*) indicating the general needs of the given branch as a whole. It need hardly be said that the applications of lower links are not binding on their superior agencies. Equally apparent is that composite applications are not binding on *Gosplan*. If consumption is the goal of distribution, then the ultimate result depends on discretion of *Gosplan*. In cases of production goals, *Gosplan* must coordinate the volume and character of distribution with the volume and character of each applicant's production plan. Otherwise, the applicant cannot be responsible for failing to fulfill the production plan or the corresponding portion of the distribution plan in which the applicant designated not as a purchaser but as a supplier.

In contrast to *Gosplan*, *Gossnab*, which implements distribution, performs its principal function restricted only in two respects: by the jurisdiction of *Gosplan* and by the goal of distribution. *Gossnab* may not distribute objects included in *Gosplan*'s nomenclature. It also may not plan the distribution of goods designated for consumption. Only objects designated for production purposes are distributed by *Gossnab*, unless their distribution is allocated to *Gosplan*. Soviet terminology uses the phrase "material-technical supply" for what American economists would call "supply of goods for use in production." Therefore, the distribution plan compiled by *Gossnab* is entitled "The Plan of Material-Technical Supply."

In order to work out the plan of supply, *Gossnab* must have at its disposal data of two kinds: the purchasers' requirements and the suppliers' projected output. The purchasers' requirements are brought to the notice of *Gossnab* by means of the same procedure that is employed with respect to *Gosplan*. In comparison with *Gosplan*, there is only one peculiarity of the structure of *Gossnab*. The latter's local agencies—administrations of material-technical supply—supervise, in connection with supply, the economic entities of All-Union significance situated in the areas of these local agencies' jurisdiction. Therefore, the applications of lower entities can be checked by *Gossnab*'s local administrations even before the composite applications of the highest agencies of various economic branches are examined by *Gossnab* itself. *Gossnab* receives preliminary information concerning the suppliers' projected output from the suppliers themselves and a final report from *Gosplan*. Since *Gossnab* deals only with the distribution of objects designed for production purposes, the coordination of distribution and production plans is in this case an even more significant issue than it is in the activities of *Gosplan*. In all other respects, *Gossnab* has a substantial amount of discretion.

Mintorg as a planning agency deals only with the distribution of consumer goods. Therefore, the distribution plan compiled by *Mintorg* is entitled "The Plan of Distribution of Goods for the People's Consumption." In this plan, producing entities are indicated as suppliers and trade entities appear as purchasers. Although producing entities are not subordinate to *Mintorg*, nevertheless it is *Mintorg* that plans the distribution of that portion of their output which is consumer goods. Trade entities are subordinate to *Mintorg* as a rule or are organized by consumer cooperatives as an exception to this rule.

Mintorg receives the data required for making the consumer goods distribution plan from two sources. *Tsentrosoiuz* presents a composite application outlining in general the demands of consumer cooperative trade enterprises. *Mintorg* itself compiles a composite application with respect to the demands of the Ministry's own trade enterprises. These sources, taken together, supply the data required for the determination of the needs of purchasers. Other information, provided by producers and by *Gosplan*, make available data concerning all suppliers and their planned output. This should be sufficient to compile the plan of distribution of consumer goods. Despite, however, the consumer goals of this plan, and the concomitant absence of the need to coordinate planned distribution and production consumption, the discretion of *Mintorg* as a planning agency in regard to this distribution is not unlimited. As emphasized above, the Soviet authorities have categorized various regions of their country from the viewpoint of their priority in the area of food supply. In addition, Party directives insist that every locality be provided with the bare necessities (bread and several other products) required to ensure the maintenance of human life. In elaborating the distribution plan, *Mintorg* may not disregard these indicators. Should the scarcity of consumer goods attain an alarming level, at which even the modest indicators of the distribution plan cannot be satisfied, the Soviet authorities resort to extraordinary measures in the appropriate cities or provinces, and sometimes throughout the entire country. They create a so-called *chrezvychainaia troika* (an emergency committee of three persons) at the All-Union level consisting of the Minister of Trade, a representative of the Central Committee of the Party and one additional official, or made up of the chief of the local department of trade, a representative of the local Party agency and one more local official. After its creation the "*troika*" resolves the day-to-day problems of food distribution in the given locality within the limits of the available resources and in accordance with the established system of priority: first of all kindergartens and then hospitals must be supplied, etc., while the general population is last in line. It is noteworthy that, even in situations where a "*troika*" has been created, the issue of the "closed" supply of the Soviet elite is not discussed, and, consequently, it is apparent that this supply remains intact even under extraordinary circumstances. In any event, when a "*troika*" is established the plan of distribution loses its force with respect to matters decided by the "*troika*."

Upon the confirmation of distribution plans, those who are to implement the plans must be notified of the plan indicators addressed to each of them. Notification is implemented by means either of a *nariad* (order) or of a *plan prikrepleniia* (plan of attachment).

The first method is employed almost exclusively in the area of material-technical supply. Ministries and other central agencies receive from the agency that has confirmed the plan of distribution allocation certificates (*fondy*). These are documents indicating the entire quantity of certain objects allocated to each addressee for the planned period. The allocations received must be distributed among subordinate entities as potential purchasers, and data concerning this distribution must be forwarded to the agencies planning supply. These agencies, relying upon the information received, issue *nariady* (orders) addressed both to potential purchasers and suppliers. The orders contain all of the planned indicators within the planned quota that has been allocated for a specific purchaser and supplier. As a result, the latter become participants in administrative ("vertical") relations with a planning agency and of civil law ("horizontal") relations with one another.

The second method is employed for consumer goods distribution and to some extent also for material-technical supply. In accordance with planned indicators established for one year (or, sometimes, for a shorter period of time), planning agencies attach each potential purchaser to a potential supplier. Both the purchaser and supplier receive from these agencies the required notification informing them of the *prikreplenie* (attachment) implemented and of the plan indicators determining in general the supply for the entire time-period during which *prikreplenie* (attachment) is to be in force. Relying upon the notification received, the potential purchaser sends its own order (*zakaz*) to the potential supplier, thereby specifying the general indicators of an annual plan. Administrative ("vertical") relations between planning agencies and addressees of the plan and civil law ("horizontal") relations between addressees of the plan arise immediately upon receipt by the addressees of the notification of the *plan prikrepleniia* (plan of attachment). These relations are further developed on the basis of the order (*zakaz*) sent by the potential purchaser to the potential supplier.

As a matter of course, planning notification can function efficiently only if it is issued in a timely manner. The law in force establishes the deadlines for the fulfillment of these duties by planning agencies.[5] However, a violation of these deadlines does not have significant financial consequences: the law requires the payment of a daily fine of only 25 rubles and the sum total of all such payments cannot exceed 250 rubles. It might seem at first glance that Soviet legislation strives to ensure the stability of confirmed plans, precluding any modification of plan indicators after an established date before the execution of contracts of delivery dictated by plan commands. But the same legislation actually capitulates, obliging suppliers and purchasers to modify their executed contracts in accordance with changes in plan indicators implemented by planning agencies after the deadline set by the law. In practice such changes usually occur more often than one can imagine, especially in cases where the most important objects are distributed. Thus, a *nariad* (order) for the supply of oil received by a Leningrad production association was changed six times in one year. Taking into consideration the fact that each change makes it necessary to modify the corresponding contract, to adjust the production process to the new contractual terms, and to modify a number of derivative legal connections, one will understand the degree to which the absence of stability in distribution plans is detrimental to the entire Soviet economy.

From the viewpoint of the distribution of the output of goods, agricultural production presents an extremely peculiar situation.[6] In all other cases, the distribution of a product is a prerequisite to its sale. But in the case of agricultural production, distribution is employed in order to determine what may be retained by the producer and what must be transferred to the state. Previously this distribution was regulated by a number of legislative acts, among which the following were the most important: the decree of the USSR Council of Ministers of April 23, 1970 "On the Unification of the Decrees of the Government of the USSR Concerning the Organization of the State Purchase of Agricultural Products,"[7] and the decree of the Central Committee of the Communist Party of the Soviet Union and the USSR Council of Ministers of July 7, 1983 "On the Improvement of Economic Relations Between Agriculture and Other Branches of the National Economy."[8] At the present time, one must also take into account a 1986 decree of the Central Committee of the Communist Party of the Soviet Union and the USSR council of Ministers, "On Further Perfection of the Economic Mechanism of Economic Activity in Agricultural-Industrial Complexes of the Country,"[9] and Soviet legislation addressed to the USSR *Gosagroprom* and its local agencies. Through these agencies the USSR *Gosagroprom* notifies all collective farms and other agricultural production entities of the relevant indicators from the confirmed plan of state purchase of agricultural products. This plan contains annual indicators, which are required to be stable for five years. On the basis of the plan indicators thus received, which have mandatory force, district agricultural-industrial associations, together with collective farms and other interested producers, draft plans for the sale of agricultural products to the state. Because the centrally-determined plan tasks are unconditionally binding, the draft plans only specify and supplement the imperative commands issued from "above." However, in order to formally observe so-called collective-farm democracy, collective farmers discuss and approve the suggested drafts at their general meetings. The law in force "recommends," in addition, that collective farms adopt, along with the planned obligations, also obligations to sell agricultural products to the state in a quantity over and above that called for in the plan. Despite the use of the word "recommendation" instead of the word "order," there are no collective farms that have ever refused to adopt a "recommended" part of a procurement plan. The 1986 decree mentioned above emphasizes the voluntary character of additional obligations and doubles the state procurement prices with respect to additional portions of agricultural produce sold to the state. In turn, the procurement plan is only a part of a collective farm's general plan, which encompasses all aspects of the distribution of the farm's output, indicating those portions that: (1) must be sold to the state in accordance with and above the planned quantity, (2) must be retained for the producer's current economic activity and for the replenishment of property funds required by law, and (3) may be freely sold at collective farm markets or through the trade enterprises of consumer cooperatives. In this way, the entire output of the collective farm is distributed in advance, and, in the subsequent process of performance, a principle that allows for deviation only on rare occasions must be observed: obligations toward the state are performed first, and only if these are fulfilled may the other portions of the farm's output be utilized.

The All-Union plan of agricultural procurement elaborated by the USSR *Gosagroprom* must be confirmed by the Government of the USSR. A similar situation exists with respect to the relations between republican governments or provincial executive committees, on the one hand, and republican or provincial *agropromy*, on the other hand. At the district level, where local *agropromy* have direct connections with collective farms and other agricultural producers, the situation is somewhat different. A draft plan coordinated with each collective farm and every other agricultural entity must be presented by the local *agroprom* to the district executive committee for confirmation. Once a draft has been transformed into a plan two types of relations are created: "vertical" or administrative (between the district executive committee and each collective farm or each other agricultural entity), and "horizontal" or civil law (between each collective farm or other agricultural entity and the appropriate state or consumer cooperative enterprise functioning as a procurement organization in behalf of the Soviet state).

Among the conflicts arising in the sphere of agricultural distribution, the problem of balancing the demands of the state with the needs of producers is the most significant. The deplorable situation of Soviet agriculture, incapable of providing a food supply for the country (to say nothing about providing food to satellite countries), induces the Soviet rulers to try to squeeze as much as possible out of collective farms. In turn, collective farms strive to retain at least that quantity of the different objects of their production sufficient for maintaining continuity in their agricultural production and an acceptable level of payment for the labor of collective farmers. Because of the basic insolubility of this conflict, in no other branch of the Soviet economy is "fakery" (*ochkovtiratel'stvo*) so widespread as it is in the agricultural area. Not infrequently, collective farm boards and chairmen understate the level of achievable indicators in order to obtain less intensive planned tasks than would otherwise be given them. They know, however, that such tricks are hopeless with respect to grain. Since the state must ensure a bread supply that is at least sufficient to satisfy the minimal demands of the populace, and because to do so requires that the Soviet leadership spend on the world grain market large amounts of hard currency that could better be used for the acquisition of technology and other more significant objects, state officials do their best to withdraw a greater quantity of grain from collective farms than is available according to these farms' own data. Manipulations in farm reports are more practicable with respect to meat, vegetables and other similar objects of agricultural produce. These objects cannot, of course, replace the grain necessary for collective farms' agricultural activity, but, withdrawn from the system of state procurement where they would have to be sold at very low fixed prices, they can be disposed of by free sale at much higher market prices, thus serving as an additional source of income from which increased payments can be made for the labor of collective farmers. The same purpose leads collective farms to engage in activities (road-building, transportation of goods, woodcutting, etc.) which are far removed from agriculture, but the payment for which allows the farms to maintain somehow the balance between expenses and income. Thus, the unbearable procurement tasks resulting from the constant lag of Soviet agriculture are, in turn, the cause of the further undermining of agricultural production in the USSR. However, in contrast to industry, where measures are being taken for development through a science and technology program, agriculture has not yet been addressed by the new Soviet leadership with measures of any significance. It seems that this vicious circle is evaluated by them as insurmountable, just as it was by their predecessors.

Owing to the circumstances discussed above, distribution in the area of building construction is more centralized than is distribution in the area of the production of goods. Apart from having the capacity to initiate those construction projects that can be built with customers' incentive funds, the lowest links of the Soviet economy actually take no part in planning in this sphere. Economic entities can, of course, request that specific projects be included in the centralized plan. However, except for collective farms and consumer cooperatives, which undertake construction projects with their own funds or with their centrally allocated funds, such requests have no legal force and do not represent a special phase of the planning process as is the case in the process of planned distribution of the output of the production of goods. A decree of the Central Committee of the Communist Party of the Soviet Union and the USSR Council of Ministers of July 12, 1979, cited earlier, which is known in the USSR as the Decree on the Economic Mechanism, centralized construction planning to an even greater degree than had previously been the case. Subsequent changes in the the Soviet leadership have not affected the established planning regulations. Drafts of construction plans are prepared by *Gosplan* and must be confirmed by the Council of Ministers. As a rule, these plans encompass five-year periods and contain plan tasks specified for annual periods. They deal with what in Soviet terminology is called "capital construction," i.e. construction projects involving significant capital investment, as opposed, for instance, to minor repairs. There are, in fact, two plans: (1) the plan of capital construction addressed to each ministry or other central agency, or to the Council of Ministers of each Union republic representing the potential customers, and (2) the plan of contract works, in which are determined, along with the central agencies of customers, also the central agencies of contractors. These plans include indicators concerning not only projected construction but also all of the ancillary processes connected with material-technical supply for the construction projects, financial and labor resources, etc. On the basis of these two plans, so-called title lists (*titul'nye spiski*) are confirmed. In these lists, each construction project is characterized in detail sufficient for the subsequent development of design and estimate documentation. Title lists may be confirmed: by the USSR Council of Ministers for the most important projects, and by All-Union ministries or republican governments in conjunction with *Gosplan*—or without *Gosplan*'s consent, depending on the value of the planned projects. In accordance with the value of a given project, determined by the plan and made more precise by the title list, the required financial resources must be allocated by the state budget. Thus, the planning of building production includes the distribution not only of construction works but also of capital investment provided by the state. The money allocated is usually transferred to the Construction Bank

(*Stroibank*) or, sometimes, to the State Bank (*Gosbank*). In either case the funds are deposited in the customer's account and are spent in accordance with the estimate and under the control of the bank. As to the design, which also is a planning prerequisite of capital construction, contractors and customers must, as a rule, employ one of the standard designs, and only in special cases may an individual design be ordered. Individual designs, blueprints for designs of any kind, and estimates that accompany designs are worked out by independent design entities. However, all these documents must be confirmed by the appropriate planning agency in order to complete the planning process of capital construction.

Much as for other types of planned distribution, in the area of building production, distribution plans entail two types of legal connections: administrative or "vertical" (between planning agencies, on the one hand, and potential contractors and customers, on the other hand), and civil law or "horizontal" (between contractors and customers themselves). In addition, however, a number of other legal links, both "vertical" and "horizontal," arise as a result of such planning. These links connect either the contractor or the customer, or sometimes both, with planning agencies and economic entities functioning in the spheres of supply, design, financing, etc. At the same time, the complicated set of legal relations established by the planning of capital construction is unified by one principle: maximal centralization, and minimal initiative.

The extreme centralism in the area of capital construction meets the political needs of the ruling elite to maintain its economic monopoly, but it undermines those economic incentives necessary for construction activity. While construction is under way, the customer, spending budget resources for an object under construction that will only later be transferred to it for the purpose of operative administration, has no direct interest in being as vigilant and as active as a customer should naturally be.[10] The contractor is interested in the timely completion of the construction project and in receiving payment upon completion. The proper functioning of an object after it is built is of no concern to the contractor. Moreover, since the customer is spending not its own funds, but money from the state budget, the contractor strives to exploit this situation in order to conceal the habitual lag in its work behind the planned schedule. Such results are commonly obtained by convincing the customer to acknowledge the completion of various stages of construction that actually have not yet been finished by the contractor. The absence of any economic interest on the part of those agencies that deal with preparatory work for the forthcoming plan need hardly be mentioned. But, as a result of this indifference, planning mistakes in the area of construction, though not so numerous, are far more egregious than in any other economic area. A real disaster in the area of Soviet construction is the so-called *konservatsiia* of unfinished construction projects.

Konservatsiia, semantically, means temporary closing. Sometimes, construction is temporarily halted quite legitimately because of unforeseen economic needs that require the redistribution of resources, or because of natural events impeding the construction process, etc. However, more often *konservatsiia* leads to the termination of the entire project. This sometimes occurs owing to the high-handedness of the Soviet rulers. Muscovites will never forget, for example, a splendid church that stood in the center of Moscow until it was destroyed shortly before World War II by order of Stalin, who had planned to build the Palace of Soviets in this location. Instead of the promised Palace, however, the Muscovites received a winter swimming pool. Yet such illustrations are extraordinary or even unique. Other events occur much more frequently and cause far more damage. Before including any given construction project in building plans, all of the circumstances that might negatively affect the proposed project are supposed to be studied carefully and assessed seriously. These requirements are, however, disregarded in a number of cases, and the consequences are truly deplorable. New buildings for a university had already been erected on the outskirts of a major city, when it was discovered that there was an insufficient source of drinking water at this location. Upon completion of the construction of a new plant, situated far from the sources of raw materials, the construction engineers finally made the calculations that should have been taken into consideration before planning the construction of the plant. According to the results of the calculations, it was found that it would have been cheaper to build a new plant close to the sources of raw materials than to deliver the required materials to the place where the plant had been built. In some eastern regions of the USSR, there are newly-constructed but entirely uninhabited cities surrounding plants and factories which cannot be exploited because of the absence of a labor force, the unbearable climate, etc. If the decisions regarding whether to construct these cities were left to the nearest local government agencies, such projects would never have been seriously contemplated. But the planning of capital construction is one of the most centralized functions in the USSR, and therefore certain preposterous results are inevitable.

As mentioned above, the distribution of the output of the production of goods and building construction is supplemented by the distribution of transportation services. Plans that govern the production of transportation services regulate carriage of all kinds: transportation of goods as well as of passengers. However, the planned distribution of transport services is directed only toward the transportation of goods and is aimed at transport enterprises as carriers and other economic entities as shippers. Plans for the carriage of goods are compiled separately for each type of transport. But, in the USSR, railroad transport retains the principal role in the area of goods transportation, and the system of planning employed in this case serves as a model for the planning of the carriage of goods by other types of transport. This allows us to limit our analysis of planned distribution of transport activities to a discussion of distribution in the railroad transport context.

Speaking abstractly, since the distribution of the output of the production of goods and building construction has already been planned, there should be no difficulty in drawing up a plan for the transportation of goods. The actual situation is, however, more complicated. On the one hand, demand for the carriage of goods stemming from the production of goods and building construction must be satisfied through the coordinated activities of all kinds of transport organizations. Thus, the distribution of the output of goods and construction must be supplemented by distribution of the corresponding transport needs among all types of functioning transport in order to form a basis for the planning of transport services. On the other hand, plans distributing the output of goods and construction have never been confirmed in a timely fashion. And if the planning of transport services were postponed until the issuance of other plans, the delay in the latter would cause such a delay in the former, that transport planning would be pointless. Bearing in mind these factors, the Soviet authorities employ with respect to the carriage of goods the same methods of planning that are common in the area of supply: first, information is sent from the bottom of the system, and then indicators are issued from the top.

Here too, planning practice is a more reliable source than are the legal provisions embodied in Articles 18–36 of the Statute of Railroads of the USSR.[11] In analyzing the law in force and current practice, one must bear in mind that, similar to production associations and independent enterprises of industry, the lowest links of railroad transport are "railroads." These are economic entities that administer and exploit strictly defined sections of the rail system and all of the equipment connected with these sections. Other establishments (railroad stations, railroad warehouses, etc.) can represent a railroad as an independent enterprise, but they are not entitled to function as juridical persons in relations with transport clients. Consequently, planning information is received from and planning tasks are addressed to railroads as transporters and other economic entities as shippers. Because the Ministry of Railroad Transport functions as the planning agency in this area, administrative ("vertical") relations are established between this Ministry and its railroads on the one hand and clients on the other hand, while railroads and clients are connected by civil law ("horizontal") relations. However, certain kinds of plans are confirmed by the railroads themselves. Under such circumstances, the railroad is connected to its client by administrative ("vertical") relations as a planning agency and by civil law ("horizontal") relations as a carrier.

There are annual plans of goods transportation including quarterly indicators and quarterly plans providing monthly indicators. The entire procedure begins with timely requests (*zaiavki*) produced by shippers, then transformed into composite requests by shippers' ministries or other central agencies, and finally presented to the USSR Ministry of Railroads. Shippers' requests must be based on confirmed plans for the distribution of industrial or agricultural output indicating the shippers as suppliers or as purchasers. Relying upon the data received, the USSR Ministry of Railroads prepares the annual plan of transportation including quarterly indicators. This plan, confirmed in substantial part by the USSR Council of Ministers and ultimately issued by the USSR Ministry of Railroads, outlines the general volume of planned transportation and specifies indicators for the transportation of different goods classified among homogeneous groups (nomenclatures). Annual plans, with their quarterly indicators, serve as prerequisites for the development of quarterly plans, with their monthly indicators. In contrast to annual planning, implemented only by the USSR Ministry of Railroads, quarterly planning is a function that can be carried out either by this Ministry or by each railroad, depending on the classification of the type of goods.

The USSR Ministry of Railroads notifies each ministry or other central agency of shippers of the indicators of the annual plans. In turn, the railroads inform each railroad station of its task of carriage, and the central agencies of shippers inform each shipper about their tasks of dispatch for the upcoming year. The indicators of quarterly plans are ultimately transmitted to their performers by the agency that has confirmed these plans, i.e. either by the USSR Ministry of Railroads or by the appropriate railroad which itself acts as a planner. Quarterly plans are more specific than annual plans, indicating the average norm of daily loading for the entire quarter, and the distribution of a quarterly volume of transportation over each month of the quarter and for each kind of goods expressed in terms of either the number of tons or the number of cars to be shipped.

On the basis of quarterly plans including monthly indicators, each shipper is required to present to the appropriate railroad detailed monthly plans of transportation that must be confirmed by the railroad with or without corrections. The monthly plan specifies the specific types of goods designated for transportation, the railroad stations of dispatch, and the destination railroads or sometimes even the destination railroad stations. Within each monthly period, the shipper presents a request (*zaiavka*) to the chief of the railroad station from which good are to be dispatched. This request is for the loading of goods during the following ten days. The shipper supplements these requests with daily loading schedules. Just prior to the beginning of each ten-day period, the chief of the railroad station informs the shipper of the transportation capacity that will be available during the following ten-day period and of the volume and types of goods which will be accepted daily for transportation. At this moment, the process of planning is finished and the performance of the plan can begin.

As is obvious, in transport planning, the lowest links of the Soviet economic system are more active than in other planned areas. This occurs simply because it cannot be otherwise under the prevailing circumstances. Central agencies may formulate a task of transportation, but if a shipper has no goods for transportation during a certain time-period or if the goods it is prepared to transport are of types different from that called for by the plan, much of the transport capacity of the appropriate transport enterprise, and many material resources would be wasted if the transporter and shipper were allowed no flexibility in their relations. Owing to the direct relations between the performers of transport plans during the planning process immediately preceding transportation, railroads can ascertain the amount of transport capacity that cannot be employed in accordance with the original plan and that therefore can be used for other purposes. This opportunity is extremely important, bearing in mind that Soviet transport in general, technologically backward and quantitatively insufficient, is one of the permanent bottlenecks of the Soviet economy. Therefore, while maintaining centralized management of transport as well as of the entire economy, the Soviet authorities allow to a certain extent for initiative on the part of the performers of transport plans in order to stimulate the utilization of any means of transportation that might otherwise remain unemployed because of the divergence between plans and reality. A certain loosening of centralized planning also results from the unpredictability of the quantity of additional transport services that might become necessary in the future. Therefore, annual and quarterly plans contain what are called reserve norms, putting certain capacity at the disposal of the chiefs of railroads and of railroad stations. Reserve norms can be employed in cases where shippers' demands increase in comparison with the plan indicators, and therefore these indicators must be correspondingly modified. In addition, one must take into consideration that a great many goods (those of Soviet institutions, individuals, etc.) are not transported according to mutually binding plans, and this too necessitates allocation of a reserve norm, which, though at the disposal of transport entities, plays an important role in the satisfaction of clients' needs.

In comparing distribution planning with production planning, one notices substantial distinctions between the former and the latter. As has been emphasized more than once, the more comprehensive planning is, the stricter plan coordination must be. This is true with respect to any type of planning, regardless of whether it governs production or distribution. However, a production plan is unilateral, i.e. it is issued by planning agencies and addressed only to producers. The planning agencies must, of course, ensure the required proportions between the indicators of interdependent producers, taking into account the Soviet economy as a whole, since the latter's output is planned *in toto*. But the producers themselves are not legally connected with one another on the basis of production plans, and, as a result, they cannot exercise any control over the degree of coordination achieved by planning agencies, nor can they seek to increase their control in the area discussed. In contrast, a distribution plan is bilateral, i.e., it too is issued by planning agencies but it is addressed to both producing and consuming entities. Therefore, in such cases any deviation from the required coordination will be ascertained immediately, and, through the legal means that are at the disposal of both addressees, each of them may strive to rectify any planning problems that negatively affect the normal rhythm of economic activity. Unfortunately, these legal means are not always efficient in practice because of economic or purely bureaucratic obstacles. But, at any rate, legally the interests of planned entities adversely affected by mistakes on the part of planning agencies can be protected in the area of distribution. The situation is more complicated in cases where distribution plans are not reinforced by consistent production plans. First of all, any divergence between these plans can be noticed only by producers, not by customers. But even if customers were informed of the absence of the required planning coordination, they could not employ any remedial measures with respect to the agencies planning production and thus dealing only with producers or the agencies planning distribution and thus dealing only with supply. Producers, on the other hand, may appeal to those agencies planning both production and distribution, in order to obtain modifications either of a production plan to bring it into accordance with a distribution plan or of a distribution plan to bring it into accordance with a production plan. If its appeal is successful, the producer's problem is solved. However, if success has been achieved through the modification of a distribution plan, the same problem (lack of coordination between production and supply) will immediately be felt by one or several customers. The latter, of course, may also appeal under these circumstances to the agencies planning either production or distribution. But a customer has this opportunity only long after the producers' demands have been submitted for consideration, and to be informed of the planning agencies' solutions, one must wait for an uncertain period of time. Meanwhile, the economic year is progressing, time is lost, and the performance of plans is running the risk of failure. As a result, the unwieldy method of planning plagued by unpredictable failures proves to be even more ineffectual by the complexity and the insufficiency of the legal remedies available for the rectification of the mistakes made by planning agencies.

All types of planning implemented in the USSR—production or distribution, unilateral or bilateral—are addressed to legal entities. Individuals have never been addressed directly by Soviet plans. This does not mean, however, that plans are irrelevant for individuals. Plans addressed to Soviet entities must be fulfilled by Soviet citizens—the workers and officials of these entities. The more demanding a plan, the more difficult its fulfillment and the less chance for an increase in the workers' salaries by means of bonuses or other incentives. Plans determine the distribution of economic resources between the production of consumer goods and the production of means of production. In Soviet practice, the latter has always prevailed over the former. The Principal Directions, adopted by the 1986 Party Congress, provide, for the period 1986–1990, an increase in the production of means of production by 20–23%, while production of consumer goods is to be increased by 22–25%.[12] But even if this task is implemented, the production of consumer goods will remain far behind the production of means of production. At any rate, the relative proportions of the resources allocated for each of these two areas of production may be different, but the degree to which consumer demands are satisfied directly depends on the proportions established between them. This is why Soviet citizens, though aware that there is a great distance between the plan and reality, pay such close attention to official information concerning those plan indicators that outline projected increases in the production of consumer goods in comparison with increases planned for the production of means of production. From the citizenry's viewpoint, the planning of retail trade is especially important. Each retail trade enterprise receives goods in accordance with a plan of distribution, and by selling the goods received each such an enterprise fulfills its trade plan. As a matter of course, neither of these plans is binding on citizens. They cannot be compelled by plans to buy anything, and their decisions depend on their own choice. But it is this planning that ultimately determines whether they will have an opportunity to make such choices. Therefore, Soviet plans, while addressed to legal entities, are not without effect upon the fulfillment of the desires of individuals. Citizens feel the weight of these plans on their backs, not legally but (and this is even more palpable) economically. In addition, one must not forget that organized distribution, always having an administrative character, can be planned and unplanned. Planned distribution, as discussed, is only economically significant for individuals. Unplanned distribution has legal importance for both organizations and individuals.

Unplanned Distribution

In contrast to planned distribution, applicable only with respect to legal entities, unplanned distribution deals to some degree with these entities, but is employed for the most part in relations between Soviet organizations and Soviet citizens. Similar to planned distribution, unplanned distribution is a form of administrative activity; however, the implementation of unplanned distribution is a function not of planning agencies, but of other administrative bodies.

In relations between legal entities, Arbitrazh performs the function of implementing unplanned distribution. As discussed in Chapter 2, Arbitrazh is an agency specifically created to resolve legal disputes between economic and other organizations. However, it would be incorrect to categorize Arbitrazh as an economic court. Such a point of view is at odds with a number of facts. Most significant among these facts are that Arbitrazh decisions depend on instructions received from planning agencies and that Arbitrazh participates to a certain extent in the administrative distribution of economic output. This participation, though quite limited, relies upon specific legal provisions governing supply in the USSR.

As a rule, the output of economic entities is distributed by planning agencies. If a product produced is included in the area of planned distribution, planning agencies regulate this distribution, regardless of whether a producer functions within the limits of a production plan or overfulfills its mandatory tasks. From the viewpoint of planning, the difference lies in the fact that planning agencies distribute a product to be produced within the limits of a production plan before it is actually made, while these agencies can only plan the distribution of above-plan production after they have been informed that such production has taken place.[13] If a product produced is not subject to planned distribution, it may be sold by a producer to any entity as a purchaser without reference to planned distribution, which is inapplicable under these circumstances. A producer acquires the same right with respect to products distributed according to a plan in cases where the entity designated by the plan as a potential purchaser refuses in the established manner to buy the allocated goods in whole or in part, and where the planning agencies fail to appoint another purchaser within a legally fixed period of time. However, some products not subject to planned distribution are distributed in an unplanned manner, and in such cases Arbitrazh plays a very important role.

The law distinguishes in the area of supply between long-term economic relations and those that cannot be considered long-term.[14] Long term economic relations are defined as those intended to continue for periods longer than one year, either on the basis of one contract or on a number of contracts consecutively executed. In cases where economic relations between a supplier and a purchaser of a product not subject to planned distribution are not long-term, upon the termination of these relations, neither party may be compelled to establish new contractual obligations. The situation is different if there are long-term economic relations between the parties. The purchaser retains its discretion even in this case, being entitled either to maintain or to terminate the previously established relations. If the purchaser decides to terminate, the supplier cannot coerce it to continue the relations. On the other hand, the purchaser has the right to maintain economic relations with the same supplier, despite the fact that the product is not subject to planned distribution. To exercise this right, the purchaser must send its order for goods (*zakaz*) to the supplier by a deadline specified by law, and, because the previously established relations are long-term, the supplier may not reject the purchaser's offer. Any attempted rejection can be challenged in Arbitrazh, which may decide that the contract offered by the purchaser and declined by the supplier must be considered executed and binding. It seems obvious that, even if Arbitrazh decisions only prolong preexisting contractual relations, this signifies that Arbitrazh does implement distribution of some products excluded from planned distribution. Such a conclusion is even more evident when one looks to disputes arising in connection not with the execution of a new contract but with the quantity of supply negotiated by contractual parties. It sometimes occurs that the supplier is ready to execute a new contract but for a quantity less than that provided in previous years, or that the purchaser insists not only upon the execution of a new contract but also upon an increase in the quantity of supply. In such disputes Arbitrazh unilaterally determines the quantity terms of the compulsory contract, functioning, consequently, as an agency that carries out the administrative distribution of products for which the procedure of general planning is not employed.

In relations between Soviet organizations and Soviet citizens, administrative distribution is employed far more widely than one might suspect. In innumerable cases, the satisfaction of citizens' needs actually depends on the decisions of administrative agencies. If a decision is positive, it is certified by an administrative order addressed to an entity that must fulfill it, and by a related document with a different name that entitles the individual concerned to receive the goods or services involved. This type of administrative distribution is, consequently, bilateral. Yet it is also peculiar, at least insofar as one addressee, a Soviet entity, is only an obligor, and the other addressee, a Soviet citizen, is only a rightholder.[15]

There exist two types of administrative distribution involving Soviet citizens: general and special. In turn, special distribution comes in many forms, while general distribution is applicable in only a limited number of specific cases. As a rule, the existence of neither general nor special distribution can be directly or logically deduced from published legal provisions, though in some cases the applicable provisions can be found in published sources.

The principal area in which special distribution comes into play has already been mentioned above as distribution in connection with activity that ensures the Soviet bureaucracy with preferential supply. It is implemented by the creation of various "closed" establishments, to which the members of the Soviet bureaucracy are assigned according to their rank. And it is in conformity with officials' ranks that the limits of supply are determined, except for the top of the political hierarchy, whose access to goods of all kinds and in any quantity is subject to no limit. In cases where the demands of the ruling bureaucracy must be satisfied by establishments open to all (theaters, transport enterprises, etc.), special reservations, special coupons or other similar devices are employed for the same purpose.[16]

Beyond the limits of the Soviet bureaucracy, special distribution is applicable in a great number of other cases, connected with privileges that depend on the respective grounds for which the distribution is implemented. Thus, holders of titles of honor of the highest ranks (Heroes of the Soviet Union, Heroes of Socialist labor, People's Artists of the USSR, etc.) have special access to food unavailable in common stores, to other scarce consumer goods, to transport services, etc. If these persons do not belong to the Soviet bureaucracy, the goods thus distributed are of a lower quality but far better than those supplied to other, somewhat less privileged groups within the Soviet population. The next of these groups comprises persons with war disabilities. They too are specially supplied with various items, though only within the lists of goods secretly confirmed. War veterans from time to time receive coupons entitling them to acquire certain goods of comparatively durable use (for example, two pairs of underwear a year or certain other objects which are scarce during a given time period). In various Soviet cities, extraordinary events in city history also can serve as grounds for the creation of privileges for certain inhabitants. In Leningrad, for instance, the 900 days of the German blockade during World War II is such an event. Therefore, individuals who received a special medal as a reward for having survived the blockade acquire certain not very significant rights in the area of distribution unavailable to other individuals.

Sometimes, administrative distribution is general in appearance and special in substance. For example, certain periodical publications, owing to their scarcity or to the undesireability of their broad dissemination, can be subscribed to only at the establishment where the subscriber works. This procedure necessitates the allocation of all copies of such publications to Soviet establishments even before the process of printing begins. However, at each establishment subscriptions are available only to persons included by the organization's trade-union committee on a special list. Another procedure governs the distribution of automobiles. Any citizen can buy a car at dealers open to all on the basis of a first-come, first-served waiting list. However, a citizen must wait for years to get an automobile in this manner. At the same time, relatively important entities (universities, large plants or factories, etc.) are annually allocated a number of cars for sale to their workers. In these cases, the managers of such establishments decide, together with the Party and trade-union committees, who specifically will be granted the right to buy these administratively-distributed cars. A mixture of general and special distribution can be ascertained in connection with what are called *zakazy* (orders). The same relatively important establishments also use *zakazy* (orders), however, exclusively in connection with scarce food (meats, sausage, cheese, butter, etc.). A certain quantity of such food is distributed among these establishments, and within the limits of this distribution the representatives of the appropriate food stores receive orders from workers of the privileged establishment. Because, however, the quota allocated is insufficient to satisfy all of the workers' demands, different establishments employ different procedures: either the usual rule of first-come, first served (as in "open" stores) or the listing of persons entitled to order food (as in "closed" stores).

In contrast to special distribution, which ultimately results in distribution among specially designated groups of persons, general distribution is applicable to all inhabitants either of the entire country or of the locality where general distribution is employed.

In a great number of Soviet cities and other localities, as mentioned above, each family receives coupons entitling it to acquire an indicated quantity of goods during a month. In Bratsk, Irkutsk, and Khabarovsk in the spring of 1986 one coupon ("*talon-zakaz*") allowed the purchase of one kilogram of ground meat, one chicken, two kilograms of "pel'meni" (small meat-filled dumplings), etc. Actually such distribution is a thinly veiled form of rationing. Since, however, this rationing is not comprehensive for the entire country, it can be legalized in each location by means of separate "directives," instead of promulgating general provisions.

At the same time, certain kinds of general distribution are regulated, at least in part, by published legal rules. Sometimes, this occurs owing to certain peculiarities of the Soviet system. For example, land may be owned only by the state, and therefore it is quite natural that individuals can receive plots of land only in accordance with the conditions established by the state as the owner and exclusively on the basis of the administrative decisions rendered by the agency entitled to deal with the land. The 1968 Fundamental Principles of Land Legislation of the USSR and Union Republics[17] and the republican land codes,[18] supplemented by numerous unpublished regulations, develop in great detail the procedure for granting land to users. And because plots of land are granted as objects of use, not of ownership, legislative acts, both published and unpublished, provide the grounds and procedure for terminating the right to land use. For the same reason, special legislation regulates the availability for use by citizens of forests and certain minerals, since these also are objects possessed exclusively by the Soviet state.

Usually, however, administrative distribution of a general character results from the insufficiency of the resources thus distributed. Two examples can illustrate this assertion. The first example relates to the purchase of prefabricated houses by citizens from special enterprises.[19] In the USSR only those prefabricated wooden houses that are allocated by distribution plans for retail sale may be bought by citizens. But to be entitled to buy such a house an individual must obtain an "order" in writing either from the establishment where he works or from the executive committee of the community in which he lives. Relevant, and for the most part unpublished, legislative acts list the prerequisites necessary for a citizen's application and for the official decision to issue the necessary order. And even if all these prerequisites are satisfied, one must observe the principle of priority and wait one's turn before the order will be issued. Only then is the holder entitled to buy and the indicated enterprise obliged to sell a house of the specified size. This does not, however, mean that the purchase can be effected immediately. If the seller has no houses of the type indicated in the order, the purchaser must wait until such houses are delivered by their producers. Should the expected delivery be inadequate to cover the number of issued orders, the principle of first-come, first-served once again comes into play.

The second example can be found in the area where bank credit is extended for individual housing construction.[20] The credit activity of Soviet banks is planned, just as is economic activity of all other types. Annual plans of credit, prepared by the USSR Ministry of Finance in conjunction with the management of the appropriate USSR Bank (the State Bank, the Construction Bank, the Foreign-Trade Bank) and confirmed, within substantive indicators, by the USSR Council of Ministers, determine the volume of credit that may be extended by each bank establishment during the plan year. The general volume thus determined must then be distributed by each bank establishment among the economic entities whose accounts are handled by the distributing establishment. On the basis of the distribution that has been approved, each account-holder receives what is called a limit notice (*limitnoe izveshchenie*) indicating the amount of credit that may be received during the plan year. The entire amount of the allocated credit limit is divided into two unequal portions: the larger portion can be requested by the account-holder for its own economic needs, and the other, far smaller portion is earmarked for the extension of credit to the same entity's workers for individual housing construction. One must bear in mind that the preparation of the credit plan is preceded by an economic entity's request (*zaiavka*), and that the portion of the credit limit earmarked for individual housing construction appears if at all only on the condition that the entity has included individual housing credit in its request. Furthermore, all indicators of a credit request must be supported with relevant data by the compiler of this document. A special list of workers is a prerequisite to obtaining the portion of credit requested for individual housing construction. The compilation of this list is a complicated procedure. A worker who wishes to be included on the list must prove that his housing conditions are worse than an established minimum standard and that housing construction is possible for him from all other viewpoints (allocation of a plot of land, supply of construction materials, etc.). Relying upon these data, the trade-union committee prepares the list, which enters into force only after approval by the trade-union committee and confirmation by the manager of the economic entity. If the appropriate portion of the credit limit is equal to the amount calculated in accordance with the list produced, each worker will receive the requested credit. Otherwise, either certain workers must be excluded from this list or each worker will receive credit in an amount less than he has requested. A worker entitled to bank credit must provide a specified portion of construction expenses from his own funds. The remaining allocated credit is extended by the bank, not immediately but gradually in accordance with the progress of the work. If an individual is a worker at an institution, which in contrast to an economic entity does not receive bank credit, he must be included on a list that the institution itself issues and presents to the bank office. Where such a list is accepted by the bank office, that office itself enters into a direct credit relation with the individual worker.

In studying administrative distribution applicable with respect to individuals and publicly legalized in the USSR one must pay special attention to the distribution of housing in state apartment buildings—one of the most crucial issues for both Soviet citizens and the Soviet regime. The principal rules regulating this distribution are embodied by the 1981 Fundamental Principles of Housing Legislation of the USSR and Union Republics[21] and in the republican housing codes.[22] Unpublished rules adopted by executive agencies also play a substantial role in this area. Some of these rules are issued by local executive committees and adjusted to the peculiarities of the cities or other localities within these committees' jurisdiction. The entire procedure is initiated by registering those persons in need of housing. Registration is one of the functions of the local executive committee. In order to be registered, an individual and his family, while having a permanent residence status in the given city or other locality, must possess no housing at all or insufficient housing. To possess no housing means to live in the apartment of a friend, relative, or other citizen not as a tenant but as a subtenant (*podnanimatel'*), and thus to be subject to eviction at any time upon notification from the actual tenant in writing.

The definition of insufficient housing depends on local rules established by the local executive committees. Mostly these rules declare housing to be insufficient in cases where there are less than five square meters per family member. Along with these objective criteria, registration depends on the recommendation of the labor collective of which the applicant is a member. This subjective criterion ensures that the shortage of living premises can be used as yet another means of strengthening labor discipline in the USSR.

As a rule, an individual's registration will remain in effect until he and his family receive an apartment or a room in a state apartment building. Only in cases provided by law, for instance, if the documents presented by an individual in applying for registration are misleading with respect to his current housing situation, can annulment of registration be effected. Distribution of living premises is on a waiting-list basis; usually one must wait for 8–10 years until one's opportunity to obtain housing finally arises. However, certain persons (for instance, the holders of the highest titles of honor) have a preferential right to distribution, and certain other persons (for instance, those whose living premises have been destroyed by natural disasters) have the right to distribution outside the waiting-list system. It is noteworthy that the relevant legal rules calling for preferential or non-waiting-list distribution indicate that such irregular distribution may be appropriate in other cases provided by law. These "other cases," though not mentioned in published legislation, disguise the fact that representatives of the Soviet bureaucracy receive state apartments without having to observe the complicated formalities and not on the basis of the general waiting-list system.

Soviet law distinguishes between the norm of housing space and the norm for the distribution of housing space. The norm of housing space is established by the housing codes of the union republics. In the RSFSR this norm is twelve square meters per family member.[23] This norm is the basis for determination of the amount of surplus living space occupied by each family. Space in excess of twelve meters per family member is considered surplus and must be paid for at higher rate than that established for living space within the limits of the norm. However, local executive committees are not obliged to rely upon this norm in the process of distributing living premises. Representatives of the Soviet bureaucracy receive state apartments far larger than what would be calculated from such a norm. On the other hand, a registered individual does not have the right to demand an apartment of the size indicated by the same norm. His priority only gives him the right to demand living space within the limits of the norm of distribution. The establishment of this norm is within the jurisdiction of local executive committees, and the size of this norm varies between seven and nine square meters per person. It is true that housing legislation proclaims, as a general rule for the distribution of housing, the principle: one family—one apartment.[24] The practicability of this principle can be assessed with reference to the fact that Khrushchev's promise to implement such distribution by 1980 has been postponed by Gorbachev to the year 2000.[25] The law in force, determining the norm of distribution of living premises, is also an eloquent demonstration of the inconsistency with reality of such propagandistic proclamations, even if these are expressed not merely by political documents but by legal provisions.

The allocation of living premises in state apartment buildings in accordance with the rule of waiting-list priority (as well as in cases of preferential or other non-priority distribution) must be finalized by a decision of the local executive committee. This decision is preceded by a discussion at a meeting of the executive committee's housing commission and is followed by the issuance of an order in writing, the unconditional prerequisite of occupancy in a state apartment. In the absence of an order, occupancy is deemed arbitrary and eviction may be carried out in an administrative rather than a judicial manner. In contrast, once an order addressed to an individual and his family members is issued, they become rightholders and the management of the appropriate building an obligor. Rightholders may either exercise or abstain from the exercise of their rights. The obligor is obliged to make available to the rightholder those living premise specifically designated in the order.

Such are the most important cases of unplanned distribution, sometimes applicable to relations between legal entities but more often employed with respect to relations between legal entities and Soviet citizens. Although planned and unplanned distribution are implemented by different agencies, both represent administrative activity, and each of these types of distribution has its own particular features.

Planned distribution is a general method of Soviet economic management. It follows from the planning of production and creates the planning prerequisites for exchange. In other words, Soviet planning affects all phases of the economic cycle, and planned distribution, as one of the stages of economic planning, governs distribution as one of the phases of the economic cycle. In contrast, unplanned distribution is a specific method of Soviet economic management, limited with respect to the areas and the circumstances in which it is applied. It does not represent a planning stage connected with a certain phase of the economic cycle. Usually, unplanned distribution either has no connection with production and exchange (for instance, in the distribution of land plots), or it connects production and exchange, but not directly and only in the final analysis (for instance, where unplanned supply is coerced through Arbitrazh by a purchaser despite objections on the part of a supplier).

Planned distribution is centralized: it is implemented by decisions of the highest governing agencies. Of course, the degree of actual direct involvement by such agencies varies depending on economic significance of the planned objects. Thus, distribution of the most important products is more strictly centralized than is the distribution of products remaining beyond the limits of the special "nomenclature." However, by means of generally outlined indicators, the highest government agencies affect the process of planning directed toward the distribution of even the least significant goods. In contrast, unplanned distribution is decentralized: it is implemented by the activity of only those agencies whose specific jurisdiction includes the appropriate function. For example, the distribution of land plots and state living space is within the jurisdiction of local executive committees; the trade departments of these committees distribute automobiles among important establishments and arrange for relations between those establishments and food stores that are to receive and perform individual employees' food orders (*zakazy*), etc.

Planned distribution serves the purpose of maintaining and strengthening the economic monopoly of the ruling elite. Therefore it is highly centralized. And the more this monopoly is connected with a particular area of distribution, the stronger must be the centralization of planning in the given area. Therefore, the distribution of capital investments is more centralized than is the distribution of the output of industrial entities, and the output of these entities also is not homogenous from the viewpoint of methods of distribution. Of course, the degree of centralization in distribution planning also depends on the correlation between supply and demand for products of different character. Scarce objects are subjected to more stringent distribution planning than are those whose supply is not far behind demand. However, it is not the scarcity of produced goods but rather the strengthening of the Soviet leadership's economic monopoly that is the most significant factor leading to distribution planning. In contrast, unplanned distribution results either from the creation of exclusive state ownership with respect to certain objects (land, minerals, etc.) or from the shortage of certain goods (apartments, food, etc.). Of course, in ensuring privileges to representatives of the ruling bureaucracy, unplanned distribution also serves the purpose of strengthening the unlimited political power of the Soviet leadership. However, were food of all kinds produced in a quantity and assortment corresponding to the people's demand, unplanned distribution would be pointless. Perhaps, the Soviet elite would continue to maintain "closed" stores even under such circumstances, however, only in order to have access to goods at lower prices or simply to avoid daily contact with the man in the street—bearing in mind Solzhenitsin's quip, concerning the Soviet rulers, to the effect that they like the people and hate the population. But were the shortage of various goods eliminated, the principal reason for the existence of unplanned distribution would disappear.

Planned distribution as an expression of the economic monopoly of the ruling summit has been developed through a unified system of planning agencies and by means of interdependent forms of planning procedures. The lowest links of the Soviet economy supply information at the start of planning and are the addressees of plans at the end of the planning process; middle links, performing administrative functions, collate information received from the bottom of the economic system and distribute the tasks formulated at the top; the highest links receive the collated information, and elaborate and confirm distribution plans. In contrast, unplanned distribution, not intended as a means of ensuring the continued existence of the established economic monopoly, relies neither upon a unified system of distribution agencies nor upon interdependent forms of distribution procedure. The distribution of plots of land and of state apartments is implemented by the same agency, but the formal procedures are different and not interdependent. The agencies involved and the procedures employed with respect to the distribution of food depend on the nature of the distribution (general or special), the type of objects distributed (available to all or only to those of rank), and the peculiarities of the different methods utilized (coupons or orders), etc.

Distinctions between planned and unplanned distribution must not be disregarded in the process of assessing the potential for the restructuring of Soviet distribution activity.

The Soviet leadership has proclaimed a "new deal" in the area of economic management, first of all in the sphere of economic planning. This policy has been expressed in a number of documents and speeches. It actually became one of the principal issues discussed at the Congress of the CPSU in 1986.[26] One could even hear calls for the restructuring of the entire system of Soviet planning.[27] However, it was emphasized more than once that no essential modification of the economic system as such should be considered necessary.[28] The economic system was praised, not criticized. Thus, relying on the Soviet declarations, one can expect only a within-system change. But such a change is, as already indicated, only a routine move into a different phase of the common cycle. At this point the country is moving from extreme centralization to relative decentralization. Moreover, insofar as one deals with distribution, the policy proclaimed calls for changes only in planned distribution, and there are no indications that there will be any relaxation in the area of unplanned distribution. And, as Soviet experience proves, it cannot be otherwise: since the abolition of NEP not a single economic reform has been addressed to unplanned distribution.[29] The causes of the stability of unplanned distribution are rather clear.

Unplanned distribution results either from the peculiar features of the Soviet system or from a shortage of goods. The Soviet regime, deprived of its peculiarities, would lose the character of the Soviet regime. Therefore, in this direction no change can be seriously expected to be implemented by the Soviets themselves. Shortage are not a specific Soviet problem. Unfortunately, this disastrous phenomenon is widespread in the world today, and is much more menacing in a number of countries. Nevertheless, a shortage of goods has accompanied the Soviet regime throughout its history and often becomes worse upon transition from one historical period to another. Therefore, this reason for the existence of unplanned distribution is no less permanent than are purely Soviet peculiarities. The shortage of certain goods can be eliminated. Such events sometimes occur. There was a time, for instance, when sewing machines could be bought only in accordance with the rule of priority. Now these machines are commonly available. However, the long history of shortages persuasively demonstrates their inevitability. As a result, unplanned distribution is inseparable from the Soviet system.

Actually the same conclusion must also be formulated with respect to planned distribution and economic planning in general. The Soviet authorities have not denied this even when reforms are discussed, as at the 1986 Party Congress.[30] In fact, insisting that the principles of planning be strengthened and developed, the Soviet rulers have in mind their own ideas of plans as the directive commands of central agencies binding on addressees and performers. The transition from extreme centralization to relative decentralization always has been reduced to the following measures:

(1) A decrease in the number of planning indicators. In 1965, for example, only the indicator of profit was retained for economic entities engaged in production. However, this weakened the opportunities for centralized control to such a degree that within a very short time the eliminated indicators were restored. The present leadership will certainly take into account this experience, eliminating in all probability only those planning indicators that affect unnecessary details, and leaving the indicators unchanged in areas of production where even details are deemed important;

(2) The liquidation of superfluous intermediate links of planning. Production associations, for instance, can deal directly with economic ministries without the interference of industrial associations. Brezhnev created industrial associations as new administrative agencies in 1973–1974 for the purpose of strengthening centralization. It is quite clear that Gorbachev, acting in a period when a return to relative decentralization is imminent, cannot help but oppose industrial associations and recommend their liquidation. The history of the Soviet economy is marked by the constant creation and liquidation of superfluous intermediate links, and neither Brezhnev's initiative nor Gorbachev's counter-measures can be considered the last step on this path;

(3) Allowances for greater participation by the lowest links of the Soviet economy in the process of planning. The legislation dedicated to the 1965 economic reform, for instance, even allowed for the development of plans on the basis of executed contracts. To some extent this method is employed at the present time, especially in the area of planned distribution of consumer goods. However, if the indicators of distribution plans are lower than those expressed by the quantity of executed contracts, the latter must be modified in accordance with the former. Genuine initiative on the part of the performers of plans can be developed only on the condition that their suggestions will be at least relatively binding on planning agencies. But this seems incompatible with the principle of the primacy of plans, a principle protected by the present leadership to no less degree than by its predecessors;

(4) Ensuring the stability of plans. Actually, however, from the economic point of view, flexibility in plans is less detrimental than stability, owing to the inevitable mistakes of planning agencies. And from the legal point

of view, the stability proclaimed cannot function without the imposition of property liability in cases where this stability is violated. Yet, the introduction of property liability collides with the usual immunity of the planners and the reluctance of performers to employ this type of legal sanctions.

Therefore, planned and unplanned distribution will be retained in substance, despite the changes promised by the new Soviet leaders.

Notes

1. Model Collective Farm Charter, art. 29.

2. Collective farmers most often take part in goods-money relations not as purchasers but as sellers, and usually in such transactions they sell their own products, as opposed to their shares in kind from the collective farm.

3. *Izvestia*, June 12, 1985.

4. *SP SSSR*, 1985, part 1, no. 23, item 115.

5. *SP SSSR*, 1981, part 1, no. 9–10, item 62.

6. In contrast, the material-technical supply of agricultural producers, including collective farms, is subordinated to the same rules which are in general employed to other purchaser of machines, equipment, etc. Like economic ministries and other central agencies representing the various economic branches, USSR *Gosagroprom* represents agricultural and other subordinate entities, in drafting composite orders and in distributing appropriated funds.

7. *SP SSSR*, 1970, no. 8, item 63.

8. *SP SSSR*, 1981, sect 1, no. 19, item 104.

9. *Izvestia*, March 29, 1986.

10. The situation is even worse in cases where it is not the enlargement of an existing operation but the building of a new enterprise that is to be undertaken. In these cases, a special entity, the "management of the enterprise to be constructed" is created solely for the purpose of exercising the rights and fulfilling the duties of a customer. Upon the completion of the construction project this temporary entity must immediately be liquidated.

11. *SP SSSR*, 1964, No. 5, item 36.

12. *Izvestia*, March 9, 1986.

13. *SP SSSR*, part 1, 1981 no. 9–10, item 62.

14. Ibid. Fundamental Principles of Civil Legislation, Art. 34.

15. We do not speak here of distribution based upon Party discipline, which, for example, obliges each Party member to subscribe the Party's leading newspaper, *Pravda*.

16. For details, see Mikhail Voslensky, *Nomenklatura—Gospodstvuiushchii klass Sovetskogo Soiuza* (London: Overseas Publication Interchange Ltd., 1985) pp. 281–343.

17. Art. 10.

18. RSFSR Land Code, arts. 12–19.

19. *SP RSFSR*, 1960, no. 14, item 60.

20. *SP SSSR*, 1981, part 1, no. 29, item 170.

21. Arts. 18–21.

22. RSFSR Housing Code, art. 28–37.

23. Ibid, art. 38.

24. Fundamental Principles of Housing Legislation, art. 18.

25. The 1986 Fundamental Directions, *Izvestia*, March 9, 1986.

26. *Izvestia*, February 26-March 9, 1986.
27. Speech by V. V. Shcherbitsky, *Izvestia*, Feb. 27, 1986.
28. In this respect the Chairman of the USSR Council of Ministers N. I. Ryzhkov was the most eloquent. He emphasized the task "to strengthen and to perfect the centralized planned administration of the economy" and pointed out: "We have not justified and we will never justify the hopes of bourgeois ideologists that we should refuse this fundamental principle." *Izvestia*, March 4, 1986.
29. The abolition of official rationing in the mid–1930's and in the late–1940's cannot be categorized as economic reforms in the Soviet interpretation.
30. Above, note 28.

8

Exchange: Its Legal Regulation

General Principles

Examined from the viewpoint of legal regulation, exchange in the USSR is based upon contracts of many different kinds. The common law system and the civil law system view the notion of contract differently. For there to be a contract in the common law system, there must be a promise and either consideration or reliance. Consideration involves a bargained-for exchange between the parties. Reliance involves a promise by one party upon which the other party has substantially relied. Contracts in the civil law system require an agreement by two parties, but do not require a promise, consideration, or reliance. Therefore, for instance, the making of a gift is not regarded as a contract under common law, but is regarded as a contract under civil law. An agreement is considered a contract under the civil law system only if it: entails the imposition of mutual duties (*causa credendi*); is executed for the purpose of liberating both parties from their mutual duties (*causa solvendi*); or if one party seeks to enrich another (*causa donandi*).[1] Despite the absence of the corresponding concept, *causa credendi* in the civil law system is identical to the consideration of the common law system. At the same time, exchange is a sphere of businesslike activities, and therefore it demands that only contracts based on consideration in the common law system or on *causa credendi* in the civil law system be employed. Consequently, though Soviet law derives from the civil law system, and, instead of consideration, it recognizes the three types of *causa* listed above, Soviet contracts in the sphere of exchange should be understandable to persons familiar with either the civil law or the common law systems, because of the identity of consideration and *causa credendi.*

Similar to the civil law system and in contrast to the common law system, Soviet law provides for and regulates in detail dozens of specific contracts. For the most part, such regulation is provided by the Fundamental Principles of Civil Legislation and civil codes, while details are determined by other acts the Soviet legislation. Certain contracts not dealt with by the Fundamental Principles or the civil codes are provided for by special legislative acts. However, the direct regulation of specific contracts by Soviet law does not mean that the concept of *numerus clausus* is applicable. Rights and duties can arise from "legal transactions provided for by law, and also from legal transactions that, although not provided for by law, are not contrary thereto."[2] In practice, one does sometimes come across contracts not provided for by law but which, nevertheless, have been executed by individuals or even by organizations and do have legal force. But in order to present a general picture reflecting the Soviet system of contractual obligations,[3] it seems useful to outline this system by classifying those contracts which are regulated by the Fundamental Principles and the republican civil codes.[4]

There are nine groups of contracts provided for by these legislative acts: (1) contracts for the alienation of property for a charge (purchase and sale, delivery, state purchase of agricultural produce, barter, maintenance for life); (2) contracts of the transfer of property for use for a charge (lease of property, lease of housing); (3) contracts for the transfer of property to another person's ownership or use without charge (gift, gratuitous use); (4) contracts for performance of work (independent work, capital construction); (5) contracts of rendering services (agency, commission, deposit); (6) contracts of carriage (railroad carriage, maritime carriage, river carriage, automobile carriage, air carriage); (7) contracts of credit and accounts (loan, bank credit, bank account); (8) contracts of insurance (property insurance, personal insurance); (9) contracts of joint activity (joint activity of citizens, joint activity of organizations).

Certain of these contracts, (for instance, gift) are not employed in the sphere of exchange, and, therefore they will not be discussed further. All of the other contracts serve either as legal forms of exchange (for instance, purchase and sale) or as accessory components of the same activity (for instance, carriage of goods). However, among both types of contractual obligations, there are contracts indigenous to the Soviet system (for instance, state purchase of agricultural produce or planned carriage of goods) and those common, if not to all countries of the world, then at least to the countries of the civil law system (for instance, maintenance for life or agency). In studying exchange as a stage of the Soviet economy, we will concentrate on those types of contracts peculiar to the Soviet system.

While Soviet contracts may be classified in accordance with their legal purposes, the same contracts are also grouped with reference to the sphere of their application. In this respect one can distinguish between ordinary contracts and economic contracts. Ordinary contracts are those that can be executed between individuals, between individuals and organizations, or between organizations themselves (purchase and sale, lease of property, etc.). A contract also necessarily qualifies as ordinary, either if both of the parties are individuals (for instance, maintenance for life) or if at least one of the parties is an individual (for instance, lease of living premises). However, the mere fact that a contract is classified as ordinary does not deprive it of Soviet peculiarities. Contracts of retail sale are known throughout the world, but in the USSR they have features that one would hardly expect to find in a Western contract of the same name. Contracts for the lease of living premises have even more special Soviet features. Certain contracts qualify as ordinary not because they have direct counterparts in Western systems but to distinguish them from economic contracts.

In contrast to "ordinary contracts," a term introduced by Soviet scholarly writers, the term "economic contracts," is found in Soviet legislation.[5] Nevertheless, the validity of the latter notion and its theoretical interpretation continue to provoke controversies in Soviet literature.[6] One of the authors of this book has expressed his viewpoint in a Soviet publication.[7] The same point of view is maintained in the present book.

The definition of the phenomenon discussed must indicate that economic contracts can be executed only between Soviet organizations and ought to be related to the economic needs of these organizations. However, not all contracts employed between Soviet organizations for the purposes mentioned can be considered economic contracts. Therefore one must point out additional features of such contracts in order to ensure the requisite degree of precision and certainty in the definition developed. And in this connection the distinctions between the planned and the unplanned contracts of Soviet entities are especially important.

Of course, since the Soviet economy is comprehensively planned, at least within the limits of production activity, all contracts connected with the economic tasks of Soviet entities are affected by planned purposes. This does not mean, however, that all of these contracts are economic from the legal point of view. And if a contract is an economic one because of its planned character, it is subject to legal rules inapplicable to non-economic, unplanned contracts: the invalidity of a planned contract contradicting mandatory plans;[8] the termination or modification of a planned contract owing to changes in the appropriate plan,[9] etc. One must, consequently, distinguish between planning as an economic phenomenon and planning as a legal phenomenon. Economically speaking, a contract is planned regardless of whether it results from a plan directly or indirectly. Legally, a contract is planned only in cases where a plan is the necessary prerequisite of the contract's execution as a legal command binding for one or both of its addresses. All contracts planned in the legal sense and executed by Soviet entities for economic purposes are clearly economic contracts.

However, because of two circumstances, economic contracts cannot simply be equated with planned contracts.

On the one hand, there are two groups of unplanned contracts employed by Soviet entities for economic purposes in their mutual relations. Unplanned contracts of the first group are contractual types independent of planned contracts. For example, purchase and sale, an unplanned contract, can be executed between Soviet entities in pursuit of economic goals. But there exists no planned contract of purchase and sale. The contract of purchase and sale can be only unplanned, and therefore as a contractual type it is independent of planned contracts. Such unplanned contracts are not economic contracts. Unplanned contracts of the second group have direct counterparts in the area of planned contracts. For example, delivery can be planned and unplanned.[10] Unplanned delivery is regulated exactly as is planned delivery, except that the validity and stability of the former do not depend on established planned tasks. Thus, delivery as a unified contractual type comprises planned and unplanned contracts of the same name. Such unplanned contracts are economic contracts.

On the other hand, Soviet entities make certain contracts that, though unplanned, are required to be executed, similar to the most stringently regulated planned contracts. Bank account contracts serve as a perfect illustration. These contracts are not planned, since no planning act predetermines their execution. However, the law mandates that these contracts be executed by every newly created Soviet entity and the State Bank (*Gosbank*) office in the appropriate location.[11] As a result, these and other similar contracts acquire features analogous to those intrinsic in planned contracts. Therefore the former as well as the latter should be classified as economic contracts.

Thus, the notion of economic contracts encompasses planned contracts as well as unplanned contracts that are subject to the same contractual regime or to the same coercive execution as planned contracts. The great number of types of economic contracts employed in the USSR can be reduced to six groups.

The first group is composed of contracts concerning the alienation of property for a charge. These are, in particular, contracts for the delivery of products and consumer goods, state purchase of agricultural produce at collective farms and state farms, and supply contracts for gas, heat, and electricity. All of these contracts are either planned (planned delivery, planned state purchase of agricultural produce at collective farms and state farms, planned supply of gas, heat, and electricity) or unplanned but endowed with the same legal characteristics as those of planned contracts (e.g. unplanned delivery or unplanned purchase of agricultural produce).

The second group includes contracts for the nongratuitous use of property. This group is limited to contracts for the planned lease of property (e.g. rental of means of transport), and it does not include unplanned property leases. Although the contractual terms of unplanned lease contracts are identical to those of planned contracts, the former can be executed not only between Soviet entities but also between such entities and individuals or between individuals themselves.

The third group comprises contracts of production, for example, contracts for capital construction, and contracts for the fulfillment of project work for scientific research, construction, or skilled construction work. All of these are planned contracts. Therefore, they fall, without need of further analysis, within the category of economic contracts.

The fourth group includes contracts for transport services, for example, contracts for carriage of goods, towage, and for the exploitation of spur lines. The first two are characterized as economic contracts because of their planned nature; the last as a result of its application only in relations between Soviet entities and because the legal requirement that every owner of a spur line enter into contractual relations with the railroad enterprise in possession of adjoining railroad[12] is just as strong as in the case of a planned contract.

The fifth group encompasses contracts for banking services. These include contracts for bank credit and the bank accounts of Soviet entities. A contract for the extension of bank credit to a Soviet entity is an economic contract because it is based on a planning act; the bank account contract, because its execution is compulsory for all Soviet entities to which the rights of a juridical person have been accorded.

The final, sixth, group includes contracts concerning the performance of other services. Such are, for example, contracts for freight forwarding and for warehouse storage. The contract for freight forwarding is a planned contract. The contract for warehouse storage may be either planned or unplanned. But both are economic contracts as they are only applied in relationships between Soviet entities.

Economic contracts must be characterized from two points of view. As contracts, they ensure the establishment and implementation of goods-money relations between legally equal entities functioning in their capacity as juridical persons. As economic connections in substance, these same contracts are subject to a special regime of economic discipline providing a greater or lesser degree of strict centralized control over their execution, performance, alteration, and termination. The former feature indicates that economic contracts belong to the class of civil law contracts. However, the latter feature shows that they constitute a specific group of civil law contracts separated in practice and in doctrine because of the peculiarities of their legal regulation.

This conclusion made with respect to economic contracts is challenged by the same Soviet scholars who refuse to accept the interpretation of goods-money relations as a prerequisite of *khozraschet* and the institution of the juridical person as a legal expression of the economic autonomy of production and trade entities.[13] Even more peculiar is the fact that these authors employ the same approach with respect to economic contracts as they employ in attempting to substantially modify the longstanding and deeply rooted Soviet notion of *khozraschet*.

The authors of the book *Khoziaistvennoe pravo*,[14] use the term "economic obligations," instead of "economic contracts." This modification of terminology pursues quite definite practical goals: to introduce three types of economic obligations (similar to their three types of *khozraschet*[15]) and to dispense with economic contracts as a phenomenon of goods-money relations in a general definition of economic obligations that is entirely unrelated to monetary exchange (here too, similar to distortion of genuine *khozraschet*, by means of artificial generalizations linking phenomena that are actually different.[16])

These authors' general definition is extremely vague, as is always the case where attempts are made to doctrinally unify that which actually is heterogeneous. The authors assert that an economic obligation in general is an obligation directed toward the achievement of planned results by means of one party undertaking a duty to perform for the benefit of another "certain economic/operative and/or economic/administrative actions."[17] They define the peculiar term "Economic/operative actions" as the supply of goods, the construction of new objects, the transportation of goods, and other types of economic services usually connected with the execution and performance of economic contracts. They define the equally peculiar term "Economic/administrative actions" as actions embodied in planning tasks or other administrative orders, formulated by superior agencies and addressed to economic entities. Thus, the supply of goods and administrative orders are included in the same class of potential objects of economic obligations in general. However, goods can be bought and sold, while administrative acts, even those which impose monetary duties upon their addressees, by their nature cannot be bought or sold. These distinctions result from the fact that "economic/operative" actions are conducted as goods-money relations, while "economic/administrative" actions are carried out outside the sphere of monetary exchange. How can both be combined as homogeneous objects of economic obligations? Logically, this is, of course, impossible, but teleological arguments often can be illogical. Since these authors' goal is to undermine the firmly-based connection between economic obligations and goods-money exchange, they must proclaim the similarity of very different activities: exchange of goods and administration. Acceptance of this illogical postulate, however, logically does lead to several obvious conclusions: economic obligations can exist without goods-money relations, and, vice versa, goods-money relations are not the only possible types of economic obligations. Despite its doctrinal vulnerability, this conception has proven to be quite efficient as a weapon in the fight against "market socialism," which is an *alter ego* of "socialism with human face."

Having formulated the general definition of economic obligations, these authors then turn to classification, distinguishing between three types of economic obligations: economic/operative obligations, economic/administrative obligations, and internal economic obligations. Economic/operative obligations are those which in normal terminology are called economic contracts. Even these authors at certain points use the terms "economic/operative obligations" and "economic/contractual" obligations interchangeably.[18] They prefer, however, to employ the word "obligations," even with respect to indisputably contractual relations. "Economic/administrative" obligations are different. They do not and cannot have a contractual nature, because they are legal connections based not on the equality of the participants but rather on the subordination of one participant to the other. Therefore, the definition of "economic/administrative" obligations indicates that these obligations arise from planning tasks and involve a distribution of rights and duties, according to which the agency that has established a planning task may demand its performance, and the entity to which this task has been addressed must effect its performance.[19] The authors also mention the duty of the planning agency to provide the performer with the requisite material and financial resources as well as the right of the performer to demand presentation of these resources.[20] Yet, although the authors know quite well that neither the performance of this "duty" nor the exercise of this "right" are enforced by legal sanctions or afforded legal protection, they make no attempt to fill this substantial gap in their legal construction. Goals are more important to them than sound legal reasoning: by disingenuously positing that such non-existant property rights and duties are included among "economic/administrative" obligations, the authors can demonstrate once more that "socialist" obligations are not dependent on market relations, and that goods-money exchange is not an inevitable consequence of the establishment of economic obligations.

Special attention must be paid to "internal economic obligations." A number of large economic associations and independent enterprises engage, as a method of strenghthening internal *khozraschet*,[21] in bookkeeping practices that call for the maintenance of records monitoring the allocation of the entity's property between its subdivisions, written orders for materials and semifinished products, and certification in writing of the delivery of these objects by one subdivision to another. If one of an entity's interdependent subdivisions cannot fulfill its plan because of another subdivision's failure to implement required operations, not the former but the latter loses, entirely or in part, the right to share in the incentive funds distributed by the entity's management. In order to free themselves from the duty to analyze and to resolve each disputed case of this nature, the managements of a number of large associations and enterprises have created their own "internal" arbitrazh, whose decisions are taken into consideration in the distribution of incentive funds, though management is free to abolish or disregard these decisions.

This practice has been referred to by those legal scholars who attack "market socialism" in order to reach completely unexpected conclusions. First of all, they characterize these bookkeeping practices, which are purely formal, as a manifestation of internal/economic operative administration supplementing the operative administration of property of each economic entity as a whole.[22] The entity's operative administration, the authors then claim, is supplemented by the operative administration purportedly exercised by planning and other government agencies. Thus, following this approach to its logical conclusion, a general notion of operative administration emerges that leaves no room for interpretation of this phenomenon in the light of goods-money relations: the administrative agencies as such and the internal subdivisions of economic entities do not participate in goods-money relations, yet both, it is claimed, possess the right of operative administration. Hence, operative administration must share the fate of *khozraschet* and of the institution of the juridical person owing to the insistent desire to tear these phenomena away from goods-money relations. Moreover, the managerial technique of directing the activities of internal subdivision employed by certain economic entities has been elevated to the status of "internal economic obligations."[23] This phenomenal legal invention seems especially well-suited for the struggle against "market socialism": "internal obligations" are of a property nature and connect equal participants, but, nevertheless, no goods-money relations arise in this case, and no market activity results from such obligations.

However, speculative deductions based on illogical premises must themselves be illogical. This illogicality can be proven in the present case by the absolute discrepancy between the theoretical constructions and economic reality. It is true that a centralized economy cannot function without "vertical" relations in which one participant commands and another performs. But these simply are administrative relations, not "economic/administrative" obligations. It is also true that the subdivisions of economic entities are interdependent in their economic activities. But technological interdependence, directed by an entity's management and resulting from the administrative subordination of each subdivision to the head of the entire organization, requires no other legal connections, and, consequently, "internal economic" obligations are more patently fictitious than even "economic/administrative" obligations.

The actual situation is quite different from the picture painted by these authors. Economically, distribution, following production, precedes exchange. Legally, exchange can be implemented only by means of contracts. To the extent that production and distribution are subordinated to centralized direction, exchange requires economic contracts relying on certain administrative prerequisites, regardless of whether these contracts are planned or unplanned. In contrast, within the limits of exchange that, though connected with planned production, is not preceded by planned distribution or does not preclude the participation of individuals along with organizations, non-economic contracts are sufficient, regardless of whether or not these contracts are affected by administrative orders.

Economic Contracts

As discussed above, economic contracts may be planned and unplanned.[24] However, it is planned contracts that play the decisive role in the Soviet economy. Therefore, an analysis of economic contracts must concentrate on planned contracts, i.e. those the execution of which relies on appropriate planning prerequisites.

Since contracts assume the participation of no fewer than two parties,[25] planning must be not unilateral but correlative[26] in order to acquire the legal force necessary for the formation of contractual obligations. As has already been mentioned, correlative planning is employed only in the area of distribution, not in that of production.[27] Consequently, only those planning acts that concern distribution can serve as legal prerequisites of economic contracts. Let us also remind the reader that the planning of distribution has two kinds of legal consequences: "vertical" and "horizontal" relations.[28] "Vertical" relations are of an administrative nature: planning agencies may demand the performance of planning acts from their addressees. "Horizontal" relations are of a civil law nature: the addressees of planning acts are simultaneously entitled and obliged to execute economic contracts. This is the abstract characterization of the civil law consequences of centralized planning in the area of distribution—the issue which Soviet legal theory calls the problem of the correlation of the plan and the contract.[29] This problem is, however, differently resolved with respect to different groups of economic contracts. In analyzing the dependence of contracts on plans, one must distinguish between four types of contract-plan relationships.

The first type: planning acts unconditionally oblige their addressees to execute dictated contracts, and therefore none of the performers of plans may avoid the establishment of contractual obligations; however, the specific economic operations provided for by the plan must not be implemented until the contract itself is executed. If one of the addressees of the planning act attempts to avoid the execution of a contract, the other addressee may compel it to establish a contractual obligation in accordance with the procedure provided for by law.[30] In cases where both addressees of a planning act fail to perform their mutual duties, Arbitrazh may employ compulsory measures on its own initiative. The performance of planning acts without or before the execution of contracts is a violation of law involving administrative responsibility for the guilty officials of the offending economic entities. In addition, the addressee of a planning task who performs this task by providing goods or services for the other addressee without or before the execution of the contract will not receive payment for the goods or services. This rule is enforced by the supervision exercised by bank offices over the observance of contractual discipline, which must be strictly adhered to in monetary accounting between Soviet economic entities. This first type of correlation between plans and contracts entails the highest degree of dependence of contract on plan, and, as one might surmise, it is used in that sphere of economic activity where planning is the most centralized. As indicated above,[31] Soviet planning possesses such a character in the area of capital investment. The relation between plans of capital construction and contracts for capital construction represents the only case of the type of correlation above described.

The second type: planning acts oblige both addressees to execute planned contracts; however, one party is bound conditionally, while the other party's duty is unconditional. The addressee conditionally bound may avoid performance of a planning act if it fulfills the conditions established by law. On the contrary, the addressee bearing an unconditional duty may not unilaterally avoid executing the contract. If this addressee tries to avoid performance of its duty, the other party can employ compulsory measures to ensure that this duty is fulfilled. However, the performance of economic operations, mandated by the plan but not yet called for in a validly executed contract, is prohibited, and the same consequences ensue from a violation of this rule as arise from the violations of identical rules applicable in the area of capital investments. This prohibition is mitigated in only one respect with regard to the situation now being discussed. To maintain continuity of the economic activity involved, and bearing in mind that planned tasks are usually communicated to their addressees after long periods of delay, leading to a similar delay in the execution of economic contracts, the law allows, as an exception to the general rule, for precontractual performance at the beginning of each new year in accordance with the contractual terms of the previous year. This type of correlation between plans and contracts is specific to the area of supply of goods. Plans of supply unconditionally oblige the seller to execute a contract of delivery, while the purchaser may avoid execution of a contract under conditions specially provided by law.

The third type: planning acts oblige both addressees to conclude planned contracts; however, certain economic operations are to be performed directly on the basis of the plan, while the implementation of other economic operations is precluded until after execution of the contract. In addition, the performance of economic operations with reference only to the plan simultaneously effects the execution of the contract required for the fulfillment of the other economic operations. Such a relationship occurs between plans and contracts in the area of carriage of goods. The plan of transportation mandates the presentation of certain means of transport by the carrier and the transfer of certain goods for the purpose of carriage by the shipper. The documents certifying the transfer and receipt of goods, respectively, by the shipper and the carrier qualify as a contract of carriage executed in writing. Having thus executed the contract, the parties fulfill other economic operations: carriage of goods, their unloading, etc.

The fourth type: planning acts oblige one addressee to execute a specified contract, while the other addressee is entitled but not obliged to do so. If the former attempts to avoid the execution of the contract, it can be compelled to establish contractual obligations by the latter in the manner provided by the law. On the contrary, the latter may refuse to execute the contract indicated by the plan, and in this case the former cannot force the establishment of contractual obligations. Only after the contract has been validly executed, are both parties obliged to perform the economic operations indicated by the plan, and only after the execution of the contract can such operations be implemented. The correlation outlined is characteristic of plans and contracts in the area of bank credit. The appropriate bank establishments are obligated to execute contracts for the extension of credit included in credit plans. However, if an economic entity entitled to receive credit according to a credit plan has no desire to avail itself of this opportunity, it would be senseless to require it to accept credit. Therefore, plans of credit provide economic entities with the right to receive credit, but not the duty to exercise this right.

Despite the differences between the various types of correlations between plans and contracts, they all have one feature in common: in all cases either one or both of the parties have the right to compel the other to execute the contract dictated by the plan. However, the applicable measures of compulsion are not identical. Their features depend on the character of the contracts involved and on the procedures for the execution of these contracts.

The most general procedure is outlined by the legislation governing contracts of capital construction.[32] Within one month after the arrival of planning documents, the contractor must present to the customer a draft of the contract. This draft must be signed by the customer under all circumstances within ten days. If the customer has any objections, the latter will be registered in a statement of disagreements (*protokol raznoglasii*), attached as a supplement to the contractual draft. The contractor has ten days to settle any disagreements by negotiations with the customer. If these negotiations do not succeed, the contractor may bring the dispute to Arbitrazh. Otherwise, the expiration of the ten-day period is considered the legal equivalent of the contractor's acceptance of all counterproposals formulated by the customer. The only exception to this rule involves those counterproposals that contradict the planning documents. Such proposed changes will be invalidated by Arbitrazh even if the ten-day period has expired. Disputes, timely transferred to Arbitrazh and called precontractual disputes (*preddogovornye spori*), are heard and resolved in accordance with the principle of economic expediency, though within the limits of the law in force and the relevant plan. If Arbitrazh finds mistakes in planning documents, it must inform the appropriate planning agency and wait for its decision. Independent alterations of planning tasks by Arbitrazh itself are illegal and thus have no binding force. Guided by these rules, Arbitrazh formulates all of the contractual terms left unsettled by the parties, and upon issuance of the final Arbitrazh decision the contract is deemed concluded with the terms agreed upon by the parties, on the one hand, and those fixed by the Arbitrazh decision, on the other hand.

The legislation on contracts of delivery provides for a far more varied procedures than does the legislation on to contracts of capital construction.[33] Contracts of delivery can be executed according to a procedure which differs from that employed in the area of capital investments only from the viewpoint of the time periods established for each precontractual stage. However, as a rule, the supplier works out a draft of a contract, though in specially provided cases this function is performed by the purchaser. Moreover, the purchaser may refuse to conclude a planned contract, entirely or in part, on the condition that the deliverer and the appropriate planning agency are informed within ten days after the purchaser's receipt of the planning documents.[34] In contrast, the deliverer acquires a similar right only in cases where the plan of delivery contradicts the plan of production, and the appropriate planning agency, informed of this divergence, adopts no decision within ten days after receiving the deliverer's information. There are also two alternative procedures for the conclusion of delivery contracts. One of these procedures, acceptance of an order (*zakaz*) for performance, is applicable with respect to contracts based on plans of attachment.[35] In these cases, the purchaser transfers an order to the deliverer with reference to the plan mentioned and the deliverer either accepts this order or initiates an Arbitrazh dispute within a time period established by law. Another procedure, acceptance of a warrant (*nariad*) for performance, is used for contracts where a planning act predetermines all of the terms of the forthcoming delivery. In these cases, the contract is deemed executed according to the terms of the planning warrant, if neither the supplier nor the purchaser expresses the desire to execute a contract according to the standard procedure within ten days after the arrival of the warrant from the appropriate planning agency.

For carriage of goods, a contract, as discussed above,[36] results from the transfer of goods by a shipper, the acceptance of these goods by a transport entity for the purpose of carriage, and the issuance by the latter of a document certifying the performance of the indicated actions.[37] These actions are so precisely outlined by the plan that disputes between the parties seem unimaginable. At the same time, any party that attempts to avoid performance of its planned duties must pay fines to the other party in an amount determined by transport legislation and representing either a fixed sum or a certain percentage of the value of the goods involved. Because such fines themselves serve as a means of coercing execution of contracts of carriage, there is no need to resort to Arbitrazh for resolution of precontractual disputes under these circumstances. Arbitrazh also may not interfere in precontractual relations between bank establishments and economic entities demanding extension of credit in accordance with plans. However, the rule that Arbitrazh does not implement precontractual dispute resolution in the area of bank credit is due to factors different from those acting in the area of good transportation. Credit plans provide for the extension of credit not indiscriminately but exclusively for certain purposes (connected with unfinished manufacture of complicated products, with goods bought but yet not paid for by purchasers, etc). To receive credit, an economic entity must not only refer to the plan but also prove the existence of circumstances that legally justify the extension of credit. In turn, the bank establishment seeks to verify the validity of the entity's request, and, depending on the results of this verification process, either extends credit or refuses to do so. The adoption of a positive or negative decision is a matter of administrative discretion; more precisely, it is one of the means of financial supervision employed by the bank. And because Arbitrazh is not entitled to resolve disputes between supervising and supervised agencies, the refusal of a bank establishment to extend planned credit may be appealed only to the superior bodies of the bank but not to Arbitrazh in the form of a precontractual dispute.

Planned economic contracts differ from ordinary contracts not only in the way they are concluded but also in the method by which the identity of the contractual parties is determined and in the time periods during which these contracts are to retain their force.

The contractual parties are predetermined by plans. However, the relevant planned indications may be mandatory either entirely or as limits upon the choices that the parties may make. Contractors and customers are mandatorily designated in capital investment plans, and nothing can be changed by the addressees of planned tasks. If a contractor cannot perform certain kinds of work, it may enter into subcontracts with other construction entities to provide the required work. But this creation of a general contractor—subcontractor relationship does not affect the legal position of the customer, who deals only with the general contractor and is in no way legally connected with the subcontractors.[38] For supply, the regulations are less rigid. The Statute on Delivery of Products for Production and Technical Use permits the conclusion of contracts of delivery either between production and consumer entities or between any of these entities and organizations of material-technical supply.[39] The Statute on Delivery of Consumer Goods provides an even greater number of opportunities for the parties' choice.[40] Although these legislative acts refer to the circumstances under which one choice or another must be made, in practice matters are more complicated than the legal provisions would suggest. It often occurs that a consumer indicated by the plan wishes to deal directly with the producer, however, the producer prefers to deal with the consumer not directly but through supply or wholesale agencies. Such cases, categorized as disputes with respect to the structure of contractual connections, are resolved by Arbitrazh, which adopts its decisions in accordance with the principle of economic expediency either independently or after consultation with the appropriate planning body. For a long time a number of Soviet scholars have been insisting on direct contractual connections between producers and consumers, considering them to be cheaper and more expedient than indirect connections through supply or wholesale agencies. These authors disregard completely the economic advantages that result from the activities of intermediate agencies, such as the freeing of producers from extremely burdensome trade functions.[41] Yet, the problem has not been finally solved with regard to the delivery of consumer goods. As to products for production and technical use, Soviet law has recognized at last that indirect connections must be maintained as a general rule, while direct connections may be established only under precisely described circumstances.[42]

The time period for which an economic contract remains in force also depends on the specific area of economic planning. A contract for capital construction must be executed so as to remain in force during the entire period of the construction process outlined in the relevant planning acts. If this period exceeds one year, the contract is called a "general contract," and its terms are particularized annually by agreements between the parties.[43] Contracts of delivery designate a single or periodic acts of performance. In the former case, the contract remains in force until it is performed or the planning act expires. In the latter case, a contract is concluded covering the entire time period during which the related plan remains in force: usually for one year, but sometimes for a quarter, a season, etc. In accordance with five-year plans of supply, the parties execute a five-year contract of delivery, annually particularized by additional agreements.[44] Contracts for the carriage of goods are made each time goods are transported, although transportation plans are established for one year, and the performance of these plans requires numerous acts of carriage.[45] Bank credit may be short-term or long-term. Short-term credit is extended for less than one year and is used to supplement circulating assets. Long-term credit is extended for more than one year and is used for the acquisition of basic assets.[46]

As a general rule, planned economic contracts can neither be altered nor cancelled while the planning acts that serve as their legal prerequisites retain binding force. Alteration or abrogation of planning acts leads, respectively, to changes in or termination of the appropriate contracts. It is true that the legislation regulating all types of planned activities obliges contractual parties to execute additional agreements in order to change or terminate their rights and duties in accordance with the alteration or abrogation of planning acts.[47] In fact, however, such agreements deal only with the consequences of the new decisions adopted by the planning agencies. The performance of an economic contracts in accordance with its original terms is prohibited once the appropriate planning act has been altered or abrogated, regardless of whether or not an agreement between the parties has been executed.[48] At the same time, also in this respect, contracts of delivery are regulated differently.[49] Although the plan of supply remains in force, the parties may terminate a contract of delivery or change its terms (without exceeding planned limits) by mutual agreement. In cases where agreement cannot be reached, either party may bring the matter before Arbitrazh.

A general rule of Soviet law states: "The content of contracts executed on the basis of a planning task should correspond to this task."[50] The consequences of violations of this general rule are determined by legislative acts on economic contracts of various types. For instance, Article 31 of the Statute on Delivery of Products provides: "contracts contradicting . . . state plans and tasks shall be deemed invalid entirely or in part." However, just what constitutes such a "contradiction" is differently determined with respect to different contracts, bearing in mind the peculiarities of the various legislative regimes that regulate economic contracts of different types. Let us compare from this point of view the contract of delivery and the contract of capital construction.

Owing to circumstances mentioned above,[51] no economic contract is more subordinated to plans than is the contract of capital construction. Moreover, not only planning acts but also numerous legislative acts mandatorily determine the rights and duties of contractors and customers with such detail that seemingly no room is left for contractual agreement: any term arrived at by the parties themselves must be deemed void, if it contradicts planning orders or legal provisions. Thus, in this case the rule of Article 34 of Fundamental Principles of Civil Legislation, abstractly formulating the absolute dependence of planned contracts on planning acts, finds its most consistent and unfailingly severe application. Nevertheless, contracts of capital construction are executed and even must be executed under the threat of legal sanctions directed against the addressees of plans (fines exacted for the benefit of the state budget) and the management officials of the entity (of the contractor or of the customer) that attempts to avoid the establishment of contractual obligations. Such stringent measures may seem incomprehensible, bearing in mind that the contract discussed, from all appearances, represents a mere formality neither supplementing nor developing centralized commands. In fact, however, restricted as it is from the viewpoint of the initiative of the performers of the plan, the contract of capital construction qualifies as an important means of ensuring the implementation of Soviet construction programs.

On the one hand, the execution of a contract allows the parties to determine whether there are errors in the plan itself. A party that discovers a design flaw or other mistake in one of the planning documents may refuse to execute a contract until the appropriate agency makes the required corrections.[52] Arbitrazh, informed by the appropriate party of the actual cause of precontractual disagreement, must suspend the hearing of such a dispute in order to notify the agency entitled either to retain or to modify the plan confirmed. Depending on the decision of this agency, Arbitrazh resolves the dispute thus suspended. On the other hand, the contract, once concluded, empowers the customer to exercise supervision over the activities of the contractor. Only as a contractual party may the customer monitor the contractor's observance of those planning indicators that determine the quality of construction, the character of each component, the time periods allowed for completion of the entire project and separately scheduled portions, the actual volume of work performed, and the conformity of the contractor's monetary claims with the sums payable according to the estimate, etc. It is true that because capital construction is financed by the state budget, the customer's lack of direct financial interest leads to decreased vigilance in monitoring the contractor's performance, in comparison with cases where the same entity pays its own money for the work performed or goods acquired. Therefore, a number of other agencies, especially the appropriate offices of *Stroibank* (Construction Bank), exercise supervision over the activities of both the contractor and the customer. This supervision is almost comprehensive, encompassing not only financial matters but also the process of construction itself. As a result, *Stroibank*'s staff includes many construction engineers as well as bookkeepers. However, without the customer the requisite supervision could not be so systematic as it actually is in daily practice. All of this indicates that the contract of capital construction has some inherent value, despite what would seem to be its purely formal character.

One must also take into consideration that matters not dealt with by the plan are provided for by means of the contract. Both parties develop contractual terms concerning their mutual services (for instance, the temporary use of the customer's buildings by the contractor), material and technical supply for the construction planned (for instance, acquisition of certain materials by the customer and their transfer to the contractor), provision by the customer for certain needs of the contractor's workers (for instance, their housing needs for the period of construction), etc. As is obvious, these terms do not directly relate to the construction of the object specified by the plan. Therefore, they are included not in the contract of capital construction, but rather in the special conditions supplementing the contract and embodying the agreements reached between the parties themselves. As to the contract *per se*, it is extremely brief and refers to the plan, design, blueprints, and estimate as to its constituent parts, although the latter derive from planning commands, not from the parties' own initiative. Deviations from the plan can occur not in the process of executing the contract, but during the performance of the construction work, and not as a general rule but only in two cases provided for by the law.[53] The contractor is rigidly bound to follow the design. However, insignificant deviations are allowed, if these do not change the established technical principles, involve no danger for the durability of the structure, and are recorded by the contractor on the appropriate blueprints. The contractor is no less rigidly bound by the estimate. However, changes reducing the price of construction are allowed, if these do not decrease the quality of the object constructed, are approved by the customer as to the materials to be substituted, and if the entity that is the architect of the project has no objection.

Because contracts of capital construction include certain substantive terms resulting from agreements between the parties, and because a limited degree of initiative remains with the parties even after the establishment of contractual obligations, the rigidity of planning in this economic area does not preclude either precontractual disputes or disputes resulting from modifications of the contract after its execution. Precontractual disputes can arise in connection with any of the terms that may be developed by the parties and that are embodied in the special conditions. It may happen, for example, that the customer, to which the plan of supply allocates the necessary construction materials, wishes to deal directly with their supplier, while the contractor prefers to be the sole master of the entire construction process and therefore insists upon the transfer by the customer of all of the rights created by the plan of supply. This is a common ground for precontractual disputes in the area of capital construction. Sometimes, precontractual disputes are more closely related to the construction itself. It occurs, for instance, that a plan, covering several components of a unified complex (two workshops, three apartment-buildings, etc.), establishes one time period for the completion of the entire project, but does not determine the sequence in which these components should be constructed. Under such circumstances, the sequence depends upon the decision of the parties, and if agreement cannot be reached, this precontractual dispute must be resolved by Arbitrazh. Finally, it also occurs that the contractor engages in practices reducing the price of construction, despite objections on the part of the customer or of the architect. If the objections are found to have been groundless, the contractor will keep the entire amount of savings resulting from the undertaking implemented. In contrast, should the objections prove to have been reasonable, the contractor must remove at its own expenses all of the consequences of its unauthorized activity. Disputes of this character are heard by Arbitrazh, however, not as precontractual matters, but as disputes related to the improper performance of the contract.

Thus, a certain degree of initiative on the part of addressees of planning tasks can be developed even in the most centralized area of economic activity in the USSR, capital construction. It is noteworthy that, in discussing the issue of capital construction at the 1986 Party Congress, Gorbachev and Ryzhkov insisted upon a new strategy in this area, emphasizing not so much the construction of new plants and factories as the technological renovation of existing economic units.[54] However, neither Soviet leader posed in connection with capital construction the question which, though in vague terms, was formulated with respect to other types of economic activity: how to reasonably coordinate centralism and decentralization? And as representatives of the Soviet system, they cannot be criticized for this omission. Since capital investment is the exclusive prerogatives of the owner and because Soviet economic entities are not owners of their property,[55] decentralization is incompatible with the very nature of capital construction. Therefore, the existing centralism must be retained in this area, despite the vague promises to reasonably combine it with decentralization in other areas of the Soviet economy.

The situation is different with respect to the contract of delivery. Even during the period of Stalin's centralism this contract was not as strictly planned as was the contract of capital construction. The present Soviet reformers, calling for a certain degree of decentralization of economic management during the period of the twelfth five-year plan (1986–1990), also emphasize supply and other types of economic activity connected with it (disposition of above-plan production, extension of bank credit, etc.). The development of Soviet legislation during the forthcoming five-year period and, to an even greater extent, economic practice as it evolves either on the basis of this legislation or independent of it will indicate the degree to which such promises are fulfilled. The following discussion will deal with the correlation between the contract of delivery and the planning of supply under the law currently in force.

Soviet entities that are not indicated by the plan of supply as potential suppliers and purchasers may not execute a contract of delivery with one another. Such a contract would be void from the moment of its execution, and its performance would entail, along with personal responsibility for certain officials, also financial liability for both parties.[56] Even those entities that do have the right to execute a contract according to the plan may do so only with respect to objects indicated by the plan. Substituting other articles for planned objects is a violation of the same law and entails the same legal consequences as does the execution of a contract between parties that are not connected by the plan. Furthermore, addressees of the plan of supply may not in the contract increase the quantity to be delivered above the level fixed by the plan. To the extent that this rule has been violated, the contract is void, and the sanctions employed against violators are identical to those resulting from the execution of contracts of delivery without planning prerequisites. In all these respects, contracts of delivery depend on the planning of supply.

However, supply cannot be planned on the basis of the extreme centralism that dominates in the area of capital construction. Designs and blueprints outline all the details of a planned construction project. As a rule, similar details are unavailable to the planners of supply. They can, of course, predetermine, for example, all of the characteristics of fuel such as petroleum earmarked for certain consumers, and therefore, the delivery of petroleum relies not upon genuine contracts but upon a simplified substitute for a contract: the acceptance of a warrant for performance.[57] But even such plans sometimes disregard the specific needs of their addressees, containing gaps which can be filled only by the parties themselves. Soviet law takes this situation into account, entitling each party to demand the conclusion of a formal contract despite the apparent comprehensiveness of the planned indicators.[58] At the same time, the diameters of drills or colors and sizes of shoes required by each purchaser cannot be predetermined by the plan, and only its addressees may develop these or analogous terms relating to the forthcoming delivery. Further, plans of supply remain in force for long time periods, while the purchaser requires periodic delivery from the supplier. The most convenient times for actual delivery are known only to the contract parties, and, consequently, only the contract between them can ensure a mutually optimum solution. Therefore, the law entitles the parties to establish this term, by mutual agreement, though limiting the parties' freedom by the rule that the annual quantity must be equally divided among quarters, and the quarterly quantity must be delivered in equal monthly portions.[59] Lastly, the process of planning of supply begins long before actual delivery. The economic circumstances prevailing at the time when plans are drafted naturally can change substantially before the time of performance, and, as a result, the previous needs of purchasers may either entirely disappear or their level may not be so high as is indicated by the plans. Soviet experience has demonstrated the inefficiency of coercive measures compelling the purchaser to acquire objects which, though provided for by the plan, are no longer required. Therefore, the law currently in force entitles the purchaser to refuse to execute a planned contract either completely or to the extent that the quantity called for in the plan exceeds the purchaser's actual needs.[60]

All these circumstances lead to considerably broader discretion for addressees of the plan of supply than for addressees of the plan of construction. However, the discretion of the parties concluding a contract of delivery is not the same with regard to different contractual terms. From this point of view, the contract of delivery contains four types of terms, namely those which are: (1) subject to no discretion of the parties (for instance, the specific articles and maximum quantity), (2) unconditionally subject to the parties' discretion (for instance, the specific dates of delivery), (3) conditionally subject to the discretion of at least one of the parties (for instance, a complete or partial refusal to buy planned objects announced within the established period of time), or (4) subject to the parties' discretion to choose from among established alternatives (for instance, the parties' right to choose one of the modes of carriage listed in special conditions [*Osobye usloviia*] regulating the delivery of goods of the type involved). Relying upon the classification suggested, one can predict the character of additional decentralization that may be acceptable to the Soviet rulers in the area of supply.

Terms that are now not subject to the discretion of the parties may be affected by two changes, mentioned but not developed by Ryzhkov at the 1986 Party Congress.[61] First, products manufactured over and above the plan, though planned in the area of supply as a general rule, may be left at the disposal of the producers and excluded from the planning of distribution. But there is no doubt that such an innovation will never be employed with respect to goods short in supply, and since scarcity prevails in the Soviet economy, one cannot expect broad development of the suggested innovation, at least in the near future. Second, planning of supply must rely on data accumulated by means of concluded contracts. But if all needs expressed in contracts could be satisfied, only political, not economic factors, would govern centralized distribution in the USSR. Under present circumstances, the Soviet authorities cannot abolish centralized distribution not only because of their political interests but also owing to the lag of supply behind demand. Therefore, Gorbachev's innovations will, at best, mirror in this regard Kosygin's reform: planning should follow contracts, however, executed contracts must be modified in accordance with confirmed plans.

Terms that are completely subject to the parties' discretion cannot be affected by the projected reforms. With respect to these terms, contractual freedom has already attained its zenith, and no reform could be able to ensure further development in the same direction. But can the Soviet leadership increase the number of such terms? The right of the purchaser to refuse to execute a planned contract, completely or in part, formulated by the law as conditional, has in fact been transformed into an unconditional right by Arbitrazh practice.[62] As to the abrogation of legal alternatives restricting the parties' discretion, it is difficult to reach a satisfactory conclusion. Sometimes such alternatives are obviously unnecessary. For example, among a dozen methods of monetary accounts between Soviet entities provided for by legal provisions, the parties could themselves choose the most convenient method, instead of being restricted by alternatives laid down in the mandatory rules of the applicable Special Conditions (*Osobye usloviia*). For the most part, however, the restrictions result from economic necessity. For example, limitations on the types of available transportation are required in order to ensure the optimum distribution of carriage of goods between means of transportation of different kinds, bearing in mind that the volume of transport services in the USSR is inadequate to meet the needs of producers, let alone of consumers. Thus, the projected reforms aimed at decentralization, while changing nothing in the area of capital construction, do not seem significantly more promising with respect to supply.

Looking to the relation between plans and contracts, carriage of goods differs substantially from supply and construction. This results both from the technological peculiarities of transport activity and its specific regulation by legal provisions.[63]

Technologically, the means of carriage must be appropriate to the types of goods transported. It is impossible definitely to ensure the necessary matching at the stage of centralized planning, but, under the Soviet system, it is also unacceptable to ignore carriage of goods at the planning stage and to rely exclusively on contracts. Specially assigning all transported goods to designated means of transportation directly in the process of planning would render it virtually impossible to adhere to the plan because, at the time of the performance of plan tasks, the shipper may have goods that are not identical, even though similar to those indicated by the plan, just as the carrier may have the means of transportation provided for by the plan but earmarked for transportation of other goods of the same type. As a result, the planners must avoid such an extreme. However, they also cannot resort to the opposite extreme by declining to carry out any planning in this specific area. Goods that have been produced must be transferred to their consumers. Thus, the planning of transportation logically follows the planning of production and distribution. The latter would be senseless without the former. To employ plans of transportation and to simultaneously avoid rendering their performance impracticable the Soviet authorities have found it necessary to depart from their standard planning approach. Instead of precise indicators, they establish classes of goods that a shipper legitimately may present for transportation, and types of means of transportation that the carrier must be able to ensure in each planned period. These types are binding for both parties, but within the established types the choice is subject to each party's discretion.

Legally, a contract of carriage may be made not only by agreement but also through the implementation of certain economic operations: the transfer of goods by the shipper and the acceptance of these goods by the carrier. Both parties prepare and perform the actions required of them at the precontractual stage and at the stage of the conclusion of the contract. Therefore, the problem of the dependence of the performers' activities on the plan must be formulated differently with regard to transportation than it is usually characterized in connection with construction or supply. The planning either of construction or of supply creates only one "horizontal" link between its performers: the right and the duty to execute the appropriate contract. Consequently, in these cases, the problem is reduced to the relation between plan and contract. In contrast, the planning of carriage of goods creates between its addressees two "horizontal" links: a precontractual link based only on the plan, and a contractual link based simultaneously on the plan and on the contract. Therefore, dealing with the carriage of goods, one must analyze the relation between the binding force of the plan and the free initiative of its addressees in the performance of both planned and contractual operations. As discussed above, the performance of planned operations specified by the parties' choice within the limits of confirmed types of goods and means of transport leaves more room for discretion than is common in other economic areas subordinated to the plan. Since, however, these same operations lead to the conclusion of a contract, the parties' discretion is significant in the relation between transport contracts and plans.

Depending on the specific features taken into consideration, the planning of carriage can be characterized either as stronger or as weaker than the planning of supply. It is stronger, because, in contrast to purchasers, shippers have no right to refuse to make a contract. Nevertheless, the discretion of shippers is not so limited as is that of the customer in the construction contract. The customer who attempts to avoid concluding a contract can be compelled to enter into contractual relations by taking the matter to Arbitrazh as a precontractual dispute. The shipper is not subject to similar compulsion. The latter's refusal to use the means of transportation allocated by the plan leads to the payment of penalties, and the earlier that the carrier is notified of the refusal the lower the penalty that must be paid by the shipper. However, if the shipper does not have the goods, whose transportation is called for by the plan, it would be preposterous to compel him to execute a contract with the carrier. Continuing the same comparison from another viewpoint, one will come to the conclusion that the planning of transportation is weaker than the planning of supply. The quantitative indicators of the contract of delivery may not exceed the highest quantitative limits determined by the plan. For transportation exceeding the quantity designated by planned indicators is quite possible in cases where the shipper presents a request for additional means of transportation in advance and the carrier timely accepts such an offer.

Thus, the addressees of transport plans are far more independent of planned commands than are the performers of other plans. This results not from subjective inclinations toward decentralization in this specific area but from the objective features of transport activities dictating specific methods of legal regulation. Does the present Soviet leadership have any desire to see further decentralization in this area? Economically, such a tendency would be pointless, taking into account the notorious backwardness of all types of Soviet transport. Politically, the weakness of centralized regulation stemming from the nature of transport activity has already attained a level contrary to the interest of the ruling elite, and only the "standard forms" (waybills, transport receipts, etc.) employed for the purpose of governing various types of carriages serve as a centralistic counter-balance to inevitable decentralization. Legally, no sign of further decentralization has ever been expressed or noticed. At any rate, all of the speakers at the 1986 Party Congress, incessantly calling for the reconstruction of economic administration, did not utter a word about the same idea addressed to Soviet transport and its upper-level or subordinate entities. Actually, transport troubles the Soviet rulers not in the methods of its administration but because of its underdevelopment. Recent appeals for scientific and technical progress do relate, of course, to transport as well as to other economic branches. Transport is, however, entirely disregarded insofar as organizational improvement of the Soviet economy represents the principal matter of official concern.

The legal implementation of the organizational improvement of the Soviet economy proclaimed by the 1986 Congress of the Communist Party of the USSR is just beginning. However, even the first Soviet decrees emerging in this area demonstrate a devotion to stale methods rather than a desire for substantial innovation. As an eloquent illustration one need only look to the Party and Government decree "On the Improvement of Planning, Economic Stimulation, and Perfection of the Administration of Production of Consumer Goods in the Area of Light Industry," published in *Izvestia* on May 6, 1986. This decree addresses not production in general, but only the production of consumer goods, and not all consumer goods, but only those produced by economic entities of light industry. Moreover, notwithstanding the restricted scope of its application, the decree does not substantially strengthen the economic independence of subordinate entities. It calls for the implementation of genuine *khozraschet*, yet refers only to the requirement of selfsufficiency and abolishes numerous forms of state subsidies. The decree emphasizes the broadening of the property rights of production associations, yet outlines only a procedure for the use of profit and allows for more freedom only in the disposition of monetary funds earmarked for technological innovations. It increases property liability, yet deals only with contractual violations committed by production associations and disregards improper actions on the part of planning agencies.

Of the principal types of economic contracts, the decree simply does not mention the contract of carriage of goods. Also, a new provision connected with capital investments proves that no substantial change can be expected in this area. "As an exception," the decree states, economic entities of light industry may employ production development funds for the expansion of enterprises built before 1950, if the cost of such expansion does not exceed three million rubles. This limited exception, which is only a temporary measure, represents the sole change effected in the established system of capital investments. The edict's provisions concerning the supply of consumer goods, which in isolation might seem promising, are also insignificant, as a comprehensive analysis of all the relevant provisions will indicate.

On the one hand, "the volume of supply . . . shall be independently determined by production associations (enterprises), with reference to executed contracts of delivery." But, on the other hand, plans of production of consumer goods must be "based on confirmed indicators," and the assignment for supply must emanate from centralized planning agencies.

In addition, "Production associations (enterprises) are allowed to sell independently consumer goods produced over and above the plan." It follows, then, that within the limits of the plan the same goods can be sold only to planned purchasers in accordance with planned indicators. Hence, the independence of contracts from plans is not so broad as it might seem at first glance. Furthermore, long-term direct connections between deliverers and purchasers, in principle rejected with respect to products of production-technical use, are proclaimed by the decree as the most desirable for the supply of consumer goods. But "long-term direct connections" ensure contractual freedom to no greater extent than do "plans of attachment" applicable in other cases where consumer goods are distributed. Thus, the decree seems heavy with declarations but light in substance. And this impression remains unchanged, despite the "revolutionary" measure of "freedom of prices" introduced by the decree. This freedom signifies that deliverers and purchasers may increase prices of "especially fashionable" goods under the control of the State Committee of Prices until supply corresponds to demand. As is quite obvious, the actual goal of such "freedom" is the increase of retail prices, not the improvement of the production efficiency of light industry, although this goal is disguised in the form of monetary stimuli ostensibly established for the benefit of producers.

In free market countries, the execution and performance of contracts, while regulated by legal provisions, result from economic inducements. In countries in which the economy is subject to mandatory planning, economic inducements are not sufficiently strong to stimulate the same activity. Here, legal provisions, accompanied by administrative coercion, play a more important role both in causing the establishment and ensuring the fulfillment of contractual obligations. The entire complex of such measures is called economic discipline, and it includes three interdependent, though different, branches: financial discipline, planning discipline, and contractual discipline.[64] All of these branches of economic discipline, even contractual discipline, impose numerous duties upon the addressees of planning tasks not in their mutual relations but in the relations between each addressee and the Soviet state represented by different agencies in various cases.

Financial discipline is of a general nature, revealing its force in all planning or contractual obligations which connect the lowest links of the Soviet economy. The functions of financial supervision ensuring financial discipline are implemented by agencies of the Ministry of Finance and by establishments of the State Bank (*Gosbank*) or the Construction Bank (*Stroibank*) depending on the character of the activity supervised (production and trade work or construction work).[65] Financial supervision can be either episodic or systematic. Episodic supervision assumes only one form—financial audits, the purpose of which is to ascertain the status of the property funds[66] of the entity inspected, the conformity of their volume with established norms, the accordance of the spending of monetary resources with their designation as funds of circulation, investment, amortization, etc. Violations of financial discipline discovered through episodic control lead to personal responsibility for the individual culprits and, in cases where these violations affect contracts, the latter must be either invalidated or corrected by modifying or deleting the illegal terms. Systematic supervision is carried out with respect to all monetary accounts maintained between contractual partners as well as in the processes of bank credit extension and the spending of extended credit. Bank establishments will honor an entity's order to make a payment to another entity only if both are connected by a contract executed in conformity with the plan, if the payor has monetary resources earmarked for the acquisition involved, and if the entity receiving the payment has already performed its duty or is prepared to perform it without delay. Sometimes systematic supervision includes a comparison of the prices officially established and those requested by the performer, inquiries whether performance has been rendered in fact or only on paper, etc. Before extending credit, the bank first checks all of the prerequisites substantiating the entity's request,[67] and after that the bank will make a payment from a credit account only if the payment does not contradict the entity's goals justifying extension of credit.

Plan discipline is of a specific nature, being applicable only where an act adversely affects the process of planning or the performance of plans. Various agencies deal with the enforcement of plan discipline: those which issue plans or which are superior to the addressee of a planning task, Arbitrazh in cases where it is entitled to initiate a dispute with reference to the non-observance of plan commands or where such non-observance is ascertained during the hearing of a dispute initiated by one or both parties, a procurator as an official supervising the absolute and uniform adherence to the laws by all individuals and establishments, including economic entities subject to plan discipline,[68] etc. A great number of actions or failures to act qualify as violations of plan discipline. These violations encompass the execution of a contract without the necessary planning prerequisites; the failure to execute a contract mandatorily dictated by planning acts; deviations from planned indicators in formulating contractual terms; disregard of these indicators in the process of performing contracts; failure to carry out economic operations directly called for by the plan; undertaking these operations in a way contrary to the planned indicators, etc. Violations of plan discipline may be deemed official crimes under certain circumstances.[69] As to the financial consequences of such violations, one must consult the legislative acts regulating the various types of economic activity: supply, construction, transportation, etc. Sometimes, violations of planning discipline simultaneously signify that the interests of one addressee of a planning act have been adversely affected by another addressee. Then, the defendant's liability toward the plaintiff also satisfies the appropriate administrative agency representing the state as the rightholder in the area of planning discipline. For example, a supplier or a contractor who refuses to execute a planned contract violates both plan discipline and the right of its prospective contractual partner. The compulsory execution of the contract resulting from the settlement of a precontractual dispute and the payment of a fine by the defending party to the party adversely affected (in an amount determined respectively by the legislation on delivery or construction) will be considered satisfactory also from the viewpoint of guardians of plan discipline. Not infrequently, however, violations of plan discipline either leave intact the parties' interests or even are committed by one in favor of the other. Under such circumstances, the offenders must be held accountable to the appropriate state agency, while mutual liability between the parties is precluded. For instance, Article 88 of the Statute of Delivery of Products for Production and Technical Use provides for cases where such products are sold to a purchaser not indicated by the plan of supply. Although the supplier has violated plan discipline, the purchaser hardly suffers from this violation. Therefore, fines equal to anywhere from 25% to 100% of the price of products thus sold must be paid by the supplier not to the purchaser but to the appropriate agency of material-technical supply.

Contract discipline is also of a specific nature, and an entity becomes subject to such discipline only upon execution of a contract with another entity.[70] However, similar to other types of economic discipline, contract discipline connects not the contract parties with one another (they are connected by contract rights and duties) but each of these parties with the state (the parties as obligors, and the state as the rightholder, represented by the appropriate agency). There exist the following important forms of contract discipline.

First, the mandatory rules of the legal provisions regulating any given type of contract have the force of contract terms, regardless of whether they are reproduced in a specific contract or not. In failing to observe such terms, a party violates contract discipline. Thus, legislative acts dealing with various types of economic contracts provide for penalties which must be paid by the offender to the other party. For instance, the legislation on delivery includes sanctions for delay, and for deviations from established requirements of quality, assortment, tare, packing, etc. Delay qualifies as a ground for the imposition of penalties under either the legislation that regulates construction or that which governs transportation. Both types of legislation also discourage other violations by means of specially established sanctions. The party damaged by a violation of an economic contract has the right to demand the payment of penalties from the offender and additionally bears the duty toward the state to exercise this right in practice. One can imagine the degree of material interest connected with a right, the exercise of which must be compelled by the state. And how can any material interest arise, if at the end of each economic year all sums exacted as contractual fines must be transferred to the state budget? But the replacement of material stimuli by coercive discipline is a tested method of Soviet economic administration. It is truly astonishing that a legal rule can provide for the payment of penalties to the state for failure to exact penalties from a contractual party.[71] But such is the substance of contractual discipline, and no one has suggested that it be changed, despite the virtues of economic stimuli extolled by the latest forum of Soviet communists.

Second, contractual parties may agree to employ measures strengthening but not weakening their responsibility for nonperformance or improper performance of an economic contract. For instance, the inclusion in a contract of penalties that are not provided for by law is valid, while the refusal in a contract to employ the sanctions called for by law is invalid.[72] Contractual parties have the right to increase but not to decrease the size of penalties established by legislation. A decrease may be ordered only by Arbitrazh and only under extraordinary circumstances, in contrast to increases applicable in all cases, where Arbitrazh assesses the violation committed as an especially malicious act.[73] An agreement between a purchaser and a supplier for the delivery of goods of a higher quality than that called for by the applicable standard in return for the payment of an accordingly higher price than the established norm is allowed. In contrast, the delivery of products of a quality lower than that required by the applicable standard in return for the payment of proportionally lower price than that officially established is prohibited, despite an agreement to this effect between a supplier and a purchaser.[74] The economic arguments inducing contractual partners to employ any such agreements cannot be taken into consideration, because even reference to these arguments contradicts the principle of contract discipline. In observing the principle indicated, Arbitrazh must declare void all such agreements, and in cases where the agreements have not only been concluded but also performed, both parties will be obligated to pay penalties to the state.

Third, contract discipline assumes that mutual control will be implemented by both participants in contractual obligations. In disregarding this function, an economic entity neglects its duty toward the state. If the failure of one party to exercise vigilant control furthers the commission of a violation by the other party, the former will be punished to no less extent than the latter. For instance, both statutes on Delivery[75] state that "the purchaser is obliged" to refuse to accept delivered goods whose quality does not correspond to the indicators of confirmed standards. As a matter of course, the purchaser bears this duty toward the state and not to the supplier, since the latter as an offender cannot be a rightholder. However, failure to fulfill such a duty conceals but does not further a violation of law on the part of the supplier. Therefore, the purchaser cannot be fined for the benefit of the state, though the individual responsibility of guilty officials is not precluded. Another situation arises in cases where a contractor represents that it has performed more work than is in fact the case in order to receive more money than it deserves, and the customer certifies this padding, thus opening the path to illegal enrichment at the state's expense. Under such circumstances, 7% of the amount of padding must be paid to the state by both parties in equal proportion (3.5% each).[76]

Like other civil law contracts, economic contracts are enforced by general measures of civil law liability: compensation for damages caused by the non-performance or improper performance of contractual duties.[77] At the same time, in contrast to other civil law contracts, whose sanctity is only occasionally protected by certain special sanctions (penalties or fines) as supplements to the general measures, economic contracts are protected by means of both the former and the latter types of sanctions in accordance with the legislation regulating delivery, construction, transportation, etc. Although the state is the owner of the monetary resources moving from one economic entity to the other along the channel of civil law liability, and despite the fact that all payments resulting from breaches of contractual obligations are ultimately transferred to the state treasury, one cannot challenge the definite effectiveness of the monetary sanctions used in enforcing economic contracts. As a consequence of being subjected to such sanctions, the offender loses a portion of its monetary resources, but it must nevertheless perform the plan *in toto*. And it will strive to do so in order to avoid additional negative consequences: a decrease in its incentive fund, the withholding of bonuses, etc. However, from the viewpoint of the Soviet state as the monopoly owner of the entire economy, the performance of plans in monetary form is senseless, if at least in part the money received represents not an accumulation in kind but employment of monetary sanctions. An excess of monetary accumulation in comparison with accumulation in kind means, under the specific structure of the Soviet economy, that within the limits of this excess money has been moved from one pocket to another, but that the owner of both pockets has suffered a loss, instead of making a profit. Therefore, in providing measures of liability for breach of contract, Soviet law also proclaims the principle of so-called real performance.

In its general form, the principle referred to maintains that "the payment of a penalty (or fine, forfeit) established in the event of delay or other improper performance of an obligation and compensation for losses caused by improper performance shall not release the debtor from specific performance of the obligation, except for instances when a planning task on which an obligation between socialist organizations is based has lost force."[78] As is clear, only the last provision is addressed exclusively to economic contracts. However, even without it there would be no doubt that a contractual obligation cannot be performed once the plan upon which it is based loses binding force, irrespective of whether or not this has been preceded by a breach of the contract and the application of property sanctions. Thus, the rule cited applies to all civil law contracts and establishes in general, that even the payment of compensation for damages and the payment of penalties will not free the offender from its duties, nor will it deprive its partner of the rights connected with the performance of the contract according to its terms as originally formulated. As an abstract regulation this rule is in no way defective. However, applied to economic contracts without any modification, it is obviously unsatisfactory. Certain types of economic activity are quite compatible with a legal provision that retains after a breach of contract only the duty of the offender to implement and only the right of its partner to demand specific performance. But in the absence of other regulations, the rightholder might refuse to exercise its right, thus liberating the obligor from its duty, and, as a result, the state's desire to ensure the proper correlation between monetary accumulation and accumulation in kind would be defeated by the failure to implement fully the principle of real performance. In order to avoid such undesirable consequences, the Soviet legislator stresses the essential nature of the principle discussed with respect to economic contracts of various types.

The strongest commands in this regard are addressed, as one could guess from previous discussion,[79] to the contract of capital construction. While entitling the parties to recover penalties for various violations, the legislative acts that regulate capital construction make no provision whatsoever for the cancellation of a contract nor for the irrevocable refusal to accept even partial performance as a legal sanction for improper conduct on the part of either the customer or the contractor. Consequently, the principle of real performance is mutually binding in the area of construction: whatever violations may have been committed and whatever sanctions may have been imposed, both the customer and the contractor retain not only the right but also the duty to demand and to implement specific performance. The extreme centralization of capital investments and the designation of these investments not for the satisfaction of current demands but for the achievement of long-term goals leads to certain peculiarities in the legal provisions that apply the general principle of real performance to delays in construction contract performance. Usually delay is punished by penalties, and the eventual fate of the appropriate part of real performance depends on the concrete peculiarities of the specific regulations. In capital construction, the contractor must pay penalties for failure to complete each stage of the work according to the schedule outlined, yet at the same time the mutually binding principle of real performance remains in force. However, if, despite the previous delay, the contractor manages to complete the entire project on time, the penalties previously recovered must be returned by the customer.[80] Owing to the same circumstances, special provisions are addressed to the completion of capital construction projects ahead of schedule. As a rule, in relations between Soviet entities, premature performance of an obligation by the debtor is permitted only if the creditor has consented to such activity.[81] In contrast, the construction contractor is encouraged to render performance in advance of schedule by the law itself. Profit made from the exploitation of the structure during the period beginning upon actual completion and ending at the time indicated as the completion date by the construction plan must be transferred to the contractor.[82] Certain privileges are also established for the contractor in cases where the quality of construction does not correspond to the plan. In accordance with the principle of real performance, all defects must be eliminated by the contractor at its own expense.[83] Because, however, this duty is by itself very expensive, the contractor is not required to pay penalties.

The contract of delivery is less affected by the principle of real performance than is the contract of capital construction. A customer may not refuse to accept performance tendered by a construction contractor guilty of delay. On the contrary, a purchaser of goods does have such a right, but he may exercise it exclusively with respect to that portion of the goods not delivered on time and only on the condition that the supplier is informed of the refusal before it dispatches these goods.[84] Since the contract of delivery is designed to satisfy the current demands of the purchaser, under no circumstances can the penalties recovered from the supplier for violations of its duties be returned. Moreover, if the purchaser has not exercised its right to refuse to accept goods not delivered on time, and, if the supplier's delay has exceeded a monthly or a quarterly period, the quantity of goods still outstanding must be added to the quantity due for delivery during the following month or the following quarter, and additional sanctions established to ensure real performance will be imposed for delay during a subsequent period.[85] Such a procedure is repeated until the expiration of the time period for which the plan of supply has been confirmed. The right to collect unpaid penalties can be exercised after the expiration of the plan within the period established by the statute of limitations; however, the principle of real performance loses its force upon expiration of the plan period. In the future the economic demands of the supplier must be ensured not by the real performance of the violated contract but by contracts executed on the basis of the new plan.

The contract of carriage of goods is the most peculiar from the viewpoint of the principle of real performance.[86] In order adequately to explain these peculiarities, precontractual and contractual duties must be examined separately. As discussed above,[87] it would be pointless to compel a shipper who does not possess the goods indicated by the plan to present these goods for carriage. Therefore, the violation of this precontractual duty by the shipper must lead to a fine rather than to specific performance. The situation is different with respect to a carrier who cannot provide the requisite means of transportation at the present time but can supply them in the future. Therefore, specific performance remains applicable to the carrier. However, the application of this rule is reasonable only if the shipper possesses the goods that are to be transported according to the transport plan. All of these considerations have affected the approach taken by the Soviet legislator. Only upon the shipper's demand is the carrier obliged to specifically perform its duty to present means of transportation in accordance with the monthly planning indicators. The shipper has the right to repeat its unsatisfied demand each month and each quarter until the expiration of the economic year. For the following economic year, the rights and the duties of the shipper and the carrier will be based on new plans and new contracts. In comparison with the precontractual stage where the principle of real performance is applicable to at least one party, the carrier, at the contractual stage neither the shipper nor the carrier is subject to this principle. The only contractual duty of the shipper is to receive or to ensure the receipt of goods delivered, and the increase in fines that results from continuing delay itself renders fulfillment of this duty actually unavoidable. The only contractual duty of the carrier is to deliver transported goods intact and on time. But delay in delivery cannot be remedied by specific performance, and the replacement of lost goods with like objects is both impractical and illegal for the carrier. This signifies that the contractual duties of the carrier as well as the shipper, while enforced by monetary sanctions, are not affected by the principle of real performance.

In sum, one comes to the conclusion that all planned contractual relations are initiated either upon the execution of an economic contract on the basis of confirmed plans or upon the performance of certain operations dictated by planning acts. A contract must be performed in accordance not only with its own terms but also with the stipulations of law and the indicators of plans. Legal obligations created by the plan and the appropriate contract can be terminated either by proper performance or through the combined employment of financial sanctions and the principle of real performance, except in cases where this principle is inapplicable owing to the peculiarities of certain types of economic activity.

A similar, though not identical, process is found also in the legal form of unplanned economic contracts that have direct counterparts in the area of planned contracts.[88] A comparison of planned and unplanned delivery may serve to demonstrate this assertion.

Both planned and unplanned delivery are regulated by the same frequently-referred-to statutes,[89] though there are rules addressed exclusively to planned delivery just as there are certain other rules affecting only unplanned delivery. The number of such cases, however, is actually insignificant, and all of these few distinctions stem from the fact that the execution of one contract results from the plan, while the other contract is not based upon a plan.

In the context of planned supply both the supplier and the purchaser are obliged to execute a contract of delivery. However, the purchaser is only conditionally bound by the law, and actually is liberated from observance of its formal conditional duty by Arbitrazh practice. On the other hand, if certain parties have been involved in long-term economic connections, the supplier of unplanned products may not refuse the purchaser's demand for the conclusion of a new contract.[90] In addition, the compulsory conclusion of an unplanned delivery contract can be effected through resort to Arbitrazh, where the parties, while failing to overcome other disagreements, have managed to jointly determine the quantity, assortment, and schedule of the forthcoming delivery. These rules smooth over the distinctions between the binding and discretionary character of the execution of contracts for planned and unplanned supply.

Modification or abrogation of planning prerequisites entails, respectively, changes in or termination of contracts of planned delivery. Because contracts of unplanned delivery do not depend on planning prerequisites, the identical sequence of legal events cannot arise in this area. However, putting aside the information that must be submitted to planning agencies by the participants in planned contracts, the latter may be changed or terminated by agreement between the parties just as may be unplanned contracts.

Moreover, regardless of whether the contract is planned or unplanned, if one of the parties ignores the other party's request that the contract be changed or terminated, the dispute is resolved by Arbitrazh.

The penalties established by the legislation on delivery have binding force regardless of the planned or unplanned character of the contract involved. Of course, penalties assessed for failure to send planning documents on time to the entities entitled to receive them are penalties that by definition cannot apply to unplanned contracts. Also, a party that maliciously refuses to conclude a planned contract may be fined by Arbitrazh, while the same sanction is precluded with respect to an unplanned contract, even where conclusion of the contract is mandatory for the supplier or also for the purchaser. But these quite comprehensible exceptions aside, no other differences can be found. Neither planned nor unplanned contracts can provide for the inapplicability of any sanction required by law, decrease their amount, mitigate the conditions calling for their application, etc. The right to recover penalties, proclaimed as a duty by the law, is just as much a duty of both parties to an unplanned contract as it is of parties to a planned contract. In both cases the parties may provide higher penalties than those mandated by legislation and may provide additional sanctions to protect their rights. All amounts received through the collection of penalties and compensation by the participants in either planned or unplanned contracts must be transferred to the state budget at the end of the economic year.

The principle of real performance functions with the same force with respect to both planned and unplanned deliveries: the quantity of objects not delivered during a given month or quarter must be added to the quantity to be delivered during the following month or quarter, except in cases where the purchaser timely informs the supplier of its refusal to accept those goods where delivery has been delayed. Only one distinction between planned and unplanned contracts seems significant from the viewpoint of the principle discussed. Planned contracts are affected by the principle of real performance until their planning prerequisites are abrogated or lose legal force because of the expiration of the plan periods. For unplanned contracts, the principle of real performance ceases to function upon expiration of the period for which the contract has been executed, unless the parties have stipulated otherwise in their contract. In both cases, however, penalties of any kind may be recovered despite the expiration of the plan or the contract, subject only to the statute of limitations.

Other problems arise in connection with unplanned economic contracts that are similar to planned economic contracts not in type but in the mandatory requirement that they be concluded. Unplanned economic contracts of this class possess two features that distinguish them from other economic contracts: they are permanent, not temporary, and one of their parties administratively supervises the activities of the other. The application of these contracts is either selective or comprehensive.

Contracts for the exploitation of railroad spur lines[91] are selective: they may be concluded only between an economic entity that possesses such a line and a railroad that as an independent enterprise administers the appropriate main line. Without a contract, the owner of a spur line has no right to use it, and the railroad must refuse to render any services requested by the owner. At the same time, the simple fact that a spur line has been constructed or acquired creates mutual duties on the part of both the owner and the railroad controlling the adjoining main line to execute the requisite contract. In cases where one of the parties fails to fulfill this duty, the other party may compel it to execute the contract through Arbitrazh. Arbitrazh also makes the final determination with respect to contractual terms that, having been grounds for dispute between the parties, could not be resolved by their superior agencies. Thus, the mandatory execution of such an unplanned contract does not differ from the coercive performance of planning duties with respect to entrance into planned contractual relations. In addition, since the technical attachment of a spur line to a main line is intended to be permanent, the contract for the exploitation of a railroad spur line must be unlimited in duration as well. And this is in fact the case. Bearing in mind, however, that transport technology is constantly developing, and also that substantial renovation of a spur line may be necessary periodically, the law requires the replacement of the previous contract by a new one every three years.

Examined as such, the contract discussed is a legal form designed to introduce administrative supervision by a railroad over the owner of a spur line. The owner is obliged to observe all transport rules governing the exploitation of spur lines, and it must permit inspection by the railroad at any time when this is required. The railroad has the right to inspect a spur line at its discretion, and, if any violations are found, to prohibit further exploitation of the spur line until the situation is rectified. It is obvious that none of these rights and duties directly relates to economic activities, and, what is more, not equality, but the subordination of one party to the other is the dominating principle in their mutual relations. Thus, within these limits, one deals not so much with a civil law contract as with an administrative institution, in contrast to an economic contract, which is civil law in nature. But one must not forget that planned contracts, though related to civil law, are also permeated with administrative elements, at least with regard to their planning prerequisites. Nevertheless, they qualify as economic contracts because of these contracts' economic purposes, which both equal parties are obliged to further in conformity with planning commands. The contract for the exploitation of a railroad spur line is discussed here in detail not because of its economic significance but as an excellent illustration of an economic contract combining civil law attributes with administrative components of an undiluted character, i.e., of a purely administrative, rather than planning-administrative, nature.

If the railroad-spur contract were reduced only to the duties mentioned above, it would have none of the features of an economic contract. These features are, however, apparent, if one takes into consideration that the same contract governs, along with administrative supervision based on the principle of subordination, also economic activity based on the principle of equality. Such activity can be seen in the joint efforts of the owner of a spur line and the appropriate railroad at the initial and the concluding stages of goods transportation. The direct exploitation of spur lines, relying on this special contract, expresses itself in a specific legal form peculiar to all economic contracts that are mandatorily dictated by law and that are assumed to be of unlimited duration.[92] Specifically, the principal permanent contract, providing stable terms for its fulfillment, must be performed on the basis of numerous sporadically executed contracts employed for the achievement of separate goals. Thus, in accordance with the contract for the exploitation of railroad spur lines, the owners of these lines provide for the presentation and transportation of railroad cars, observe the established terms and schedule for the performance of these operations, follow the unified norm of allowable demurrage of cars on spur lines and at railroad terminals, etc. The monetary sanctions for violations of these contractual duties provided for by transport legislation enter into force for the parties involved upon execution of the contract for the exploitation of a railroad spur line. However, in order to demand that the railroad entity supply locomotives and other services, the owner of the spur line must, relying on the parties' principal and permanent contract, enter into specific contracts, and the execution of the latter is simultaneously a method of performance of the former. On the other hand, the expiration of these derivative contracts does not affect the legal force of the principal contract. Such a contractual structure ensures continuity of administrative supervision, despite the periodic discontinuation of civil law links.

Bank account contracts[93] are comprehensive: every Soviet entity, upon its creation, must execute such a contract with the appropriate bank establishment. The bank may not refuse to enter into contractual relations, once the legality of the creation of the applicant has been verified. All of the terms of the contract are specified by legislative acts. These terms can be neither modified nor supplemented by the parties. The only possible disagreement that can arise is a refusal on the part of a bank establishment to open an account requested by a legal entity. This refusal, following from the exercise of financial control as a purely administrative function, may be challenged not in Arbitrazh but only before the establishment's superior bank agency. Usually, bank accounts are opened at the appropriate office of the State Bank. However, construction entities have their accounts at offices of the Construction Bank. In both cases, bank accounts are used for the financing of current economic activity. If an economic entity is a customer in the area of capital construction financed by the state budget, a special account for this purpose must be opened in an office of the Construction Bank. Also as a rule, each legal entity holds its account at the bank office nearest the location where this entity is situated. However, a production unit of a production association, if the former and the latter are situated in different places, may be allowed to have a separate account, maintained in the nearest bank office, although this account, while at the disposal of the production unit, is utilized only on behalf of the production association.

Similar to the contract for the exploitation of a spur line, the bank account contract serves as a means of ensuring administrative (financial) supervision[94] by the bank over the economic activities carried out by the account holder. Consequently, in this case too, the contract apparently is not so much a civil law as an administrative institution. On the one hand, the holder of an account must deposit its money in and implement its monetary operations through the bank, and, on the other hand, the bank must make sure that these requirements are strictly observed,[95] putting an end to any violations. At the same time, however, bank offices provide economic services to account holders, honoring their payment orders and receiving money paid to the account holders. These services, the most significant of the bank's economic activities, are a necessary component of the economic activity of every entity in the USSR. Therefore, within the limits described, the bank account does qualify as an economic contract under Soviet law. Legislative acts, regulating bank accounts as economic contracts,[96] exhaustively list the parties' rights and duties, accompanying this listing by a specification of the penalties that must be paid by an offending party to its contractual partner in cases where the established rules are violated.

Another similarity between bank account contracts and contracts for the exploitation of spur lines is that both are performed by means of derivative contracts. With respect to bank accounts these derivative contracts are called "forms of monetary settlements." If a holder of a bank account must pay for received goods or for any services, it either gives the appropriate order to the bank or accepts the appropriate demand of its creditor transferred through the bank. Both of these acts may be approved by the bank on the condition that there are no legal or financial obstacles to their performance. Thus, in every case where monetary transfers are to be made, a specific contract must be executed between the bank and the holder of the bank account. The same procedure is employed by the bank and a legal entity entitled to receive money for goods sold or services presented: this entity either addresses its own demand or accepts an order of its debtor. Each such episodic payment contract is first executed and then terminated by performance. Nevertheless, the bank account contract retains binding force, regardless of the number of monetary transfers that are made on the basis of payment contracts.

Soviet legislation provides for a great number of forms of monetary settlements in economic relations between legal entities. The peculiarities of each of these forms are of little interest. However, two substantial features characterizing monetary accounts are very important to the comprehension of the Soviet economic system and its legal organization.

The first feature can be seen in the fact that the structure of monetary payments in the USSR prohibits any elements of credit in mutual relations between economic entities. During the period of NEP when goods-money relations were the most developed in the USSR,[97] economic entities frequently sold goods or presented services to one another on credit. Such transactions strengthened the entities' economic independence and simultaneously undermined the rulers' economic monopoly. One of the measures employed by Stalin in order to establish and confirm his personal dictatorship was the credit reform of 1929–1931.[98] This reform introduced bank accounts binding for legal entities and rigidly controlled by bank establishments. It was, however, called a "credit reform," because the most substantial innovations related to extension of credit in the Soviet economy. From this time forward, economic entities were entitled to receive credit only from the bank, in accordance with established plans and exclusively for the purposes enumerated by the law. Mutual credit in relations between Soviet organizations was strictly forbidden under threat of personal responsibility for any economic managers disregarding this ban. However, the ban could, in the absence of certain special rules, be neutralized in a roundabout way, namely, by means of delivering goods or presenting services and then failing to demand the required payments for a comparatively long period of time. In order to prevent such abuses, Soviet law obliges all entities entitled to monetary payments to submit the documents necessary for the collection of payments within rigidly limited time periods. The observance of this requirement leads to monetary payments without delay and entitles the creditor to receive bank credit until the debtor transfers the money owed. Should the delivery of the appropriate documents be delayed, the bank will refuse to accept the documents themselves, and will also deny any requests for bank credit from the same entity. As a result, the interests of the creditor would be adversely affected not only by virtue of the refusal of bank credit but also because a more complicated procedure for the exaction of payments from the debtor is employed where the creditor has thus delayed collection.

The second feature of the various forms of monetary settlements is connected with the role these procedures play in ensuring adherence to financial plans and in maintaining contractual discipline.[99] All monetary documents submitted by economic entities to the bank for the purpose of collecting or paying sums due must refer to the financial resources (funds) from which each specific payment is to be made, to the planning acts that serve as the requisite preconditions of performance of the appropriate operations, and to the economic contracts executed in order to ensure the fulfillment of planning tasks.[100] A bank establishment will refuse to approve the payments ordered or requested if any one of the references is left out or if the bank, in carrying out an independent check of the relevant data, discovers groundless references in any of the documents submitted. As a general rule, an entity that is a supplier or a performer of other services first dispatches its goods or renders its services and then submits monetary orders addressed to the payor through its bank office. The latter may refuse to pay, entirely or in part, should the document received in itself prove the complete or partial groundlessness of the requirement submitted. If the goods arrive before the documents, the payor may refuse to pay if defects have been discovered or if certain articles are missing from the shipment. If no such justifications for the refusal to pay exist, the debtor having refused payment, must pay penalties to the creditor. It can also occur that the debtor may violate its duty not by illegally refusing to pay but by failing to have sufficent funds in its account to cover a request for payment. If such violations are committed more than once, the contractual partner or the bank office may introduce for this payor a form of monetary settlements in accordance with which the transfer of money must precede the transfer of goods. Usually, the application of this sanction ensures only that the creditor will receive payment upon the dispatch of goods, even though the debtor has made the requisite transfer before the time of dispatch. This result stems from the rule that, while obliging the debtor to transfer money to the creditor's bank before the dispatch of goods, at the same time allows the creditor to receive this money only upon proof by transport documents that the goods have already been dispatched. Sometimes, however, payments do precede the presentation of services, when this form of monetary settlements is employed not as a sanction for past violations but as a regular procedure established for certain types of economic activity. For instance, the shipper pays the full carriage price at the moment when the carrier receives the shipper's goods for transportation. To ascertain the cause of this deviation, one must bear in mind the purpose of the general principle. Generally payment must not precede the dispatch of goods in order to prevent replacement of bank credit by monetary credit extended by the customer to the seller or other performer. But in the area of carriage goods this danger does not exist, since the carrier, once the shipper's goods have been loaded in freight cars, cannot delay their carriage without suffering losses resulting from the downtime of the freight cars. Therefore, the payment of freight by the shipper simultaneously with the receipt of goods by the carrier does not precede performance but rather accompanies the initial stage of performance. In addition, because consignees and consignors usually are different entities, the postponement of payment on the part of the shipper is technically impracticable. This is why Soviet legislation establishes a special form of monetary accounts for these economic relations, ensuring at the same time strict observance of all types of economic discipline.

As the previous analysis demonstrates, unplanned economic contracts, whose execution is dictated not by the plan but by the law, are a special class of economic contracts. Ultimately, they lead to the achievement of economic goals on the basis of property relations between equal partners. This serves as the ground for including them among economic contracts. However, their *causa proxima* is not an economic purpose itself but rather is ensuring the execution of other economic contracts, connected with the presentation and removal of cars in the process of exploitation of railroad spur lines or the making of monetary payments from bank accounts. The economic operations finally resulting from these contracts are auxiliary with regard to the direct goals of delivery, construction, and other economic contracts of an analogous character. The auxiliary nature of these operations precludes exercise over them of the kinds of administrative control that exist with respect to more basic forms of economic activity. To fill this gap, a very substantial one, taking into account the Soviet authorities desire to maintain extremely centralized economic management, the mandatory execution of the respective economic contracts combines two purposes: the implementation of specific types of economic activity and the subordination of the latter to special forms of administrative control.

Taken together, all economic contracts—planned and unplanned, principal and auxiliary—are the most important legal component of Soviet exchange in which economic and other entities participate. But these are not the only types of contracts that serve the economic needs arising in the process of exchange in the USSR. Along with economic contracts, there are other civil law contracts, called "non-economic," but just as subordinate to economic goals.

Non-Economic Contracts

Contracts executed between Soviet entities have always possessed one of the features typical of economic contracts: their participants are not individuals but organizations. If a contract between these entities nevertheless is classified as non-economic, this classification must be based upon one of the following two causes: either the contract is of a type that may also be entered into by individuals (for example, purchase and sale, lease of property, etc.) or the contract lacks features requisite for economic contracts (planned character, mandatory execution, etc.). For example, an economic entity is entitled to sell its surplus equipment and materials, if this entity's superior agency or the appropriate agency of supply refuses to exercise the right to redistribute such unutilized resources. Although the acquirer also must be an organization, the act implemented actually is a purchase and sale, i.e. a contract that may also be entered into by individuals, and therefore is subject to ordinary civil law rules, not to the special regime established for economic contracts. Non-economic contract relations can also be seen in cases where producers whose goods have been refused acceptance by planned purchasers sell these goods by means of contracts for sale on commission. These contracts are used only in relations between producing entities and special organizations of the state supply (*Gossnab*) system, i.e. in an area inaccessible to individuals, and from this point of view they share a common feature with economic contracts. However, the sale of goods on commission relies neither on planned prerequisites nor on legal commands of a mandatory nature. Also, it is not one of those contracts that, though unplanned, are a contractual type that also encompasses planned contracts. Thus, the special regime addressed to economic contracts cannot be employed with respect to sales on commission. Therefore, this type of contract belongs to the class of ordinary, not economic, contracts under Soviet civil law.

The two illustrations given are at the same time the two most important cases where non-economic contracts result from the economic activity of legal entities. These entities not infrequently conclude other non-economic contracts either in their mutual relations or in their relations with individuals. However, putting aside organizations created specially for the purpose of satisfying the demands of individuals, Soviet organizations do not directly fulfill their economic functions by means of such contracts. Incentive funds, for instance, result from production achievement, but the expenditure of the monetary resources included in these funds for the purchase of goods to reward in kind the winners of "socialist competition," or for the "satisfaction of the cultural needs of workers and office workers" with a concert by a philharmonic orchestra is not a part of the entity's production process. A well designed park area around a factory affects the workers' state of mind and thus stimulates their production work, but neither the park area itself nor its recreational use are direct components of economic activity.

Among the non-economic contracts employed by economic entities, the independent work contract deserves special attention. A certain amount of money can be spent by Soviet organizations to pay for independent work. But this amount is extremely limited and strictly earmarked for a narrowly defined range of purposes. This rigidity is intended to prevent the increase in personnel beyond confirmed numerical limits which might otherwise result from the execution of labor contracts disguised as independent work contracts. The Soviet authorities consider such concealed increases in personnel dangerous, because these increases conflict with the centralized planning of wages and, consequently, threaten to disturb the balance sought to be maintained between the monetary income of the population and its cover by goods produced. Therefore, all contracts of independent work that are really disguised labor contracts are declared void immediately upon their discovery, and the officials who violate this legal prohibition are held personally responsible. The actual efficiency of these regulations can be illustrated by a notorious case from Soviet practice.[101] Once a Leningrad textile plant encountered an unforeseen problem: a river vessel bringing in perishable raw materials was caught in the ice. The vessel had no chance of reaching the wharf where it was to have been unloaded, and the ice was not solid enough to permit unloading where the vessel was stuck. A cargo worth several hundred thousand rubles seemed doomed. Then a small group of workers offered to unload the ship at their own risk for thirty thousand rubles. The director of the textile plant had no authority to make such an agreement, which, according to Soviet law, would be considered an independent work contract. An appeal to the local Party agencies proved fruitless. Official letters and telephone calls to the responsible ministry led to nothing but promises to "clear things up" and "come to an agreement." The process of "coming to an agreement" continued all winter, until navigation on the Neva River was restored. By that time there was nothing to unload—the valuable goods had spoiled. Throughout this long series of negotiations, no one had thought to suggest breaking the rule in order to save the cargo. This is no isolated incident. Occurrences of such a kind are endemic in the economic life of the USSR. And the availability to legal entities of certain non-economic contracts that leave the negotiating parties more room for contractual freedom than do economic contracts changes nothing. The regulation of non-economic contracts is more liberal but the prerequisites of their execution are no less stringent than those outlined for economic contracts.

The largest area in which non-economic contracts are employed is that of relations in which one or both participants are individuals. The objects of exchange in these relations are either goods, services, or the use of property. Accordingly the most important non-economic contracts are purchase and sale, independent work, and lease of property. Each of these contracts is regulated by a separate chapter of the republican civil codes,[102] except for the housing lease, which is governed by rules of the republican housing codes. In cases where special economic entities of retail trade, domestic services, or domestic rental deal directly with their clients, a great many ministerial or local regulations are applicable, sometimes adversely affecting the legal positions of individuals as these are guaranteed by civil codes or current laws.[103] Substatutory administrative regulations (i.e. regulations that are issued by departmental or local agencies and that therefore must not contravene the law) function to some extent in the area where individuals sell various products of their own economic activity by contract.[104] The principal goal of these acts is to outline the limits and thus to restrict the employment of non-economic contracts by citizens acting as producers, rather than consumers.

The legal regulation of non-economic contracts of these groups varies, depending on three factors: the identities of the subjects engaging in the economic activity involved, the status of supply and demand in the given economic area, and the specific nature of the economic area where supply lags behind demand.

The participants in the economic activity that is the subject matter of non-economic contracts may be either specialized entities[105] or individuals, regardless of whether they implement such activity occasionally or on a regular basis.[106]

A specialized entity may engage only in those economic activities for whose performance it was created. The combination of activity of different types, for instance, of retail trade and rental or services, is strictly prohibited. Moreover, a specialized entity of retail trade must not deal in wholesale trade since wholesale trade may only be between organizations. Sale on commission is also incompatible with retail trade in new goods, because old articles and new objects cannot be sold in accordance with identical legal provisions.

The economic activity of specialized entities is planned, and though some of these entities fulfill production functions (for instance, enterprises providing domestic services) while other engage in retail trade (for instance, department stores and smaller shops), they are governed not by production plans but by plans of commodity turnover (*plany tovarooborota*). This occurs because in all cases they either sell or rent out goods or services, and if they sell, the objects of sale are either ready-made or produced in accordance with the order of a specific acquirer. Thus, in substance, the plan of commodity turnover is a species of distribution plans: it indicates not that which must be produced but that which must be sold or presented for the use of citizens. However, in contrast to distribution plans, which are bilateral,[107] plans of commodity circulation are unilateral. Issued by planning agencies, they address specialized entities, entailing the establishment of "vertical" (administrative) relations: the planning agencies are entitled to demand and the specialized entities are obliged to ensure the performance of the given planning tasks. Individuals in their capacity of potential purchasers, lessees, or customers are, of course, not bound by these plans and, consequently, do not take part in "horizontal" (civil law) relations, entitling and obliging both parties to execute a contract in accordance with planning commands. Instead of mutual obligations, unilateral rights and duties arise in these cases. A specialized entity is obliged to enter into a contract with any customer, though there are certain restrictions: the prohibition against selling liquor to minors, the right of priority of members of consumer cooperatives to buy goods in the trade enterprises of these cooperatives, etc. An individual, however, has no duty to buy, rent, or contract for services. Consequently, the execution of a contract depends exclusively on the individual's discretion. What should be the normal correlation between offers of good and services and the demands of those to whom the offers are made is subject to the abnormal consequences of "planning interference." The problem is that plans of commodity turnover must correspond to the resources allocated to the retail or service system, irrespective of the extent to which these resources are in accordance with consumer demand. Meanwhile, in the USSR the scarcity of that which is really required "peacefully co-exists" with an overstock of that which almost nobody wishes to acquire, while the right to receive bonuses is based upon fulfillment and overfulfillment of planed tasks. Therefore, the managers of specialized entities act with might and main to procure the resources required to satisfy consumer demand at least partially, thus ensuring an improvement in the relevant economic indicators before the expiration of each planned period. Among the methods employed for this purpose, bribery is far from the least important. If, however, scarce resources have been procured, the entities' managers do not feel obligated to make all of them available to ordinary customers. For the most part, these resources are sold "on side" to "reliable" persons who pay the official price plus an under-the-table bribe. As a result, the payor of the bribe gets a scar commodity, the recipient extracts a profit, and only the situation of ordinary customers remains unchanged.

The practice described is so notorious that the ruling officials of the Party have long observed something of a Party tradition: a newly appointed leader of a province or district party committee begins his "mingling with the people" with sudden inspections of retail enterprises. His inspections end with the discovery of concealed goods, their immediate transfer to the store's counters, and the imposition of sanctions upon the culprits.

After a while, however, the fighting spirit of the new leader evaporates, tranquility returns, and the habitual practices are resumed in full force. Quite aware of these practices, a great many customers strive to establish close ties with salespersons, as more reliable, though more expensive, sources of supply than those provided by the official system. It is not without reason that in a Soviet vaudeville show, that miraculously escaped the censors, keepers of supply and managers of goods are depicted as being among the most respected persons, but as fearing that, should scarcity be overcome, "mere" engineers would be held in higher esteem. On the other hand, if a crime such as blackmarketeering ("the buying and reselling of goods or other articles for the purpose of making profit"[108]) in general results from the constant scarcity prevalent in the USSR, "close ties" with salespersons sometimes lead to a combination of blackmarketeering with official crimes. Collusion between a salesperson who secretly provides the requisite goods, and a black marketeer, who sells these goods no less secretly to individuals paying "through the nose," exemplifies just such a combination. These phenomena, presenting a merger of various crimes from the legal point of view, are from the economic point of view one of the means of supplementing the official economy by the underground economy in the USSR. Such are the "side effects" of the scarcity connected with Soviet planning. And the situation is even more staggering, if one remembers that the scarcity of goods is one of the primary reasons for their centralized distribution, but, at the same time, the centralized distribution of goods, owing to these "side effects," itself exacerbates the already severe problem of scarcity.

With respect to planning, two other peculiar circumstances must be pointed out. First, collective farms themselves determine the amount of produce that they will sell at collective farm markets. Since, however, such discretion, in fact, depends on the quantity of produce required to be supplied to the state and on the satisfaction of requirements concerning the maintenance of collective farm property assets in kind,[109] the decisions made by collective farms in this regard actually are less free than might seem to be the case. Other restrictions also exist. For example, a decree of the Party Central Committee and the USSR Council of Ministers of August 5, 1982[110] "allows" collective farms (this is the word actually used, despite the formal independence of collective farms as separate proprietors) to sell at collective farm markets a quantity of fruit and vegetables that cannot exceed 10% of the volume of planned procurements of the same items. Second, rental of space in state apartment buildings is based upon administrative distribution,[111] but by itself is not planned. Of course, the performance of construction plans for state apartment buildings affects the volume of living space available for administrative distribution. However, these plans govern the construction of apartment buildings, not their distribution, and, at the same time, the distribution of dwelling premises encompasses also existing apartment buildings, space in which has been left vacant by departing tenants. As a matter of course, no plan may be addressed to citizens functioning as sellers, lessors, or contractors. However, legal lists of allowed trades and legal prohibitions on dealing in other trades, as well as purely objective obstacles resulting from the scarcity of goods required for the exercise of certain kinds of available trades, put limits on private initiative. And, in contrast to the planned sector of the economy, where some flexibility is allowed, the limits on private trades are firmly fixed.

But whatever the legal and planning preconditions for non-economic contracts may be, as soon as the former appears, the latter may be concluded. In analyzing economic contracts, we have ascertained that either their parties are entirely deprived of contractual freedom or that this freedom is severely restricted.[112] How do matters stand with non-economic contracts in this regard? The answer differs from contract to contract, and this is so, of course, not only in connection with the Soviet economy. Nevertheless, even in these cases the latter's peculiarities do not seem inconsequential. It is clear that contractual freedom must be broader in relations between individuals than between individuals and organizations. However, Soviet law either predetermines or precludes certain contract terms even in individuals' obligations. For instance, Article 131 of the RSFSR Housing Code, predetermining a contract term, provides that the amount charged for the rental of apartments in individual houses must not exceed an established rate. In contrast, Art. 351 of the RSFSR Civil Code, precluding a contract term, prohibits even partial performance of an individual contractor's duty by persons other than the contractor himself. It is, further, clear that the independent work contract allows broader discretion to the participants than do other non-economic contracts. However, in Soviet practice in this area model contracts are employed in cases where state entities function as contractors,[113] and, consequently, the opportunities for choice remaining to customers are more restricted than seems economically necessary. It is, finally, clear that if state entities are sellers, freedom of contract cannot be as broad as in cases where things are sold by individuals. State entities, dealing with innumerable customers, cannot conclude each retail contract by means of separate negotiations. All contract terms are publicly announced, and customers must act in accordance with the rule of "take it or leave it": the choice of what to acquire remains their decision, while the other contract terms, predetermined by the sellers, cannot be modified on the basis of an agreement between the parties. Auxiliary agreements are possible only in cases where a retail seller performs special services such as the temporary safekeeping of purchased goods, delivery of goods to a customer's place of residence, etc. But the existence of these supplementary agreements does not affect the basic economic principle that separately negotiated contracts are incompatible with mass merchandising, both in the USSR and in other countries.

Purely Soviet peculiarities lie in the fact that the rule of "take it or leave it" is universal, embracing all retail entities, large or small, without exception, and that unilaterally elaborated contract terms do not originate with the seller, but are established by the central agencies. The seller may not modify these terms in accordance with changing "market conditions," and, as a result, the contradictory combination of scarcity and overstocking arising from the specific administration of Soviet production is exacerbated by the no less specific administration of Soviet trade. One can also point out, as side effects of Soviet trade administration, that workers in this economic area make from it an illegal income as significant as that resulting from the exploitation of the scarcity of consumer goods. One illustration will suffice. Fruit and vegetables are sold by grocery stores at seasonal prices that are periodically decreased from spring through the late summer and periodically increased from the late summer through the fall. In winter, prices are stable, but vegetables and fruit are scarce. Upcoming seasonal price changes are officially brought to the notice of retail entities only two or three days before they go into effect. But grocery store employees know approximately when a change will occur, and they zealously prepare to take full advantage of such an important event. On the eve of an expected change fruit and vegetables are accumulated in great quantities at retail entities' warehouses, and subsequent actions depend on whether prices are to be decreased or increased. All the accumulated produce will be sold on the day preceding a decrease or on the day of a declared increase. The fact that demand always exceeds supply makes both operations easily practicable. If there is a price decrease, food sold the day before the decrease is reported as having been sold the following day; if there is a price increase, food sold on the day of the increase is reported as sold the day before by appropriate alterations in the books. As a matter of course, the difference between the reported prices is used to line the pockets of salesmen and their superiors. It is true that either an internal inventory, or even an inventory conducted by an outside agency, precedes the introduction of new prices. But this changes nothing. An internal inventory can be simply adjusted to the criminal purpose, while an outside inventory may be neutralized by reliable means—bribery. The Soviet authorities are aware of the exploitation of retail trade as an unlimited source of income by trade workers. A great number of criminal cases in this area prove the existence of an intensive fight against these phenomena. But to some extent the insurmountability of the problem has been recognized, judging from the fact that salaries in the area of retail trade are lower than in other branches of the Soviet economy. This a practice results from the idea that since trade workers have at their disposal uncontrolled sources of income, the salaries of these workers must be lower than average, and the difference will be recovered many times over at the expense of the customer.

In comparison with state entities, which have almost no freedom of contract in dealing with the public, private individuals are in principle free in their mutual contract relations, except for restrictions provided by law or established in practice.[114] This freedom is important not so much with respect to individuals' occasional contracts (such as the sale of used articles) as in connection with their regular contract activity (such as that exercised at collective farm markets). The collective farm markets, notwithstanding their name, may be used not only by collective farmers but by all individuals selling agricultural produce grown by them personally. Even state retail entities sometimes sell certain goods at collective farm markets. There is, however, one reason for keeping the word "farm" in the name: among collective producers, only those engaged in agricultural production may sell their produce at these markets. And since collective farms are the principal producers in the agricultural area, these markets establishments are designated "collective farm markets." However, while certain entities function as sellers at these markets, only individuals may act as buyers. Even enterprises of consumer cooperatives, generally entitled to purchase collective farm produce, may not do so at collective farm markets. Such rigidity is quite understandable. Collective farm markets are allowed and even encouraged by Soviet law in order to strengthen, at least to some extent, the woefully inadequate supply of food to the Soviet population provided by the state system of retail trade. Therefore, at collective farm markets as well as at retail establishments, not organizations but solely citizens may act as purchasers. Within the limits of agricultural produce, citizens, not entities, in fact, are also sellers. The retail entities operating at collective farm markets sell only industrial articles: shoes, clothes, etc.; however, as of 1986, consumer cooperatives are entitled to sell at these markets agricultural produce transferred to them by collective farms. Actually, collective farms prefer to sell their produce through enterprises of consumer cooperatives functioning as commission agents. Sale at collective farm markets is less convenient to collective farms, since their representatives must unfailingly observe the binding prices established by the management of their respective farms, while free and flexible prices are important in trade of this type. The right to employ such prices is granted to some extent to consumer cooperatives and without restriction only to individuals that therefore are not only purchasers but also the principal sellers.

As an essential source of food supply, collective farm markets possess a number of significant peculiarities. First, they are not subject to scarcity. Food such as meat, homemade sausage, butter etc. can be found in a great number of localities solely at collective farm markets. In Moscow, Leningrad, Kiev or other of the most important cities one can buy these objects in retail shops early in the morning, standing in line for several hours, if one's turn comes in time. In contrast, at collective farm markets, one has regular access to these goods constantly, and, what is more, the scarcity in the official retail system positively affects the abundance at collective farm markets. In the winter months, for example, onions, garlic and sometimes potatoes periodically disappear from the state shops in all cities, including the capital and industrial centers. Collective farm markets react as a sensitive barometer to these economic oscillations, immediately becoming overfilled by objects temporarily unavailable to consumers through the common channels. Second, the quality of food sold at collective farm markets is incomparably higher than in retail shops. Therefore, in certain cases, purchase at collective farm markets is preferred to acquisition of the same goods at trade enterprises even when there is no problem of scarcity. Relatives of sick persons strive to feed these persons with food bought at the markets. Well-to-do individuals who do not belong to the Soviet elite, and who therefore have no rights to privileged supply, rely entirely on collective farm markets, resorting to the state retail system only with respect to articles of non-agricultural production. Incidentally, this has purely psychological consequences that must seem very peculiar to a stranger: in the country of officially proclaimed universal equality, an habitué of collective farm markets looks down on those who must be content with official supply. Third, prices at collective farm markets, resulting from freely reached agreements between sellers and buyers, are higher than those mandatorily established for retail shops. This is quite natural in all cases, regardless of whether the objects involved are available in trade entities of the retail system (here, one pays more for higher quality), or the retail system does not provide the population with certain objects or cannot ensure their adequate supply (here, one pays more because of scarcity). Since not centralized planning but individual adjustment to economic circumstances is the only functioning factor in this area, prices, though higher than in retail shops, depend on the correlation between supply and demand at any given time. Therefore, these prices are always susceptible to change, even during the same day, to say nothing of longer periods of time.

The economic peculiarities of retail trade at collective farm markets, as these have been described above, are legally recognized and officially encouraged. In no other sphere of economic activity is Soviet law as liberal as it is with respect to collective farm markets. Putting aside the small fee exacted by the management of markets for the space used, and the sanitary control to which foods brought for sale are subjected, only one restriction is relatively significant: citizens may not sell objects produced by other persons. Violations of this rule qualify as commercial middleman activity or even as blackmarketeering, i.e. as crimes punished by criminal law.[115] However, if collective farmers or other individuals have agreed to take turns in selling the produce of all of the participants of such agreements without charge, no violations of these legal rules can be established. Apart from this single restriction, trade by individuals at collective farm markets is free in all other respects. Even the distance between the place of production and the place of sale is not regulated. Many resourceful persons take advantage of this fact. For instance, collective farmers from Kirghizia transport early fruit and vegetables to regions of the Extreme North when winter is at its worst in these places. The transport costs are, of course, very high, but by maximizing the quantity sold and the prices, the seller can ensure such a high level of profit that these costs easily can be disregarded. The same practice is exercised by individual producers from other southern areas of the USSR. Certain forms of the underground economy are palpable also in these cases. Sometimes, there arise secret associations including, along with the producers of goods earmarked for sale in remote regions, transport officials providing the requisite carriage, inhabitants of the localities of destination making their apartments available as warehouses, persons who sell the goods at the place of destination, etc.[116] In engaging in such illegal economic activities, one commits violations considered crimes. But the sale of agricultural produce in regions remote from individual producers' places of residence and the extraction of high profits by means of such sale are, though reluctantly, deemed legal by the Soviet authorities, yielding to the pressure of economic necessity. All of these circumstances indicate that sellers at collective farm markets enjoy a special legal position in comparison with other subjects of non-economic contracts connected with the products of individual economic activity. Referring to this fact, good natured, though unsolicited, Western advisers of the Soviet authorities have an excellent solution to their economic problems: simply render the form of exchange allowed at collective farm markets all-embracing and at least the food problem will be resolved. The acceptance of such advice would, of course, resolve the food problem. But it would also "resolve" the problem of the Soviet system itself. Therefore, collective farm markets can be permitted only to a limited extent, depending on the achievements of the state economy. But the transformation of this exception into general rule may be conceived only by especially benevolent Western dreamers. As realistic politicians, the Soviet rulers will never allow for economic renovations that, for them, are fraught with political peril.

The legal peculiarities of non-economic contracts result not only from the nature of their subjects but also from the character of their objects. The more scarce these objects, the less available they are to the customer. We have already discussed various manifestations of scarcity reflected in phase of distribution: concealed rationing of certain foods, preliminary registration of the potential acquirers of certain other articles, etc.[117] As a matter of course, scarcity or the absence of scarcity likewise cannot be ignored in the phase of exchange. In the system of retail trade, local executive committees resort to limiting the number of scarce goods that may be sold to each purchaser and to lifting the established limits in cases where scarcity is no longer a problem. Enterprises providing services announce the number of orders that will be accepted on a given day, and contracts will be executed only with a corresponding number of persons standing in line. Should, however, demand be less than supply as is the case with respect to laundries, which are eager to present their services, phenomena extraordinary in Soviet practice can be observed: the taking of telephone orders, the pick-up of dirty laundry at customers' apartments, the delivery of clean laundry to customers' places of residence, etc. Entities of domestic rental usually rent out such articles the outright purchase of which would not really be difficult. Therefore, individuals resort to their services not in order to rent what they cannot buy, but to have temporary use of what they do not need to own. However, even within these limits, supply can be either higher or lower than demand. For instance, one Model Contract governs the renting of various types of used articles.[118] Some of these articles are demanded by customers in greater numbers than are at the disposal of lessors. Therefore, Article 2 of this Model Contract establishes that, upon expiration of the time period for which the contract is to remain valid, it can be renewed for an equal time period "by agreement between the parties." Relying on this rule, the lessor can avoid renewing contracts connected with objects that are in great demand.

The actual correlation between supply and demand is employed by the Soviets in manipulating established prices in cases where price increases are implemented not in a disguised form (the replacement of goods in high demand by identical goods of purportedly improved quality), but by means of a government decree or of a substatutory act of the State Committee on Prices of the USSR. An increase in retail prices for scarce objects always has been accompanied by a decrease in the retail prices of goods that are not in great demand. From the viewpoint of propaganda, such an approach serves as a pretext for contending that the actual losses incurred by customers are not as great as they would be if prices in one area were increased without price decreases in other areas. In fact, however, such a combination of increases and decreases allows the Soviets to kill two birds with one stone: to negatively affect a high level of demand through an increase in prices and to positively counteract a low level of demand by decreasing prices. This open secret as to the genuine goals of the undertaken manipulations was once indirectly recognized by the Soviet rulers. In 1975, they increased payments for services to consumers, asserting that the previous price level did not compensate service entities even for their operating costs. In this instance the increase of prices in one area was not accompanied by a decrease of prices in any other area, and thus no grounds for propagandistic demagogy were created. However, one fact could not be concealed because it was too obvious: payments, while increased for services in high demand, were left intact for services not very popular among Soviet customers. In addition, if necessary, the Soviets employ the method of "double prices." Occasionally, this method is implemented by the establishment of so-called commercial stores (*kommercheskie magaziny*). Most recently such stores appeared during the time of Andropov's rule. The goods available at commercial stores are more varied but the retail prices far higher than in the regular retail system. However, in contrast to previous experience, this latest introduction of commercial stores was a failure due to circumstances that prevail today in the USSR. The accumulation of monetary resources by a number of Soviet citizens, owing to circumstances mentioned above,[119] deprived the Soviet authorities of the opportunity to exceed demand by supply in the commercial stores. Long lines became common in these stores as in other retail enterprises. As a result, a short time after their creation, the commercial stores were liquidated. The method of double prices is systematically employed in the form of commission sales of collective farms' produce through trade enterprises of consumer cooperatives. The law allows a cooperative enterprise as a commission agent and a collective farm as a principal to set by mutual agreement retail prices that are higher than those employed in the state retail system.[120] Aside from the fact that this practice leads to increased profits, the Soviet authorities resort to it in order to remove well-to-do customers from state retail enterprises to cooperative trade entities and thus to diminish to some extent the scarcity of agricultural produce dominating in the state retail system.

Along with common non-economic contracts, the phase of exchange includes certain peculiar species of such contracts, whose regulation also is important for a comprehensive legal analysis of the Soviet economic system.

In the area of retail trade, there is one contract deserving of special attention: the sale on credit.[121] Economically, the higher the price of an article the more such a contract is desirable. However, the Soviet authorities resort to this legal form, bearing in mind not so much the interest of customers as the state's interest in disposing of goods that are not in great demand. The law provides that credit may be extended for a time period no longer than twelve months, that the sum of credit may not exceed an amount equal to four months of the salary of the purchaser, and that only articles enumerated on a special list can be objects of sale on the installment plan. All of these articles are of durable use but none is scarce. It also is noteworthy that, in contrast to retail sale, assuming, as a rule, immediate payment for articles sold, consumer services, in principle, involve payments advanced by the customer for the benefit of the contractor. However, in cases where consumer services are performed with materials that are not in great demand, the contractor may provide these materials to the customer on credit sale.

In the area of consumer rental, there are certain peculiarities involved in the rental of various articles, (except for pianos) that are reflected in the 1965 Model Contract.[122] The reader of this Model Contract immediately notices a great number of formal requirements that must be satisfied in order to rent anything. However, from the formal point of view, the renting of pianos is no less complicated. The distinctions between these contracts are connected with liability for damages caused by the lessee to the lessor. Only lessees of articles other than pianos are subject to punitive liability: they must pay double the price of those rented articles that are not returned to the lessors. The reasons for this distinction are clear. Pianos are delivered by the rental shops to the customers' places of residence, and therefore neither forgery at the time of the execution of contracts nor the appropriation of rented objects is possible under the circumstances. Other articles are picked up by customers at the place of the execution of contracts, and therefore forgery and misappropriation have reached such a level that the inventories of the rental shops must be replaced almost annually. Therefore punitive property sanctions are employed along with criminal punishment in order to prevent this genuine disaster. As discussed, objects of domestic rental are not scarce, and their appropriation because of the impracticability of purchase hardly ever occurs. It is otherwise with library books borrowed by readers for home reading. Unfortunately, the number of copies of books in print depends least of all on the readers' demands in the USSR. The political significance of a publication, the official position of its author, and other circumstances irrelevant to the substance of the work play the decisive roles. As a result, books that individuals truly do want to read are more readily available in libraries than in stores, and the scarcity of certain books in the retail system leads to the illegal appropriation of the libraries' copies. Therefore, the penalties for appropriate library books are not double the price of the books, but ten times the price. Furthermore, the most important Soviet libraries either refuse to lend out their books for home reading or require that the establishment where a reader works provide a guarantee that books lent will be returned.

In the area of providing consumer services one must analyze separately the peculiarities of obligations connected with the construction of individuals' houses in accordance with a 1981 Model Contract.[123] Demand for this service outstrips supply even though in urban areas the building of new individual houses is not common and in rural areas construction of housing is usually done by peasants with their own labor. The Soviet legislator obviously takes this imbalance of supply and demand into consideration, judging from the heavy burden imposed upon the customer in favor of the contractor. Usually, the construction of an individual house takes no less than one year and not infrequently consumes an even longer time period. However, the customer is obliged to pay the contractor for all materials that are required for the entire construction process within ten days after the execution of the contract, i.e. long before the contractor itself will spend money for the acquisition of these materials. In addition, according to the general rule of Article 226 of the RSFSR Civil Code, delay in the performance of a monetary duty is penalized by payment of interest at the rate of 3% per annum. Yet, the customer, obliged to make full payment for the completed house within three days after taking possession, is penalized for delay at the rate of 0.1% per day, i.e. 36% per annum. Even violations of the payment terms of economic contracts executed between Soviet organizations do not entail penalties at such a high rate as that established for similar violations of this non-economic contract. Finally, one of the provisions addressed to the same non-economic contract is so ambiguous that it could reasonably be interpreted either in favor of the customer or of the contractor. The Model Contract states that the customer is entitled to submit his claims concerning the quality defects directly to the contractor within five months after taking possession of the house. In accordance with Article 365 of the RSFSR Civil Code, however, the period of limitation for a judicial petition begins to run at the time when the appropriate claim has been actually submitted by the customer to the contractor. But what if a claim has not been submitted at all, and the five-month period has already expired? When does the period of limitation begin to run? With respect to purchase and sale this question is resolved by Article 249 of the RSFSR Civil Code: the period of limitation begins to run at the time when the period for the submission of claims by the purchaser to the seller has expired. The legislation regulating the independent work contract includes no such provision. Therefore, this legislation allows for different interpretations, connecting the starting date of the period of limitation either with the expiration of the period during which the customer may bring claims directly to the contractor, or with the time when the former has received the house from the latter.

The last factor affecting the Soviet regulation of non-economic contracts that involve relations between individuals and organizations is the specific nature of the economic area involved where supply lags behind demand.

The worse, almost critical, disparity between supply and demand can be found in the sphere of consumer services. This has resulted from the view that the development of such services cannot be a primary objective of economic policy in a country where an incomparably more important problem, the problem of food supply, is far from being resolved. Therefore, only a relatively insignificant portion of the monetary resources earmarked by the state budget for the satisfaction of individual demands is allocated for the enlargement of existing or the construction of new consumer service enterprises. Cities with hundreds of thousands of privately-owned cars have only a few automobile repair garages. Tailors and shoe repair shops exist in ridiculously limited numbers. In medium-sized communities, where apartment bathrooms are a rarity, no more than one or two public bath houses are provided for the use of the inhabitants. Soviet leaders have never mentioned such objects in their "program" speeches, perhaps considering this issue to be less than advantageous from the propagandistic viewpoint, or possibly realizing that in this case propagandistic efforts are pointless, since for decades no construction of such a character has been implemented in almost any area in Soviet territory. The Soviets were, however, forced to carry out certain measures in rural areas, where state service entities simply did not exist, and collective farms were not permitted to divert human or economic resources from agricultural production to the performance of service functions. In 1966, the Party Central Committee and the USSR Council of Ministers issued a decree "On the development of Subsidiary Enterprises and Trades in the Agricultural Area,"[124] which not only allowed but mandated the creation of collective farm workshops to ensure the provision of domestic services to the rural population. The decree itself and its commentators[125] refer to the seasonal character of agricultural production as the principal reason for this innovation, which works to ensure full utilization of collective farmers' labor. Actually, however, a no less important role was played by the completely dismal lack of services in rural regions.

In both rural and urban areas, except for certain sporadic measures and the promulgation every three or four years of decrees calling for improvement in consumer service but providing no serious means for carrying out those mandates, the Soviets demonstrate almost complete indifference toward these individual needs, not only economically but also legally. The success of an individual trying to establish contract obligations with a special entity, the services of which are in great demand, entirely depends on his own ability. Neither preliminary distribution nor official registration or other forms based on the principle of priority can be used by customers. Sometimes customers themselves resort to unofficial registration, but such arrangements are not binding for the servicing entities and can be disregarded even by their organizers or participants. The increase in the number of permissible individual handicrafts by current law[126] must soften the sharpness of the situation but only the future can prove to which extent these legal innovations will be efficient under specific Soviet circumstances.

An essentially different official attitude can be observed in retail trade, especially within the limits of food supply. And this is quite comprehensible: the Soviet system would have collapsed long ago, if the food supply were constantly at the same level as that of the supply of consumer services. The entire history of the Soviet regime proves the inability of this regime to cope with the food problem. One cannot, however, contend that the Soviet leadership expresses almost complete indifference also in this area. At least in appearance, things are otherwise. In May of 1982 the Plenum (meeting of the full membership) of the Party Central Committee adopted the Food Program of the USSR for the period until 1990.[127] The 1986 Party Congress maintained and developed the ideas contained in the 1982 document in the Fundamental Directions, which deal with the time period up to the year 2000. In accordance with the Food Program, a great many legislative acts have been promulgated.[128] However, with the exception of an edict addressed to collective farm trade and containing no essential innovations,[129] all of these legislative acts are concentrated on the production, distribution, and exchange implemented by economic entities. Non-economic contracts that can be executed between these entities and Soviet citizens are not mentioned at all. But independent of the Food Program, contracts of retail sale have always been regulated in consideration of the scarcity of goods relative to consumer demand. The relevant legal provisions accommodate, in part, the customer's needs, and, in part, the state's interests. Thus, special rules established by the USSR Ministry of Trade[130] use different approaches to the regulation of retail sale connected with food and that involving other goods. In principle, such differentiation is quite justified. One can hardly object to provisions that preclude, as a rule, the return of purchased food, although the same provisions allow in many instances for the return of other goods after their acquisition. However, putting aside the problem of *onus probandi*, one cannot reconcile certain other rules that, while concerning only the retail sale of food, nevertheless contradict one another. For instance, on the one hand, goods of poor quality may not be sold at all. But on the other hand, the buyer of food is entitled to return it only if "concealed" defects have been discovered. References to the probability that other defects can be caused by the purchaser are not persuasive: not infrequently the character of these defects by itself supports the opposite assumption. But even if such a reference is reasonable, it does not justify the establishment of an abstract rule in favor of retail enterprises to the detriment of their customers. Nevertheless, Soviet law maintains a similar policy in cases connected not only with food but also with other goods, where the purchaser's fault is not in question. For instance, the republican civil codes establish that a purchaser who discovers defects in an object bought may demand at his option the replacement of the object, a proportionate reduction in the price, the removal of defects by the seller at his own expense or reimbursement to the buyer for the cost of correcting the defects himself, or the rescission of the contract along with reimbursement for the buyer's losses.[131] Civil codes are codified laws, and, consequently, they can in theory be modified only by the legislator. In the case discussed, however, changes have been introduced by the Ministry of Trade that have adversely affected the purchaser's legal position, in replacing his free choice with a restricted mandatory sequence: first repair must be implemented, and only if this proves to be futile, can replacement of the object or the return of money be effected.[132]

In comparison with retail sale and domestic service, the renting of state housing is subject to peculiar regulation, which takes into account the legal adjustments necessary to cope with a demand that substantially exceeds supply. Housing space is an indispensable prerequisite of human life. Therefore, even a social system based on the primacy of politics over economy cannot be indifferent with respect to this issue. As a result, housing construction is far more developed in the USSR than is the construction of service enterprises. It is true that Stalin managed to bring the Soviet public housing economy to an extremely deplorable state. This, however, compelled Khrushchev to proclaim housing construction to the one of the most important objectives of his economic policy and to initiate a massive program of housing construction, the likes of which had never before been undertaken by the Soviet regime. At the same time, the housing situation is not so important as is the food supply. Therefore, the former has never attracted such official attention as has the latter, and, notwithstanding Khrushchev's achievements in this area, his successors have been less concerned with the problem, decreasing state expenditures and simultaneously increasing the monetary share that individuals must contribute in housing construction. If an apartment building is built by a housing cooperative, the individual's right to a separate apartment arises from cooperative membership. A non-economic contract of housing lease is applicable only in cases where citizens live as tenants in state apartment buildings or in individual houses.

The contract of lease connected with individual houses plays an important role in the regulation of housing relations between owners and tenants. However, bearing in mind the shortage of dwelling premises in the country, Soviet law maintains that while the execution of this contract exclusively depends upon agreement between the parties, the contract terms are dictated by legislation. The legal predetermination of the rental rate has already been mentioned,[133] though its goal is rather to prevent the extraction of so-called non-labor income by homeowners than to ensure favorable contract terms for the benefit of tenants. But in a number of cases tenants' interests prevail from the viewpoint of the compilers of housing legislation.[134] The tenant is entitled to settle his closest relatives into the apartment rented without the consent of the homeowner, and members of the tenant's family have the same rights with respect to this apartment as does the tenant himself. Upon expiration of the time period for which the contract has been executed it must be renewed at the request of the tenant, except in cases where a contract executed for less than one year provides otherwise or where the court ascertains that the rented premises are required for the personal use of the homeowner or his family members. Also, the contract remains in force even where the owner of the house transfers his property rights to another person. Eviction of the tenant and his family members may result only from gross violations of the tenant's duties and exclusively in cases enumerated by the law. As a rule, however, the contract, once executed, cannot be disolved by the homeowner.

The rent of housing space in state apartment buildings also requires the execution of a contract of lease between the tenant and the entity that manages the appropriate building or group of buildings and that is called the housing exploitation entity. However, the ultimate execution of such a contract depends on the distribution of housing space by local executive committees and the issuance by these same agencies of documents allocating specific housing each tenant and his family members.[135] Moreover, though Article 51 of the RSFSR Housing Code provides that the parties' rights and duties are fixed by the contract, in fact, all contract terms are specified by the relevant legal provisions. The contract plays a subsidiary or even a purely formal role, if one speaks about the contract in writing provided for by housing law, not about the mere fact of presentation of housing space by the housing exploitation entities and receipt of these premises by entitled tenants. Not infrequently contracts in writing are not executed at all, but, nevertheless, housing obligations arise, and both parties acquire quite definite rights and duties. In assessing these rights and duties, one must come to the following conclusion: it is difficult for the tenant to receive housing space from the state; however, once such space has been granted, it is almost impossible for the state to rid itself of the tenant. The size of the typical housing accommodations presented by the state to individuals is extremely limited, but the rights of the users of this space are sufficiently protected and, in principle, irrevocable.[136] Eviction without providing for relocation in other dwelling premises can occur only in cases indicated by law where the tenant grossly violates his duties toward the state. In general, however, eviction is either impossible or requires the presentation of other dwelling premises, should the withdrawal of living space result from extraordinary circumstances (demolition of apartment buildings, their transformation into public buildings, etc.). The stability of housing rights engenders other privileges in favor of tenants: temporarily absent tenants as a rule retain their rights for six months, delay in payment of rent cannot serve a ground for a tenant's eviction, reconstruction or remodeling of dwelling premises is allowed only with the consent of the tenants, etc. In addition, tenants in state apartment buildings have certain other privileges. They are entitled to receive temporary living space during periods when major repair of the rented dwelling premises is undertaken.

So long as the appropriate legal procedure and special requirements are adhered to, one tenant may exchange his room or apartment for the dwelling premises occupied by another. Rented living space can be an object of sublease in accordance with terms provided by law. Each adult member of the tenant family may contractually replace the tenant, and he may also demand to be separated from his family by means of executing a contract with the lessor with respect to a separate room of the family apartment. Usually the exercise of these rights requires the consent of the lessor and the other family members. In cases where the required consent cannot be obtained, any of the interested parties may make the dispute the subject of a judicial hearing. Sometimes, the court deviates from the law, but for most part housing rules are more strictly observed than are a great many other legal provisions functioning in the USSR.

Such are the most important types of non-economic contracts. One cannot deny the peculiarities of these contracts in comparison with economic contracts. Differing from one another in their availability to various subjects of Soviet law, in the preconditions required for their execution, and in the purposes for the achievement of which each group of contracts can be employed, they also have essential distinctions from the viewpoint of the parties' initiative in the process of their execution, performance and termination. This initiative, almost nonexistent with respect to certain economic contracts, is in fact inseparable from all non-economic contracts, the execution of which has always depended on the discretion of both or of at least one of the parties and functioning of which also leaves more or less restricted room either for mutual agreement or unilateral consent. Insofar as non-economic contracts are entered into by a Soviet entity, on the one hand, and a Soviet citizen, on the other hand, a specific problem irrelevant to economic and other non-economic contracts arises: to what extent must the interests of Soviet entities prevail over the interests of Soviet citizens, and to what degree will the latter be protected against arbitrary action on the part of the former. Although this problem is differently resolved in different cases, nevertheless, as discussed, each non-economic contract of such a specific class contains peculiar terms favoring to a greater or lesser degree one party or the other. Owing to the participation of individuals, non-economic contracts, even where one party is an organization, are not subject to the economic discipline so important for economic contracts. Therefore, the principle of real performance has never been mutually binding in cases of unilateral violations of these contracts, and the penalties established by the law are employed not as a rule but only as infrequent exceptions to the general rule.

At the same time, it would be a mistake to qualify economic and non-economic contracts as opposite or even fundamentally different phenomena. Apart from the fact that in the USSR both regulate property relations and rely on agreements between their parties, the homogeneity of economic and non-economic contracts in general can be argued legally as well as economically.

Legally, contractual freedom is not entirely precluded with respect to economic contracts just as it is not completely unlimited in the area of non-economic contracts. As has been demonstrated, certain economic contracts (delivery, for instance) allow the parties broad initiative, while at the same time certain non-economic contracts (the housing lease, for instance) cannot be executed without adhering to strict administrative prerequisites. Moreover, all economic contracts contain at least several terms stemming from agreements between the parties, and not a single non-economic contract executed between organizations or between organizations and individuals lacks at least several terms mandated by relevant legal provisions.

Economically, contracts of one group must be supplemented by contracts of the other group in order to complete the economic cycle initiated by production and leading through distribution and exchange to consumption in the final analysis. Consumer goods first moving along the channels of delivery must ultimately reach the consumer through retail trade. Apartment buildings erected by means of capital construction are utilized on the basis of housing lease. The transportation of goods from producers through wholesale entities to retail enterprises connects the sphere of state production with the area of individual consumption.

Thus, both economic and non-economic contracts as legal forms, employed in the phase of exchange which follows the phases of production and distribution, constitute a system of Soviet contracts both dichotomous and unified at the same time. The dichotomy of this system results from the different purposes that various sections of the Soviet economy are expected to serve. The system's unity corresponds to the character of the Soviet economy as "a single national economic system,"[137] irrespective of whether this system is represented by organizations or individuals.

Notes

1. For greater detail see, e.g., Jean Carbonier, *Droit civil, les obligations* (Paris: Presses Universitaires de France, 1979) p.106–123.

2. Fundamental Principles of Civil Legislation, art. 4.

3. One must bear in mind that Soviet law, like the civil law system, does not distinguish a law of contracts and a law of torts, as does the common law system, but rather recognizes a law of obligations, which provides for contractual and non-contractual obligations, including obligations arising from causation of damage. In addition, rightholders and obligors, the participants in obligations, are called creditors and debtors irrespective of the monetary or non-monetary character of each obligation.

4. RSFSR Civil Code, chapters 21–38.

5. E.g., an unpublished decree of April 21, 1949 had the title "On the Conclusion of Economic Contracts."

6. For a review of these controversial conceptions, see A. G. Bykov, *Plan i khoziaistvennyi dogovor* (Moscow: Izd-vo MGU, 1975) p.3–25.

7. O. S. Ioffe, *Plan i dogovor v sotsialisticheskom khoziaistve* (Moscow: Iuridicheskaia literatura, 1971) p. 71–74.

8. RSFSR Civil Code, art 152, para 2.
9. Ibid., art. 234.
10. See the section of Chapter 7 ("Distribution and its Legal Forms") on "Planned Distribution."
11. *SP SSSR*, 1981, part 1, n. 3, item 12.
12. *SP SSSR*, 1964, No. 5, item 36.
13. See the section of the Chapter 4 ("Production: Its Legal Organization") on "Agencies of Production."
14. V. V. Laptev, ed., *Khoziaistvennoe pravo* (Moscow: Nauka, 1983).
15. Above, note 12.
16. Ibid.
17. Laptev, *Khoziaistvennoe pravo*, p. 175.
18. Ibid, p. 188–190.
19. Ibid, p. 196.
20. Ibid.
21. Above, note 12.
22. Laptev, *Khoziaistvennoe pravo*, p. 108–116.
23. Ibid., p. 204–208.
24. See the previous section of the present chapter.
25. Soviet law provides for only one type of contract—joint operation—that may be executed by more than two parties (the RSFSR Civil Code, art. 434–438).
26. See note 24.
27. Ibid.
28. See note 10.
29. E.g., N. I. Ovchinnikov, *Poniatie i klassifikatsiia khoziaistvennykh dogovorov* (Vladivostok: Izd-vo Dal'nevostochnogo Universiteta, 1970), p.3–8.
30. See below, in the present section.
31. Above, note 10.
32. Rules on Contracts for Capital Construction (*SP SSSR*, 1970, n. 2, item 11), articles 13–20.
33. Statute on Delivery of Products for Production and Technical Use, articles 21–30; Statute on Delivery of Consumer Goods, art. 17–25 (*SP SSSR*, 1981, part 1, no. 9–10, item 62).
34. In fact, Arbitrazh practice allows for refusal on the part of the purchaser even after the expiration of this ten-day period.
35. See note 10.
36. See above, in the present section.
37. E.g., the Statute of Railroads of the USSR, art. 38–39.
38. Fundamental Principles of Civil Legislation, art. 68.
39. art. 21.
40. art. 17.
41. E.g., R. O. Khalfina, *Pravovoe regulirovanie postavki produktsii v narodnom khoziaistve* (Moscow: Izd-vo AN SSSR, 1963) p. 142.
42. Above, note 39.
43. Above, note 32.
44. Above, note 33, art. 25 and art. 19, respectively.
45. Above, note 37.
46. Principal Rules on Bank Credit (*SP SSSR*, 1982, part 1, no. 32, item 160), Chapters II and III.
47. E.g., Statute on Delivery of Products for Production and Technical Use, above note 33, art. 31.

48. Therefore, the contract of delivery may be changed or cancelled as a result of alterations of plans in the same form which is employed for execution of a contract by means of acceptance of a warrant for performance (Ibid.).
49. Ibid.
50. Fundamental Principles of Civil Legislation, art. 34.
51. See note 10.
52. Where a contractor discovers a mistake of such nature during the process of construction, it must halt this process, inform the customer, and wait for the latter's new instructions issued by planning agencies, (Rules on Contracts for Capital Construction, art. 61).
53. Rules on Contracts for Capital Construction, art. 37–52.
54. *Izvestia*, Feb. 26 and March 4, 1986.
55. See the section of Chapter 3 ("Ownership and Law of Ownership") on "The State's Right of Ownership."
56. *SP SSSR*, 1981, part 1, no. 9–10, item 62.
57. See above, in the present section.
58. Ibid.
59. Above note 56.
60. See above, in the present section.
61. *Izvestia*, March 4, 1986.
62. See above, in the present section.
63. E.g., the Statue of Railroads of the USSR, articles 18–77.
64. Among the more recent works by Soviet scholars dealing with the mentioned problem, the following provide a general analysis: I. Kh. Kalmykov, *Pravovoe regulirovanie khoziaistvennykh otnoshenii*, (Saratov: Izd-vo SGU, 1982); B. I. Pugynskii, *Pravovye sredstva obespecheniia effektivnosti proizvodstva*, (Moscow: Iuridicheskaia literatura, 1980). For an analysis dedicated to the specific aspects of economic discipline, see, e.g., A. Lebed, "Distsiplina postavok—vazhnoe uslovie povysheniia effektivnosti proizvodstva," *Khoziaistvo i pravo*, 1981, no. 11, p. 10–16. "Discipline" is sometimes included in titles of edicts (e.g., a 1983 edict of the Party Central Committee and the USSR Council of Ministers "On Strengthening of Discipline in the Area of Deliveries," *SP SSSR*, 1983, part 1, no. 11, item 195).
65. *SP SSSR*, 1981, part 1, no. 3, item 12 and No. 30, item 176.
66. Above, note 55.
67. See above, in the present section.
68. 1977 Constitution, art. 164–168.
69. RSFSR Criminal Code, art. 170–172.
70. Pre-contractual negotiations are subject to contractual discipline only where contractual terms are dictated not by the plan but by the parties' choice within the limits of appropriate legal provisions.
71. E.g. the Statute on Delivery of Products for Production and Technical Use, art. 101.
72. *SP SSSR*, 1967, no. 26, item 186.
73. Ibid.
74. Statutes, above, note 33.
75. Above note 33, articles, respectively, 72 and 69.
76. *SP SSSR*, 1973, no. 18, item 106.
77. Fundamental Principles of Civil Legislation, art. 36.
78. Ibid.
79. See note 10.
80. Above note 32, art. 68.

81. RSFSR Civil Code, art. 173.
82. *SP SSSR*, 1969, no. 15, item 82.
83. Above note 32, art. 65.
84. Above, note 33, arts. 35 and 32 respectively.
85. Ibid.
86. E.g., The Statute of Railroads of the USSR, art. 29, 144.
87. See above, in the present section.
88. See above, in the present section.
89. Above note 33.
90. See above, in the present section.
91. The Statute of Railroads of the USSR, art. 79–95.
92. Compare, for example, this contract with the bank account contract.
93. *SP SSSR*, 1981, part 1, no. 3, item 12 and no. 30, item 176; 1983, part 1, No. 27, item 155.
94. See above, in the present section.
95. Only in certain cases provided for by the law may Soviet organizations keep cash on hand or make payments in cash.
96. Above, note 93.
97. Above, note 55.
98. *SZ SSSR*, 1930, no. 8, item 98, and 1931, no. 4, item 52 and no., 18, item 166.
99. See above, in the present section.
100. If an economic contract is unplanned, the reference to planning acts is, of course, not required.
101. Olimpiad S. Ioffe, "Law and Economy in the USSR," *Harvard Law Review* 95 (1982): 1599.
102. Chapter 21 (Contract of purchase and sale), Chapter 30 (Independent work contract), and Chapter 27 (Lease of Property) of the RSFSR Civil Code.
103. *Sbornik normativnykh aktov po grazhdanskomu zakonodatel'stvu*, vol. 2, p. 4–13, 149–153, 113–118.
104. Ibid., pp. 15–16. See also vol. 1, pp. 41–43.
105. In the discussion that follows we will deal only with specialized entities to which all citizens have access, putting aside "closed establishments."
106. Apart from the underground economy, private economy as a permanent business is permitted within restricted limits only to individuals who as housewives, pensioners, or students are freed from the performance of publicly recognized work. In all other cases, citizens may only combine their official work and individual economic activity.
107. See note 10.
108. RSFSR Criminal Code, art. 154.
109. See note 10.
110. *SP SSSR*, part 1, 1982, no. 22, item 112.
111. See the section of Chapter 7 ("Distribution and its Legal Forms") on "Unplanned Distribution."
112. See the previous section of Chapter 7.
113. E.g., *SP RSFSR*, 1981, no. 11, item 71.
114. See above, in the present section.
115. RSFSR Criminal Code, articles 153–154.
116. Olimpiad S. Ioffe, *Soviet Law and Soviet Reality* (Dordrecht: Martinus Nijhoff 1985) p. 102–103.
117. Note 111.

118. *SP RSFSR*, 1965, no. 1, item 2.

119. See the section of Chapter 1 ("The Fundamental Structural Elements of the Soviet Economic System") on "Exchange."

120. *Grazhdanskoe zakonodatel'stvo*, compiled by A. I. Kabalkin (Moscow: Iuridicheskaia literatura, 1974) p. 911–915.

121. *SP RSFSR*, 1965, no. 4, item 19.

122. *SP RSFSR*, 1965, no. 1, item 2.

123. *SP RSFSR*, 1981, no. 11, item 187.

124. *SP SSSR*, 1966, no. 7, item 71.

125. E.g., *Sub'ekty grazhdanskogo prava*, ed. S. N. Bratus' (Moscow: Iuridicheskaia literatura, 1984) p. 206.

126. See the "Afterword."

127. *Prodovol'stvennaia programma. Normativnye akty* (Moscow: Iuridicheskaia literatura, 1984) p. 9–45.

128. Ibid.

129. Ibid., p. 138–139.

130. *Sbornik normativnykh aktov po grazhdanskomu pravu*, vol. 2, pp. 4–10.

131. RSFSR Civil Code, art. 246.

132. Above note 131, pp. 8–10.

133. See above, in the present section.

134. RSFSR Housing Code, art. 131–136.

135. Above, note 111.

136. RSFSR Housing Code, art. 50–99.

137. 1977 Constitution, art. 16.

9

Legal Protection of the Soviet Economic System

General Principles

Legal protection of the Soviet economic system is designed both to deter conduct that threatens the system and to provide compensation for damage caused to the system. Legal protection is more necessary and more extensive in the Soviet system than in a capitalist system, because the very nature of the Soviet system creates more temptations and more possibilities for abusive conduct, and, moreover, because such conduct is not only economically but also politically dangerous for the Soviet system. Legal protection has a variety of goals. It is designed to prevent theft of government property, to encourage plan discipline, to discourage mismanagement of government property, and to restrain private enterprise activity.

Theft of state property is a major problem in the Soviet Union for a number of reasons. First, because the percentage of property owned by the state is much higher than in a capitalist country, the chances that a given theft will involve state property are much higher also. Second, the extremely low wages create a strong temptation to steal. Third, the system of distribution of goods makes many products unavailable to the average citizen even with money. This system is governed by long-term plans, which often misestimate the correlation between supply and demand. Furthermore, the best goods are shunted off into special stores for the elite (e.g., Party officials, state officials, military officers, top managers and scientists, ballet stars, sports heros) or are sold in regular stores only to citizens with special permits obtained on the basis of their status, not need. A citizen repairing his home, for instance, may discover that the necessary supplies are impossible to find in any store, but easy to steal from where he works. The managers of state property lack the incentives that private property owners have to care for property and prevent its theft.

Because the incentives provided automatically by private ownership of means of production have not been fully replaced by the system of incentives for plan fulfillment by managers of the state-owned economic system, mismanagement is a constant problem. In many cases, the combination of irrationalities in the system of plan incentives and an arbitrary non-market pricing system actually encourage managers to take action contrary to the interests of the economic system as a whole. Because of the complexity or even the impossibility of maintaining a rational pricing system in the absence of a free market, solutions are sought not through reform of planning and pricing, but through coercive measures, such as criminal and administrative penalties.

The inability of the Soviet economic system to fill the needs of the Soviet people creates numerous opportunities for private enterprise. However, to allow this enterprise to flourish would threaten the Soviet system, so legal measures must be used to keep it in check. These legal measures are difficult to enforce, because the enormous profits of illegal private enterprise provide large amounts for bribery of law enforcement officials.

Institutional Basis of Protection of the Economy

A number of important institutions devote much or even most of their time to the protection of the economy. These include the Procuracy, the Ministry of Internal Affairs, the Committee on State Security, the People's Supervision Organization, banks, safety organizations, and environmental protection agencies. Special protective roles are played by the legal counsel and accountants of organizations.

Because there is no institution in English-speaking countries with powers exactly corresponding to those of the Procuracy, most English-speaking commentators on this institution denote it with the word "Procuracy," the direct English equivalent of the Russian word "Prokuratura." One part of the Procuracy's duties corresponds to that of the public prosecutor's office; however its duties go far beyond that.[1] With respect to protection of the economy, a number of aspects of the Procuracy's work are of great importance: the investigation of crime; the prosecution of crime; the investigation of activity that is not necessarily criminal, but amounts to a violation of economic legislation; the stopping of such illegal activity; and the securing of civil compensation for economic entities harmed by illegal activity.

The Procuracy is organized in a manner designed to make it independent both of local governmental bodies and of economic ministries and their subordinate production associations and enterprises. The Procurator General of the USSR is formally appointed by the Presidium of the Supreme Soviet. This means that he is in fact selected directly by the Politburo. Thus, he owes no loyalty to anyone except the Politburo. Procurators at the republic, province, and city levels are appointed by higher levels of the Procuracy. Local governments and industrial enterprises have no authority over them. While it is by no means unknown in practice for a local procurator to join with other local officials in a scheme directed against the economy, the combination of professionalism and the threat of severe punishments creates a powerful pressure for a local procurator to place institutional loyalty to the Procuracy over local personal connections. Even the extremely powerful provincial Party secretaries sometimes cannot be sure of preventing investigations by the Procuracy, insofar as the Procurator General is exercising his important function of reporting to top Party officials on local corruption.

The Procuracy has primary responsibility for pretrial investigation in criminal cases. Soviet law follows the continental European system of having an elaborate and formal pretrial investigation, leaving few or no surprises for the trial itself. Unlike Western Europe, where pretrial investigation is conducted by an independent "investigation judge" and where the party under suspicion may be represented by counsel during the investigation, in the Soviet Union, the pretrial investigation is conducted by the Procuracy, and, with some exceptions, the accused is denied access to counsel during the investigation. The investigator of the Procuracy has procedural powers that greatly aid in the uncovering of the facts of crimes against the economy. These include the right to hold the accused incommunicado and without access to an attorney for months, the right to call any person for questioning, to demand production of documents, and to conduct searches. Investigations of complex economic crimes often last many months and produce dozens of volumes of investigative records. In addition to preparing a detailed case for the prosecution to present at trial, the investigation serves a preventive purpose. Often, in the course of uncovering an economic crime, the investigator will discover that the crime was made possible by lax accounting controls, poor physical security, or other shortcoming on the part of the government organization that was the victim of the crime. In such cases, the investigator will make a formal recommendation to the agency to mend its ways.[2] If the pretrial investigation ends in a decision to bring formal criminal charges, a prosecutor of the Procuracy will handle the actual prosecution of the criminal case, performing a role quite similar to that of the prosecutor in most other countries.

Another quite different, but important role of the Procuracy is that of securing civil compensation for harm done to the economy. The Procuracy has the right to bring civil cases on its own initiative or on the request of economic entities to secure compensation for damages caused to these entities. A very large number of these cases are brought to secure compensation from enterprise employees for harm intentionally or negligently done by the employees to the enterprise. In criminal cases, the procuracy can also present claims for compensation for entities that are victims of economic crime. Typical cases will involve prosecutions for embezzlement or theft from state enterprises.

Also important is the general supervision power of the Procuracy. Under this power, the Procuracy supervises all activities of Soviet economic entities. When an illegal activity is discovered, the Procuracy calls the illegality to the attention of the entity and requests that it be stopped. This request may take various forms. The most serious is a formal "protest" against a specific illegal action. Milder is a "representation" in which the Procuracy calls the attention of an enterprise, organization, or governmental body to a pattern of illegal activity. Often these requests are made informally by telephone. In many cases, local Party authorities are informed of the protest. In the vast majority of cases enterprises "accept" the recommendation of the Procuracy. If an enterprise disputes the Procuracy's request, the procurator can refer the matter to a higher level in the procuracy, which can take the matter to the next higher administrative level above the offending enterprise. The power of the Procuracy to stop illegal activity is greatly aided by the fact that it is not subordinate to the republic or local governments, and thus is, in theory, and to some extent in practice, free of local influences. Statistics show that enforcement of labor law and protection of state property account for most of the total general supervision activity of the Procuracy.[3]

The Ministry of Internal Affairs has several rather different functions, some of which directly involve the protection of the economy.[4] Unlike the Procuracy, and unlike many other ministries, the ministry is a "union-republic" organization meaning that there is a Ministry of Internal Affairs in each republic, simultaneously subordinate to the government of the republic and to the USSR Ministry of Internal Affairs. This "dual subordination," a common feature in Soviet government structure, works because overall Party control means there can be no policy differences between the government of a republic and the government of the USSR. Functions of the Ministry include ordinary police work, administration of labor camps, fire safety, highway safety, administration of the passport system, administration of the permit system for dangerous items (firearms, fireworks, printing presses, and copying machines).

The local police force ("*militsiia*" in Russian) is responsible for apprehending criminals and for pretrial procedures for crimes of lesser importance than those investigated by the Procuracy.[5] Pretrial procedures for economic crimes that are of high frequency but low seriousness, are handled before trial by a police inquiry rather than a full-fledged preliminary investigation. Such crimes include petty theft of state property, possession of homemade liquor, illegal hunting and fishing, and residence permit violations. Preliminary investigation is required for economic crimes of greater seriousness, but in most cases this may be conducted by police rather than procuracy investigators.

The traffic police (called the "State Auto Inspectorate") direct traffic and fine violators of traffic regulations. Since most Soviet traffic is by government-owned vehicles involved in economic operations, most of the ordinary traffic control functions could be said to be directed toward protection of the economy. Certain aspects of the traffic rules enforced by the traffic police directly affect the economy, e.g., rules on diversion of gasoline from state-owned vehicles to private car owners, and rules on use of state-owned vehicles to transport black-market merchandise.

The fire safety function of the Ministry of Internal Affairs involves both fire safety inspection and fire-fighting. Since all major structures belong to the government, these functions also directly involve protection of the economy.

The enforcement of passport and residence permit legislation, discussed in Chapter 6, provides direct protection of the economies against the upheavals that would be caused by free movement of labor.

During the 1960s, the Committee on State Security (KGB) was given a rather broad role in the investigation of economic crime. However, the current law gives it investigative powers only in cases involving state security (e.g. espionage) or smuggling, though it may investigate other crimes if they are discovered in the course of an investigation of crimes within its jurisdiction.[6] Most legislation on the KGB is unpublished. This unpublished legislation may give it additional functions in the protection of the economy.

The People's Supervision system is a system of government inspection and supervision agencies whose paid staff is augmented by a large number of "volunteers."[7] The system is designed to enlist large numbers of members of the public for unpaid work on the task of detecting shortcomings in the operation of government agencies. The structure of People's Supervision parallels that of the Party; there is a national People's Supervision Committee with headquarters in Moscow; there are republic-level and local people's supervision committees; there are people's supervision groups at enterprises and organizations. At the top levels, the staff consists almost entirely of paid government employees. At the bottom level, most work is done by unpaid volunteers. However, in the Soviet Union "volunteer" work is rarely entirely voluntary. The local Party organization may strongly suggest to its members that they "volunteer" to work for People's Supervision. While People's Supervision is a nationwide agency, like the Procuracy, the Ministry of Internal Affairs, and the Committee on State Security, its mission is different. Its employees and volunteers are generally not lawyers, but many (about one-third) are Party members.[8] Unlike the local agencies of the Procuracy, local agencies of People's Supervision are subordinate to local government, and, by implication, to local Party officials. People's supervision committees are encouraged to work together with other organizations, for instance with the Young Communist League in mass inspection projects, with "trade unions" in checking labor conditions, and with collective farm auditing committees on agricultural matters.

People's Supervision committees are charged with hunting out not only actual violations of the law, but also mismanagement and inefficiencies. They check plan fulfillment, particularly in areas that are given little weight in formal evaluation of management performance. Most managers are interested in fulfilling their production and financial plans, but have comparatively little incentive for quality control or introduction of new technology. One function of People's Supervision is to press for plan performance in areas such as these where the legal sanctions for poor performance are weak. Likewise, managers interested in plan performance pay little attention to waste of material, money, or manpower, since the planning system puts emphasis on results rather than costs. People's Supervision also checks these neglected areas. People's Supervision also looks for waste in the government bureaucratic system. Inspections may take place on orders from higher agencies, on the initiative of local bodies, or response to letters and complaints received from citizens.

People's Supervision has a number of enforcement powers. It can reprimand officials, order them to pay for harm done to the state, or in extreme cases remove them from their positions. However, if it discovers criminal activity, it is supposed to report to the Procuracy. The People's Supervision groups in individual enterprises lack these enforcement powers and can only report to the local committees with recommendations for enforcement action.

The State Bank has a regulatory, an operational, and a supervisory role.[9] In its regulatory role, it issues "Instructions" on banking matters binding upon all organizations in the USSR. In its operational role, it maintains bank accounts, transfers funds, makes loans, and performs other banking functions. In its supervisory role, it ensures that transactions for which it performs funds transfers or makes loans have been conducted in accordance with plan and law. A similar operational and supervisory role belongs to the Construction Bank and the Foreign Trade Bank, for construction and foreign trade operations respectively. In some cases operational and supervisory functions are performed by the savings bank network, although the main purpose of this network is to maintain accounts of funds voluntarily deposited by private individuals. The Construction, Foreign Trade, and savings banks are subject to the regulatory authority of the State Bank. Like the Procuracy, the banking system is completely independent of local authorities, and of government administrative organizations, industrial ministries and their subordinate enterprise. Thus, local branch banks take their orders only from their vertical superiors and ultimately from the head Bank office in Moscow. This means that the banking system, like the Procuracy, can provide an effective check on local abuses.

The Basic Provisions on Payments in the National Economy of the USSR provide that, with some exceptions, payments are only to be made *after* shipment of goods, completion of work, or rendering of services.[10] Payments require the consent of the payor and that the payor have sufficient funds in its account. Thus, the bank has the power to check the legality of a payment both with respect to the payee (Has the payee become entitled to the payment?) and the payor (Does the payor have funds authorized for this payment?). In this way, all transactions are essentially preaudited for legality and conformance to plan. Further control over payments is ensured by the bank's duty to enforce priorities for payment in case an enterprise has insufficient funds to meet all of its obligations. Payments must be made in the following order: wages, social insurance, payments to the treasury, insurance, payments for goods and services, payments into enterprise funds and payments of penalties for breach of contract, repayment of bank loans, and all other payments.[11] When a construction project is authorized by the planning authorities, the necessary funds are transferred to the Construction Bank, which releases them in installments, upon receipt of documentary proof that specific stages of construction have been completed.[12]

The State Committee of the USSR for Supervision of the Safe Conduct of Work in Industry and for Mining Inspection (*Gosgortekhnadzor*), which is organized on a union-republic basis, is responsible for industrial safety inspection and enforcement.[13] Since it is independent of the industrial ministries, it may have some capability of exercising independent supervision. It has general rulemaking and supervisory powers in the area of industrial safety and very specific powers in areas involving particular dangers. Areas where it exercises detailed supervision include boiler inspection, elevator inspection, mining, oil and gas, mineral fertilizers, gas pipelines and urban gas systems, explosive and flammable substances, and construction and operation of nuclear power plants. It is responsible not only for preventing injuries to employees but for protecting equipment and mineral reserves from accidental damage.

This Committee's rights include those of making inspections at any time of installations under its supervision, making proposals for improving safety and giving binding instructions for the correction of safety violations. In extreme cases, it can stop work and evacuate personnel. The Committee has the right to fine enterprise personnel for violations, and even to recommend that they be discharged or suspended (though actual discharge or suspension can be conducted only in accordance with labor legislation).

The RSFSR Code on Administrative Violations mentions a "State Committee of the USSR for Supervision of Safety of Work in Atomic Energy" (*Gosatomenergonadzor*).[14] Because most legislation on nuclear power is secret, it is difficult to unravel the exact system of nuclear safety agencies in the USSR, though an excellent start has been made by Professor Donald Barry.[15] The aftermath of the Chernobyl disaster will probably lead to a major reorganization of this system, and also will force the Soviet authorities to release more information.

Inspectors of the State Insurance Organization (*Gosstrakh*) have the right to verify the observance of veterinary health and fire safety rules and to cancel policies if these rules are not observed.[16] However, the Soviet insurance industry does not seem to have developed the elaborate risk measurement and risk prevention functions of insurance in capitalist countries. Rather it sets flat rates by regions and republics. Thus, for instance, it will cost 25 rubles a year to insure a camel worth 500 rubles if it is kept in Estonia, regardless of the care with which it is kept.[17]

State Energy Supervision is subordinate to the Ministry of Energy and Electrification of the USSR. This ministry is responsible for nonnuclear electric power plants and for central heat plants, which, in many Soviet cities pipe hot water or steam to individual buildings. This organizational structure, in which the supervising agency is subordinate to the agency supervised obviously threatens the independence of the supervisory process. State Energy Supervision itself is responsible for safety inspection of non-nuclear electrical plants and power lines, and also of heat plants and systems.[18] This organization also has responsibilities with respect to the prevention of wastage of energy.

As both Soviet and foreign authors repeatedly have noted, the system of environmental protection agencies in the Soviet Union is weak. These authors have pointed to two fundamental problems. The first is that there is no single powerful centralized environmental protection agency independent of the industrial ministries and local government authorities. The second problem is that many environmental protection functions are assigned to the same agencies whose main duty is natural resource exploitation.

Soviet authors argue that effective environmental protection will only be possible if there is a single centralized government agency with powers: (1) to make environmental rules binding on all other agencies; (2) to monitor observance of these rules; and (3) to impose sanctions for the violation of these rules.[19] These authors advocate the creation of such an agency, to be called something like the State Committee on the Environment. However, because the Soviet Union has a planned economy, it is doubtful that the creation of a government body similar to the Environmental Protection Agency in the United States would be particularly effective. It would do little good to monitor environmental pollution and punish the polluters if the polluters' economic plans call for production that can only be obtained by creating a certain amount of pollution and do not provide the resources necessary to prevent or clean up this pollution. Therefore effective protection of the people and the economy against pollution must come from central planning agencies, not from monitoring and enforcement bodies.

This may be why the only centralized environmental agency of general jurisdiction lacks monitoring and enforcement capabilities. The Commission of the Presidium of the Council of Minsters of the USSR on the Protection of the Environment and the Rational Use of Natural Resources has the power to request reports and to make policies binding upon other organizations.[20] However, it does not have its own staff or facilities for monitoring environmental quality or enforcing sanctions for violation of environmental legislation. The actual planning decisions that determine what measures will be taken for protection of the environment are made by the State Planning Committee and the State Committee on Science and Technology. The State Committee on Construction is responsible for implementing these decisions in new plant construction. The Ministry of Chemical and Petroleum Machinebuilding is responsible for the manufacture of "scrubbers."

The role of monitoring and enforcement agencies is a limited one. They cannot force an enterprise to install environmental protection equipment not provided to it by the plan, no matter how bad the environmental effects of operating the enterprise. In the most extreme cases, they could close down an enterprise that presented immediate danger to human health;

however, important government policies of full utilization of productive facilities and full employment would mitigate against use of this power. Monitoring is needed to make sure that enterprises are in fact maintaining and using the equipment provided to them by plan. Air quality is monitored by the State Committee on Hydrometeorology and Monitoring of the Environment;[21] the use of scrubbers is monitored and enforced by The Main Administration for the Supervision of the Work of Gascleaning Installations of the Ministry of Chemical and Petroleum Machinebuilding;[22] and water and air quality are monitored by the State Sanitary Inspection of the Ministry of Health and other organizations.[23] A serious problem is the political power of the major industrial ministries. Thus, while local inspectors of the Ministry of Health may have the theoretical power to enforce environmental legislation upon a factory under the jurisdiction of an industrial ministry, they are likely to find it hard to ensure compliance in practice.

There are serious problems with the organization of natural resource protection in the Soviet Union. The problem is that typically the agency assigned to protect a resource is the same agency whose main task is to exploit the resource. This agency may do an excellent job of protecting the resource against outsiders, whether they are private citizen poachers or other state agencies, but the agency assigned both to exploit and protect a resource is unlikely to do a good job of protecting the resource against its own depredations. Soviet commentators have frequently pointed out the difficulties with this mode of organization and have suggested that agencies never be given the task of protecting the economy against their own excesses.[24]

Conservation of the fish population is the duty of the Main Administration for the Protection and Reproduction of Fish Stocks and the Regulation of Fishing of the Ministry of Fisheries.[25] But the main duty of the Ministry of Fisheries is to meet ever-growing plan targets for fish catch. The Ministry of Irrigation and Water Supply is responsible both for protecting and exploiting the water supply.[26]

Larger enterprises and organizations have their own legal departments. Smaller enterprises do without legal counsel or hire a local lawyer as a consultant on legal matters. For those enterprises that have legal counsel, the chief legal counsel is appointed by the superior organization and is responsible not only for ordinary legal work, but also for ensuring the legality of enterprise operations.[27] He (or she—half the lawyers in the Soviet Union are women) is not supposed to approve any documents that involve a violation of the law. While the chief legal counsel is in practice heavily subject to the influence of the enterprise director, he also must take into account the disciplinary consequences he might suffer for approving illegal actions. Furthermore, there is no conflict involved when the legal counsel points out to the director the possible sanctions for illegal actions the director proposes to take.

The Ministry of Finances and the Central Statistical Administration have the power to issue instructions binding on all enterprises and institutions. These instructions provide rules for implementation of the accounting requirements set by law and prescribe the accounting forms which must be completed.[28] These rules are very detailed, so the individual enterprise has essentially no discretion in accounting methods. This unification of accounting methods is necessary both to give planners comparable information from different enterprises, and to provide a ready basis for dealing with problems such as disobedience to plan directives, waste of resources, and embezzlement. The accounting rules help detect embezzlement; criminal sanctions to be discussed later in this chapter help deter embezzlement. There is currently a great deal of discussion in the Soviet Union about how accounting and reporting rules can be revised and computer systems can be employed to provide central planners with more prompt and useful information.

Accounting is the responsibility of the chief accountant of each enterprise or organization. The rights and duties of the chief accountant are stated in 1980 legislation.[29] This legislation continues the longstanding Soviet practice of attempting to make the chief accountant a spy and watchdog in the enterprise, with loyalties to the superior organization, not to the enterprise where the accountant works. This is done by legislation providing that the chief accountant is appointed and discharged by the superior agency, not by the head of the enterprise or organization where the accountant works. In addition, this legislation provides that members of the staff of the chief accountant can be discharged only with the permission of the chief accountant. The legislation provides for two modes of control by the chief accountant. All accounting reports submitted to the superior agency must be prepared and signed by the chief accountant. In addition, the law provides that many types of transactions with third parties must have the formal approval of the chief accountant.

Each ministry maintains an auditing department, responsible for regularly auditing the books of subordinate organizations. It is responsible for annual formal audits of all economically-accountable subordinate organizations. The auditors are required to report not only to their superior organization, but also, in the case of apparent criminal violations, to the appropriate investigatory agencies.

Types of Protection

Both the Party discipline system and various branches of Soviet law are used to protect the Soviet economic system. The vast majority of persons in important managerial positions are members of the Communist Party. The Party discipline system provides a flexible way to punish those whose actions threaten the economic system without exposing the fallibility of the Party membership to the public. Labor law provides a method for disciplining rank and file workers. Criminal law provides major sanctions for serious offenses. The law on administrative violations provides minor sanctions for minor offenses. Legislation on the Comrades' Courts provides an alternative set of sanctions for minor offenses. Civil law allows recovery for harm caused to the economy. The economy is protected not only against actions by individuals, but also against actions by state enterprises or other entities. Administrative and finance law are used to prevent improper action by enterprises. Civil law provides a means for recovery of damages caused by such improper action. However, while in the United States, corporations may be convicted of crimes, in the Soviet Union only individuals may be subject to criminal responsibility.

Responsibility under the "law" of the Party parallels and often substitutes for responsibility under the law of the state. Managers guilty of illegal or incompetent activity may be subjected to sanctions ranging from a "comradely criticism" to expulsion. The Statute of the Communist Party of the Soviet Union contains some very vague provisions giving a general outline of the procedures for imposing responsibility on a Party member.[30] Under the formal procedures described in the Statute, except for cases involving certain high party officials, who can be expelled only by the Central Committee, questions of Party discipline are decided by the primary party organization. The disciplined Party member may appeal to higher Party bodies, up to and including the Central Committee of the Party. Because the democracy with power flowing from the bottom to the top depicted by the Party Statute does not correspond to the reality of oligopoly with power exercised downward from the Politburo, the procedures formally described in the Statute cannot be considered to correspond to those in real life. Since Party meetings are secret, it is hard for an outsider to learn how Party discipline procedures actually work in practice.

With respect to criminal offenses, the Party Statute states: "For the violation of Soviet laws, a Party member bears double responsibility—before the State and before the Party. Persons who have committed offenses punishable as crimes shall be excluded from the ranks of the Communist Party of the Soviet Union."[31] Actual practice is different. When it appears that a Party member has committed a crime, one of several things may happen. Party authorities may decide to overlook the crime in the light of the member's political importance; they may suggest to the primary Party organization that it hold a meeting and apply a sanction short of expulsion; or they may suggest expulsion. In general, the Procuracy will only bring a Party member to trial if he has been expelled from the Party. Thus, the Party has, and apparently often exercises the *de facto* power to provide amnesty for its members. However, Party members cannot count on amnesty. If they get caught in the midst of an anti-corruption campaign, or lose the protection of powerful officials in higher Party organizations, they may find themselves expelled from the Party and subjected to severe criminal punishment. In recent years a number of instances have been reported where Party members engaged in large scale theft of state property have been expelled and have received death sentences in the criminal trials that followed their expulsion. Ordinary Party members enjoy no such immunity from punishment for minor administrative violations. Since perhaps half of all car owners are Party members, to grant them immunity for traffic violations would lead to chaos. Moreover, many of the economic offenses defined as administrative violations, for instance, failure to observe environmental standards by industry, can be perpetrated in practice only by enterprise directors, who are almost invariably Party members.

Even where the only punishment imposed by the Party is a reprimand, the effect on the Party member's career may be severe. Under the "nomenklatura" system, there are two important lists maintained by the Party. One is a list of jobs for which Party approval is required for hiring or firing. The other is a list of persons who can be considered candidates for managerial jobs. The Party maintains a dossier for each person on the latter list; any Party disciplinary action will be entered into this dossier.

Criminal law protection of the Soviet economic system is very highly developed. About one-third of all criminal convictions are for crimes against the economic system.[32] These include theft of state property, maladministration of state property, and black market activities. Each Soviet Republic has its own criminal code. However, in the area of economic crime the differences among the codes are trivial. The most serious crimes are defined by USSR legislation, whose definitions are then copied verbatim into the codes of the republics. Often there are "campaigns" against particular types of economic offenses. As part of these campaigns USSR legislation will require uniform amendments to the criminal codes of the republics or the Party will order the amendments. In addition, there is a tendency for draftsmen in other republics to follow the law of the Russian Republic, because of its overwhelming importance in the Soviet system. All criminal offenses are found in the codes; there are no criminal provisions to be found scattered among other legislation. Thus, while this chapter will only discuss crimes defined in the Criminal Code of the Russian Republic, what is said applies to all Soviet criminal law.

The Russian Republic Criminal Code follows classic continental European criminal code organization. There is a general part dealing with bases of criminal responsibility, the applicability of the code in time and space, intent, negligence, responsibility of minors, nonimputability, self-defense, necessity, attempt, participation, punishment, and compulsory medical and rehabilitative measures. There follows a special part, consisting of somewhat more than 200 articles, each defining a specific crime and the range of punishment for the crime. Often the article will define less and more serious variations of the same crime and give the punishments for each. The following is a typical article of the RSFSR Criminal Code.

> Article 161. Violation of Rules Established for Combatting Plant Diseases and Pests.
>
> The violation of rules established for combating plant diseases and plant pests resulting in grave consequences shall be punished by deprivation of freedom for a term not exceeding one year or by correctional tasks for the same term.[33]

This article illustrates some of the typical features of Soviet legislation against economic crimes. It refers to rules which are probably unpublished and not easily available to those who are supposed to obey them. It depends upon a classification, "grave consequences," which is not well-defined by the law. Often, however, such vague terms are given more precise definition by binding interpretations handed down by the Supreme Court of the Russian Republic or of the USSR. The combination of the dependence of criminal code articles on rules issued by administrative authorities, and the presence of vague terms in the articles, allows considerable latitude for the expansion or contraction of the use of criminal penalties in connection with the starting or stopping of campaigns against particular types of crimes without the necessity of amending the criminal code.

The authoritative commentary on the RSFSR Criminal Code indicates that Article 161 (quoted above) may apply to failure to act as well as to taking actions contrary to agricultural regulations.[34] This principle illustrates another aspect of Soviet economic criminal legislation, that it goes beyond punishing actions that actively harm the economy to include failure to take actions required by law.

Offenses too minor to be considered crimes are punished in the Soviet Union as administrative violations. Administrative violations are generally punishable only by small fines and do not lead to a criminal record. The accused has much more limited procedural rights than the accused in a criminal case. The law of administrative violations is unified by the USSR Fundamental Principles of Legislation on Administrative Violations, which serves as the basis for the Codes on Administrative Violations of the republics.[35] If one examines a typical code on administrative violations, such as that of the Russian Republic, one finds that most of the offenses listed are economic offenses.[36] Specific offenses will be discussed below, in connection with an analysis of the legal protection of the economy against specific types of threats.

The Code on Administrative Violations specifies a simplified enforcement procedure. Unlike criminal sanctions, which may be imposed only by courts, penalties for administrative violations may be administered by a wide variety of agencies. If no agency is specified, the administrative violation is addressed by the administrative commission attached to the local government body. In many instances a particular agency is given power to impose sanctions for violation of a specific code article because of the knowledge or expertise of the agency. In some cases jurisdiction is split further, with different agencies responsible for violation of a single article of the code under different circumstances. In a few instances, administrative violation cases are tried by a court. In the vast majority of cases, however, the decision is made by the appropriate administrative agency or its representative.

In some cases, such as minor traffic offenses, the official that catches the administrative violator has the right to impose a fine on the spot. In other cases, the official must make a written statement containing the relevant circumstances, to serve as the basis for the initiation of a later administrative proceeding. In these cases an open hearing is conducted at which the accused has the right to present his side of the case. The process is speedy—the hearing is supposed to take place within ten days after the offense. In most instances, the accused has the right to appeal to a court if he considers that he is innocent of the violation.

The law on administrative violations allows the handling of the massive number of minor violations of regulations for protection of the economy without the delays and expense of criminal trials and without the branding of large numbers of citizens as criminals for minor offenses. At the same time, the mildness of the sanctions for administrative violations often prevents them from having the desired effect. A Soviet manager may well prefer to risk paying a small fine out of his own pocket rather than delay production operations in order to meet safety or environmental requirements, and thus risk failing to fulfill his plan. In the short run, failure to fulfill the production plan might cost the manager much more in lost bonuses than would the fines for a few minor violations. In the long run, the violations will be completely forgotten, while the plan fulfillment will serve as an important stepping-stone in the manager's career.

The civil law provides major protection to the economic system. Most important are the rules for enforcement of contracts and recovery of damages for breach of contract. The civil law also serves to protect the economy through what Soviet law calls "obligations from the causing of harm" and "obligations from the unjustified obtaining or saving of property."

Other chapters have already pointed out the particular features of contract enforcement in specific areas of the economy. There are also some important general principles. The vast majority of contracts between state entities provide for payment of specific penalties in case of breach. Such penalty clauses are required by law, because actual damages are typically impossible to calculate, given the lack of a free market in which substitute goods or services could be bought, or improperly rejected goods could be sold. For the same reason, in practice, recovery is often limited to the penalties specified by law and contract, since further damages cannot be shown. Article 189 of the Civil Code provides for three possible combinations of penalties and damages: only the penalties may be recoverable; damages may be recoverable; or the victim of the breach may choose between damages and penalties. The first alternative applies to many types of transportation contracts. The second alternative applies to most other contracts, but, as mentioned above, actual damages are hard to prove in practice. Legislation reported in *Izvestia*, August 12, 1986, introduced stricter rules for breach of performance of supply contracts. Procedures for the collection of penalties were simplified and penalties paid late were increased by 50%. The size of bonus funds was closely tied to the percentage of contract fulfillment.

The duty to compensate for causing harm applies to both negligently and intentionally caused harm. If a citizen driving a private care negligently runs into a truck belonging to a government agency, the government agency can recover damages from the citizen. The law applied is identical to that applicable to an automobile accident involving two privately-owned cars. If a citizen steals government property in addition to any possible criminal liability, there is liability to the organization whose property was stolen. Employees are responsible for harm done intentionally or negligently to the property of their employers. However, responsibility of employees for harm negligently caused to the employing organization is limited by labor legislation. Harm may also be caused by one organization to another. The simplest example might be an accident caused by a vehicle belonging to one enterprise running into a vehicle belonging to another enterprise. An enterprise might receive a shipment of goods by mistake and use them rather than returning them. A paper mill might pollute a river in violation of environmental legislation, causing harm to a fishing organization downstream.

There are several possible procedural channels through which the injured organization may recover damages. If both parties are state organizations or are cooperatives other than collective farms, the claim must be brought through State Arbitrazh. If at least one party is an individual or a collective farm, the normal channel is the regular court system. Procedures in the case of harm caused by an employee to his employer are governed by labor legislation. If a claim is brought in court, it may be filed as a civil complaint or, under the procedure of Soviet law (similar to the procedure in many European countries) that allows a civil claim to be brought by the victim in a criminal trial. The injured organization itself may bring a court claim, or the Procuracy may present a claim on behalf of the organization. The latter approach is particularly common when the Procuracy is already involved in a criminal prosecution in the case. Finally, very small claims may be brought before a Comrades' Court. Soviet law provides for organization of Comrades' Courts at places of work or residence.[37] The Comrades' Courts are made up of ordinary citizens, not law-trained judges.

Claims of employers against employees that involve more than one-third of one month's wages are handled by regular court procedures.[38] Those involving less than one third of one month's wages are handled unilaterally by employer deduction from the employee's wages. If the employee is dissatisfied with the deduction, he may bring a grievance through the channels specified by labor law, as discussed in the chapter on that topic.

Sanctions for actions contrary to the interests of the economy may be imposed through the disciplinary procedures provided by labor legislation. Disciplinary procedures and grounds are different for managerial employees and ordinary employees, reflecting the fact that the hiring, firing, and discipline of managerial employees is subject to detailed Party control, while that of ordinary workers is not. The job categories that are considered to be managerial are defined in Appendix 1 to the Statute on Labor Disputes.[39]

Discipline of managerial employees is governed by a 1929 decree that is still in force with respect to them.[40] These employees may be disciplined for actions "incompatible with their dignity and position" even if these actions do not constitute violations of their service obligations or the rules of labor discipline. While the law does not say so, managerial employees may be subjected to Party discipline in addition to labor discipline. They may fear Party discipline much more than ordinary labor discipline, because they must have Party recommendation for any future job advancement. Ordinary employees may be disciplined only for violations of the rules of labor discipline. In either case the only permissible legal disciplinary measures are those provided by the labor code.[41] These are a reproof, a reprimand, a severe reprimand, a transfer to lower paying work or a lower position for up to three months, or discharge.

Protection of State Property

So far we have considered the institutions and legal provisions that protect the economic system. Now we will turn to specific threats to the economic system and examine, with respect to each, the way the law protects the economy against the threat. We will start with the problem of theft of state property.

More persons are convicted of crimes against state property than of any other type of offense against the economic system. The Criminal Code devotes an entire chapter to such crimes, and this chapter is placed immediately after the chapter on Crimes Against the State, to signify its importance. In addition to the fifteen separate offenses defined in this chapter, a number of articles in other sections of the code are in some way related to the protection of state property. The scanty criminal statistics that are available suggest a gradual decline in the ratio of convictions for theft of state property to that of convictions for theft of personal property. If this is so, it may be because many alternative forms of sanction have become available for theft of state property, but not for the theft of personal property—Party responsibility, labor discipline, administrative penalties, etc.

In an earlier chapter, we pointed out that despite the division of "socialist" owernship for ideological reasons into the separate formal legal categories of state ownership and social ("*obshchestvennaia*") ownership, for all practical legal and economic purposes, social ownership is treated as state ownership. Thus the theoretical dividing line between state ownership and social ownership is of no practical significance in the criminal law, since the two terms are invariably combined into a single phrase in the relevant articles of the Criminal Code. On the other hand, the division between state ownership and individual ownership is of considerable importance, since this determines whether a crime will be classified as theft of socialist property or theft of personal property, a classification which may be of considerable importance to the defendant. For instance, theft of "socialist" (i.e., state) property on an especially large scale may be punished by death, while theft of personal property, no matter how large-scale, carries a maximum sentence of ten (or in a few cases fifteen) years of deprivation of freedom.

The severity of the penalty for theft depends upon the magnitude of the stealing. Each of the Criminal Code articles defining a type of theft of state property provides a substantially higher penalty for large-scale theft. Article 93–1 provides a possible death penalty for theft on an especially large scale. The Criminal Code does not provide an objective criterion as to what constitutes large-scale theft. However, the RSFSR Supreme Court has issued an instruction, binding on the lower courts, to the following effect:

> [I]n judicial practice the theft of state and social property is considered large-scale, as a rule, if the price of what is stolen is over 2500 rubles. In addition, in defining the size of the theft, courts should proceed not only from the monetary price, but also from the volume, quantity, and nature of the goods stolen. The theft of state and social property that is of particular importance for the economy, has a high market price, or is committed in a particularly large quantity or volume, also is large-scale, even if the retail price of the goods is somewhat under 2500 rubles.[42]

Theft on an especially large-scale is likewise undefined by the Criminal Code. Judicial practice, however, suggests that 10,000 rubles is the dividing line between large-scale and especially large-scale theft, but that other factors should also be taken into account as in the case of the ordinary/large-scale theft distinction.[43] Why does Soviet law adopt these subjective distinctions, in contrast to the harsh, but objective line drawn by traditional English law between petit larceny and grand larceny, where the thief could be hanged if what he stole was worth more than 12 pence? The explanation lies in the fact that the artificial nature of Soviet prices means that the official retail prices of goods do not accurately reflect the market value of the goods, and thus do not reflect the harm to the economic system if the goods are stolen.

The Criminal Code distinguishes a number of categories of theft crimes and provides different penalties both for different types of crimes and for different gradations of the same crime. Four articles of the Criminal Code define theft crimes. Article 89 defines "secret theft"; Article 90 defines "open theft"; Article 91 defines theft by force or threat of force; Article 92 defines theft by embezzlement or abuse of official position.

Minor thefts of state property may be punished as administrative violations rather than as crimes. Article 49 of the Code on Administrative Violations provides for punishment of "Petty Theft of State Property." Factors considered in determining if a theft is petty are price (i.e., under 50 rubles), quantity, weight, volume, and significance for the economy.

Physical protection of state property against theft is an important function of the local police. In addition, it is not unusual for enterprises to use guards or to contract with the police for additional guard services above and beyond normal police patrols. Cases occasionally arise in State Arbitrazh of suits by enterprises against such contract guard services for failing to properly protect the enterprise property.

One of the most serious threats to the Soviet economy is the embezzlement or misuse of state funds for private purposes. This threat is much greater than in capitalist countries where most businesses are small. In a small business, the owner cannot embezzle from himself and he can keep a close watch over the few employees. The Soviet legal system employs a wide variety of accounting and auditing controls and criminal and administrative penalties to prevent embezzlement of state funds. These controls are administered by a number of the institutions mentioned at the start of this chapter. The vast majority of payments are subject to at least a triple audit: by the chief accountant, the State Bank (or other bank), and by the auditing department of the superior enterprise. Particular care is taken with cash. Other than for payroll funds, enterprises are allowed to have almost no cash.[44] Substantial embezzlement of payroll funds is difficult because employees would immediately complain if they were not paid. In retail establishments that take in substantial amounts of cash from the public, regular inventories and audits are designed to ensure that all this cash is in fact deposited. Employees that handle cash in such establishments must sign contracts making them fully responsible, without limit of liability, for all cash that passes through their hands.[45]

The taking of bribes is a crime closely related to the theft of state property. The fact that almost nothing can be done without the permission of some state official creates numerous possibilities for bribery that would be absent in a free enterprise system. A state official who takes a bribe to violate his duties to the state is unjustly enriched by the abuse of his state office, so in the eyes of the law the bribe money must be forfeited to the state. Often the bribe is given to secure the diversion of state property for private benefit, another form of theft of state property. Penalties for bribery were strengthened as part of a 1986 campaign against "nonlabor income."[46]

Counterfeiting is really theft of state property, because counterfeit money is mainly used to buy state property. The same is true of counterfeiting stamps and tickets, a lesser offense, because these are used to buy services from the state. Counterfeiting is relatively rare in the Soviet Union because of the strictly enforced prohibition of private ownership of printing equipment.

While poaching presents no really serious threat to the Soviet state, the huge forested areas of the country afford numerous opportunities for illegal gain and recreation through unauthorized hunting, fishing, and trapping. The result is that poaching is one of the most commonly prosecuted crimes and administrative violations. Freshwater and ocean fish form a major part of the Soviet diet. Fishing is conducted in a planned manner by authorized organizations such as fishing collectives (organized like collective farms) and fishing enterprises. Furs are a major export commodity. In addition to fur ranches, there is a well-developed system of authorized professional hunting and trapping. In these authorized systems, wildlife exploitation is conducted along the same lines as the other aspects of the Soviet planned economy. Unauthorized fishing and hunting represents an economic threat to this planned operation. In addition, unauthorized hunting presents dangers of accidents with firearms, and unauthorized possession and use of firearms present security problems.

Sport fishing and hunting are quite legal, provided the sportsmen obtain the necessary licenses and obey government regulations. However, particularly in the case of hunting, these regulations are quite restrictive, so there is a strong temptation to violate them. Hunting and fishing violations probably rank next after traffic and passport violations in the number of administrative fines imposed each year.[47] Hundreds of thousands of fishing penalties are handed out each year, along with tens of thousands of hunting penalties. The relevant legislation is found in Articles 85 and 86 of the Code of Administrative Violations. These articles provide punishment not only for ordinary citizens, but also for officials, presumably those who violate conservation rules in their effort to meet planned quotas for their catch. In some instances, it is legal to hunt or trap valuable furbearing animals, but the pelts must be turned over to the state. Violations are punished under Article 189. State officials who buy goods obtained from illegal hunting may be punished under Article 190.

Criminal punishment for illegal hunting is rarely imposed and is usually limited to a fine. Illegal fishing for or catching of sea mammals is subject to strict sanctions under Article 163 of the Criminal Code. Under national and international wildlife protection programs, the Soviet Union has an obligation to restrict the hunting of seals and sea otters. This obligation is fulfilled by the provisions of Article 164 of the Criminal Code.

The huge Soviet land area contains more natural resources than that of any other country in the world. All of these resources are supposed to be exploited only in accordance with the national economic plans. Natural resources may be used illegally, however, by state enterprises seeking shortcuts to plan fulfillment or plan overfulfillment or by private individuals seeking to make money from these resources. For instance, officials of state lumbering enterprises may be liable for the illegal cutting of trees under Article 169 of the Criminal Code, if, for instance, they cut trees in a national park preserve. Private individuals may also be held responsible under this article or under Article 167, which punishes persons who find gold or precious gemstones and fail to turn them over to the state as required by law. More minor violations of the rights of the state to natural resources, water, and forests are punishable under Articles 46–48 of the Code on Administrative Violations.

Responsibility for Mismanagement of State Property

Article 172 of the Criminal Code punishes negligent fulfillment of official obligations causing substantial harm to state or social interests or to the legally protected rights and interests of citizens. While this definition is broad enough to cover non-economic offenses, the majority of prosecutions under this section of the Code are undoubtedly for offenses against the economy. In addition to this article, a number of articles of the Criminal Code punish more specific crimes of negligence in areas related to the economy. Article 140 punishes violation of labor safety rules; Article 152 punishes output of defective goods; Article 157 punishes selling defective products; Article 214 punishes violation of mining rules; Article 215 punishes violation of construction rules; and Article 216 punishes violation of explosive safety rules. Seemingly in an attempt to combat a tendency to prosecute for mismanagement any time something went wrong, the USSR Supreme Court has published a number of decisions in individual cases to the effect that a person may only be convicted for mismanagement with respect to matters for which he had responsibility and had a real opportunity to control.

Wasting energy is a particular form of mismanagement. Because energy is paid for out of enterprise funds, managers have only limited reason to try to conserve it. In order to pressure them to try to conserve energy, penalties for failure to exercise conservation measures are included in the Code on Administrative Violations. Article 90 deals with wasting electricity, while Articles 93 and 94 deal with wasting natural gas.

Acts that harm the environment may be considered to be a form of mismanagement. While environmental protection legislation applies to individuals as well as to state enterprises, because of the state monopoly of major means of production individuals in the Soviet Union are incapable of causing significant harm to the environment. Even managers of production associations and enterprises have only limited control over the harm they may cause to the environment. Key issues of environmental protection are decided at the planning stage, not at the later enforcement stage. Decisions made at the planning stage control, for instance, the designed level of pollutants in waste water from paper mills and whether or not effective containment buildings will be constructed at nuclear power plants. However, there is also an enforcement aspect to environmental protection. Managers of enterprises, or in rare cases, private citizens, through their own intent or negligence may cause pollution above the levels assessed by planners as acceptable. In such cases administrative and even criminal liability may ensue.

Air pollution is punishable under various articles of the RSFSR Code on Administrative Violations. Enforcement is the task of State Sanitary Inspection of the Ministry of Health. The effectiveness of this enforcement appears doubtful, both because of the relatively low political influence of the Ministry of Health and because of the extremely small size of the fines provided by the Code on Administrative Violations—usually a maximum of 100 rubles for offenses by officials and less for offenses by private citizens. Offenses under this code include release of atmospheric pollutants above levels allowed by regulations, release of pollutants into the atmosphere without obtaining required permission (Article 77); putting enterprises into operation without observing air quality protection requirements (Article 78); violation of rules for the use of "scrubbers." (Article 79); putting means of transport into operation without complying with exhaust pollution requirements(Article 80); operation of means of transport in violation of exhaust pollution requirements (Article 81); failure to observe pollution rules in waste burning (Article 82); improper release of pesticides, herbicides and other chemicals (Article 83); and failure to follow orders of air protection supervision organizations (Article 84).

Criminal punishment for air pollution provides more serious sanctions. Article 223 of the Criminal Code punishes "pollution of the atmosphere with industrial production waste harmful for individuals," with corrective tasks (a fine deducted from salary) for up to one year or a cash fine of up to 300 rubles. The same offense if it causes substantial harm to the health of people can be punished by deprivation of freedom for up to five years. The application of this article was the subject of a binding instruction of the Full Bench of the Supreme Court of the USSR.[48]. This instruction indicated that a necessary element of a violation was exceeding the limits set by administrative regulations for the level of atmospheric pollutants. It also indicated that in cases where a plant was forced to stand idle, because pollution control equipment was omitted due to the intent or negligence of administrators, criminal charges could be brought for causing the losses to the state by not having the plant in operation.

Water pollution is subject to administrative punishment under various articles of the RSFSR Code on Administrative Violations. Article 57 punishes water pollution and putting enterprises into operation without required water protection equipment. Criminal punishment is provided by the same article of the Criminal Code that prescribes penalties for pollution.

Article 88, part 2, provides for a fine for failure to follow safety regulations at plants under the supervision of agencies of State Atomic Energy Supervision. The fine, as in other cases of actual or potential pollution, is a ridiculously small: 100 rubles.

Failure to take good care of state property is another major form of mismanagement that poses a threat to the economy. It is human nature to take better care of one's own property than that of others. A visitor to a small Soviet city is likely to see decaying public buildings with rusting equipment parked next to them. On the outskirts of the city he will see private houses with carefully scrubbed windows, mended fences, and brightly painted shutters. Because most property is owned by the state rather than private parties in the Soviet Union, the government faces a serious problem in persuading people to care for this property or even to refrain from damaging it. A large number of articles of the Code of Administrative

Violations and a few articles of the Criminal Code are designed to encourage the protection of state property from physical mistreatment.

Among the offenses punishable under the administrative code are damage to freight and freight stations (Articles 129 and 130), railroads, roads, and road drainage strips (Articles 131–134), pipelines (Article 135), communications lines (Article 139), housing (Article 142), and urban plantings (Article 145). The Criminal Code punishes more serious offenses against state and social property. Intentional destruction or injury to state or social property is punished by Article 98 of the code; however, deprivation of freedom may be imposed only where aggravating circumstances are involved, such as arson, large-scale damage, human casualties, or intentional burning of forests (Article 98). Negligent destruction of state property is normally handled as an administrative offense and is criminally punishable only when there are human casualties, other serious consequences, or burning of forests. Article 103 punishes a bad-faith attitude toward the preservation of state property on the part of one charged with protecting it.

Agriculture presents particular problems of conservation of state property. The educational level of farm managers and workers is substantially below that of their urban counterparts. Urban employees seek to advance largely by doing well on the job. Farm workers seek only to perform minimally on the job, while attempting to maximize their income from the small-scale private agriculture permitted by Soviet law. The combination of lack of education and lack of interest presents serious problems with respect to the preservation of farm property. Administrative fines cover such offenses as trampling of fields (Article 96), violating rules for dealing with plant pests and diseases (Article 97), failing to fight weeds (Article 99), poor care of machinery (Article 100), and violating quarantine and veterinary health rules (Article 101). Criminal punishment is also imposed. Crimes include criminally negligent use or storage of agricultural equipment (Article 99–1, added by Khrushchev, as one of his many attempts to solve the problems of the economy by short term campaigns rather than long-term reform); and violation of veterinary rules (Article 160), violation of plant pest and disease rules (Article 161).

Prevention of Violations of Plans and Rules

Even where an action does not directly involve theft of or physical harm to state property, it may harm the economy. Violations of plans, trade rules, quality control rules, safety rules, and health rules are examples of the types of activity that may cause such harm. Violations of plan discipline may take a number of forms. Mere failure to fulfill a plan is not a criminal or administrative offense, though it will have negative consequences for the manager involved. Falsification of plan fulfillment data is a common and serious criminal offense.

Failure to fulfill obligations under a plan set for an enterprise typically has two negative consequences for the manager involved. First, under the complex scheme whereby payments to enterprise incentive funds and bonuses are calculated, it is likely to reduce both general management fringe benefits and individual bonuses. Second, repeated failure to fulfill plans has the same effect on the career of a Soviet manager that repeated losing seasons have on a football coach in any country. Plan fulfillment, like a won-lost record, is the one clear and objective measurement of management performance. The pressure to fulfill a plan is compounded by pressure from above. Superior agencies also have a plan, which is the sum of the plans of their subordinate organizations. This heavy pressure from above to achieve the targets set in economic plans often tempts managers to falsify reports on plan fulfillment. Obviously such falsifications are a breach of discipline, for which the managers may be subject to disciplinary responsibility. Article 152–1 of the Criminal Code provides severe penalties for such falsifications. Often such falsification also involves the more serious offense of theft of state property, since by inflating figures of plan performance management personnel indirectly inflate their own bonuses.

Economic violations in retailing are also common. They fall into three basic categories. The first involves items whose sale is restricted for some reason of public policy, such as liquor or firearms. Store personnel may violate these restrictions to fulfill a plan, to please a friend, or to receive a favor in return. Such violations, depending upon their severity are punishable as crimes or as administrative violations.[49] The second situation is the common one where goods are made available to stores in quantities insufficient to meet demand at the prices set by state price-fixing authorities. The result is a temptation for store personnel to sell these items "under the counter" to friends or for favors. The third situation involves a variety of embezzlement schemes, the sanctions for which have already been discussed.

Allowing private parties to conduct foreign trade operations would create possibilities for private enrichment, would hinder central planning of the use of foreign currency reserves and would destroy the power of the government to control consumer demand by limiting knowledge of the type of goods available in capitalist countries. Allowing ordinary state enterprises to engage in foreign trade would present the same threats and would also create the possibility that poorer deals might be obtained due to incompetence of particular enterprise personnel and to competition among Soviet buyers or Soviet sellers. Therefore foreign trade has long been reserved to a small number of specially-authorized state agencies. The vast majority of foreign trade transactions are conducted by foreign trade organizations subordinate to the Ministry of Foreign Trade. These organizations operate in strict accordance with foreign trade plans and are staffed by competent international trade personnel, thus eliminating the various threats to the economy listed above. The problem with this system has been that it has creates a bottleneck that has slowed the importation of foreign technology. Therefore, as mentioned above in the chapter on research and development, the list of entities entitled to engage in foreign trade operations has been expanded to include several dozen new organizations outside the Ministry of Foreign Trade. It remains true, however, that only organizations authorized by law, or by government decree, may engage in foreign trade operations. Under Soviet law any foreign trade transaction by other than such authorized organizations is invalid.[50]

In a capitalist economy, there is little need for legislation on quality control. If goods are of poor quality, customers will not buy them and the company manufacturing them will have to change its ways or face bankruptcy. In the Soviet economy, however, as long as an enterprise can perform the tasks required by the plan, it has little interest in quality. Its customers will either be required to take the goods produced or will have no practical alternatives to taking them, even if the goods are of poor quality, because they will have no other sources of supply. For this reason, the state must take a variety of steps to protect the economy from substandard goods.

One possible step would be to introduce a system of strict liability for defective products, allowing very high recoveries for victims and high fees for their lawyers, patterned on the products liability system of the United States. This has not been done and is not likely to be done in the USSR, because it would transfer large quantities of state property into private hands and create private centers of wealth. The absence of such liability means that the economic accountability system cannot be counted upon to enforce product quality.

Instead, a variety of administrative and punitive measures have been adopted to attempt to improve product quality. These measures include the setting and enforcement of quality standards, the awarding of a "mark of quality," and imposing of criminal and administrative punishment upon those responsible for poor quality goods. One visit to a Soviet department store will show how far short these measures fall of reaching their goal.

Standards for technical characteristics and quality are set by the State Committee of the USSR on Standards for products of major importance and by republic, branch, and other levels for products of lesser importance.[51] These standards are enforced in a number of ways. Legislation effective in 1987 created an independent system of quality control inspection. Products not meeting standards may not be counted when calculating plan fulfillment or contract performance. In addition, there may be administrative or criminal sanctions for not meeting standards.

Article 170 of the Code on Administrative Violations provides for officials to be fined up to 100 rubles by local government administrative commissions for the production of goods not meeting government quality standards. The combination of the weak political power of local officials and the low fine suggest that this article is unlikely to be effective.

Article 152 of the Criminal Code also provides for punishment for production of poor quality goods. This article applies only to: (1) repeated production of poor quality goods; (2) large scale production of poor quality goods; (3) production of goods that fail to meet standards, do not comply with technical conditions, or are incomplete. Only certain persons, however, can be punished for this offense: directors, chief engineers, heads of technical supervision departments, or others carrying out their duties.

Goods that are of unusually good quality may be awarded a "mark of quality."[52] Enterprises whose goods qualify for this award receive additional payments into their bonus funds.

Violation of safety regulations obviously can lead to injury to individual citizens. It can also damage the economy through causing the destruction of equipment and the temporary or permanent disability of employees. Safety protection is implemented through civil liability, inspection, administrative fines for minor violations, and criminal penalties for violations with serious consequences.

Entities whose activities cause danger to the public are subject to civil liability independent of their fault under the ordinary rules of the Civil Code concerning obligations for the causing of harm. These rules would apply, for instance, if a citizen were run over by a truck belonging to a state enterprise. The liability of economic entities to their own employees raises more complex questions. If an entity was not at fault in an accident, the employee is compensated by a type of workmen's compensation under the social insurance system, and there are no negative financial consequences for the employer. If an injury to an employee was caused by safety violations by the employing entity, the employee receives social insurance benefits and can sue the employer for losses not covered by social insurance. The employer who has violated safety rules must pay these excess losses and in addition must reimburse the social insurance agency for workmen's compensation payments made to the employee.[53] However, as mentioned above in connection with products liability, both the amount of damages awarded and the potential lawyers' fees are too small to exert real pressure for obedience to safety rules.

Each of the state inspection agencies mentioned earlier in this chapter has responsibility for inspecting for compliance with safety rules in the area under its jurisdiction. Typically its inspectors have the power under the Code on Administrative Violation to impose fines for violations of rules without going through the cumbersome procedure of bringing the violator to court. A large number of articles of the RSFSR Code on Administrative Violations provide sanctions for violations of safety rules. Article 88 provides for the fining of officials who repeatedly violate safety rules concerning objects subject to the jurisdicition of the State Committee for Supervision of the Safe Conduct of Work in Industry and for Mining Inspection. A fine may also be imposed for any violation, repeated or not, of nuclear safety rules. Article 89 provides for a fine for any violation of rules concerning use of explosives under the jurisdiction of the same agency. Transport safety is dealt with by Articles 103–104 (railroad), Articles 105–107 (air), Articles 110–111 (water), Article 113 (fire safety on transport), Article 126 (dangerous shipment), and Article 169 (fire safety).

In sufficiently serious cases, violation of safety rules can lead to criminal liability. In the Criminal Code there are articles dealing with transport safety (Article 85), damages to railroad tracks (Article 86), and lumber floats and explosives (Article 165).

Prevention of Other Threats to the Economic System

Private enterprise operations threaten the state monopoly on economic planning and, most importantly, the policy against allowing citizens to have substantial independent sources of income. On the other hand, a complete abolition of private incentive would stop provision of various essential services. The line between forbidden and permitted private enterprise is drawn by both administrative and criminal law. Even in the limited situations where private enterprise is permitted, income tax law provides for extremely high taxes on profits from private enterprise. In 1986, legislation strengthened the penalties against illegal private enterprise operations and against tax evasion. It introduced important new requirements designed to prevent the use of money earned through illegal private enterprise activities. Transactions between citizens and government organizations involving more than 5000 rubles must be conducted by bank transfers.[54] Citizens concluding transactions involving over 10,000 rubles or building houses worth over 20,000 rubles are required to file a declaration indicating where they got the money. Local executive committees may require such declarations even in cases where transactions involve lower amounts.

A statute on the artisan and handicraft business, divides such work into three categories: (1) forbidden; (2) permitted only with a license; and (3) freely permitted.[55] The choice of which occupations to forbid appears to have been more political than economic. Citizens may not make and sell printing equipment or engage in the printing, copying, or tape-duplication business (all threatening government control of who reads what). Artisan and handicraft businesses not on the forbidden list require a license. A license covers the registrant and members of the family working with him. To prevent the creation of private factories, not more than two licenses can be issued for work to be done at a single location. Adherence to license requirements and license restrictions is enforced by local finance departments and local police, who are required to turn in violators to the appropriate authorities for administrative or criminal punishment in case of violation. Income from private activities is subject to heavy tax rates.[56] Earnings of over 5000 rubles per year from private handicraft activities are taxed at the rate of 65%; earnings over 7000 rubles a year from private professional practice is taxed at a rate of 69%. Other types of legal private enterprise activity are taxed at a rate of 81% of income over 7000 rubles a year. Tax disputes may be appealed to higher financial agencies, but are not subject to judicial review. Tax enforcement is difficult; emigré lawyers report widespread tax evasion.

For violating regulations on engaging in handicraft and artisan work, an administrative penalty of a fine of up to 50 rubles, with or without confiscation of the violator's raw materials and product inventory, may be imposed. For engaging in a prohibited trade, there may also be a fine of up to 50 rubles. Confiscation of raw materials, products, and means of production is obligatory in this case.

Criminal liability for private enterprise activity requires something beyond merely engaging in such an activity without a license. The definition of criminal private enterprise is found in Articles 153, 154, and 162 of the Criminal Code.

Article 162 provides criminal punishment for engaging in a forbidden trade by persons already subjected to administrative fines, for conducting such a trade on a large scale, or with the use of hired labor.

Article 154 punishes purchase and resale of goods for the purpose of making a profit. This crime in Russian is called "spekulatsiia" and is often mistranslated by the English word "speculation." However, unlike a capitalist who speculates on market fluctuations, the Soviet blackmarketeer is virtually guaranteed a profit and only speculates on getting caught and punished. The crime exists because of the unresponsiveness of the Soviet retail system to market demand. By pricing goods in many instances below market price, the system creates golden opportunities for blackmarketeers, who through connections obtain high quality goods and then resell them at inflated prices. This crime is committed only when there is an intent at the time of purchase to resell the goods at a profit. Thus the Supreme Court ordered the acquittal of a defendant who bought goods while abroad as a present for a relative, and then resold them at a profit when he returned home to find that the relative had just died.[57] There are gradations in the penalty depending upon whether the crime was committed on a large scale (over 200 rubles of profit) or an exceptionally large scale (over 1000 rubles of profit).

Article 153 of the Criminal Code punishes two separate crimes: private enterprise activity with the use of state, cooperative, or other social forms, and acting as a commercial middleman. Some instances of violation of the first part of Article 153 are clear. Such, for instance, was the case where a black market entrepreneur took over the sheltered workshop of a mental hospital and turned it into a slave labor factory for making scarce consumer goods, which he sold at high prices through kiosks set up at railroad stations (with appropriate bribes to the station officials), while keeping all the profits for himself. However, there have been quite a few problems in applying the first part of Article 153 because of the difficulty of drawing the line between innovative public enterprise incentive schemes and the illegal use of forms of public economic operations for private activity. The typical problem arises with "shabashniki," groups of migrant workers who contract with state enterprises and collective farms to do heavy construction jobs that local workers are unwilling or unable to do. Typically these workers work as a "brigade" under a leader. All receive very high salaries, with the leader receiving the highest salary of all. Actual formal arrangements vary. All involved may work as individual outside contractors; there may be a single contract with the leader; or all may be taken on as temporary employees under exceptionally favorable pay and bonus conditions.[58]

Finally, some of the more enterprising illegal private entrepreneurs may find themselves in violation of Article 154 (illegal use of a trademark). For instance, smugglers of foreign jeans must contend with underground operations where fake foreign trademarks are attached to Soviet-made jeans. The gradual spread of photocopying machines in the Soviet Union has opened up a new type of black market activity—the copying of trashy American novels (e.g. the works of Harold Robbins), which lamentably have the same popularity with Soviet readers as with American readers. Such copying violates Article 171 of the Code on Administrative Violations, and also typically involves theft of state property (paper and toner).

In the private service area a particularly common offense is the use of state means of transportation for private profit. Drivers of public vehicles frequently transport passengers or goods for payment, and this offense is punishable under Article 125 of the Code on Administrative Violations. Penalties for this offense were increased as part of 1986 campaign against "non-labor" income.[59]

Two particular problems involving private agriculture have attracted the attention of authorities. Both are due to the fact that while peasants are allowed to own livestock and poultry, they are often unable to obtain the necessary feed for them legally. The first offense, trampling of fields, typically occurs when livestock are allowed to roam to graze, or are driven across state or collective farm fields to off-limits grazing grounds. The second offense, feeding bread to livestock or poultry, is caused by the interaction of the inadequacy of feed supply with the state policy of subsidizing low bread prices. Depending upon their seriousness, these offenses may be either administrative violations or crimes.[60]

Home distilling appears from the criminal statistics to be the most widespread of black market activities. Knowledge of the technique of home distilling is part of the Russian peasant tradition. Urban dwellers, while gradually losing this traditional knowledge, benefit from the high quality of Soviet secondary, technical, and higher education in physics and chemistry. From the 1950s to the 1970s, home distilling declined as a percentage of all crimes, while nevertheless remaining the principle type of illegal private economic activity. This decline may have been due to social factors—the urbanization of the Soviet population, and the fact that during this period wages rose faster than vodka prices. The incidence of the crime has varied widely from republic to republic, being low in republics such as Georgia, where vodka is not part of the national tradition, and high in the Slavic republics.[61] The sharp increase in vodka prices and restriction on vodka sales under Gorbachev's anti-alcohol campaign will undoubtedly have the effect of increasing the quantity of home distilling, while prosecutors and police, in the spirit of the campaign, will increase their efforts to obtain convictions for this crime or punishments for the related administrative violation.[62]

The Soviet regime considers unauthorized foreign currency operations to be very dangerous threats to the economic system. Such foreign currency operations pose two different types of threats to the Soviet economic system. First, they might hinder the planned use of foreign currency reserves, by diverting part of the reserves to unplanned uses. Second, they might allow individual citizens to be enriched by engaging in private import and export transactions and they might allow these citizens independence of the government by giving them possession of a currency not controlled by the government.

Foreign currency operations may be divided into three categories: those in which a Soviet citizen is a participant, those involving foreign visitors to the USSR, and those involving international trade transactions. Foreign currency operations between private citizens are the most restricted. When on the territory of the USSR, private citizens may conduct only three types of transactions involving foreign currency or its equivalent: (1) give its equivalent to a spouse, child, parent, grandchild, grandparent, brother, or sister (or to another person with permission of the Ministry of Finances); (2) leave it by will; or (3) subject to compliance with regulations established by the Ministry of Culture by agreement with the Ministry of Finance, buy or sell a single item of currency for collection purposes.[63] Foreign visitors can exchange foreign currency for rubles at branches of the State Bank of the USSR and can use foreign currency to obtain goods and services from organizations that have special approval to accept foreign currency.[64] Authorized foreign trade organizations may conduct foreign trade transactions involving foreign currency.

Illegal operations with foreign currency involving less than 25 rubles are punishable as administrative offenses under Article 153 of the Code on Administrative Violations. However, since 25 rubles is only six or eight dollars at the black market rate of exchange, most illegal operations would be too large for this section to apply. Article 154 of the same code punishes the illegal sale of "payment documents" denominated in rubles, but obtained for foreign currency. These documents are coupons sold to Soviet citizens and foreigners who legitimately have foreign currency. They allow the holders to buy goods at special stores closed to the Soviet public, where the goods are of much higher in quality (often imported) and are much lower in price than the goods in regular Soviet stores. Article 88 of the Criminal Code provides liability for violation of foreign currency regulations, including a possible death penalty for repeated or large scale violations.

Soviet customs attempts to control closely the import and export of foreign currency and rubles. Every traveler must fill out a currency form. It is common for customs inspectors to count the money travelers are carrying to verify what is written on the forms. These forms are filed away permanently when the traveler leaves the country, and are available to agencies investigating violations of foreign currency regulations.

Along with violations connected with foreign currency, international smuggling presents threats to the state monopoly of foreign trade and to state control of citizens' sources of income. Smuggling of books and video tapes also threatens state control of information. The vast majority of international freight shipments are planned as part of the overall international trade planning process. However, it is important to the authorities to be sure that what is actually shipped is what is planned. In addition, there is a substantial amount of unplanned shipment, such as goods brought in by travelers and presents sent through the mail. Comparing the huge quantity of fashionable foreign clothes worn by Soviet citizens on the streets of Moscow with the total absence of such clothes in the stores, it is easy to see that smuggling is occurring on a large scale. Nevertheless, there would be much more smuggling without substantial efforts made by the government to catch smugglers and the severe penalties imposed upon those who are caught. In one notorious case some years ago, officials of the Ministry of Fisheries shipped out caviar in cans marked "SARDINES." The foreign recipients deposited money in Swiss bank accounts in the name of the high Ministry officials who were part of the conspiracy. By mistake, some of the sardine cans found their way into an ordinary Moscow grocery store, and when customers discovered that they could get caviar for the price of sardines, the store was mobbed, leading to the discovery of the scheme by the authorities. The Soviet mastermind of this scheme was executed for large scale theft of state property.

The customs rules are set out in the Customs Code of the USSR.[65] Customs are administered by the Main Customs Administration subordinate to the Ministry of Foreign Trade. It is in charge of inspection of all goods entering and leaving the USSR. Customs has the right to impose fines (of up to 10 rubles on ordinary citizens or up to 50 rubles on officials) for violations of customs regulations. In addition, it has the right to confiscate undeclared goods or goods banned for export or import, and in such cases to impose fines of up to 50 rubles on citizens or up to 100 rubles on officials guilty of intentional attempts to smuggle contraband. Confiscations and fines may be appealed to the Chief Customs Administration and from there to the courts. Violation of rules may be punished under Article 186 or 187 of the Code on Administrative Violations. Serious smuggling attempts are punished under the criminal law. Article 78 of the Criminal Code defines criminal smuggling as that "accompanied by hiding items in special containers, or with the fraudulent use of customs and other documents, or on a large scale, or by a group of persons organized for smuggling activities, or by an official using his official position, or for the smuggling of explosive, narcotic, strongly-active, and poisonous substances, arms, ammunition, and weapons." This article provides for punishment of three to ten years deprivation of freedom plus possible banishment for a period of two to five years.

As discussed in the chapter on Labor Force and Labor Law, the residence permit system is of great importance in the balancing of jobs with labor and population with housing. However, it requires substantial enforcement efforts from the legal system. It seems likely that computerization of police and employment records in recent years has strengthened the enforcement of passport legislation. Excluding traffic offenses, violation of passport rules appears to be the most common type of administrative violation.

Minor infractions of residence rules are punished as administrative violations. In Moscow and Leningrad, where the number of violations are particularly high, fines are administered directly by the police. In other localities, the fines are imposed by administrative commissions. Article 178 of the Code on Administrative Violations punishes intentional habitation in violation of passport rules with a 10 ruble fine. Article 180 of the Code on Administrative violations punishes those who allow a person to reside without a passport or registration; Article 181 punishes hiring a person who does not possess the appropriate passport or registration. Penalties are light: a warning or 10 ruble fine for violation of Article 180, and a 10 ruble fine for violation of Article 181, with a 50 ruble fine for officials who commit a repeat violation in the same year. Because of the large number of passport violations in Moscow, Leningrad, and Tashkent, special legislation allows these fines to be administered on the spot by police in those cities, without the usual formalities.[66] After receiving two administrative penalties for living without a passport or residence permit, a Soviet citizen may be criminally punished under Article 198 of the Criminal Code, which provides for up to one year of imprisonment. In enforcing this article, the court is supposed to review the legality of the prior administrative actions. No statistics are available on the frequency with which this article is applied.

Notes

1. Law on the USSR Procuracy, *Svod zakonov SSSR*, 10.41; Gordon B. Smith, *The Soviet Procuracy and the Supervision of Administration* (Alphen aan den Rijn: Sijthoff & Noordhoff, 1978).
2. RSFSR Criminal Procedure Code, art. 140.
3. Smith, *The Soviet Procuracy*, pp. 88–104.
4. Statute on the Ministry of Internal Affairs, *Svod zakonov SSSR*, 10.281.
5. Statute on the Soviet Police, *Svod zakonov SSSR*, 10.236.
6. RSFSR Criminal Procedure Code, Art. 126.
7. Law on People's Supervision, *Svod zakonov SSSR*, 1.329; V.M. Makarov, *Narodnyi kontrol': organy i pravovye formy deiatel'nosti* (Moscow: Iuridicheskaia literatura, 1975).
8. D.A. Kerimov, N.G. Kobets, and G.V. Mal'tsev, ed., *Sovetskoe gosudarstvennoe stroitel'stvo i pravo* (Moscow: Mysl', 1984), p. 305.
9. Statute of the State Bank of the USSR, *Svod zakonov SSSR*, 5.399; G.C. Gurevich, ed., *Sovetskoe finansovoe pravo* (Moscow: Iuridicheskaia literatura, 1985), 226–255.
10. Basic Provisions on Payments in the National Economy of the USSR, *Svod zakonov SSSR*, 5.545.
11. Ibid., Art. 6.
12. Rules for Financing Construction, *Svod zakonov SSSR*, 6.116; Charter of the All Union Bank for Financing Capital Investments (Stroibank), *Svod zakonov SSSR*, 6.145.

13. Statute on the State Committee of the USSR for the Supervision of Safe Conduct of Work in Industry and for Mining Supervision, *Svod zakonov SSSR*, 6.542.

14. RSFSR Code on Administrative Violations, *Ved. RSFSR*, 1984, no. 27, item 909, Art. 212.

15. Donald D. Barry, "Political and Legal Aspects of the Development and Use of Nuclear Power in the USSR and Eastern Europe," in Peter Maggs, Gordon B. Smith, and George Ginsburgs, eds., *Law and Economic Development in the Soviet Union* (Boulder: Westview, 1982), p. 159.

16. Model Statute on Agencies of State Insurance in the Union Republics, *Svod zakonov SSSR*, 5.625, Art. 22.

17. On State Obligatory Insurance Belonging to Citizens, *Svod zakonov SSSR*, 5.645, Art. 6.

18. Statute on State Energy Inspection of the USSR, *SP SSSR*, 1967, no. 19, item 135.

19. A.E. Lunev, *Priroda, pravo, upravlenie* (Moscow: Nauka, 1981), p. 122.

20. Statute on the Commission of the Presidium of the Council of Ministers of the USSR on the Protection of the Environment and the Rational Use of Natural Resources, *Svod zakonov SSSR*, 4.30.

21. Statute on the State Committee of the USSR on Hydrometeorology and Monitoring of the Environment, *Svod zakonov SSSR*, 4.32.

22. Statute on State Supervision of the Work of Gascleaning and Dustscrubbing Installations, *Svod zakonov SSSR*, 4.476.

23. Statute on State Sanitary Inspection in the USSR, *Svod zakonov SSSR*, 3.115.

24. E.g., A.E. Lunev, *Priroda*, p. 121.

25. Statute on the Ministry of Fisheries of the USSR, *Svod zakonov SSSR*, 6.513.

26. Statute on the Ministry of Irrigation and Water Supply, *Svod zakonov SSSR*, 6.269.

27. General Statute on the Legal Department (or Bureau), Chief (or Senior) Legal Counsel, Legal Counsel of a Ministry, Department, Executive Committee of a Soviet of People's Deputies, Enterprise, Organization, Institution, *Svod zakonov SSSR*, 10.124.

28. See T.V. Koniukhova, ed., *Sbornik po finansovomu zakonodatel'stvu* (Moscow: Iuridicheskaia literatura, 1980).

29. Statute on Chief Accountants, *Svod zakonov SSSR*, 5.309.

30. Statute of the Communist Party of the Soviet Union, Pravda, March 7, 1986, pp. 8–10., Arts. 8–12.

31. Statute of the Communist Party, Art. 12.

32. Ger P. van den Berg, *The Soviet System of Justice: Figures and Policy* (Dordrecht: Martinus Nijhoff, 1985), pp. 331–332. (Adding the figures for "Crimes Against Socialist Ownership," "Economic Crimes," "Official Crimes," and "Violations of Labor Safety."

33. This article is quoted from the excellent translation of the RSFSR Criminal Code by Harold J. Berman and James W. Spindler in Willam B. Simons, Ed., *The Soviet Codes of Law* [*Law in Eastern Europe*, No. 23] (Alphen aan den Rijn: Sijthoff & Noordhoff, 1980), p. 53.

34. Iu. D. Severin, ed., *Kommentarii k Ugolovnomu kodeksu RSFSR* (Moscow: Iuridicheskaia literatura, 1984), p. 329.

35. Fundamentals of Legislation of the USSR and the Union Republics on Administrative Violations, *Svod zakonov SSSR*, 10.375.

36. Specific offenses are defined in the RSFSR Code on Administrative Violations, Arts. 41–193.

37. Statute on Comrades' Courts in the RSFSR, in Butler, ed., *Basic Documents*, p. 238.

38. Statute on Monetary Responsibility of Workers and Office Workers for Damage Caused to an Enterprise, Institution, or Organization, *Svod zakonov SSSR*, 2.327.

39. Statute on the Procedure for Consideration of Labor Disputes, *Svod zakonov SSSR*, 2.451.

40. On the Fundamentals of Disciplinary Legislation of the USSR and the Union Republics, *Svod zakonov SSSR*, 2.341.

41. RSFSR Labor Code, Art. 135.

42. *Biulleten' Verkhovnogo Suda RSFSR*, 1963, no. 1, p. 9.

43. Severin, ed., *Kommentarii*, pp. 221–222.

44. Statute on the Conduct of Cash-handling Operations by State, Cooperative, and Social Enterprises, Organizations, and Institutions, *Svod zakonov SSSR*, 5.566.

45. Statute on Monetary Responsibility, Articles 10–11.

46. "Ob usilenii bor'by s izvlecheniem netrudovykh dokhodov," *Ved. VVS*1986, No. 22, item 364.

47. Van den Berg, *The Soviet System of Justice*, p. 73.

48. *Biulleten' Verkhovnogo Suda SSSR*, 1983, No. 4, p. 9.

49. Administrative violations—Art. 146 (Trade Rules), Art. 147 (Liquor), Art. 148 (Guns); Crimes—Art. 156-1 (Liquor sales), Art. 156-3 (Trade Rules), Art. 156-4 (Gasoline Sales), Art. 157 (Selling Poor Quality Products).

50. For an excellent historical study, see John Quigley, *The Soviet Foreign Trade Monopoly; Institutions and Laws* (Columbus: Ohio State University Press, 1974).

51. Statute on the State Committee of the USSR on Standards, *Svod zakonov SSSR*, 5.253.

52. On Improving Planning and Strengthening the Influence of the Economic Mechanism on Raising the Effectiveness of Production and the Quality of Work, *Svod zakonov SSSR*, 5.32, Art. 52(c).

53. RSFSR Civil Code, Art. 456.

54. "Ob usilenii borby," above note 46. Decree of the Central Committee of the Communist Party, "O merakh po usileniiu borby s netrudovymi dokhodami," *SP SSSR*, 1986, part 1, no. 21, item 119. Decree of the Council of Ministers of the USSR, "O merakh po usileniiu borby s netrudovymi dokhodami," *SP SSSR*, 1986, part 1, no. 21, item 121.

55. Statute on Handicraft Trades of Citizens, *Svod zakonov SSSR*, 2.49.

56. On Income Tax from the Population, *Svod zakonov SSSR*, 5.459, Articles 20–27.

57. *Biulleten' Verkhovnogo Suda SSSR*, 1983, no. 2, p. 28.

58. Patrick Murphy, "Soviet *Shabashniki*," *Problems of Communism* 34 (1985): 48.

59. "Ob usilenii borby," above note 46.

60. Administrative violations—Art. 96. (Trampling Fields), Art. 152 (Feeding Bread); Crimes—Art. 154-1 (Feeding Bread), Art. 168 (Trampling Fields). Penalties for buying bread or other foodstuffs in foodstores to feed to livestock were strengthened by the decree mentioned in note 58.

61. Van den Berg, *The Soviet System of Justice*, p. 44.

62. Home distilling may be punished either as an administrative violation—Art. 160—or a crime—Art. 148.

63. On Transactions with Foreign Currency Equivalents on the Territory of the USSR, *Svod zakonov SSSR*, 5.577, Art. 2.

64. Ibid., Art. 1.

65. Customs Code of the USSR, *Svod zakonov SSSR*, 5.140.

66. Moscow—*Svod zakonov SSSR*, 10.493; Leningrad and Tashkent—*Svod zakonov SSSR*, 10.494.

Conclusion

Our legal analysis of the Soviet economy thus comes to an end. This analysis has demonstrated that the Soviet economy is an integral part of the Soviet system. This system in turn is a regime based on the unlimited political power of the ruling elite. This elite relies upon its economic monopoly to maintain unlimited political power.

Any economic monopoly assumes centralized management. A monopoly encompassing the economic system of an entire country must be centralized at the national level. In the USSR three factors support such centralization: (1) unified state ownership; (2) centralized planning; and (3) economic discipline. Each of these factors is camouflaged by official dogmata as well as by the law in force. Officially there exists in the Soviet economy not only state ownership but also collective farm/cooperative ownership, and the ownership of trade unions and other social organizations. Accordingly, Soviet law distinguishes between the rights of state ownership personified by the whole people, the right of collective farm/cooperative ownership held by each collective farm or other cooperative, and the right of social ownership held by trade unions and other social organizations. As a result of this camouflage, the ruling elite does not appear to be an owner at all, and its economic monopoly is hidden because of the replacement of state ownership, actually the only dominant form of ownership, by three forms of ownership connected with different collective bodies, beginning with the people as a whole and ending with small societies. Further, centralized planning is officially said to be an expression of democratic centralism. Accordingly, Soviet law proclaims not only the rights but also the duties of planning agencies, and not only the duties but also the rights of entities subject to planning. As a result of this fiction, planning, which is extremely centralized in fact, is depicted as being decentralized, and its genuine role in the exercise of economic monopoly is distorted by reference to the purported participation of all economic links in the planning process. Finally, in its official interpretation, economic discipline is nothing but a means of maintaining reasonable economic order in the interests of the entire economic system and each of its components or links. Accordingly, Soviet law outlines economic discipline as a system of rules ensuring control from the "top" in accordance with the genuine demands of those at the "bottom." As a result of such wording, one of the most powerful means of centralized suppression is presented as a moderate method of establishing harmony between the "center" and the "periphery."

Using Hegelian language, one can say that here the Soviet economy contains a contradiction between its appearance and its essence. Is there an avenue leading to the elimination of this contradiction? One can formulate only two suggestions: either to sacrifice the essence for the sake of appearance or to reject the appearance and retain the essence. The former suggestion would mean the abrogation of the economic monopoly that is in the grasp of the ruling elite, through dismantlement of unified state ownership, mitigation of centralism in favor of decentralization, and relaxation of discipline for the benefit of subordinates. The consequences of such an abrogation would be the undermining or even the liquidation of the unlimited political power of the Soviet leadership. Therefore this approach is completely unacceptable within the limits of the dominant system. The same system also precludes acceptance of the latter suggestion, which would entail official acknowledgment of the anti-democratic nature of the Soviet form of political organization of human society, instead of covering this form with a democratic disguise. Thus, in fact, one deals in this case not with a contradiction that must be eliminated in order to improve the system established, but with a phenomenon whose elimination would mean the destruction of the system itself. Consequently, despite the ingenuous expectations arising upon the coming to power of each new Soviet leader, it is clear that no such leader, no matter who he may be, can break down the domination of the factors discussed. Rather he will seek to strengthen all of the factors that serve to maintain the rulers' economic monopoly.

However, while being the principal source of unlimited political power, economic monopoly does not directly involve economic activity. Such activity is available not to the political organization that maintains economic monopoly but to the economic entities that have been created by this organization in order to produce, to sell, to transport, etc. Separate economically, the same entities must also be legally independent as holders of the rights of juridical persons. At the same time, the legal independence of separate entities can be tolerated by the political rulers only to the extent that such independence does not infringe upon the rulers' economic monopoly. And this monopoly remains intact only where the factors ensuring its exercise are not adversely affected by the creation of the legally independent economic entities. This has been taken into consideration in the process of establishing the appropriate correlation between economic independence and economic monopoly in the USSR. Therefore, (1) the unified ownership of the Soviet state is supplemented by the derivative operative administration of Soviet entities; (2) centralized planning leaves some room for initiative on the part of the performers of planned tasks; and (3) economic discipline directly affecting "vertical" relations (between agencies of control and subordinate entities) is combined with certain economic discretion directly affecting also "horizontal" relations (between the subordinate entities themselves). Similar to factors of economic monopoly, the attributes of economic independence are camouflaged by official dogmata and by the law in force. Officially only state entities lack the capacity to be owners, while collective farms, cooperative and social organizations qualify as holders of ownership. Accordingly, Soviet law connects the right of operative administration with state entities and the right of ownership with collective farms, cooperative and social organizations. As a result of such camouflage collective farms, cooperative and social organizations appear to be economically more independent than are state entities, although the former's right of ownership is in fact identical to the latter's right of operative administration. Further, initiative on the part of performers of planned tasks is officially assessed as an expression of their economic freedom. Accordingly, Soviet law provides for economic contracts as agreements based on the free consent of both parties either within the limits of plans or even with reference to the data accumulated by economic entities for the purpose of economic planning. As a result of such distortion, the actual subordination of contract to plan is officially characterized simply as a reasonable combination of the two, and the actually minimal role of economic contracts is exaggerated, while the comprehensive force of economic planning is intentionally obscured. Finally, in its official interpretation, a certain degree of discretion on the part of of economic entities means the independent management of their current economic activity. Accordingly, Soviet law establishes rights of economic entities toward planning agencies, leaving, however, those rights without legal protection, and entitles the same entities to be free in their contractual relations, providing, however, that the requirements of economic discipline are strictly observed. As a result of this wording, the full power exercised from "above" and the rigid subordination required from "below" are depicted as only restrictions on that which functions as a rule in all other respects.

In this case, too, one can speak about a contradiction between essence and appearance. However, this contradiction is more propagandistic than substantial. Soviet law uses the title "ownership" with respect to the property rights of collective farms, cooperative and social organizations. All the same, a great number of special rules addressed to these entities limit their property rights to those of operative administration and protect the interests of the state as the actual owner. The importance of economic contracts can be formally extolled. However, in the absence of comprehensive regulation of planning activity, subordination of contract to plan results from the established practice of planning. In legal provisions, the discretion of the administrative agencies seems restricted, insofar as these provisions acknowledge the independent discretion of economic entities. But because the discretion of the economic entities is not legally protected, the discretion of the administrative agencies actually is not restricted. Thus, the subservience of operative administration to ownership, of contract to plan, and of economic discretion to economic discipline is an immutable fact of the economic system in the USSR. But degree of this subservience is not immutable. There is some flexibility, leaving room for maneuvering between centralism and decentralization. The Soviet leadership engages in such maneuvering, being compelled periodically to resort to increased decentralization, thus avoiding economic collapse, and to the restoration of centralism, thus preventing a political cataclysm. In such forms the specific law of the cyclical development of the Soviet economy manifests itself in Soviet practice. However, the opportunities for this maneuvering have their limits, which preclude two opposite extremes: the abolition of economic decentralization and the rejection of economic centralism. The abolition of economic decentralization, corresponding to Soviet political centralism, is prevented by the threat of a complete economic collapse, because the economy simply could not function without a certain degree of decentralization. The rejection of economic centralism, suggested by good-natured critics of the Soviet regime, is made impossible by the threat of complete political collapse, because unlimited political power of the type established in the USSR cannot be maintained without a very high degree of centralism. Thus, the perfection of the Soviet economy within the limits of the Soviet systems cannot be effected through the abolition of decentralization or the rejection of centralism but only through maneuvering between centralism and decentralization. From this it follows that the only efficient methods of economic management are those actually employed by the Soviet rulers and criticized by their unsolicited advisers.

Such efficiency is quite compatible with the generally recognized inefficiency of the Soviet economy. The criteria of economic efficiency depend on correlation between economic and politics. Where politics is subordinated to economics, growth of production, income, common welfare, etc. constitutes the principal criterion of economic efficiency. One can also take into consideration other factors: the strength of the country's external independence, the prevention of situations provoking internal dissatisfaction, etc. However, the status of these other factors are indirect results and not direct indicators of economic efficiency, where economics has primacy over politics. But in the USSR politics prevails over economics, and this changes the criteria of economic efficiency, which must be considered to be higher, the stronger it maintains the leadership's political power. Of course, to be unlimited, political domination must rely on economic growth. However, not all forms of economic growth correspond to the needs of the dominating rulers. The latter require the increased development of heavy industry, in order to strengthen their internal and external power, but the accomplishment of this goal cannot be ensured if light industry substantially diverts material resources from politically more important areas of economic activity. Therefore, a concomitant result for the market economy (political reinforcement) is for the totalitarian economy the principal indicator of its efficiency, and, vice versa, the totalitarian economy admits only as a concomitant result that which is the principal indicator of efficiency of the market economy (the common welfare). Within the limits of thus distorted correlation between economic efficiency and concomitant results, the Soviet leaders do their best also to improve the country's common welfare. They strive to increase the production of consumer goods and the citizenry's average income. Scarcity of goods, which remains an insuperable problem for Soviet production is mitigated by means of administrative distribution. With the same purpose in view, Soviet law regulates non-economic contracts employed by individuals in their mutual relations, especially in the area of the centralized supply. Nevertheless, the common welfare of the Soviet population cannot even be compared with the economic might of the Soviet state. Why does this occur? Is it not possible to combine reinforcement of the state's economic might with an equal improvement in the citizenry's economic well-being? Or, perhaps, the malicious intent of the Soviet leadership is the principal cause of the deplorable state of affairs?

Malicious intent is absolutely irrelevant to this issue. Moreover, even if it existed, it could never be as constant as is the economic scarcity that prevails in the USSR. The low level of individual well-being results not from the subjective peculiarities of the Soviet rulers, but from the objective substance of the Soviet system. Once again we encounter a contradiction, operating, however, not between essence and appearance, but within the essence itself, examined in its reality, without a propagandistic veil. The level of individual well-being could be raised only if this would not affect the state's economic might. Such a miracle could occur as a result exclusively of comprehensive economic prosperity. The latter is not subjectively undesirable for the Soviet leadership, because, while ensuring further reinforcement of the state economy, it would also eliminate the economic causes of individual dissatisfaction. But in order to achieve the requisite upsurge, it would be necessary to replace direct administration in the form of commands stemming from the politically ruling "top" with indirect regulation in the form of incentives intended to encourage development of an economically emancipated "bottom." This, in turn, would assume complete rejection of centralism and the establishment of entirely unfettered decentralization, which, of course, would lead to the rulers' loss first of their economic monopoly and then of their political domination. Conversely, in order to retain political dominance based on economic monopoly, the Soviets cannot look to economic freedom indirectly regulated by means of material incentives but must resort instead to administrative subordination of economic activity directly aimed at achieving the desired results by means of mandatory commands. This, in turn, assumes complete rejection of decentralization and the establishment of absolute centralism, which, of course, would lead to equally unacceptable results: first economic disaster and then political collapse. The only remaining way out of this vicious circle is maneuvering back and forth between dominant centralism and subordinate decentralization. But such maneuvering precludes prosperity at a level that could provide both the strengthening of the country's economic might and the improvement of individual well-being. Because of this fact one must inevitably be oriented to the strengthening of the former as a subjectively chosen purpose and to the improvement of the latter as an objectively restricted dream. And the further the Soviet regime drifts away from the time of its creation the larger the abyss between the degree of economic strengthening of political power and the level of material satisfaction of individual demands.

In this respect, the Soviet food supply is the most illustrative. Other consumer goods are historically variable depending on industrial developments, and if now a Soviet peasant has a refrigerator, instead of a root cellar, this is due not to an increase in his welfare but to the appearance of new, previously unknown industrial products. It is otherwise with food. Now, as before, food is bread, butter, milk, meat, vegetables, fruit, etc., no matter how substantial their industrial processing may actually be. And from a great number of comparable indicators just two seem more than sufficient: in the 1920s the Soviet Union could feed the country's population with its own bread, though they did not produce nuclear weapons; yet in the 1980s, when the Soviet Union represents one of the world's nuclear superpowers, in order to feed the country's population it must buy bread abroad.

In the USSR, the development of the food supply is as cyclical as is the development of the economy: periodically, government rationing replaces free sale, and eventually free sale replaces government rationing. However, while the level of output of heavy industry has always increased at least to some degree with each economic cycle, even the previous level of food production has never been restored as a result of cyclical economic process. The time of NEP is generally known as the Soviet epoch of food abundance. The abolition of NEP led to food rationing in the late–1920's. In 1935, free sale replaced food rationing, and the supply of food to the population was significantly improved, but the food abundance of the period of NEP had become a purely historical fact. Pre-War circumstances entailed concealed food rationing, which was publicly introduced upon the German invasion. Only in 1947 was free sale again established, and the citizens could buy more food than previously, though not so much as they could in the second half of the 1930's. Since the early 1960s a gradual shrinkage in the food supply relative to demand has been taking place, and the situation has deteriorated to such an extent that concealed rationing is being employed at present. It is difficult to predict whether this concealed rationing will be replaced by public rationing or the new Soviet leaders will manage to restore free sale in cases where now they must resort to secret distribution. However, judging from Soviet experience, the level of balance of food supply and demand attained in the late 1940s is at present indubitably unattainable. From this point of view, the cyclical development of the Soviet economy truly can be characterized as a spiral development, should one prefer to use Hegelian-Marxist-Leninist terminology. But the spiral discussed inversely mirrors the philosophical spiral: the latter assumes a certain upward movement upon the completion of previous cycle, in contrast to the former, which involves a consistently downward motion before the beginning of each subsequent cycle. This signifies that the cyclical development of the Soviet economy has its insurmountable limits, because the sources maintaining a dependable circular movement are gradually depleted by this all-consuming spiral-like movement, and since, as a result, the exhaustion of these sources is inevitable, the system itself is definitely doomed to failure. No measures are adequately efficient to prevent its final collapse, though the course of events may be slowed, or quite possibly accelerated, by various circumstances.

Any factor allowing for the supplementation or economization of domestic resources by means of foreign contacts delays the system's ultimate demise. Increase in prices favorable for Soviet dumping at the world oil market, foreign trade purchases of grain compensating for domestic agricultural underproduction, industrial espionage ensuring the acquisition of technological innovations without a substantial waste of time and money—all of these and a great many other events and actions delay the system's movement toward its inevitable fate. Similar assessments must also be made with respect to the Soviet policy of detente. Those Western Sovietologists who consider detente as simply allowing for Soviet a military build-up are not mistaken. But their conclusion is obviously lopsided. The Soviets are in need of detente not exclusively for their program of military build-up but also because a unilateral arms race is less expensive than a bilateral one.

In contrast, there are factors leading to depletion of domestic resources because of unfavorable external or internal circumstances and thus accelerating the destruction of the Soviet regime. Declining prices in the world oil market deprive the USSR of an important source of influx of hard currency and, consequently, diminish the state's capacity to acquire needed goods through foreign trade. An American embargo cutting off grain shipments could entail catastrophic consequences for the Soviet system, should it remain in force for an extended period of time and be unanimously maintained by other exporting countries. The capture of numerous spies, sent out by Soviet intelligence, is not only a political but also an economic defeat for the USSR, insofar as this jeopardizes its industrial espionage. Similar conclusions must be reached regarding the Soviet policy toward the American program known as "Star Wars." Those Western Sovietologists who think that the purpose of the Soviet policy in this area is geared toward maintaining a military balance, if not Soviet military superiority, are indubitably correct. However, their conclusion does not take all factors into account. The Soviets are indeed frightened by the challenge to their military might, but far more frightening to them is the exorbitant burden upon their economic resources that an adequate response to this challenge would entail.

Only bearing in mind that cyclical development upon a model of a contracting spiral is accompanied by counteracting factors, which, on the one hand, delay and, on the other hand, accelerate an economically destructive process, can one correctly outline the genuine perspective of the Soviet economy and, consequently, the final fate of the Soviet system. It seems, however, necessary to emphasize at least two points, in order to avoid quite predictable misinterpretations of the result of this analysis.

First, the economy is not the sole cause of Soviet predicaments. The country also experiences severe political stresses, which sometimes manifest themselves in the form of strikes, disobedience, and dissent, despite the harsh measures of suppression. The notorious "cooperation of socialist nations" disguises concealed national hostility, which grows stronger as coercive programs of Russification are stepped up. Even the problem of population has acquired a political coloring since the birth rate in the Southern and Eastern union republics is higher than it is in the European part of the USSR, and this fact will undoubtedly work to gradually undermine the Russian majority and threaten Russian dominance. All of these issues are extremely significant and deserve separate scrutiny and special research. However, a book dedicated to a legal analysis of the Soviet economic system may contain only such deductions that follow from *this* analysis and that are relevant to *this* system.

Second, economic predicaments, economic stagnation and even economic regression, no matter how substantial these may be, have never brought any system of human society to collapse in and of themselves. These occurrences as well as numerous others can create a favorable situation for the overthrow of a dominant regime. However, the overthrow itself assumes political actions available only to political forces that are sufficiently interested to plan and sufficiently strong to achieve both destructive and constructive ends: the dismantlement of one system and the creation of another. To anticipate an exemplary scenario for the happening of such events and to indicate the specific forces that will carry it out are the tasks of sociologists, political scientists, and futurologists. As to economic factors expressed in legal forms, and their role in forthcoming political changes, this motive power of the irrepressible development can and must be ascertained by means of legal analysis of the Soviet economic system.

Afterword

In writing this book, the authors strove to take into consideration all relatively substantial changes of Soviet legislation concerning the Soviet economy. Only draft or experimental modifications were omitted. Theoretical analysis also seemed premature in cases where new legal provisions did not immediately enter in force because these provisions had to be supplemented by subordinate normative acts and ensured by creation of appropriate economic resources. We think, however, that correctness of our general conclusions must be additionally checked on the basis of the most important drafts, experiments, and incomplete innovations that have been announced recently by Soviet officials or have been promulgated in Soviet legislation.

Among various items of draft legislation, the idea of restoration of trade cooperatives (*promyslovaia kooperatsiia*) is especially significant. According to the Washington Post,[1] information on this idea was presented by a leading Soviet economist Leonid Abalkin in New Delhi where he accompanied Gorbachev on a state visit to India. Abalkin said that in the nearest future Soviet citizens would be allowed to create cooperatives providing services and engaging in manufacturing, for local distribution, such items as furniture, crockery, simple utensils, national costumes and products made from materials "left over" at state enterprises. It is assumed that these cooperatives would pay the state a certain sum as a fee for a license or as income taxes or even in both forms, and the rest of the profit would be distributed among the members of the cooperatives in accordance with their work contributions. Judging from Abalkin's predictions, the revived and expanded cooperatives would constitute between 10% and 12% of the national income within the next decade.

In his general assessment of a forthcoming innovation Abalkin emphasized that it would not signify depart from basic principles of socialism: new cooperatives would not be allowed to hire other workers; that would remain purely a state function. In other words, it is a question of "a within-system reform" (using Professor Nove's words), not of a change of the system itself. However, this system relies upon economic monopoly of holders of unlimited political power that administer economic activity by centralized methods and resort to certain decentralization only under threat of economic collapse. What does the restoration of trade cooperatives mean with respect to these features of the Soviet system as a single whole?

Trade cooperatives are not new phenomena for the Soviet economy. These cooperatives existed in Stalin's time, when economic centralization reached the highest possible level, and they were liquidated in 1959, i.e., in Khrushchev's time, when the first post-Stalin attempts of economic decentralization were implemented. Moreover, in the Baltic republics (Estonia, Latvia, Lithuania) trade cooperatives were left intact in 1959 and have continued to function up to the present. Thus, neither creation nor liquidation of trade cooperatives can be used as evidence of centralization or decentralization. There also is no proof that restoration of these cooperatives will undermine economic monopoly of the Soviet state. Past and present trade cooperatives have been based on the same organizational and financial principles that Abalkin suggests for expanded employment of these economic entities in the future. Nevertheless, like collective farms and consumer cooperatives, trade cooperatives have indirectly personified not their own property but the property of the Soviet state. The income of trade cooperatives' members resulting from distribution of cooperatives' profit after performance of all financial duties toward the state has always been as low as average salary of state workers. Only actual practice can prove to what extent and in which direction the restored trade cooperatives will differ from those known to Soviet law and the Soviet economy in the past, and in some area even at the present. The direct purposes of this undertaking, may easily be ascertained by studying the law on individual labor activity adopted by the Supreme Soviet of the USSR on November 19, 1986.[2] This law allows, within the certain limits, private labor activity by those individuals who are not connected with state or cooperative production: housewives, invalids, pensioners, and students. Workers and officials of state and cooperative entities and institutions may also engage in private labor activity, but only when they are free from their principal duty. Because of the nature of their primary employment, these workers and officials remain in the "socialized" sector of the economy. The situation is different with respect to those for whom private labor activity is the only source of support. Economic difficulties have compelled the Soviet leadership to enlarge the area of permissible private labor, but because of peculiarities of the Soviet system a certain form of "socialization" of this labor also must be developed Therefore, the law of November 19, 1986 itself declares in Article 1 that "the state will encourage citizens who conduct individual labor activity to join . . . cooperatives, voluntary societal entities and societies." This means that, in contrast to the opinions expressed by some Western media, the restoration and expansion of trade cooperatives are earmarks not of the creation of private enterprises for the first time since Lenin's NEP, but of the limitation of private activities to less than the scope apparently allowed by the new legislation.

The new experiments include the application of so-called full economic accountability (*polnyi khozraschet*) to several economic ministries, including the Ministry of the Light Industry, on January 1, 1987.[3] The combination of the two words "*polnyi*" (full) and "*khozraschet*" (economic accountability) has been more than once employed in Soviet legal and economic practice.

Each time the phrase has been given a different interpretation. Before the 1965 economic reform full *khozraschet* was contrasted to internal *khozraschet*: goods-money relations were available to enterprises subject to full *khozraschet* and unavailable to separate shops subject to internal *khozraschet*.[4] Legislation on the 1965 economic reform uses the word "full" to mean "genuine" *khozraschet* as opposed to fictitious *khozraschet*, as this reform characterizes previous methods of economic management.[5] Neither the pre–1965 nor the 1965 interpretation was taken into account in the process of preparation of the 1987 experiment dealing with certain economic ministries. An economic ministry as a unified system of economic entities and administrative agencies cannot enter as such into goods-money relations. On the other hand, as a unified system an economic ministry is a single whole, not an internal department. Thus, neither full *khozraschet* nor internal *khozraschet* as contrasting methods of economic administration can be compatible with *khozraschet* of economic ministries. At the same time, legislation providing for the experimental application of full *khozraschet* to economic ministries does not mean replacement of fictitious *khozraschet* by the genuine article. As this has been already discussed,[6] *khozraschet* of ministries is a fiction by definition, and the Soviet leadership has introduced this fiction to pursue not the goal of economic incentive, but that of pervasive distribution of administrative expenses between the state budget and the branches of the state economy.

However, the 1987 experiment includes a new component in the full *khozraschet* of the economic ministries affected. This component never was previously a part of the concept of ministerial *khozraschet*. And the word "full" with respect to participants of the experiment reflects the peculiarities of this component. Let us take as an example the Ministry of Light Industry. As Abalkin explained at the same interview in New Delhi, this ministry would not receive its plan of production from the government. It itself would have to determine its plan in accordance with contracts executed between enterprises or associations of light industry and trade or other organizations. Taking this statement at face value, one could come to the conclusion that full *khozraschet* of the Ministry of Light Industry means separation of ministerial *khozraschet* from centralized planning. If so, then centralization is not simply loosened but entirely replaced by decentralization, because centralized planning at the governmental level would be supplemented by decentralized planning at the ministerial level, as a result of this experiment. However, if one assesses the relevant circumstances realistically, one immediately sees the vulnerability of such a conclusion.

As is generally known, shortages, a permanent disease of the Soviet economy, are nowhere as prevalent as in the area of light industrial production. If trade and other organizations, that reflect consumer demand, execute economic contracts in strict accordance with this demand with economic entities of light industry, the production plan of the Ministry of Light Industry thus established will exceed considerably the material resources that are at disposal of agencies of supply. Therefore, the Ministry of Light Industry must plan production relying not only on executed contracts, as Abalkin contends, but at any rate also on the planning of supply. However, in decentralizing planning of production on the level of the ministries involved in the experiment, the Soviet leadership retains intact the previous, mainly centralized system of planning of supply on this level by either the USSR Council of Ministers, the State Planning Committee (*Gosplan*), or the State Committee on Supply (*Gossnab*). As a matter of course, in cases where a discrepancy arises between centralized distribution of material resources and the contracts executed by production and trade organizations, the ultimate solution must depend on distribution, not on contracts. This is only one of numerous illustrations that could be used in order to disprove the new interpretation of full *khozraschet* maintained by propagandists of the 1987 ministerial experiment. The experiment obviously does involve a certain trend toward decentralization. And this is easy to understand, bearing in mind the turn of the economic cycle at the start of Gorbachev's rule after Brezhnev's administration. But even under these circumstances, centralization clearly prevails. And is also easy to understand, bearing in mind that in each Soviet economic cycle, centralization has played the guiding role while decentralization has only saved what has been jeopardized by the arrogant guidance.

In dealing with recently announced, but incomplete innovations, we must return to the law of November 19, 1986, on individual labor activity. This innovation is incomplete in at least two ways.

On the one hand, a number of the types of individual labor activity allowed by the new law cannot be actually implemented in accordance with the law until the requisite economic resources are created and the appropriate procedure is established for distribution of these resources among those engaged in individual labor activity. For example, the new law provides for private repair of privately-owned cars. However, many kinds of spare parts needed for such repairs cannot be found in auto parts stores. Previously both problems—those of spare parts and private repair—were resolved by the illegal methods of the underground economy. Now, since this activity is legalized, these problems must be eliminated by strong economic efforts, not merely by legal prescriptions. The new law does not take effect until May 1, 1987. One can predict without risk of being mistaken that the necessary substantial improvement in supplies hardly will be achieved during six months in a country that has proved incapable for decades of coping with this task. As a result, the combination of legalized and underground private activities will be inevitable despite any extraordinary innovation of legal and economic character. The Soviet leadership foresaw that from the outset. This is why the November law on individual labor activity was preceded by three special decrees directed against extraction of non-labor income, and why the concept of non-labor income was broadly interpreted (income is prohibited if it is not permitted) and intentionally criminalized (as a source of non-labor income, unlawful actions are equivalent to criminal behavior).[7] By means of these decrees Soviet rulers will be able simultaneously to encourage private initiative and to keep these activities in check.

On the other hand, a number of provisions that the new law contains cannot be employed in accordance with the leadership's goals before administrative regulations—governmental, ministerial, or local; public, secret, or semi-secret—establish the necessary special procedures. I. Gladki, a speaker at the meeting of the Supreme Soviet of the USSR dedicated to adoption of the law on individual labor activity, indicated that one of goals of this law was to attract additional manpower as a means of strengthening economic development.[8] It is needless to say that attraction of additional manpower cannot be meant to involve the migration of workers from state or cooperative economic entities to private economic activity. To prevent such migration the law emphasizes that its principal addresses are those not connected with the sphere of societal production (housewives, invalids, pensioners, etc.). However, the problem is not as simple as it appears at first glance. Certain invalids and pensioners may be workers at state or cooperative entities. Could they leave these entities in order to engage in private economic activity? Because such a shift is officially undesirable, the new law must be supplemented by carefully elaborated formal obstacles. "Housewives" is a noun of the feminine gender. But this does not mean that only women can keep house. With reference to the Constitutional principle of equality of women and men, such an interpretation easily could be rejected. Do working men or even working women acquire the right to replace their jobs by housekeeping, and thus make themselves available for themselves individual labor activity? Since this is not formally precluded by the law, application of this new law must be postponed until the Supreme Soviets and Councils of Ministers of the USSR and the republics implement edicts or directions on putting the law on individual labor activity into effect, so as to adjust the legislation of the USSR and the union republics to this law.[9] And the law of November 19, 1986 indicates itself how this adjustment must be made. Article 6 provides: "Citizens that have expressed a desire to engage in individual labor activity are obliged to receive permission from the executive committee . . . at the place of permanent residence." This permission remains in effect for the time it specifies, but not longer than for five years. Thus, local executive committees, by granting, refusing, or not renewing permissions, may regulate the number of persons engaged in individual labor. These committees are not obligated to give reasons when they reject applications. But administrative regulations, public or more probably secret, will, of course, list these reasons. Prohibitions against shifting from societal production to individual labor are sure to be high on the list.

Relying upon all of these approaches, the new Soviet leadership is attempting to mitigate at least some economic difficulties by enlarging the application of individual labor without modifying the Soviet system. Can these goals be achieved? Are they contradictory with one another? These questions can be answered only on the basis of detailed analysis of the new provisions.

First, the new law increases the number of types of private undertakings. They are allowed in such areas as the handicraft trade (production of clothes, footwear, hats, etc.), services (construction and repair of private houses, repair of automobiles, etc.), the social/cultural sphere, (certain forms of teaching, translation of foreign works, medical practice, etc.), and in a number of other cases. However, the newly established broad permission is not unrestricted. Not only are occupations prohibited that seem dangerous politically, ideologically, or from the viewpoint of state security (production of weapons, teaching of subjects outside the official curriculum, etc.), occupations are also prohibited if they could lead to high profits, for example production of jewelry. The law also allows other restrictions, regardless of whether these are established by legislation of the USSR or of the republics, by statute or administrative regulations. As a matter of course, individual labor activity will be prohibited in cases where it relies upon hired workers.

Second, previously there were no legal provisions explicitly providing for individual production that could be exercised for the purpose of sale, though implicitly such a permission was contained by legal regulations addressed to collective farm markets and individual agricultural production. Now a general permission is in force with respect to individual labor activity in the handicraft trade. In addition, whatever is the nature of the individual labor, the new law allows those dealing with this activity to use customers' materials, in contrast to the old regulations which, as a general rule, did not allow the use of customers' materials.

Third, individual labor activity is not only allowed more broadly, but specially encouraged within the limits newly outlined by the law. Local executive committees as well as economic and other entities are obliged to assist development of this activity in the process of acquisition of materials and equipment, sale of produced products, lease of premises for workshops, etc. At the same time, individual labor activity is subordinated to rigid control on the part of local governmental agencies in the form of permissions and registration, licenses or franchises. This control is combined with the system of income taxes, and it is backed up by legal sanctions (confiscation of income, prohibition against an offender's continuing to engage in individual labor, etc.) applicable to those who exceed the established limits or who violate the established procedure.

These are the innovative characteristics of the law of November 19, 1986. Even referring only to these innovations, one hardly can contend that the Soviet system is going the way of substantial reformation. Apart from making small utensils that do not play a significant economic role, individual labor activity is restricted to the area of consumer demand, while production of means of production remains a monopolistic function of the state economy. But even in the area of consumer demand the private economy obviously depends on the state economy: the former can be developed in the most essential directions only to the extent to which the latter will ensure it with the necessary supplies. It is also far from certain that the newly permitted activities will remain legal. Soviet peasants have not forgotten how Khrushchev enlarged collective farmers' plots of land in 1954 because of the deplorable situation of Soviet agriculture and how he restored the previous limits in the early 1960s to prevent the further enrichment of the peasantry. Are there guarantees against a similar retreat with respect to individual labor activity? Is not the opposite assumption more realistic in a country of cyclical economic development and subordination of law to unlimited political power? Regardless, however, of whether such a retreat occurs and when it takes place, the economic dependence of individuals on the state strengthened by their legal dependence isolates the Soviet system from changes of substance as a result of the enlargement of the area of private economic activity. This conclusion also follows from certain other features of the new law.

This law, listing specific goals that must be achieved, mentions in its Preamble the creation of an opportunity for Soviet citizens to receive "additional income" by means of their individual labor. If such income is "additional," then what is the principal income? As a matter of course, the principal income must result from implementation not of individual but of societal labor—either previously (for pensioners), or at the present time (for workers of state or cooperative entities and members of their families), or in the future (for students). Thus, the nature of so-called personal ownership, as it is interpreted by Soviet law,[10] remains unmodified, despite the legal innovations we have discussed. Article 10 of the law sets the amount of the fee for a franchise as a percentage of the average income of state or cooperative workers engaged in a comparable activity. Those who receive licenses, instead of patents, must pay taxes in amount of 13% of income, as Abalkin said in New Delhi and as is generally established in the USSR for salary exceeding 100 rubles per month. Thus, it is assumed that income resulting from individual labor activity will be at the same level as that from state and cooperative entities and institutions.

We can, therefore, conclude that this incomplete innovation, despite all its significance, like the new economic ideas and new economic experiments described previously, leaves the Soviet system intact. The process of "reconstruction," as it is called by Gorbachev and other Soviet leaders, is under way in the USSR. Therefore, one can expect a number of other provisions designed to modify the regulation of the Soviet economy. Judging from the plan of legislation for the time-period 1986–1990, confirmed by the Presidium of the USSR Supreme Soviet and the USSR Council of Ministers,[11] such expectations are not groundless. After this development reaches the a stage of maturity, reflected not only in new legislative acts but also in broad economic practice, explorers of the legal organization of the Soviet economy will be in need to renew their analysis. The legal innovations that had been published, but had not been put into effect, just as this book went to press cannot be disregarded. But, as we have tried to demonstrate, their carefully limited nature confirms rather than undermines the final conclusions of our research.[12]

Notes

1. *Washington Post,* November 27, 1986.
2. *Izvestia*, November 21, 1986. More detailed characterization of this law see below.
3. E.g., *Izvestia*, November 29, 1986
4. See the section of Chapter 4 ("Production: its Legal Organization") on "General Principles."
5. Ibid.
6. Ibid.
7. *Izvestia*, May 28, 1986
8. *Izvestia*, November 18, 1986.
9. *Izvestia*, November 21, 1986.
10. See the secton of Chapter 3 ("Ownership and the Law of Ownership") on "The Right of Personal Ownership."
11. *Ved. SSSR*, 1986, no. 37, item 782.
12. This manuscript was already set in type when the Soviet press (*e.g., Izvestia,* February 8, 1987) published, for discussion, a draft Law on the State Enterprise (Association) approved by the January (1987) Plenum of the Central Committee of the Communist Party of the Soviet Union (*Pravda,* January 29, 1987). The draft suggests a number of changes in legal status of economic associations and independent enterprises concerning property rights, planning, contractual and other obligations, etc. However, these changes could not be taken into consideration not only because the manuscript was finished but also because the document published was only a draft. In a work dedicated to analysis of legal innovations in economic activities in the USSR obsolete legal provisions will be, of course, replaced by new legal norms, including those that will enter into force with the enactment of a new law resulting from discussion of the draft. Now, however, such a replacement cannot be justified. In addition, the draft itself, referring to the broadening of so-called economic methods of administration, emphasizes that it "deepens the centralized principles of development of the national economy." Thus, a projected law must strengthen, not undermine, the most important ideas formulated and argued in this book.

Index

Abalkin, Leonid, 311
Academy of Agricultural Sciences, 141
Academy of Sciences, 136, 141, 142, 143, 144, 150
Accountability. *See Khozraschet*
Accountants, 278
Administration for Services to the Diplomatic Corps, 164
Administrative distribution, 69
Administrative law, 51–52
  defined, 48
  See also Administrative violations
Administrative violations, 56–57, 281–282, 285
Agricultural agency. *See Gosagroprom*
Agricultural distribution, 187–190
Agriculture
  political organization of, 103
  See also Agricultural distribution; Collective farm/cooperative ownership; Collective farms; Farm families, movement of; *Gosagroprom*
Alcoholism, 28–29
Andropov, Yuri, 28, 72, 104
Apartments, 202–204, 250
Arbitrazh, 54, 69, 132(n46), 197–198, 220, 221, 222, 223, 224, 225, 226, 228, 235, 239, 240, 241, 265(n34), 283
Artisan work, 294–295
Assembly lines, imported, 149
Atomic energy regulations, 289
Automobiles, 95
  distribution of, 200
  repair, 314

Banks, 201. *See also* Savings banks; State Bank; *Stroibank*
Berman, Harold H., 60, 73, 96(n4)
Birman, I., 93
Black market, 11–12, 42, 249–250, 295, 296
Blue jeans, 296
Books, 257–258, 296, 298
Bread, 39–40, 45(n66)
Brezhnev, Leonid, 6, 25, 35, 102, 104
Bribery, 286
Building construction. *See* Construction
Bureaucrats, 34–35, 205
  privileges of, 86

Capital construction. *See* Construction
Carpets, 95
Caviar, 298
Central Committee of the Communist Party, 50, 89–90, 105, 129, 183, 186, 188
Central Council of Trade Unions, 157, 158
Centralism, 6, 102, 130
  and decentralization, 101–102, 103–105, 110–111, 114, 305–306, 314
  and democracy, 101–102
Centralization. *See* Centralism
Central Statistical Administration, 277
China, 16(n14)
Civil law, 52
  See also Fundamental Principles of Civil Legislation
Code of Laws, 47–48
Collective farm/cooperative ownership, 19–20, 20–21, 23, 25, 62, 79–81, 82. *See also* Cooperative organizations
Collective farmers, 26–27, 208(n2)
  and labor contracts, 170
  See also Collective farms
Collective farm law, 55
Collective farm markets, 41–42, 252–255
Collective farms, 31, 102, 103, 128–130
  and agricultural distribution, 188
  deficits, 32–33
  labor force, 26–27
  land rights, 67
  and Ministry of Social Security, 80
  produce sales, 250
  young people on, 163
  See also Collective farm/cooperative ownership; Collective farmers; Farm families, movement of; Model Collective Farm Charter
Collectivization, 9–10, 11
Commission of the Presidium of the Council of Ministers of the USSR on

the Protection of the Environment and the Rational Use of Natural Resources, 276
Commission on Labor Disputes, 175
Commissions on Affairs of Minors, 163
Committee on State Security. *See* KGB
Commodity turnover, 248–249
Communist Party, 21, 23, 173
and criminal offenses, 279–280
and economic entities, 131(n16)
Computer chips, 149
Comrades' Courts, 167–168, 283
Constitution, 34, 60
and individual labor activity, 85–86
and personal ownership, 84
and planning, 105
See also Constitution (1936); Constitution (1977)
Constitution (1936), 8, 10, 11, 15(n10), 19–20, 21, 22
and individual labor, 83
See also Constitution; Constitution (1977)
Constitution (1977), 12–13, 15(n10), 21, 22, 23–24, 62, 65, 73, 104
and individual labor, 83
and personal ownership, 92
See also Constitution; Constitution (1936)
Construction, 27, 208(n10), 220, 223–226, 266(n52)
contract terms, 258–259
and distribution, 181–182
planning of, 190–192
unfinished projects, 191–192
Construction Bank. *See Stroibank*
Consumer cooperatives, 31
Consumer services, 258–260
Contract discipline, 234–235
Contracts, 246–247, 263–264
for consumer services, 258–259, 259–260
for credit purchases, 257
for food trade, 260–261
and freedom, 251, 252, 264
housing, 261–262, 262–263
for independent work, 247–248
between individuals, 248
and law, 264(n3)
limits on, 250–251
rental, 255–256, 257, 262–263
for retail trade, 256–257, 260–261
with specialized entities, 248–249
state housing, 261
See also Economic contracts; Model Collective Farm Charter
Cooperative organizations, 89, 311–312. *See also* Collective farm/cooperative ownership; Consumer cooperatives; Housing cooperatives
Cooperatives. *See* Cooperative organizations
Council for Economic Mutual Assistance, 149
Council of Ministers, 50, 89–90, 105, 129, 183, 187, 193–194, 201, 314, 317
Bureau of Energy, 141
Conterfeiting, 286
Country houses, 86
Courts, 283. *See also* Comrades' Courts; Supreme Court of the Russian Republic
Credit, 243–244
distribution of, 201–202
Criminal law, 56–57, 280–281. *See also* Administrative violations; Criminal procedure law; Private enterprise, criminal
Criminal procedure law, 57–58
Currency. *See* Money
Customs regulations, 298

Decentralization, 6. *See also* Centralism
Democratic centralism, 101, 104, 110–111. *See also* Centralism
Discharging of employees
for criminal charges, 173
for disabilities, 171–172
for disciplinary reasons, 171, 172
for political reasons, 173
to reduce staff, 171
security against, 171–172
by third parties, 173
trade unions and, 172
for unexcused absence, 171
for unsuitability, 171
Distribution, 31–37
administrative, 198–204
of agricultural products, 32–33
and construction, 181–182, 190–192
of consumer goods, 185–186
of food, 200
general, 200–202
of housing, 201
planned, 198, 207–208
planned and unplanned, 204–206
and production, 181
special, 199–200
of surplus production, 33
and transportation, 182–183, 192–195
unplanned, 198, 206–207
See also Agricultural distribution; Distribution planning; Production
Distribution planning, 185, 186–187
agencies of, 183–186
annual plans, 193–194
and production planning, 179–181, 195–197

quarterly plans, 193–194
and transportation, 192–195
See also Distribution, planned
Drinking. *See* Alcoholism; Home distilling
Drunkenness. *See* Alcoholism
Duty to work, 26

Economic accountability. *See Khozraschet*
Economic administrative agencies, 50
Economic contracts, 214–217
for alienation of goods, 213
for bank accounts, 242–243
for banking services, 214
and civil law, 235–239
for construction, 220, 223–226, 237
for delivery, 220–221, 226–228, 237–238, 239–240
and distribution, 217
as forms of exchange, 211
and monetary payments, 243–244
and ordinary contracts, 211
parties to, 212, 221–222
planned and unplanned, 212–213, 245–246
and planning, 218–220, 223
for production, 213
for project work, 213
for railroad spur lines, 240–242
for services, 214
and supply, 226–228
time periods of, 222–223
for transportation, 213–214, 221, 228–231, 238–239
types, 211
for use of property, 213
See also Contracts; Economic discipline
Economic development, 36–37
Economic discipline, 232. *See also* Contract discipline; Financial discipline; Plan discipline
Economic growth, 134
Economic law, 47
and arbitrazh, 54
and courts, 55
Economic obligations. *See* Economic contracts
Economic plans, 132(n29)
Embezzlement, 286
Employees
discharging of. *See* Discharging of employees
liability of, 168–169
quitting, 169–170
Employment contract, 161–166. *See also* Labor contracts
Energy bureau. *See* Council of Ministers, Bureau of Energy
Energy conservation, 288
Environmental protection
agencies, 276–277
laws, 288–289
Exchange, 37–43
and distribution, 217
and economic contracts, 217
and rationing, 38–41
See also Economic contracts

Factories
hiring patterns, 28
Family law, 55–56
Family life, 55–56
Farm families
movement of, 165
Finance law, 53–54
Financial discipline, 232–233
Fire safety, 272–273
Firing. *See* Discharging of employees
Fish, conservation of, 277
Fishing, illegal. *See* Poaching
Food business
graft in, 252
return of goods, 260–261
See also Collective farm markets
Food shortages, 253, 307–308. *See also* Shortages
Foreign currency. *See* Money, international exchange value
Foreign currency operations, 297
Foreign tourism, 95
Foreign trade, 291–292
Foreign Trade Bank, 54
Free-market economy, 16(n13)
Friedman, Milton, 16(n13)
Full employment, 165
Fundamental Directions of Economic and Social Development of the USSR for 1986–1990, 67–68
Fundamental Principles of Civil Legislation, 21, 22, 52, 63, 65, 80, 82, 118, 210, 223
Fundamental Principles of Housing Legislation, 202
Fundamental Principles of Labor Legislation, 53, 157
Fundamental Principles of Land Legislation, 53, 201
Fundamental Principles of Legislation on Marriage and the Family, 55
Furniture, 95
Furs, 95

Gold, 95
Goods-money relations, 37–38, 64, 214

Gorbachev, Mikhail, 23, 25, 29, 35, 37, 38, 67, 72, 90, 93, 102, 103, 104, 183, 204, 226, 228, 296, 311, 317
Gosagroprom, 23, 80, 102, 103, 109, 141, 188
Gosbank. See State Bank
Gosplan, 50, 108–109, 136, 138, 139, 149, 151, 158–159, 164, 184, 190, 276, 314
  and *Gossnab,* 185
Gossnab, 50, 141, 185, 314
  and *Gosplan,* 185
Gosstroi. See State Committee on Construction
Grain, 45(n66)
Grain purchases, 39–40, 309

Handicraft business, 294–295, 316
Heroes of Socialist Labor, 199
Heroes of the Soviet Union, 199
Home distilling, 296, 302(n62)
Houses
  laws regarding, 84–85, 86
  See also Housing
Housing, 258
  contracts, 261–262, 262–263
  distribution of, 202–204, 250
  and labor contracts, 170
  loans for, 201–202
  permits, 298–299
  retail sale of, 201
  space allocation, 203
  See also Apartments; Housing cooperatives; Housing shortage; Residence permits
Housing cooperatives, 89–92
Housing shortage, 89–90
Hungary, 16(n14)
Hunting, illegal. *See* Poaching

Independent work, 247–248
Individual income, 92–94
Individual labor activity, 12–13, 85–86, 267(n106), 314–315, 316–317
Industry, 102–103
Innovations
  rewards for, 147–148
Intelligentsia, 3
Inventors and inventions, 146–148. *See also* Society of Inventors and Innovators
Inventor's certificates, 146–147
  and patents, 148

KGB, 150, 173
  and economic crime, 273
Khozraschet, 214, 216, 312–314
  and administrative agencies, 120–122
  on collective farms, 115, 129
  and economic entities, 122–123
  features of, 117
  and goods-money relations, 124
  and juridical persons, 117–118, 125–126
  and planning, 119
  and production units, 128
  and research and development, 143–144
  and state ownership, 116
Kosygin, Alexei, 6, 103, 228
Khrushchev, Nikita, 6, 25, 35, 90, 103, 203–204, 261, 290

Labor, 25–28
  discipline. *See* Comrades' Courts
  duty of, 162
  and rehabilitation of criminals, 161–162
  right to, 26
  and technology, 37
  value of, 162
  See also Central Council of Trade Unions; People's Commissariat of Labor; State Committee on Labor and Social Problems; State Committee on Labor and Wages; Work hours
Labor collectives, 165–166
Labor contracts, 30–31, 166–173
  and discipline, 167–168
  and job assignments, 166
  termination of, 169–173
  and wages, 166–167
  and work hours, 166
  See also Contracts; Labor disputes; Labor force
Labor disputes, 174–175
Labor force, 27–28
  discipline of, 28, 167–169
  and foreign employers, 164
  planning process, 159–160, 163–164
  problem with, 27–28
  relationships with employers, 161–166, 168, 170–171, 174–175
  and temporary residence permits, 164
  See also Employees; Employment contract; Labor collectives; Labor disputes; Labor law
Labor law, 53, 157–159
Land
  ownership of, 66
Land law, 63. *See also* Fundamental Principles of Land Legislation
Laptev, V. V., 47
Law, 17(n31). *See also* Economic law; Family law; Finance law
Lawyers, 277
Legislation, 47–48
Lenin, Vladimir, 6, 9, 37, 134, 312
Libraries, 257–258

Lisichkin, G. S., 124
Loans, 88–89
Local executive committees, 2
Luxury goods, 95

Malfiet, K., 83
Management, 104, 269–270
  negligence in, 288–290
Managers, 33–34, 96(n9), 282
  accountability, 290–291
  discipline of, 284
Manpower. *See* Labor force
Market socialism, 215, 216
Marx, Karl, 19, 20, 21, 25
  on penal labor, 161–162
Marxists, 96(n4)
Metallurgical industry, 32
Military, 32, 37, 309
Military Industrial Commission, 149
Military technology, 152–153
Minister of Trade, 186
Ministries, list of, 177(n49)
Ministry of Chemical and Petroleum Machinebuilding, 276, 277
Ministry of Defense
  Main Intelligence Administration, 150. *See also* KGB
Ministry of Finance, 54, 70, 139, 151, 201, 232, 277
Ministry of Fisheries, 277
Ministry of Foreign Trade, 150, 291–292, 298
Ministry of Health, 277
Ministry of Higher and Specialized Secondary Education, 143, 144
Ministry of Internal Affairs, 272–273
Ministry of Irrigation and Water Supply, 277
Ministry of Justice, 151
Ministry of Light Industry, 313–314
Ministry of Railroads, 193–194
Ministry of Social Security, 80
Ministry of Trade, 50, 140, 185–186, 261
Mintorg. *See* Ministry of Trade
Mismanagement. *See* Management
Missiles, 149
Model Collective Farm Charter, 55, 128, 129–130
Model Rules of Internal Labor Order, 167
Modernization, 134
Monetary payments, 243–245
Monetary reform, 35
Money
  and goods, 37–38, 64, 116, 118
  international exchange value, 94
  and luxury goods, 95
  See also Foreign currency operations; Monetary payments; Monetary reform
Mutual aid funds, 88–89

Napoleonic Code, 65
Natural resources, illegal use, 287
NEP. *See* New Economic Policy
New Economic Policy (NEP), 37, 103, 117, 308, 312
1977 Constitution. *See* Constitution (1977)
1936 Constitution. *See* Constitution (1936)
Non-economic contracts. *See* Contracts
Nove, Alec, 1–2

Oil, 309
Olympics (1980), 79
Operative administration, 70–71, 116, 304–305
  amortization fund, 72
  building and installation fund, 71
  capital investment fund, 72
  charter fund, 71
  and construction, 182
  incentive funds, 72
  monetary funds, 72
  and personal ownership, 87–88
  and production, 181
  and state ownership, 73–74, 75, 82
  See also Ownership
Ownership, 9, 10–11, 19–25, 63, 304–306
  fact versus law, 59–60, 61–66, 88
  nature of, 75–76
  and operative administration, 70–71
  principles of, 59–66
  See also Collective farm/cooperative ownership; Operative administration; Personal ownership; Socialist ownership

Paris Convention for the Protection of Industrial Property, 148
Passports, 26, 160, 299
Patents, 148, 151. *See also* Inventor's certificates
Peasants, 3
People's Artists of the USSR, 199
People's Commissariat of Labor, 158
People's Supervision Organization, 273–274
Periodical subscriptions, 200, 208(n15)
Personal ownership, 10–11, 12–13, 19–20, 25, 62, 66, 67, 88, 317
  and cooperative organizations, 89
  of housing, 84–85
  and housing cooperatives, 89–92
  items, 84
  and operative administration, 87–88
  and state ownership, 86–87
  and state's economic monopoly, 83–84

See also Ownership
Peter the Great, 134
Plan discipline, 233–234
Planning
 balance in, 111
 chain of command, 107–109, 109–110
 economic, 209(n28)
 Politburo's role, 107–108
 problems, 111–114
 by production associations, 126
 stability of, 113–114
 timeliness of, 112–113
 types of, 106–107
 violations of, 290–292
Poaching, 286–287
Police, 272
Politburo, 2, 4, 49–50, 78, 79, 98(n68)
Political power, 2–3, 4–5
Pollution, 288–289
Population movement, 159–160
Pravda, 208(n15)
Presidium, 50
Prices, 35, 39–40, 50–51, 140, 256–257
 of clothing, 51
 of meat, 51
 zonal variations, 40
Private enterprise, 270, 316
 in agriculture, 296
 criminal, 295–296. *See also* Criminal law
 as threat to economy, 294–296
 See also Black market
Procuracy, 270–272
Produce business
 graft in, 252
Production, 25–31
 of consumer goods, 196–197
 development of, 140
 and distribution, 181
 and labor, 25
 of means of production, 196–197
 planning agencies, 105–114
 principles of, 101–105
 quotas, 33–34
 See also Centralism; Distribution; Production associations; Quality control; Safety regulations; Scientific-production associations
Production associations, 126–129
 and construction plans, 126
 and distribution plans, 127
 and finance, 127
 and independent enterprises, 127–128
 as planning agencies, 126
 and subdivisions, 128
Production planning, 184
 and distribution planning, 195–197
Products, new, 139–140
Program of the Soviet Communist Party, 23
Propaganda, 3–4
Property
 rights, 63–64
 state acquisition of, 68

Quality control, 292–293

Railroads, 192, 193, 240–242. *See also* Transportation
Rationing, 38–41, 44(n55), 209(n29)
Rental business, 255–256
Republic legislation
 defined, 48–49
Research and development, 135
 cost/benefit formula, 137–138
 financing, 138–140
 goals of, 151–152
 incentives, 145–146
 inter-agency cooperation, 141
 and *khozraschet,* 143–144
 and military technology, 152–153
 organization of, 141–144
 performance monitoring, 144–145
 planning, 136–138
 role of Academy of Sciences, 142–143
 role of universities, 142–143, 144
 supervision of, 140–141
 See also Inventors and inventions; Scientific-production associations; Scientific-Technical Information Center; Technological innovation
Residence, 26–27. *See also* Housing; Residence permits
Residence permits
 and labor contracts, 170
Retail trade, 248–250, 256–257
 black market in, 249–250
 economic violations, 291
 planning of, 197
Rome, ancient, 59, 60, 65
Rubanov, A. A., 83
Ruling elite. *See* Bureaucrats
Ryzhkov, N. I., 209(n28), 226, 228

Safety regulations, 293–294
Salaries
 average, 34, 35, 36
 of bureaucrats, 34–35
 See also Individual income
Savings banks, 95
Scientific-production associations, 141–142
Scientific-Technical Information Center, 145, 150–151
Shortages, 307, 313–314
 and rental business, 255–256

See also Food shortages
Singapore, 2
Smuggling, 297–298
Socialism, 8
Socialist ownership, 19–22, 23, 24, 60, 62, 65
and cooperative/collective ownership, 24
defined, 22
and personal ownership, 24
and state ownership, 82–83
See also Collective farm/cooperative ownership; Ownership; Personal ownership; State ownership
Society of Inventors and Innovators, 151
Soldiers, 28
Solzhenitsyn, A., 94
Soviet Constitution. *See* Constitution; Constitution (1936); Constitution (1977)
Soviet economy, 16(n13)
administration of, 1–2
and civil law, 282–284
and criminal convictions, 278–284
and distribution, 31–37
efficiency of, 6–7
and exchange, 37–43
inefficiency of, 306–307
and law, 8–15, 48–49
legal protection of, 269–270
and legislation, 311–318
liberalization, 5
and ownership, 19–25
and political power, 4–5, 5–6
and political system, 1–8, 303–310
and private enterprise, 294–296
problems of, 309–310
and production, 25–31
protective agencies, 270–278. *See also* KGB; Soviet system; State Bank; State property; Underground economy
reform, 317–318, 318(n12)
as state monopoly, 303–305
studying, 2
Soviet legal system
branches, 49–58
and capitalist system, 48
and economy, 48–49
structure, 46–48
See also Administrative law; Arbitrazh; Civil law; Collective farm law; Criminal law; Family law; Finance law; Land law; State law
Soviet society, 3, 16(n23), 17(n28)
Soviet system, 2–8
Soviet technology
and capitalist technology, 135
Specialized entities, 248–249
Stalin, 6, 8, 10, 25, 38, 90, 103, 162, 226, 244
Star Wars, 309
State Agricultural Industrial Committee. *See Gosagroprom*
State Bank, 54, 72, 232
State Committee for Foreign Economic Relations, 150
State Committee on Construction, 50, 136, 276
State Committee on Hydrometeorology and Monitoring of the Environment, 277
State Committee on Labor and Social Matters. *See* State Committee on Labor and Social Problems
State Committee on Labor and Social Problems, 50, 157, 158, 165
State Committee on Labor and Wages, 158
State Committee on Matters of Inventions and Discoveries, 146–147
State Committee on Planning. *See Gosplan*
State Committee on Prices, 50, 140, 232
State Committee on Science and Technology, 136, 138, 139, 140, 141, 143, 144–145, 149, 150, 276
State Committee on Supply. *See Gossnab*
State law, 49–51
defined, 48
State ownership, 19–20, 20–21, 24–25, 60–61, 62, 66, 130
and collective farms, 32
and consumer cooperatives, 32
and cooperative/collective ownership, 25
of forests, 66
of land, 66
of means of production, 67
of minerals, 66
objects of, 68
and operative administration, 82
and personal ownership, 68–69, 86–87, 92–93
and production, 31
and right of interference, 76–77
and socialist ownership, 82–83
and supreme disposition, 77–79
of water, 66
See also Ownership; Socialist ownership
State Planning Committee. *See Gosplan*
State property
in agriculture, 290
damage to, 289–290
mismanagement of, 288–290. *See also* Management
neglect of, 289–290
theft of, 269, 284–286. *See also* Administrative violations; Natural resources, illegal use; Poaching

Statute of Trade Unions, 81
Strikes, 74, 98(n57)
Stroibank, 54, 224, 232
Supply levels
  geographic variations, 40
  and hierarchical position, 40–41
Suppression, 3–4
Supreme Court of the Russian Republic, 281
Supreme Soviet, 50, 78, 312, 317

Taiwan, 2
Technical information
  clandestine importing of, 150
  importing of, 148, 150
  payment for, 151
  See also Scientific-Technical Information Center
Technological innovation, 134–135
Technology
  imported, 148–150
  modernization of, 148–153
  and technical information, 148, 150
  See also Assembly lines, imported; Military technology; Research and development; Technical information; Technological innovation
Temporary residence permits, 164
Tourism
  by Soviet citizens, 95
Trade cooperatives. *See* Cooperative organizations
Trade union ownership, 81–82
Trade unions, 21, 23–24, 157–158
  and discharging of employees, 172
  See also Labor collectives; Statute of Trade Unions
Trainin, I. P., 17(n31)
Transportation
  and distribution, 182–183, 192–195
  of goods, 192–195
  See also Railroads
Tsentrosoiuz, 80

Underground economy, 9, 11–12, 13–15, 18(n59)
Unemployment, 36
United States Congress, 4
Unity of the fund, 69–70
Urban workers, 27. *See also* Collective farmers

van den Berg, Ger P., 162
Video tapes, 298
Voslensky, Mikhail, 2–3

Wages, 51, 166–167
War Communism, 37, 103, 117
Wilhelm, John H., 1
Workers, 3
Work hours, 28, 166

Young people. *See* Collective farms, young people on; Commissions on Affairs of Minors

Zaleski, Eugène, 1

For Product Safety Concerns and Information please contact our EU representative GPSR@taylorandfrancis.com Taylor & Francis Verlag GmbH, Kaufingerstraße 24, 80331 München, Germany

Batch number: 10726013

Printed by Printforce, the Netherlands